The Scriptures of Charles Dickens

To
Sue

The Scriptures of Charles Dickens

Novels of Ideology, Novels of the Self

VINCENT NEWEY

ASHGATE

Published by

Ashgate Publishing Limited
Gower House, Croft Road
Aldershot, Hants
GU11 3HR
England

Ashgate Publishing Company
Suite 420
101 Cherry Street
Burlington, VT 05401–4405
USA

Ashgate website: http://www.ashgate.com

British Library Cataloguing in Publication Data
Newey, Vincent
  The scriptures of Charles Dickens: novels of ideology,
  novels of the self. – (The nineteenth century series)
  1. Dickens, Charles, 1812–1870 – Criticism and
  interpretation 2. Dickens, Charles, 1812–1870 – Religion
  I. Title
  823.8

Library of Congress Cataloging-in-Publication Data
Newey, Vincent
  The scriptures of Charles Dickens: novels of ideology,
  novels of the self/Vincent Newey.
     p. cm. – (The nineteenth century series)
  Includes bibliographical references and index (alk. paper).
  1. Dickens, Charles, 1812–1870. 2. Dickens, Charles, 1812–1870 –
  Criticism and interpretation. 3. Identity (Psychology) in literature. 4. Social
  problems in literature. 5. Ideology in literature. 6. Religion in literature. 7.
  Self in literature. I. Title. II. Nineteenth century (Aldershot, England).
  PR4588.N395 2003
  823'.8–dc21   2002043957

ISBN 1 85928 434 5

Typeset in Sabon by Bournemouth Colour Press, Parkstone, Poole

Printed and bound in Great Britain by MPG Books Ltd, Bodmin, Cornwall.

Contents

List of Illustrations

The Nineteenth Century Series
General Editors' Preface

The aim of the series is to reflect, develop and extend the great burgeoning of interest in the nineteenth century that has been an inevitable feature of recent years, as that former epoch has come more sharply into focus as a locus for our understanding not only of the past but of the contours of our modernity. It centres primarily upon major authors and subjects within Romantic and Victorian literature. It also includes studies of other British writers and issues, where these are matters of current debate: for example, biography and autobiography, journalism, periodical literature, travel writing, book production, gender, non-canonical writing. We are dedicated principally to publishing original monographs and symposia; our policy is to embrace a broad scope in chronology, approach and range of concern, and both to recognize and cut innovatively across such parameters as those suggested by the designations 'Romantic' and 'Victorian'. We welcome new ideas and theories, while valuing traditional scholarship. It is hoped that the world which predates yet so forcibly predicts and engages our own will emerge in parts, in the wider sweep, and in the lively streams of disputation and change that are so manifest an aspect of its intellectual, artistic and social landscape.

Vincent Newey
Joanne Shattock

University of Leicester

Acknowledgements

This book was completed during a period of study leave granted by the University of Leicester. I gratefully acknowledge this invaluable support.

I am especially indebted to Dr Rod Mengham of Jesus College, Cambridge, who gave generously of his time to consider my work on Dickens when he was in process of advancing his own. Sincere thanks are due to friends and colleagues in the Department of English at Leicester: to Professor Greg Walker and Dr Michael Davies, who commented on various drafts and so often indulged my enthusiasm for talking about Dickens; to Professor Joanne Shattock and Professor Elaine Treharne, for their thoughtful practical assistance; to Emeritus Professor Philip Collins, for his presence, his wisdom, and his long dedication to making Leicester a centre for Dickens research. The successive groups of undergraduate and postgraduate students on my Dickens courses have kept me always on my toes and have been a frequent source of fresh insight and new information. Dr Josie Billington and Dr Peter Smith invited me at opportune moments to test my ideas in the public arena, respectively at the Victorian Studies Centre, Chester College, and in a research seminar at Nottingham Trent University. Both were stimulating occasions. My salient debts to existing scholarship, where Dickens has attracted an exceptionally distinguished line of contributors, are indicated in my text and notes. One, however, I must highlight. It was a single paragraph by Philip Davis, on *A Christmas Carol*, that opened up for me the prospect of writing on a great author I had never before thought of attempting. I hope that Bernard Beatty will remember the incisive lectures he gave on Dickens on the module we once taught jointly at Liverpool: I do.

Parts of Chapters 4 and 6 are adapted from my 'Dickensian Decadents', in *Romancing Decay: Ideas of Decadence in European Culture*, edited by Michael St John (Ashgate, 1999), and are included by kind permission. I am grateful to Alec McAulay for his early interest in this project and, among the current staff of Ashgate, particularly to Erika Gaffney, Ann Donahue and Celia Hoare for their considerate help and professionalism in aiding its path to publication. The Dickens House Museum, through Florian Schweizer, assistant curator, have been most supportive in supplying the material for all the illustrations.

I have dedicated the volume to my wife, Sue, ever my best guide and stay secure.

CHAPTER ONE

Introduction

There appeared in 1880 a book by William Hurrell Mallock with the intriguing title of *Is Life Worth Living?* This is not a treatise on suicide, but it is about a demise. Its concern, like that of much contemporary discourse, is with the waning of religious faith and the consequences for existence. Mallock identifies a widespread 'crisis', at the centre of which lie a 'negation of the supernatural' and a concomitant 'intense self-consciousness . . . on the part of man as to his own prospects and his own position'. The 'old spontaneity of action', rooted in the ideals of rewards in heaven and obedience to divine law, has given way to the cultivation of this-worldly knowledge and success, 'natural happiness', under the aegis of the 'positive school' of scientific thought and progress.[1] This is a restrained version of Carlyle's strident lament for the 'Everlasting No' of a universe become 'dead, immeasurable Steam-engine', a 'machine . . . go[ing] by the wheel-and-pinion "motives", self-interests, checks'.[2] It is also a theme at the heart of Dickens's writing. The present study is, broadly speaking, an account of how this author reflects and responds to the unsettlement and stress of his era – his involvement in the question of, as Barry Qualls puts it, 'the way man might live *adequately* in a world whose only certainty was flux'.[3] 'Adequately', which Qualls emphasizes, is an important word: there is no magical or complete solution to the challenge.

In targeting the causes of nineteenth-century *angst* Mallock's aim comes to rest on the deconstructive influence of philosophic 'positivism', which had its principal source in Ludwig Feuerbach's *Essence of Christianity*, published in 1841 and translated by George Eliot in 1854, where belief in the Divine is construed as the adolescent phase of humankind's development and Christian doctrines are interpreted fundamentally as projections of our own aspirations or wants, and where, above all, the orthodox credo of 'God is love' is displaced with the humanist principle of 'Love is god'.[4] For Mallock, the spiritual losses of deconversion far outstripped any gains in benevolent sentiment or material welfare. Dickens, we shall find, has mixed feelings in such areas, and certainly to a large extent runs with the 'Religion of Humanity' that *Is Life Worth Living?* anathematizes. There is, however, a more immediately obvious and clear-cut difference between the two writers. Mallock addresses the problem of restoring stability and the quality of life amidst change and failing metaphysical assumptions by advocating a mass return to the Catholic Church, which he views as an organism capable of infinite adaptation and, in its emphasis on ritual and dogma, of supplying a refuge from self-consciousness itself. As is suggested by R.H. Hutton's incredulous arraignment of this call in an otherwise enthusiastic review,[5] the proposal seems just as improbable in its early context as it does now, in spite of John Henry Newman and the Oxford Movement. Dickens, on the other hand, is Protestant and in tune with the future, in that he centres the quest for order and value in individuals rather than in any overarching institution.

Of the works I have chosen for detailed discussion, two, *David Copperfield* and *Great Expectations*, are first-person narratives that recall, the second often very precisely, the autobiographies of Puritan tradition, with their stories of guilt and renovation, inner maturation, the search through memory for self-knowledge and unity of being. In *A Christmas Carol* the erstwhile conversion process and strategies of meditation are powerfully dramatized and adjusted to latter-day settings and needs. The theme persists in *Our Mutual Friend* in the narratives of John Harmon's discovery of identity and the inward enlightenment of Bella Wilfer and Eugene Wrayburn. Characters in Dickens can bridge epochs, tracking, more or less firmly, the paths of John Bunyan and his pilgrims but having no Celestial City in view and in themselves confirming the investiture of what Philip Rieff, considering in the twentieth century the long march of secularization that he sees as first breaking the surface of history in the period of the French Revolution, has called modern 'psychological man', in whom 'the new centre, which can be held even as communities disintegrate, is the self', existing where 'there is no longer an effective sense of communion, driving the individual out of himself', having to manage his own 'well-being' and 'personal capacity'.[6] Or, we should add, failing to manage that 'well-being'. It is important to note from the outset the dark side of the picture. The internal landscape can be as blighted as the outer. For every one who, like Scrooge or David, gets a better life, there is one who, like Pip, can only hang on desperately, and one who, like Bradley Headstone, goes under. In the arena of selving there are some wins, some draws, and some defeats.

Yet, that Dickens is a chronicler of existential struggle against a background of dissolution does not of course mean that he has no care for the relationship between self and society, or no interest in the latter's re-formation. His characters do not simply express a solitary condition, they function, selectively, as models of how to conduct oneself and one's interaction with others, and how not to. Scrooge is a concentrated case in point. His transcending of egotism for a sense of community at the levels of personal relations, the family, the local group, and the larger stage constitutes a paradigm of good practice. As we shall see, this is one of the places where we are most strongly conscious of Dickens forging a Feuerbachian position, upvaluing the species-awareness and recognition of the interdependence of 'I' and 'Thou' that arise from an anthropological creed. The novel, Carlyle proclaimed, should bring 'doctrine', 'reproof', 'edification', 'healing', 'guidance'.[7] Dickens provides all these, and does so in a variety of ways of which the use of character-as-example is but one salient method. Another is what may be termed experiential reader engagement. This happens when we are invited to play out scenes in the theatre of the mind, in keeping with the imperative towards imaginative involvement issued by Dickens in an intended epigraph to one of his novels, 'Your homes the scene, yourselves the actors, here!'.[8] Scrooge's getting of wisdom, his recall to outgoing vision, has a counterpart in those occasions where we are prompted to take a renewed interest in people, especially the vulnerable and the overbearing. We shall encounter several great set pieces in this vein: Bumble, of all men, driven to shed a tear for Oliver; Steerforth's ruthless baiting of the defenceless Mr Mell; Magwitch succoured in open court by Pip, who has trod the same path as Scrooge, from selfishness to charity.

This is Dickensian epiphany: not a leaping of the spirit in the presence of the Divine or, as characteristically for the Romantics, of Nature, but a becoming of healthy emotional and moral instincts in anthropocentric contexts. It is part and parcel of 'the Word made Novel' in Dickens and his contemporaries, or, better perhaps, of 'the Novel made Word'; an aspect, that is, of their embrace of a long tradition of teaching whose operation and ends are memorably signalled in the 'Scola Cordis' of the *Emblems* of Francis Quarles – 'Peruse this little Book; and thou wilt see / What thy heart is, and what it ought to be'.[9] Put another way, we are here, as Matthew Arnold and the Leavises famously did in their generations, witnessing to literature as the provider of a new canon, a substitute bible, a secular scripture informed by and disseminating – to quote from T.R. Wright's investigation of the interface of *Theology and Literature* – 'an alternative set of liberal-humanist values'.[10] The 'liberal humanism' of Dickens's novels comprises major elements of their still-continuing relevance and appeal; but the phrase also signals a historic reorientation of cultural authority, and brings us, now, to the matter of ideology.

That the novelist had serious mass influence was a fact fully recognized in Dickens's time. A piece in the *Westminster Review*,

'Novels with a Purpose', which appeared in 1864, the year *Our Mutual Friend* was begun, presses the point unreservedly:

> The novelist is now our most influential writer. If he be a man of genius his power over the community he addresses is far beyond that of any author. Macaulay's influence over the average English mind was narrow compared with that of Dickens; even Carlyle's was not on the whole so great as that of Thackeray. . . . The influence of the novelist is beginning, too, to be publicly acknowledged of late much more frankly than was once the fashion. For a long time his power over society, except as a mere teller of stories and provider of easy pastime, was ignored or disputed. It was, indeed, something like the power of women in politics; an influence almost all-pervading, almost irresistible, but silent, secret, and not to be openly acknowledged.[11]

There is, of course, an ideology at work in this very statement, where the 'masculine' is assumed to be open, public, respectable, while the 'feminine' acts covertly, in close ways that are somehow dangerous, perhaps disreputable, and cannot be brought into the light. The implication of the passage is that the novel has come of age, achieved a position of legitimate, manly sway mentionable in the same breath as that of the Victorian sages – which is to say that the genre is being claimed for the patriarchal establishment. In fact, Dickens's novels have never ceased to operate surreptitiously, as well as frankly, in influencing the reader. At the extreme, they are divided against themselves and call into question conventions which on the surface they uphold. Gender stereotyping itself is one of the fields in which this most forcibly happens. For the moment, however, it is enough to be reminded that his texts are, whatever else, conduits for the inculcation and reinforcement of particular attitudes and beliefs and utilize both direct and indirect strategies to this end.

A small but telling instance occurs within the well-known satire on 'Podsnappery' in Chapter 11 of Book 1 of *Our Mutual Friend*. Podsnap is a caricature of the nationalistic, self-made, upward-climbing, puritanical man of business – of 'British Philistinism'.[12] At one of his dinner parties, he patronizes an 'unfortunately-born foreigner', correcting his guest's punctuation – 'Our English adverbs do Not terminate in Mong and We Pronounce the "ch" as if there were a "t" before it. We say Ritch' – and bringing the pompous dose of education to a climax with an encomium on 'the Englishman': 'there is in the Englishman a combination of qualities, a modesty, an independence, a responsibility, a repose, combined with an absence of everything calculated to call a blush into the cheek of a young person.' The joke is on Podsnap not only because of his overblown prudishness (which, we learn elsewhere, he applies with so much zeal as to turn his own daughter into a nervous wreck) but because of the manifest gap between his own character and the traits he has idealized. Dickens's explicit purpose lies in deprecating the myopic self-regard and monocultural barbarism with which Podsnap almost explodes. Implicitly, however, he is trailing an ideology of his own, which, though not jingoistic, is certainly about bringing and holding the nation together. Qualities are qualities whether Podsnap possesses them or not, and those he lists – 'modesty', 'independence', 'responsibility', 'repose' – are among the conspicuous virtues of John Harmon, one of the two heroes of the novel, who is balanced and quietly efficient, never brash though well-to-do and good at business, kindly towards friends and the needy, the perfect family man – Harmon[ious] within and spreading Harmon[y] without. He is a paragon of the English middle class, in whom the common sense and reasonable values of liberal humanism are allied to an instinct for practical success and standing.

Dickens thus reflects and puts in place, for immediate want of a better phrase, a bourgeois ideology. This is not a matter of simply presenting a given outlook or suite of ideas, however, but of participating in their construction. Andrew Blake rounds off his study of the intersections between developing Victorian ideologies and Victorian novels by stating that the latter were concerned with

> the reproduction of society: with the integration of the new wealthy, new powerful, and new respectable groups into the already existing ruling class structure, and the modification of that culture to include within it many new ideological elements associated with those groups. . . . The novel was an arena of public information, of public debate, and of 'interpellation', helping by its concerns to form society by helping to form individuals as members of that society.[13]

This is helpfully put in respect of Dickens, though he is not one of the authors Blake considers. To 'interpellation' I shall come in a moment. Of easier note is the emphasis on modifying an existing social structure. Dickens was certainly in some ways a radical. He assailed the institutions of Government (the notorious 'Circumlocution Office') and the Law, the Church, schools, prisons, the Poor Law system. But he was no leveller or revolutionary. Indeed, his reactions to the shortcomings of, say, support for the poor seem to be rooted, if anywhere more precise than a basic Christian ethos, in a Tory paternalism such as that expressed in Fielding's novels. His socio-political stance is undoubtedly conservative in its underlying commitment to hierarchy. This too connects him with the eighteenth century, with Cowper, Goldsmith, and

Soame Jenyns's widely-circulated *Free Enquiry into the Nature and Origin of Evil*, which averred that God in his wisdom so designed the universe that 'there is such connexion between all ranks and orders by subordinate degrees, that they mutually support each other's existence, and every one in its place is absolutely necessary towards sustaining the whole'.[14]

For Dickens, the Creator has disappeared not so much to the margins as off the edge, but the structure of subordination and layered mutuality retains a firm appeal. We are meant to approve of Joe Gargery the blacksmith, for example, when we are told, in Chapter 36 of *Great Expectations*, that he 'ever did his duty in his way of life, with a strong hand, a quiet tongue, and a gentle heart'. Dickens, like Jenyns, favours an arrangement in which, to use the latter's words, individuals are 'fitted for their respective situations'; and his ubiquitous attachment to charity also recalls the earlier thinker, who saw in indigence, not any reason for reconfiguring economic power, but a call to extol this virtue as a blessing to giver and recipient alike, a way of meeting our obligation 'to promote universal happiness'.[15] In his review of *A Free Enquiry*, Dr Johnson rebuffs its ultra traditionalism, not least in actually applauding the opportunity for upward mobility engendered by 'the maxims of a commercial nation, which . . . offer every individual a chance of mending his condition by his diligence'.[16] Neither does Dickens go for stasis or fail to recognize the flux around him, including greater fluidity in class pretensions, but he takes a circumscribed line, eschewing all notion of a free-for-all. Some aspiring characters are allowed to succeed and have status and money. John Harmon is, David Copperfield is, Scrooge is, so long as he learns the right ropes; even the incorrigible Wilkins Micawber is, so long as he does it in Australia, where the disreputable go to hoist themselves and the flag. These are standard-bearers of the varied middling class. The aspirants who fail, chief among them the ruthless meritocrat Uriah Heep and the disastrous social experiment Bradley Headstone, represent a low-born threat to the correct order of things and, like the immodest and illiberal Podsnap, a deviancy over against which that order is the more sharply defined.

Commenting on the uses of popular literature, a contributor to the first issue of *Eliza Cook's Journal* in 1849 wrote that

> The province of the literary philanthropist is clear – to circulate widely, under every shape, elements of truth; to strengthen the bands of society with instruction, and to cement national union by social and domestic recreation. The love of families engendered by this potent, but quiet influence, extends and evolves itself into patriotism, and a correct sense of social and political freedom, grounded on the only safe basis – discipline of mind.[17]

The phrasing, 'to strengthen the bands of society', suggests a dedication to the principles both of gradation ('banding') and cohesion ('binding'). These are twin goals of Dickens's address to his readership, under the more general head of 'cement[ing] national union'. One working-class periodical, the *People's Journal*, did declare him its 'champion', since, in contrast to 'the feudal school' of novelists, he did not take heroes from the privileged rank and make everyone else move beneath them 'according to their station on the artificial sliding-scale of society' (no inviolable God-given organization here), but took in characters from all quarters, so that 'every man, woman or child is [his] hero or heroine'.[18] In retrospect this judgement seems both understandable and odd. Certainly Dickens democratized the cast list of the novel, and the relatively upper-class *Prospective Review*'s troubled complaint about a 'reckless and riotous profusion' implies that this popular innovation carried a definite political punch;[19] but within the spreading mass there is a 'sliding-scale' nonetheless. The lower-class characters usually follow the 'poor but happy' or 'poor but hardworking' brand, and so do not challenge standard perceptions of class. Of the two disadvantaged figures who most prominently ascend the ladder, one, Oliver, turns out to have been a scion of the middle class all along, and the other, Lizzie Hexam, daughter of a Thames body-scavenger, possesses from the beginning the credentials fitting her for higher things, including integrity and liberality of spirit, love of family, and, rather extraordinarily, as also with Oliver, genteel speech and manners. The backdrop to Dickens's novels is shot through with upheaval in the social as in the intellectual sphere, so that J.A. Froude could speak of the new 'duty' to 'push on, to climb vigorously on the slippery steps . . . , to raise ourselves one step or more out of the rank of life in which we were born', while Ruskin was more than uneasy about a situation where it was felt to be a 'veritable shame' to 'remain in the lower grades . . . [n]ow that a man may make money, and rise in the world, and associate himself, unreproached, with people once far above him'.[20] Dickens saw dangers in the shifting tide, on whose waves rode the Heeps and the Podsnaps, but he plotted in reply a steadier and steadying dispensation.

According to the philosopher Louis Althusser, no man or woman can freely shape a course anywhere, but must live out a 'reality' which is prepared for them and to which they are called. 'Interpellation', the word Andrew Blake uses, comes of course from Althusser, for whom *all ideology hails or interpellates concrete individuals as concrete subjects, by the functioning of the category of the subject*.[21] This appropriates the technical term for what happens in a European governmental chamber when the proceedings are suspended to allow a Minister to be questioned. Like the Minister, individuals are ordered to account – by ideologies. Jeremy Hawthorn succinctly explains further:

> As ideology calls them – so the argument goes – so they recognize who they are. In other words: individuals come to 'live' a given set of ideological assumptions and beliefs, and to identify these with their own selves, by means of a process whereby they are persuaded that that which is presented *to* them actually represents their *own* inner identity or self.[22]

Hawthorn refers to a sort of 'body snatching', but 'brain snatching' might be better. Ideology is not a framework of dictates, externally imposed, but something instilled, which we perform in our practices and perceptions, our ways of acting and our ways of seeing. We are inside it and it is inside us. Moreover, in Althusser's view, bodies – or brains – are always already snatched: he adds that individuals are '*always-already subjects*'; even before being born 'an individual is always-already a subject' because he or she, the one 'expected', is destined for a place in the pre-existing 'familial ideological configuration', which in turn confers an identity and a training. In his summary, Althusser chooses to underline that subjects 'work all by themselves', stripped of all freedom except that of 'freely accepting [their] submission', in a constant state of 'misrecognition/ignorance'.[23]

   Some of Dickens's greatest insights are into 'the self' as functionary of 'the system'; in this regard, as in others, *Great Expectations* emerges as a work of genius. A plainer lens of Althusserian theory, however, first prompts us to understand the novels, as Blake does Victorian fiction generally, as 'interpellating' or summoning readers as members of a society – though Blake rightly stresses the ongoing process of social change while Althusser appears to think of fixed conditions or a *fait accompli*. Thus, in our paradigmatic text, the reader's experience of Scrooge's enlightenment underpins and develops allegiance to an evolving middle-class schema; the bountiful 'literary philanthropist' (to recall the soft-centred designation used by the student of cheap periodicals in *Eliza Cook's Journal*) is working all along, quietly but potently, in the service of 'discipline of mind', drawing on and fashioning that reader's competence in cultural observance. 'Scrooge', who on the surface depicts a person awakening to a freer, more expansive life, ironically comprises in effect a lure and a construct for regulating thought and behaviour. Dickens, though wide-awake in many respects, does not know this. He too is 'interpellated' – an unconscious moulding agent.

   It must be said at once that none of this is necessarily a bad thing. The concept of ideological formation tends to carry negative overtones; largely, I think, because it is so regularly employed by Marxists to discredit capitalism and liberal democracy, which they present as a concealed tyranny feeding on illusion. Tony Bennett is a mild but definite example:

> Ideology might thus be said to consist of those myths through which individuals are reconciled to their given social positions by falsely representing to them those positions and the relationships between them as if they formed part of some inherently significant, intrinsically coherent plan or process.[24]

The word 'falsely' is key: we are being misled into accepting the prevailing order as something 'natural' and therefore inevitable. Yet Bennett's statement does usefully highlight the importance of the fictions, the 'myths', by which we are taken in, and which we take in. We cannot *be* or *do* – at any rate, coherently – without them. As T.R. Wright says, 'Some form of ideology is, of course, a necessary part of any individual's sense of belonging.'[25] Ideology can then be viewed even more positively, as that which stabilizes and lends meaning to both self and its setting – which, to use John Fiske's words, 'constitute[s] not only the sense of the world for us, but also our sense of ourselves, our sense of identity, and our sense of our relations to other people and to society in general'.[26]

It follows that an ideology can be the more or less fruitful, or damaging, in constituting these ends; since what is at stake is the quality of our being-in-the-world, it seems important to make a reckoning, and to judge between one ideology and another. Evaluation requires, of course, an angle of detachment from which the ideology can be scrutinized. Althusser, if I grasp him aright, considers the procedure impossible: for him, the only escape from blind subjection is retreat into theoretical denial, a posture of mental non-cooperation; that is, for the individual, 'from within ideology', 'to outline a discourse which tries to break with ideology, in order to dare to be the beginning of a scientific . . . discourse on ideology'.[27] One thing Althusser fails to realize, or chooses to ignore, however, is that in practice there is never a single ideology in play but a plurality. Novels are sites of competing ideologies, where choices are made, encouraged, and provoked. *Oliver Twist*, *A Christmas Carol*, and *Hard Times* downgrade one ideology, rationalistic Utilitarianism, and elevate another, (Christian) humanism. Moreover, distance automatically extends with time, and we in turn take stock. Dickens operates from his point in history, we from ours, where we engage with his novels in the form as it were of their current afterlife –

which for me includes the light thrown by Althusser's perspectives. I no longer have available to me a purely innocent experience of A *Christmas Carol*; far from being 'interpellated', I am aware of the 'interpellative' work of the narrative, and can even see the story of Scrooge as itself an account of that work – not Scrooge being reborn but Scrooge as an always-already subject being snatched by and for the purposes of ideology. But this does not prevent me either from seeking value and benefits from within the situation of which I read or from diagnosing its drawbacks. To recognize ideology is to be granted the capacity to assess its nature, the advantages it brings, the shortcomings it imposes, its worth as a way of being and living. It is, we might say, to be situated on the discriminating outside – to be 'extrapellated'.

The novels I examine in this book all promulgate ideological schemes yet, in various ways and degrees, open them to interrogation. This happens not only with broad socio-political or cultural positions – the elaboration of middle-class ideology – but in sub-areas, of which that of gender identity is perhaps the most prominent. Conventional conceptions of female personality and roles come under question on the one hand because Dickens at times pushes them so far and so transparently as to leave them vulnerable to intellectual ambush, but also, on the other, because of his intuitive apprehension of the hidden psychology of women, which finds symbolic expression, as in the repressed Mrs Joe's symptomatic appropriation of the sign of masculine power, her stick Tickler, or her habit of holding a loaf to her body, explosively cleaving it and spreading it liberally with butter. 'Extrapellated' response in this connection is best described as a capability, not so much to stand back and interpret, as to read against the grain of a surface orthodoxy – against the view of Mrs Joe as simply a damnable shrew, in contrast to the admirably demure Biddy, the Victorian ideal. Such reading can be a matter of breaking with the direction of the text or of taking direction from its own embedded signification.

Mrs Joe is an instance of a very important kind of character in Dickens – the one who does not fit in. Malcontents like the criminals in *Oliver Twist* or the would-be parvenu Uriah Heep who probe the cordon sanitaire around middle-class society are not the only misfits. Outside and inside the line, they are everywhere. It is often not so much the fact of constraint, of being subjected to the impersonal social order, that stands out on Dickens's map as the inner tensions and wounds that go with it. Mrs Joe complains about her lot, but even those seemingly most at home in the system, like Jaggers and Wemmick in *Great Expectations* who are 'natural' exponents of the practices of institutionalized predation in the growing culture of acquisition, emerge as split within themselves, incapable, for better or for worse, of complete self-surrender. Bradley Headstone, stipendiary schoolteacher, product of the recent expansion programme in mass education, makes known that his training and the demands of his job leave something in him untouched and unfulfilled, simmering, ready to burst out and assert itself: ' "Do you suppose that a man, in forming himself for the duties I discharge, and in watching and repressing himself daily to discharge them well, dismisses a man's nature?" ' (Book 2, Chapter 6). This suppressed energy in time turns literally murderous. Yet David Copperfield himself, who perhaps more securely than anyone assumes the mantle of 'middle-class-ness', with its privileges and right-minded values, has to fight off and never quite lays to rest the demon of his cruder, uncivilized side, represented in his unworthy but resilient 'double', Heep. Pip's dark 'double' is the violent and rebellious Orlick who, like Heep, is strategically exorcized from the action of the novel but not from the account of the psyche and of social reality which it bequeaths.

Some of these examples are of the good resisting the ill, others of the contrary; but the overall picture is of discontent and irresolution in both the macrocosm of society and the microcosm of psychological life. Where Althusser figures existence as a well-regulated and smooth-running machine with individuals-become-subjects as robotic components, Dickens gives us a dysfunctional field in which *individuals are never wholly snatched or snatched whole*. Conflict and incompleteness, internal or external, seem a tragic condemnation. They are nonetheless conditions of aliveness. We all suffer limits, are bounded, but are not bound down. The pains and distress of being fitted up by and for ideology are the earnest of a persisting individuality – the trace of a resistance to being 'subject'. That in some, as in Bradley Headstone, things go madly wrong makes the troublesome excess of energy, what Headstone terms his still-surviving 'man's nature', no less a mark of abiding autonomy – which helps to explain why, against the moral grain, we feel for the schoolmaster in his homicidal rage. Thoughts of Headstone's fate, however, also return us to the positive side of the picture: that of the individual in pursuit of the best options for living, which is a journey under stress and limitation but productive of order and value. In this quest Dickens himself and the readers of Dickens are as much travellers as the protagonists of his novels. If it were necessary to single out one gain along the way, it would be, for me, the ideology of 'connection', which upvalues not only romantic attachment, or family piety, or hospitable communality, but that sympathetic response to humanity that embraces even a murderer or two, and remains a quintessential benison of the Dickensian secular scripture. Though ideologies rise to possess us, we can elect to take selective possession of them.

I begin this study with *A Christmas Carol*, published in 1843, because, far from being the 'sport' it is often taken for, it brings into clear focus many of Dickens's core concerns and attitudes of mind. There follow chapters primarily on four major novels from different stages of Dickens's career, treated chronologically. These share common themes and show both consistency and developments in Dickens's thinking, yet each also strikes in new directions. *Oliver Twist* (1837–39), adapting the motif of the pilgrim's progress and elements of the popular novel of criminal life, sets out and legitimizes a middle-class hegemony, mapping society in such a way as to allow his readership at once to know, transgress and ultimately preserve the bounds of a dominant culture and socio-political authority. At the same time, however, there is a struggle, which is never fully resolved, between the Dickens who, interpellated and interpellator, is thus committed to writing the narrative of bourgeois ascendancy and the Dickens whose fictional imagination runs loose and is recruited for the dissident underworld. *David Copperfield* (1849–50) goes inwards, rendering the fraught but successful processes of self-formation in a hero for the times. *Great Expectations* (1860–61) takes a bleak turn, exploring the problems of finding identity and purpose, even of surviving at all, in a world bereft of stable beliefs and dominated by the spirit of acquisition. Pip emerges as the *anti*-hero of *our* times, holding on in the midst of a collective incoherence and in a universe out of step with his desires. In the presentation of women in this novel, we encounter perhaps the most remarkable strain of self-subverting creative energy, of art divided against itself, in Dickens. In *Our Mutual Friend* (1864–65) modernity grows darker still than in *Great Expectations*, a wasteland of dust heaps, pollution, and human birds of prey. There emerges here the figure much admired by T.S. Eliot, the artist as existentialist hero, resiliently finding inspiration in the debris of a degraded civilization; but in the larger view Dickens also returns, with renewed vigour and fresh answers, to the task of producing a blueprint for estimable selfhood and a workable society.

These are the paths we shall tread. Yet it should be said at setting out that it is no narrow or Procrustean journey. With a writer as rich as Dickens it is advisable to keep an open mind and to expect complications and surprises – not least in those places which bear witness that the individual, though confined, is alive and kicking, whether as the object of contemplation or, be it author or reader, the contemplating presence.

Notes

1. William Hurrell Mallock, *Is Life Worth Living?* (London: Chatto & Windus, 1880), pp. 19, 104, 151.
2. Thomas Carlyle, *Sartor Resartus* (1836); *On Heroes, Hero Worship and the Heroic in History* (1841), Lecture V: introduced W.H. Hudson (London: Dent, 1967), pp. 125–6, 399.
3. Barry Qualls, *The Secular Pilgrims of Victorian Fiction* (Cambridge: Cambridge University Press, 1982), p. 15.
4. Ludwig Feuerbach, *The Essence of Christianity* (1841), trans. Marian Evans [George Eliot], introduced by Karl Barth (New York: Harper & Brothers, 1957), passim. Feuerbach says: 'Is not the love of God to man – the basis and central point of religion – the love of man to himself made an object, contemplated as the highest objective truth?' (p. 58).
5. *The Spectator*, 12 July 1879.
6. Philip Rieff, *The Triumph of the Therapeutic* (1966; Harmondsworth: Penguin Books, 1973), pp. 4, 27, 34.
7. 'Sir Walter Scott', *The Works of Thomas Carlyle*, ed. H.D. Traill, 30 vols (London: Chapman and Hall, 1896–1901), XXIX (1899), 76.
8. The motto is that proposed by Dickens for *Martin Chuzzlewit*. See John Forster, *The Life of Charles Dickens* (1872–74; London: Chapman and Hall, n.d.), p. 315.
9. 'Scola Cordis' is by Christopher Harvey, but was attributed to Quarles in the nineteenth century and printed with the *Emblems*. See Qualls, *Secular Pilgrims*, pp. 1, 194. The phrase 'The Word made Novel' is Qualls's heading for his Introduction.
10. T.R. Wright, *Theology and Literature* (Oxford: Basil Blackwell, 1988), p. 5.
11. Justin McCarthy, 'Novels with a Purpose', *Westminster Review*, 82 (July 1864); quoted in Jennifer Hayward, *Consuming Pleasures: Active Audiences and Serial Fictions from Dickens to Soap Opera* (Lexington: University Press of Kentucky, 1997), p. 28. Hayward (pp. 21–83) gives a highly informative account of the importance of Dickens, and especially *Our Mutual Friend*, in the history of mass audience engagement with serial fiction, not least from the point of view of the genre's function in shaping conduct and encouraging debate on current affairs and issues.
12. Donald Hawes, *Who's Who in Dickens* (London: Routledge, 1998), p. 187, points out that 'Podsnappery' has entered the language with the meaning of 'British Philistinism'.
13. Andrew Blake, *Reading Victorian Fiction: The Cultural Context and Ideological Content of the Nineteenth-Century Novel* (Basingstoke: Macmillan, 1989), pp. 134–5.
14. Quoted from Jenyns in Samuel Johnson, 'Review of [Soame Jenyns], *A Free Enquiry into the Nature and Origin of Evil*' (1757); *The Works of Samuel Johnson, LL.D*, 12 vols (London: W. Baynes and Son et al., 1824), XI, 259–60. For Goldsmith's commitment to a system of fixed relations and 'subordinate degrees', see my 'Goldsmith's "Pensive Plain": Re-viewing *The*

Deserted Village', in *Early Romantics: Perspectives in British Poetry from Pope to Wordsworth*, ed. T. Woodman (Basingstoke: Macmillan, 1998), pp. 93–116 (pp. 95–102). William Cowper's memorable vision of the good society comes in allegorical form:

> Few self-supported flow'rs endure the wind
> Uninjur'd, but expect th'upholding aid
> Of the smooth-shaven prop, and, neatly tied,
> Are wedded thus, like beauty to old age,
> For int'rest sake, the living to the dead.
> Some clothe the soil that feeds them, far diffus'd
> And lowly creeping, modest and yet fair,
> Like virtue, thriving most where little seen;
> Some, more aspiring, catch the neighbour shrub
> With clasping tendrils, and invest his branch,
> Else unadorn'd, with many a gay festoon
> And fragrant chaplet, recompensing well
> The strength they borrow with the grace they lend.
> All hate the rank society of weeds,
> Noisome, and ever greedy to exhaust
> Th'impov'rish'd earth; an overbearing race
> That . . .
> Disturb good order, and degrade true worth.
>   (*The Task* (1785), III. 657–74)

In the garden scene is figured the image of an optimal order, where 'interest' is not that of selfish profit but more natural relations – the interdependence of young and old, weak and strong, past generations and the present. The lowly are content and uncorrupted, the higher truly noble. All on this side is fruitfully integrated, though tiered. The forces of greed, disorder, and contamination are cast as an execrable horde – but remain ever a potent threat. We might usefully keep this passage in mind as a measure of Dickens's social idealism, which lasts right through to a re-modelling in *Our Mutual Friend* in favour of the idea of a more inclusive society.

15. *Works of Johnson*, XI, 271.
16. *Works of Johnson*, XI, 267.
17. 'Cheap Reading', *Eliza Cook's Journal*, 1 (1849), 2.
18. 'The People's Portrait Gallery', *People's Journal*, 1 (3 June 1846); quoted in Hayward, *Consuming Pleasures*, p. 32.
19. Unsigned review, 'David Copperfield and Pendennis', *Prospective Review* (July 1851); quoted in Hayward, p. 26.
20. J.A. Froude, 'England and Her Colonies', *Short Studies on Great Subjects*, 4 vols (London, 1888), II, 206; John Ruskin, 'Pre-Raphaelitism' (1851), *The Works of John Ruskin*, ed. E.T. Cook and Alexander Wedderburn, 39 vols (London: George Allen, 1903–12), XII, 342.
21. Louis Althusser, 'Ideology and Ideological State Apparatuses', *Lenin and Philosophy, and Other Essays*, trans. B. Brewster (London: New Left Books, 1971); repr. in *Literary Theory: An Anthology*, ed. Julie Rivkin and Michael Ryan (Oxford: Blackwell, 1998), pp. 294–304 (p. 301).
22. Jeremy Hawthorn, *A Concise Glossary of Contemporary Literary Theory* (London: Edward Arnold, 1994), p. 97.

23. Althusser, pp. 302–03.
24. Tony Bennett, *Formalism and Marxism* (London: Methuen, 1979), p. 116.
25. Wright, *Theology and Literature*, p. 15.
26. John Fiske, 'British Cultural Studies on Television Criticism', in *Channels of Discourse: Television and Contemporary Criticism*, ed. Robert Allen (London: Methuen, 1987); repr. in Rivkin and Ryan, pp. 305–11 (p. 308).
27. Althusser, p. 300.

CHAPTER TWO

A Christmas Carol

Snatched?

Dickensian melodrama can be breathtaking. A case in point is Scrooge's encounter with the Ghost of Christmas Past in Stave Two of *A Christmas Carol*.[1] 'Long past?', ventures Scrooge defensively. 'No. Your past.' To this rejoinder, which so acutely personalizes the issue, Scrooge reacts by wanting to cover up the 'light' that emanates from the Spirit. Rebuked, he then inquires what 'business' has led the Spirit to him. 'Your welfare!' Scrooge thinks to himself that this end would be better served if he were allowed a good night's rest; but he doesn't know what's really good for him: a great deal more than physical and mental refreshment is at stake, and deeper objectives are at once indicated by the Ghost's stunning adjustment of terms – 'Your reclamation, then'.

'Reclamation' is reminiscent of the discourse of religious exhortation, where it indicates 'the action of calling or bringing back from wrong-doing' (*OED* sense 2). In Dickens the word is similarly uncompromising, suggesting a reorientation of self and conduct that is compulsory rather than optional, and is a state not so much of being freed from something as of conforming, of somehow coming into line. As the episode develops, moreover, we become increasingly aware of the pain and degree of subjection involved in the process of reformation. Having been made to observe the bitter consequences of past mistakes, Scrooge cries out 'Why do you delight to torture me?' (81) – only to be 'pinioned' again by the Ghost and treated to another bout of shock treatment.

It is always worth noting such force in the words, phrases, and scenes of *A Christmas Carol*, since, despite alert analyses by John Lucas, Joseph Gold, and others I shall mention in the course of this chapter, there remains a common assumption that the work is a merely sportive and relaxing experience, as in Michael Slater's claim (in the popular edition which I am using) that it is 'first and foremost a triumph of *tone* . . . of a jolly, kind-hearted bachelor uncle'.[2] Far from being a simple avuncular *jeu d'esprit*, the text of Scrooge's regeneration, his journey to an 'altered life' (126), is a complex and profoundly serious one, concentrating many important features of Dickens's subject matter and concerns, their background and place in history, and their continuing significance. An obvious starting-point for discussion lies with that great ontological theme of the nineteenth century and beyond – how to preserve, or reconstitute, spiritual and moral values in an increasingly secular world.

W.H. Mallock's classic assault upon Positivism in *Is Life Worth Living?*, which was published nearly four decades after the *Carol*, will help to pull the situation into perspective. Mallock, we remember, saw the decline of religion and the rising faith in material improvement as a severe threat to the quality of life. To replace the standard of 'supernatural right' with that of 'natural happiness', for him, enfeebled, perhaps fatally, the 'moral end', since that end becomes 'nothing absolute, and not being absolute is incapable of being enforced'; and, more generally, all striving in the face of the 'infinite' or of 'something beyond' having been abandoned, our being would shrink to one flat level, 'with the colours reduced in number, and robbed of all their vividness'.[3] Yet, as Mallock himself seems to sense in spite of his call for a return to the Catholic Church in the later reaches of his book, the challenge for humankind in its deconversion was, inevitably, not the resurrection of the old disappearing order but a search for adequate compensation: 'positive thought reduces all religions to ideals created by man; and as such, not only admits that they have had vast influence, but teaches us also that we . . . must construct new ideals for ourselves.'[4] Indeed, he comes to present Catholicism itself, not as a living heritage, but as recoverable in artificial form, a to-be-chosen framework of belief and guidance sufficient unto the present need.

A Christmas Carol is manifestly about 'construct[ing] . . . ideals'. To be sure, Mallock, looking back, would have judged it a part of the very problem of secularization; for, though Dickens embraces New Testament morality and even retains an element of the 'supernatural' in the visitation of the Spirits, he is actively committed to 'natural happiness' as the grounds of well-being. Duty to God and concern for the state of the immortal soul have been succeeded by an insistent interest in healthy feelings and fruitful relationships with the outer world. Yet in this, of course, the 'vividness' and purpose of life remain – are reoriented and redefined, rather than simply dissipated. The whole psychodrama of Scrooge's redemption is rich in colour; it is a momentous process of transformation in which hard-won knowledge of self and others, and of their interdependence, brings ample return in enhancing both personal and collective existence. Dickens argues persuasively that life *is* worth living – is maybe better lived – without the support – or should we say the restrictions? – of religious orthodoxy.

In considering this aspect of *A Christmas Carol* I shall keep in mind the tradition on which it draws and over against which, in important respects, it defines its philosophy and values. Dickens's plan of salvation can be the more clearly understood against the backcloth of Puritan conversion narrative and spiritual autobiography, of which John Bunyan provides central examples and, in view of the popularity of *The Pilgrim's Progress* with the Victorians, ones which many of Dickens's readers would have known.[5] The interrelationship works both ways: while Dickens displaces revealed religion with the Religion of Humanity, the former supplies the basis of the new dispensation and a residual aura that lends his text the status of transcendent wisdom. T.R. Wright talks of the 'rational' viewpoint of 'liberal humanism' and the ' "modern" secular world', that 'miracles never happen and that religious experience is an illusion'.[6] *A Christmas Carol* is not quite like that. It carries a sense of 'the religious' and 'the miraculous' to the heart of ordinary human circumstance and aspiration.

A different way of putting the same case is to say that the *Carol* replaces one ideology (old-style religion) with another (humanism); indeed, that it discernibly weans the reader from the one onto the other. *Pace* Mallock, it is hardly possible to see this, in retrospect, as anything else than a beneficial project – Dickens intervening at a point of cultural change to show a way forward.

We are reminded of Thackeray's celebration of the writing and publication of the *Carol* as the giving of a present – 'a national benefit, and to every man or woman who reads it a personal kindness'.[7] Yet, we must always beware novelists bearing gifts. We are never more in chains perhaps than when we think ourselves free. While on one level the reclamation of the miscreant Scrooge exemplifies a release into a fuller and more useful life, on another it executes the process of his and the reader's recruitment for a socio-political regime. One critic who develops this second, very important insight, Audrey Jaffe, taking her cue from Sergei Eisenstein's theory of visual representation and spectatorship in modern literary and cinematic texts as the means of instilling and sustaining allegiance to the presiding order, defines the scenes of *A Christmas Carol* as a 'culture text' which 'projects images of, has come to stand for, and constitutes an exemplary narrative of enculturation into the dominant [that is, capitalist and commodity-driven] values of its time'.[8] The work is, in other words, a masterpiece of Althusserian interpellation or body and brain snatching. To this side of the *Carol* we shall come in due course. It should be stressed, however, that, elegant as Jaffe's arguments are, her approach too has its serious limitations. Not only is she blind to the idea that 'socialization' (to use her term) may be needful or that, especially in periods of cultural uncertainty and reformation, it may bring gains, she fails to recognize the excess of energy and meaning in *A Christmas Carol* over and above those consistent with interpellative ends – that neither author, protagonist, nor reader is wholly snatched or snatched whole. The ache Scrooge feels when being 'pinioned' by the Spirits, which is the trace of his resistance to being put on the official straight and narrow, never entirely goes away, and we shall find in the final analysis that the totemic figure of the socialized self is shadowed, disruptively, as a rival centre of significance, by its raw, non-conforming, experiencing counterpart, the individual who lives to struggle and struggles to live.

*

In Stave One Scrooge is called an 'old sinner' (46). Old in years maybe, but not in type. There is no stronger manifestation of the modernity of the *Carol* than its revision of the concept of sin, which is transferred from a religious to a social plane. In Bunyan transgression is emphatically inward, involving above all refusal of the call to grace and spiritual endeavour, as in the desire to deny Christ that almost destroys the protagonist in the autobiography, *Grace Abounding to the Chief of Sinners* (1666), or the despair of God's forgiveness that traps Christian in Doubting Castle in Part One of *The Pilgrim's Progress* (1678) and similarly threatens a premature end to the path of salvation.[9] Scrooge in his counting-house, on the other hand, offends against the claims of family when he rejects his nephew's invitation to spend Christmas with him, against those of charity when he will not donate to the annual collection for 'the poor and destitute', and against those of responsibility and fairness when he berates his employee, Bob Cratchit, consigned to the cold drudgery of his 'dismal little cell', for expecting a day's paid holiday (47–52). He can think of life only in the narrowest of linear terms, as an account, or ledger record, of financial loss or gain, so that he asks his nephew, 'What's Christmas time to you but a time for . . . finding yourself a year older, and not an hour richer; a time for balancing your books and having every item in 'em . . . dead against you?' (48). There can be no occasion for stepping into a new and unselfish dimension, as there is for the nephew, who knows that 'good' and 'profit' are not necessarily the same thing – 'There are many things from which I might have derived good, by which I have not profited' (48) – and who sees in Christmas a festival of outgoing response and communality:

> 'But I am sure I have always thought of Christmas time, when it has come round – apart from the veneration due to its sacred name and origin, if anything belonging to it can be apart from that – as a good

time: a kind, forgiving, charitable, pleasant time: the only time I
know of, in the long calendar of the year, when men and women
seem by one consent to open their shut-up hearts freely, and to think
of people below them as if they really were fellow-passengers to the
grave, and not another race of creatures bound on other journeys.'
(49)

We notice here how the religious essence of Christmas appears as a
parenthesis or secondary thought and in mechanical formulations
('veneration', 'sacred name and origin'). It is the demands of a shared
mortality (not immortality) and the answering code of sympathy –
derived from the Christian ethos – that are espoused and made vitally
present to the reader.

So, as one ideology falls away, another, humanism, fills out, and is at
the same time set in ascendant opposition to a third, Scrooge's
rationalistic, sterile utilitarianism. This latter is further specified and
exposed through Scrooge's commitment to the institutions of prison and
workhouse ('Treadmill and the Poor Law') as the solution to destitution;
limited again to harsh economic criteria, he declares to the gentlemen
collecting for charity that these establishments 'cost enough: and those
who are badly off must go there' (51). Then, when he answers the
comment that many would rather die than enter the poorhouse with the
retort that 'they had better do it, and decrease the surplus population'
he is branded an adherent, whether he knows it or not, of one of the
major theoretical roots of *laissez-faire* social policy: that of Malthus,
whose proto-Darwinian *Essay on the Principle of Population* (1803)
pulled no punches in insisting on the laws of competition and the battle
for survival, where 'A man who is born into a world already possessed,
. . . if society do not want his labour, has no claim of *right* to the smallest
portion of food, and, in fact, has no business to be where he is.'[10]

While thus making his central character the reprobate expression and
critique of a particular current of contemporary thought, or of really not
thinking at all, Dickens also, however, weaves around him a network of
motifs that mark his personal life as deficient. Scrooge is associated with
the stasis of a water-plug which, its 'overflowings sullenly congealed',
has turned to 'misanthropic ice'; with the hardness of 'sharp flint'; with
the isolation of a 'solitary . . . oyster'; with the irrelevance of a house
that, playing hide-and-seek with other houses, had once strayed into a
gloomy back street and had 'forgotten the way out again' (46, 52, 54).
One word in the nephew's extolling of Christmas is that is a 'pleasant'
time, and Scrooge's cold, cut-off condition – he says quite deliberately at
one point, 'I wish to be alone' (51) – represents, whatever else, the
deprivation of being an outsider, of *not joining in. A Christmas Carol* is

an irresistible summons to be on the inside, where giving and enjoyment are happily allied, pleasing others brings pleasure to oneself. The message is a version of the famous adage of Pope's *Essay on Man* – that 'self-love and social are the same'.[11]

Even in this early phase of the *Carol* it is apparent at times that the reader is being hailed for a promised land not only of good feelings but of plenteous consumption – the bourgeois dream. The brightness of the shop windows where 'poulterers' and grocers' trades became . . . a glorious pageant' looks forward to the sumptuous display of framed, alluring images of the street scenes of Christmas Present, in which Spanish onions 'wink' from shelves, figs are 'moist and pulpy', and there are 'Norfolk Biffins [cooking apples], squab and swarthy, setting off the yellow of the oranges and lemons, and in the compactness of their juicy persons, urgently entreating and beseeching to be carried home in paper bags and eaten after dinner' (52, 90). This is 'O Come, All Ye Faithful' with a difference; and indeed just afterwards the steeples invite to church and chapel the same 'good people' who had 'tumbled up against each other' at the grocer's door, as if blessing their rush to take possession of the objects that have aroused and will satisfy worldly desire (91).

As yet, however, the accent continues to fall on the virtue of *excursive* liberality, Scrooge's lack of which, and the possible repercussions of this for his future, are underlined in his exchanges with the ghost of Jacob Marley. 'Scrooge and Marley', partners: the two men had always been interchangeably one, and now Marley mirrors a baleful captivity that Scrooge must learn to recognize and throw off:

> 'You are fettered,' said Scrooge, trembling. 'Tell me why?'
> 'I wear the chain I forged in life,' replied the Ghost. 'I made it link by link, and yard by yard; I girded it on of my own free will, and of my own free will I wore it. Is its pattern strange to *you*?' (61)

Sometimes more exaggerated than this, for instance in the description of the Ghost as wound about with 'cash-boxes, keys, padlocks, ledgers, deeds, and heavy purses wrought in steel' (57), the symbolism plainly recalls the allegorical technique of *The Pilgrim's Progress*, though re-cast in humorous and popularly accessible form. In content, there is again the familiar shift to a 'humanist mythology':[12] in Bunyan the characteristic bondage had been that emblazoned in the showpiece exhibit of the 'Man in the Iron Cage' at Interpreter's House who cannot escape the conviction that he has no share in the 'spirit of grace', while in Dickens it is the dead weight of a withdrawn and barren life.[13] All the same, both the Man of Despair and Marley's Ghost are made present to the protagonist, and to the reader, as, in Interpreter's words, 'an everlasting caution'[14] – respective states of damnation, the old and the new, that are to be avoided at all costs. What comes to matter as Stave One draws to a close is not only the track Scrooge is on but whether and how he can get off it; and the instruments of advance at his disposal are strongly reminiscent of those available to Bunyan's pilgrim. The tiles on Scrooge's fireplace 'designed to illustrate the Scriptures' – Cains and Abels, Pharaoh's daughters, Queens of Sheba (56) – are but an echo of the Puritan devotion to the Word and its guidance, the decorative remnants of a fading tradition. Yet, for God's elect not only Scripture but everything in the world had potentially carried profitable meaning, and there was a sustained emphasis on interpreting signs, characters and topography, as Christian must constantly do, and Scrooge, in his way, after him.[15] The enchained Marley is at once cautionary spectacle and explicator (like Help who visits Christian) in a series of affective and educative encounters that had begun for Scrooge with the emotional jolt of the anthropomorphic doorknocker out of which a dead man stares and will culminate in his reading of his own name on the headstone of a neglected grave. All this happens, doubtless, in Scrooge's mind, oneirically, as the narrator implies when remarking that the pictures on the tiles were all subsumed by the image of 'old Marley's head' that dominated 'the disjointed fragments of his thoughts' (56). Then, so does Christian's pilgrimage: 'I awoke, and behold it was a dream.'[16]

In plotting the course of Scrooge's regeneration Dickens acknowledges the complex dynamics of psychological process yet advocates strategies of mental self-help. The latter are already in play at the end of Stave One. When the Ghost, referring to the chain he forged for himself, asks his erstwhile associate, 'Is its pattern strange to *you*?', Scrooge is being taught to see – or is incipiently seeing – his life from the outside, and being prompted to reflect upon its shape and tendency. Shortly after, there are signs that Scrooge is a quick learner at the art of self-evaluation, for he 'began to apply to himself' the Ghost's remorseful lament for a history of 'opportunity misused'. That is good; but, not for the last time, he is caught in an error, completely misunderstanding, as Marley had once misunderstood, where true 'usefulness' lies:

> 'But you were always a good man of business, Jacob,' faltered Scrooge . . .
> 'Business!' cried the Ghost . . . 'Mankind was my business. The common welfare was my business; charity, mercy, forbearance, and benevolence, were, all, my business.' (62)

Scrooge's mistake has supplied another opportunity for Dickens to proclaim the primacy of the 'common welfare', but simultaneously highlights the importance of working things out and getting them right – of improving oneself as well as being improved.

The schooling of Scrooge in the ways and means of thinking correctly, or of more general right-mindedness, is part and parcel of the *Carol*'s design in constructing personal identity and responsibility in line with the imperatives of an evolving bourgeois society. That is not the whole truth, however. Though ever under constraint, we can nonetheless be and do more or less well in our lives; worthy can be worthwhile selves. Transhistorically understood, what happens to Scrooge still has ample power to move and inspire as a prescription for being-in-the-world. This is especially so in Stave Two, where Dickens appropriates for the secular pilgrim one of Puritan meditation's most potent devices for unlocking and directing the energies of the self – memory.

*

'Call forth thy own recorded experience', Richard Baxter advises the wavering convert in *The Saints Everlasting Rest* (1650); 'Remember what *discoveries* of thy *state* thou hast made formerly in the walks of *self-examination*.'[17] You go back in order to take stock and move on. To this prizing of memory as a means of personal stability, insight and encouragement Bunyan adds, in the preface to *Grace Abounding*, the promise of overt instruction, as he not only urges his followers to 'call forth the former days, . . . look diligently, and leave no corner therein unsearched, for there is treasure hid' but also undertakes to offer his own remembrances of 'sins' and 'grace', the whole history of his life and conversion, as a support to others.[18] The mnemonic theme of *A Christmas Carol* similarly incorporates these two strategies, the didactic and the autodidactic. Both Scrooge and the reader are taught through examples, images, discourse and dialogue, and they are guided in the art of teaching themselves – self-learning.

Departing, Marley's Ghost instructs Scrooge to be sure 'that, for your own sake, you remember what has passed between us' (63). In Stave Two the fruits of knowledge have a more distant yet also more intimate source. Scrooge's recollection of his own past is crucial to his rebirth and getting of wisdom. The high import of memory is established immediately by the imagery of 'a bright clear jet of light' flowing from the crown of the Ghost of Christmas Past (68), which not only maintains the theme of inward illumination (with an echo perhaps of the 'candle' that goes before Christian at the House of Interpreter) but implies the operation and pursuit of grace (Christian must keep 'yonder shining light' in sight along the route of his progress, and escapes the Valley of the Shadow of Death because ' "*His candle shineth on my head, and by his light I go through darkness*" ').[19] This section of *A Christmas Carol* abounds with allusions to Scripture, which sets an atmosphere for the whole book. The Ghost's 'Rise! and walk with me!' (69) conjures up the calling of Matthew (Matt. 9. 9: 'he arose and followed him'), the raising of Lazarus (John 11. 38–46) and of the man sick of the palsy (Matt. 9. 1–8: 'Thy sins be forgiven thee; . . . Arise and walk'), and Peter's healing of the lame beggar (Acts 3. 1–11: 'Silver and gold have I none; but such as I have give I thee: In the name of Jesus Christ . . . rise up and walk'). The mystique of the sacred and of New Testament *logos* informs and is absorbed into Scrooge's story, which is a re-making of holy writ, a myth of purgation, awakening and vocation for the modern world.

To be redeemed Scrooge has to rediscover his 'forgotten self as he had used to be' (72); that is, make *feeling* contact with his experiences of, and capacity for, both happiness and dereliction. When, at the Ghost's behest, the landscape of his childhood first appears, he declares that he could 'walk it blindfold' (70). In a sense this is misguided, for there are bumps and surprises lying in wait for him; and, inasmuch as he must learn to see more clearly, the whole point is that the blindfold has to come off. From another angle, however, he has hit the mark, since the scenes are buried inside him and there come back to life, comprehensively, not only visually but emotionally. The past is, indeed, initially realized in terms of sensation, as 'a thousand odours floating in the air, each connected with a thousand thoughts, and hopes, and joys, and cares long, long, forgotten' (70). This component is retained when the mind-pictures take their vivid shape; there was feeling then, and there is feeling now. The earliest memory is of the gladness of boyhood, the little market town with children on shaggy ponies, farmers driving gigs and carts, 'broad fields . . . so full of merry music' (70–71), an idyll in which Audrey Jaffe identifies a scenario of 'fellowship and . . . an idealized preindustrial world' that is one of the *Carol's* string of images encoding Victorian culture's dominant values and arousing desire, and thereby reinforcing allegiance, in the reader.[20] Or, we might say, it is the pastoral Golden Age and the unfallen Creation – and there is, too, no rift between nature and humankind as the 'crisp air laughed to hear' the boys' chorus of glee – resituated and interiorized as part of the life process, to which the individual may turn for refreshment of spirit in face of, and while accepting by forgetting, the harsh realities of the industrialized and urbanized present. Yet it is only one part of the design of the *Carol* thus to map escape routes through the loopholes of nostalgia (by which I mean in this instance, not weak sentimentality, but a strong and socially useful device), or any kind of visionary succour.

The fact of suffering must be confronted, and its lessons learned, and Scrooge is next displayed to himself as a 'solitary' and 'neglected' child, abandoned at school while the others are away for the holidays. The adult takes delight in the visions from books that brought comfort to his young self, but the end point of the episode is a priming for action and role:

> 'Why, it's Ali Baba!' Scrooge exclaimed in ecstasy. 'It's dear old honest Ali Baba! Yes, yes, I know! One Christmas time, when yonder solitary child was left here all alone, he *did* come, for the first time, just like that. Poor boy! And Valentine,' said Scrooge, 'and his wild brother, Orson . . .'
>
> To hear Scrooge expending all the earnestness of his nature on such subjects, in a most extraordinary voice between laughing and crying; and to see his heightened and excited face; would have been a surprise to his business friends in the city, indeed. . . .
>
> Then, with a rapidity of transition very foreign to his usual character, he said, in pity for his former self, 'Poor boy!' and cried again.
>
> 'I wish,' Scrooge muttered, putting his hand in his pocket, and looking about him, after drying his eyes with his cuff: 'but it's too late now.'
>
> 'What is the matter?' asked the Spirit.
>
> 'Nothing,' said Scrooge. 'Nothing. There was a boy singing a Christmas Carol at my door last night. I should like to have given him something: that's all.' (72–3)

This is one of the places in A *Christmas Carol* that can witness to Dickens's sheer prowess in rendering inner process, irrespective of historical context or particular purpose. A recent critic, Philip Davis, for example, cites it as an instance of what Doris Lessing in her autobiography calls 'real remembering', which is 'if even for a flash, even a moment – being back in the experience itself. You remember pain with pain, love with love, one's real best self with one's real best self.' 'Unlike a common autobiography', says Davis, '*A Christmas Carol* [is] not only about the past but for whole moments imaginatively present in it.'[21] This judgement, it might be argued, is itself bounded by ideology, since Davis, and Lessing, are writing – honourably and intelligently – within the liberal–humanist tradition to which Dickens helped to give substance and impetus, and which, in one of its major aspects, values art in proportion to its success in apprehending depth and resourcefulness in persons and mental life. Then, however, the eagerness and quality of Davis's response only goes to demonstrate the effectiveness and standing of Dickens's writing as timeless and self-sufficient psychodrama.

Davis's further brief analysis, though, actually helps us to see that there is, in this and comparable sections of the *Carol*, an objective over and above, or under and beneath, the realization of inward experiencing. The 'miracle' of the passage, for Davis, is that it has a 'double movement, [a] going through the scene both with the feelings the person had at the time and with the feelings and consequences it left in him later'.[22] That movement, if scrutinized, is a notation of unsettlement and re-formation in the protagonist – the working of his conversion. The gaps between sentences and phrases, which Davis terms the 'implicit microseconds' of 'inner thinking and inner recollecting', are the stutters, splutters and pauses of a consciousness breaking up and pressing on to new perceptions, or rediscovering old. Scrooge's 'Nothing' paradoxically emits the pressure of a definite 'something' that is happening to him. The profession of helplessness figures a burgeoning of possibility; anticlimax implies the stirrings of change. 'That's all' are words Scrooge would utter in the decisive business world, but transformed to uncertainty; they are a foreclosure that yet looks for a future in which the chance might arise for him to satisfy his 'wish' to be generous towards the carol-singer. In saying 'it's too late now' he declares that it not too late at all – to repent of one's mistakes, to learn from them, and to seek to make amends.

In all of this there is a doctrine at play, a message being spread. By recognizing his own wretchedness – 'Poor boy!' – Scrooge is able to reach out sympathetically to that other 'boy' who has visited him. The child-like capacity for losing oneself in visionary realms, as the young Scrooge does with Crusoe's parrot, Friday 'running for life', as well as Ali Baba, Valentine and Orson, is respected, but the grown man must pass from exhilarated absorption in the imaginary, pointed in Scrooge's 'extraordinary voice' and his 'heightened and excited face', however desirable that state might be, to self-recognition, imaginative identification with the other person, and love of humankind. The reader of Dickens is drawn into a parallel 'rapidity of transition': contemplating Scrooge looking at Scrooge seeing Ali Baba and the rest, layer upon layer, we exit the accelerando of antic make-believe to rest at last with a keener sense of the plain beauty of humane emotion and acts – 'I should like to have given him something: that's all.' This is at once the tutorial text of the 'Religion of Humanity' and 'The Religion of Humanity' as biblio-practice – reading as both the receipt of instruction and training through ritual observance.

At this point the portrayal of Scrooge's childhood takes a strange and intriguing turn. We learn of an occasion when his sister (mother-to-be of the considerate nephew) had come unexpectedly to the school to take him home, telling him that 'Father is so much kinder than he used to be' and had relented to her intercessions for her brother – 'He spoke so gently to me one dear night when I was going to bed, that I was not afraid to ask him once more if you might come home; and he said Yes' (73–4). The girl's words, together with the fact of Scrooge's desolate vacation sojourns, infer the possibility of maltreatment, a physical or mental cruelty, that would explain his later miser's introversion and defensively hostile gestures towards the world. But Dickens does not take this route. There are no primal scenes of abuse, as there are for David Copperfield, whose consolation from books, his 'reading as if for life', is linked directly to the brutality of the Murdstones which he copes with partly by taking flight into impersonating carefree heroic characters from fiction, Tom Jones or Roderick Random, and partly by exacting vicarious control and judgement by putting his tormentors 'into all the bad ones' (*DC*, Ch. 4, 105–106). Dickens is concerned in the *Carol*, not so much with psychological determinants and logic, nor so much with the structure of Scrooge's past life, as with his present forwards course and the values this highlights and projects.

Thus, the outcome of Scrooge's next memory repeats the humanitarian perspective of the 'Poor boy' segment, though with the difference that, after entering 'heart and soul' into the festive panorama at kind old Fezziwig's where he had been apprentice, Scrooge thinks, not of an unknown suppliant, but of his own man, Bob Cratchit:

> 'What is the matter?' asked the Ghost.
>   'Nothing particular,' said Scrooge.
>   'Something, I think?' the Ghost insisted.
>   'No,' said Scrooge, 'No. I should like to be able to say a word or two to my clerk just now! That's all.' (78)

'That's all' is identical to the end of the previous instalment, but the present tense of the sentence and the phrase 'just now' (which like the word 'presently' hovers between suggestions of the immediate and the forthcoming) express Scrooge's eager confidence that this time the wished-for opportunity to redeem his offence *will* arrive. Progress towards expiation is being made, as it is also in Scrooge's education and skill in knowing the true way. On this occasion he not only reacts to what he is shown but has already taken the point and is able to explicate it: the wonder, Scrooge insists, is not simply that Fezziwig has caused so much gratitude in his people by spending 'but a few pounds' – as the Spirit, testing Scrooge in mock debate, would have it – but that he has power 'in words and looks; in things so slight and insignificant that it is impossible to add and count 'em up'; it is in Fezziwig's considerable gift to render his workers happy or unhappy in their employment, to 'make our service light or burdensome; a pleasure or a toil' (78). Scrooge is now his own Interpreter and can formulate for himself and the benefit of others the lesson he has acquired, which is – reversing his former blind conviction – that satisfaction and success are *not* to be gauged in purely economic terms. Still, however, more is being taught than he knows. When all is said, Fezziwig does spend *something* in pleasing those beneath him and in his care. Well-being and well-doing are made consistent with the culture of money and subservience – with some having more and some having less. Benevolence is good for the business and for the capitalist order of which it is a part.

Three other areas of Victorian cultural idealism are on prominent display at Fezziwig's warehouse party: male friendship, enacted in the twosome of Ebenezer and his 'fellow-prentice' Dick, of whom Scrooge exclaims 'He was very much attached to me, was Dick. Poor Dick! Dear, dear'; heterosexual love, which comes out in the ritual of the dance and courtship, with twenty couples circling in 'affectionate grouping', the three Miss Fezziwigs pursued by the six followers 'whose hearts they broke'; marriage and the family, for Fezziwig and Mrs Fezziwig – she 'worthy to be his partner in every sense of the term' – preside over the gathering of kith, kin, nubile daughters and their suitors, neighbours, servants, and all the employees with fatherly and matronly aplomb and bonhomie (76–8). Two of these themes, possibly all of them, are developed in the remaining flashbacks of Stave Two, both of which involve Belle, the woman to whom Scrooge had once been betrothed.

The first spotlight falls on a recollected conversation pinpointing the turn at which the golden idol of 'Gain' had started to take command of Scrooge, displacing his worship of a dowry-less girl, from whom he agreed to separate (79–81). His face 'had begun to wear the signs of care and avarice'. The language on both sides of the exchange, however, which is strongly reminiscent of the terminology of religious conversion, is curiously relevant to the changes that are happening in the present, as if the dialogue is being projected backwards out of the miser's incipient, as yet confused urge to mend his life and at the same time dictates in cipher the road he must take. Talking of the 'contract' between them, the woman says 'You *are* changed. When it was made, you were another man':

> 'I was a boy,' he said impatiently.
> 'Your own feeling tells you that you were not what you are,' she returned . . .
> 'Have I ever sought release?'
> 'In words. No. Never.'
> 'In what, then?'
> 'In a changed nature; in an altered spirit; in another atmosphere of life; another Hope as its great end. In everything that made my

love of any worth or value in your sight . . . '

 'I would gladly think otherwise if I could,' she answered, 'Heaven knows! When I have learned a Truth like this, I know how strong and irresistible it must be. But if you were free to-day, to-morrow, yesterday, can even I believe that you would choose a dowerless girl . . . or, choosing her, if for a moment you were false enough to your one guiding principle to do so, do I not know that your repentance and regret would surely follow? I do; and I release you. With a full heart, for the love of him you once were.' (80)

Belle's reproaches confer on Scrooge a perverse revolution that is at the moment of recall being itself overturned. What the young man became, his 'changed nature' and 'altered spirit', his devotion to the 'Hope' of amassing wealth, represents a false, ignoble destiny, from which nascent 'regret and repentance' in his older self are working to 'release' him. He is getting back to what he should be – establishing a proper continuity in his life.

Yet, what seems ultimately most striking about these passages at the end of Stave Two is not the ground Scrooge is making up but that which he has irredeemably lost. Belle's opening remark is that she will have no cause to grieve if the object of worship that has replaced her will 'cheer and comfort you in the time to come, as I would have tried to do' (79). The next scenario underscores the terrible price Scrooge has paid for his waywardness – the forfeiture of erotic love, the begetting of children, the joys and support of a family. Belle now appears, a comely matron, at the centre of a pageant of domestic bliss, 'beautiful' grown-up daughter beside her, 'young brigands' all around, husband entering with presents and being affectionately mobbed (80–83). The narrator's attention lingers, at length, over the sensuous appeal of the daughter and the pleasures of physical intimacy, as he watches her being 'pillaged' by her siblings:

> What would I not have given to be one of them! Though I never could have been so rude, no, no! I wouldn't for the wealth of all the world have crushed that braided hair, and torn it down; and for the precious little shoe, I wouldn't have plucked it off, God bless my soul! To save my life. As to measuring her waist in sport, as they did, bold young brood, I couldn't have done it; I should have expected my arm to have grown round it for punishment, and never to have come straight again. And yet I should have dearly liked, I own, to have touched her lips; to have questioned her, that she might have opened them; to have looked upon the lashes of her downcast eyes, and never raised a blush; to have let loose waves of hair, an inch of which would be a keepsake beyond price: in short, I should have liked, I do confess, to have had the lightest licence of a child, and yet have been man enough to know its value. (81–2)

Of this order of desire and experience Scrooge, presumably, has neither knowledge nor expectation, but he does have a sharp sense of a comparable blessing of which he is bereft, a child's vivifying presence in his old age, as it occurs to him that 'such another creature, quite as graceful and as full of promise, might have called him father, and been a spring-time in the haggard winter of his life'. When the husband reports to the wife that he had seen an old friend of hers that day, Mr Scrooge, and that, his partner lying near death, he is 'Quite alone in the world, I do believe', Scrooge pleads 'in a broken voice' to be shown no more (82–3). He confronts us in a symbolic attitude of trauma and penitential anguish – a cautionary spectacle unto himself and others every bit as harrowing as the figure of the enchained and tormented Marley had been.

Here the reinforcement of cultural values is equally by caveat and come-on. While Scrooge's agony warns against the horrors of self-exclusion and non-participation, hearth and home are put on alluring display as a haven of lively contentment, with life-long benefits. The narrator's suspiciously drawn-out tour of the body of the teenage girl – hair, foot, waist, lips, eyes, rich in tactile and ocular excitation – is especially interesting for two reasons. It instances the inclusion of sexual excitement in the panoply of the available and allowable gratifications of Dickens's society – a gentle soft porn – and also forms an allegory of a larger element in the relation between Dickens's text and the reader. The erotic charge of the passage is repeated later in humorous rather than sentimental form in the account of Topper's usage of 'the plump sister' during the game of blind-man's bluff at Scrooge's nephew's Christmas party (104–5), but has a correspondent quality, too, in the 'moist and pulpy' figs, the grapes that make 'people's mouths . . . water', the onions 'winking . . . in wanton slyness at the girls', which adorn the shop windows (90). We see in this the commodification both of womankind and nature, and of art in the form of Dickens's book which is there to be consumed. In this aspect, the *Carol* provokes desire while deferring satisfaction, arouses the thrill of possession while denying ownership – keeps us, in both senses of the word, wanting.

It is true also, as Audrey Jaffe explains, that desire is 'barred', as well as stimulated and prolonged, by these structures of sexual dynamics, which set up 'prohibitions marking gender codes and familial relations'.[23] What the narrator imagines of the relish of touching and looking, the father, who has his daughter 'leaning fondly on him', aptly but potentially at risk, should never think; and the narrator's own thoughts, though piquant, concede, above all through reference to modest 'downcast eyes' and the wish to spare a maiden's 'blush', the imperative of honourable intentions, the proprieties of premarital contact.[24] The vignette suggests as it were a balancing act: a licensing in the realm of the imaginary of hedonistic impulses that vis-à-vis the spheres of the public and actual are censored, channelled and restricted. A similar picture is drawn when Topper, having cornered his ample quarry during blind-man's bluff, gropes her head-dress, her ring, and a certain chain about her neck – things that, as more obviously with her 'silken rustlings', advertise yet screen off the body – before the couple become 'very confidential together, behind the curtains', and we are allowed, or indeed pushed, to envision what is going on in private (105). Even the seductive fruit is ambivalently placed: tempting but behind glass, or at least at arm's length, its touchability subject to careful negotiation of the rules of give and take, pay and purchase. In the regulatory regime of the bourgeois dispensation, which the *Carol* consistently disseminates, illusion and fantasy function as both driving force and release valve.

The cult of domesticity itself is perhaps Dickens's most important contribution to that dispensation. Historians have reported that the early decades of the nineteenth century in England saw a swing in the motivation for marriage away from considerations of wealth and social advantage to romantic attachment – though in practice the former naturally remained governing factors. In the words of John Tosh: 'Not only marriage for love but marriage *as* love was the expectation.'[25] Dickens clearly favours this principle, which is, for example, built into Belle's thesis when releasing Scrooge from his engagement because he no longer centres 'worth or value' in the bequest of her 'love' (80). Tosh links the attitude convincingly to the need of men for a refuge, a haven of therapeutic retreat, in a period when daily work and business took them increasingly away from the family base. This then leads him, however, to the view that 'the comforting image of men at the fireside was about intimacy, not authority'. Intimacy there certainly was, as in the domestic pageant that so tortures Scrooge; and Belle's offspring, as we have seen, have a presence that fits well with Tosh's sense of 'the child [being] at the heart of middle-class sensibility'. On the other hand, authority too is very much in the picture. The place of comfort beheld by Scrooge is also the place of the rule of the father, who marches in – 'attended' by 'a man laden' (82), like a prince, or a hunter-gatherer, or intrepid imperial explorer, other masculine stalwarts of Victorian England – to dispense paternal largesse.

The characteristics of Belle's husband's household recur at a different social level in Bob Cratchit's, which occupies a good portion of Stave Three and comprises one of Dickens's most significant accounts of the family sanctum. Much of what remains to be said about *A Christmas Carol* concerns this and related aspects of the book's ideological content and objectives. But not all. Before leaving Stave Two, we may reprise those experiential and psychological themes which Dickens does not cultivate but which cannot be forgotten either – stories wanting to be told or pressing for centre stage. Of these, we have already touched upon hints of a shadow cast across and forwards from Scrooge's early childhood. And what of his relationship with Dick Wilkins, who was 'very much attached' to him, and who slept beside him under the counter at Fezziwig's? Were Scrooge and Marley, sharers for many years, partners in business only? Did Scrooge love these men, or repress a love for them? Either way, this could yield another explanation of his retreat into isolation and crotchety introversion, and of his curious indifference to Belle's undoubted physical charms, fresh or faded. Such threads of course are speculative, tracing what is latent or potential, rather than actualized, in the text; but they serve to highlight something real, which is the tragic interest of the history of Ebenezer Scrooge. Our sense of an absence and distress in Scrooge's life as he contemplates the bower of married bliss – 'I cannot bear it', he exclaims (83) – cannot remain just a spur to social conformity; in his being bereft of love, of whatever kind, we perceive that his life never can be fully redeemed, that there will always be in some degree a shortfall, a scar, an affliction. There is in this an ambiguity representative of a larger and unresolved tension in what Scrooge amounts to, between character as exemplum and character as state of being, a touchstone of how to live and a study in how we live.

*

By the beginning of Stave Three Scrooge has made such good progress in his rehabilitation that he takes the initiative and implores the next Ghost, Christmas Present, to keep up the pressure: 'To-night, if you have aught to teach me, let me profit by it.' In response the Spirit shows him the Cratchits enjoying Christmas and afterwards, with a step into the future, an empty chair where Tiny Tim, the crippled son, used to sit. When Scrooge, shocked, then begs assurance that the child will be spared, he has quoted back to him the very words which he had cast at the gentlemen collecting for the needy in Stave One: 'What then? If he be like to die, he had better do it, and decrease the surplus population' (97). The sins of the unreconstructed Scrooge can, as we have seen, be described as 'social', but it might also be said that for him society does not exist at all, only the individual and the State: 'It's enough', he had insisted, 'for a man to understand his own business, and not to interfere with other people's' (51). Stave Three marks an important extension in his conversion since, in a precise rejection of his former callous utilitarianism, he comes to recognize all the more deliberately – wholeheartedly – the existence of others and their claims upon his sympathetic attention. The jolt Scrooge receives in understanding, 'overcome with penitence and grief' (97), that it is real people like the innocent Tiny Tim that are at risk from the application of Malthusian population theory – which the Ghost, hammering home the critique, labels 'wicked cant' – is compounded at the end of the Stave when he is once again confronted with his own heartless dogma. 'Have they no refuge or resource?' he asks when being shown the wretched city waifs, Ignorance and Want:

> 'Are there no prisons?' said the Spirit, turning on him for the last time with his own words. 'Are there no workhouses?' (109)

As we shall discover, though, it is not only sympathy that these 'monstrous' forms arouse but also fear and foreboding.

Tiny Tim, however, is not only a catalyst for change in Scrooge but a key figure in Dickens's elaboration of the cult of the family. John Tosh tells us that foreign visitors such as Ralph Waldo Emerson from America and Hippolyte Taine from France recorded that in Victorian England 'domesticity was more evident than piety';[26] with the Cratchits it becomes itself both repository and object of piety, an article of faith for the people living on the inside and for those viewing it from without. The conduct of Bob, Mrs Cratchit and their children (six in all, including Martha, Belinda, Peter and Tiny Tim) takes on the character of a religious ceremony. The Christmas goose enters in 'high procession'; the carving-knife is 'plunge[d] . . . in the breast' with all the diligence of a sacrifice; the 'wonderful' pudding Mrs Cratchit proudly carries in is – as the word 'heresy' in the following quotation infers – a sacred item at the heart of a ritual of dedication and joy:

> Everybody had something to say about it, but nobody said or thought it was a small pudding for a large family. It would have been flat heresy to do so. Any Cratchit would have blushed to hint at such a thing. (95–6)

Bob, priest-in-charge, lays out the appurtenances of the sacrament – apples and oranges, two tumblers, a custard-cup for the punch – and intones the consecration, 'God bless us!', to which the others, in a 'circle', echo their response, followed at last by Tiny Tim, 'God bless us every one!' (97). This is not so much family prayers – a seventeenth-century practice revived by Victorian Evangelicalism – as a substitute mass and gathered church. We have the twofold effect we have noticed before: imagery drawn from religion imparts mystery to a secular endeavour, which then becomes the site of a displaced religious sensibility.

Tiny Tim is an entity that binds the unit together, all the more effectively so because he is potentially an imperfection to be eliminated. He is an icon of the love that looks beyond impairment, and beyond genetics or eugenic theory (subjects of current debate which Dickens will address as positively and more extensively in *Our Mutual Friend*). Dependent on the others in his deficiency, he in turn proves them whole. Significantly, it is Bob, the father, who is closest to the crippled boy: who, in one of the most enduring images from the book, bears him 'upon his shoulder', and who sits holding 'his withered little hand in his, as if he loved the child, and wished to keep him by his side, and dreaded that he might be taken from him' (94, 97). In Bob Cratchit is writ large the good Victorian patriarch, supporting even, indeed especially, his frailest offspring physically and emotionally, as well as financially, and thereby being rendered both literally and figuratively taller and more legitimate in his authority. The crutch and little stool in the chimney corner, left vacant in Scrooge's distraught premonition, are signifiers of this child's talismanic presence in a structure of ideal familial relations – though a structure whose rudiments only are given and which must constantly be worked for and sustained by those who live it, through actions and through acts of faith.[27]

Some words of Tiny Tim's draw direct attention to his emblematic function, his power to move and instruct, but with regard to the larger community: 'he hoped the people saw him in the church, because he was a cripple, and it might be pleasant to them to remember . . . who made lame beggars walk and blind men see' (94). This connects the *Carol*'s presentation of the Cratchits as flourishing nuclear family, inspired by Tiny Tim, with its broader concern for cohesion and well-being in society; and the rest of Stave Three portrays a spectrum of familial and other groups in the same general posture as the Cratchits, 'happy, grateful, pleased with one another, and contented with the time' (99). The sequence ends with the festivities at Scrooge's nephew's but takes in far-flung outposts: 'a cheerful company' assembled around a glowing fire in a desolate place where miners live, 'an old, old man and woman' with three generations of children about them, singing blithely in opposition to the howling wind; lighthouse keepers joining their 'horny hands' at a rough table; a ship's crew where every man had a 'kinder word for another on that day' (100–101). Images of the happy home shade into those of a happy nation. These snapshots, like much else in the *Carol*, prophesy cinematographic techniques, especially in their use of metonymic detail – singing, clasped hands, kind words – against forbidding backgrounds – flinty waste, barren rocks, heaving sea – to stand for peace and fellowship transcending hardship and inhospitable terrain. We are reminded of patriotic film documentary. Here the adaptable hymn might be 'God rest you merry, gentlemen, / Let nothing you dismay'. Harmony and joy prevail.

There is, though, one source of dismay in the midst of all this merriment, a lone fly in the ointment – Scrooge. The revellers at his nephew's make fun of him in a guessing game where the answer is some kind of disagreeable animal, but over the Cratchits his name casts, if only briefly, 'a dark shadow' (98). When Bob, loyal as ever, proposes a toast to 'Mr. Scrooge, Founder of the Feast', his wife, before relenting, denounces the employer as 'odious, stingy, hard, unfeeling'; he is 'the Ogre of the family' (97–8). But that is precisely what Scrooge finally becomes – 'Founder of the Feast'. His destiny is to be called to office in the social order, as paterfamilias, giver of gifts and purveyor of benign authority, God surrogate. He repeats, at an eminence, the fatherly role enacted in differing forms by the charitable guardians of the poor, by old Fezziwig in his business, by Belle's husband, and by Bob Cratchit himself. Before this happens, however, he must learn and illustrate one more vital lesson – how to deal with the fact of death and how to be immortal.

*

Stave Four opens with signs of Scrooge's further awakening. For the first time consciously aiming to reform, he welcomes whatever help the Ghost of Christmas Yet To Come might give: 'As I hope to be another man from what I was, I am prepared to bear you company . . . Lead on!' (111). Presented with a group of businessmen talking flippantly about someone who has died, he is confident that he will work out the 'latent moral for his own improvement', and that sightings of 'the conduct of his future self would give him the clue he missed, and would render the solution of these riddles easy' (113).

As *The Pilgrim's Progress* shows, however, thinking things are easy can be a big mistake. Vain-confidence lurks to baffle and misdirect, leading Christian and Hopeful astray into the grounds of Doubting Castle and the clutches of Giant Despair. To these travellers the guardian Shepherds of the Delectable Mountains point out troops of men below who thought they knew the road but went wrong and now forever walk up and down 'among the tombs', stumbling and bumping into the stones: 'He that wandreth out of the way of understanding, shall remain in the congregation of the dead.'[28] At the beginning of A Christmas Carol Scrooge already has at least one foot in that congregation – the living counterpart of the deceased Marley, heading waywardly for the same damnation. By the end of Stave Four he has acquired sufficient understanding to escape his seeming fate. This final stretch, however, is the one where Scrooge is most humbled and most severely put to the lash of correction. It ends with the sternest blow of all, as he is brought face to face with the inevitability of the grave and his own passing. The gain lies in his having to confront not only this stark reality but also its implications for how he should conduct himself in the here and now.

Contrary to Scrooge's expectations, the scenes through which he is led in Stave Four never do reveal 'the conduct of his future self'. Rather, they show how others will view him, although, until the climax at the foot of a neglected tomb bearing the name of EBENEZER SCROOGE (124), he does not himself realize that he is the subject of the various conversations he overhears. The first visit is to a landscape of hell, which is no far-distant place of judgement in the afterlife but a dismal corner of the city, reached through 'foul and narrow' paths, reeking 'with crime, with filth, and misery' (113–14). A charwoman, a laundress and an undertaker's assistant haggle with a dealer in ill-gotten goods over the going rate for their spoils of a dead man's belongings, from teaspoons and sugar-tongs down to the very shirt in which he was to be buried. Scrooge's response is appropriately one of horror: 'he viewed them with a detestation and disgust, which could hardly have been greater, though they had been obscene demons, marketing the corpse itself' (117). But there is in this sentiment a grim irony and condemnation turned upon Scrooge himself, for the predatory self-interest of the thieves is the subterranean equivalent of his own mercenary nature and dealings. The charwoman, reflecting on what she and her accomplices have done, makes the connection plain for the reader:

> 'What odds then! What odds Mrs. Dilber?' said the woman. 'Every person has a right to take care of themselves. He always did!'
> 'That's true, indeed!' said the laundress. 'No man more so.' (115)

Indeed, it seems less terrible to rob a corpse than to practise usury upon the living, as is brought home in the next scenario, where a young wife cannot but rejoice at the sudden death of the creditor – Scrooge – whose hard heart has driven her family to the verge of ruin:

> She was a mild and patient creature if her face spoke truth; but she
> was thankful in her soul to hear it, and she said so, with clasped
> hands. (120)

The concept of evil, so strikingly evoked in the reference to 'obscene
demons' in the report of Scrooge's reaction to the confederates in crime
and now suggested by the woman's posture of prayerful thanksgiving,
has been emphatically transferred from a religio-theological code and
iconography to the context of people's treatment of other people – the
sin of inhumanity.

During these incidents didactic critique of the pure profit principle is
served by a simple but highly effective device which is a kind of aversion
therapy. No one would want to be classed among the devils or be the
object of a gentle woman's inner loathing. Who, moreover, could bear
the thought of not being 'natural', which is how one of the conspirators
describes Scrooge, 'a wicked old screw . . . [who] wasn't natural in his
lifetime'; or of being a fool for making one's own life a misery only to
benefit others, as the same fiend contemptuously characterizes the miser
who 'frightened every one away from him when he was alive, to profit
us when he was dead!' (115, 117)? But Dickens also wins the reader
over to his viewpoint with positive incentives. A crucial moment comes
when Scrooge is alone with the abandoned corpse:

> Oh cold, cold, rigid dreadful Death, set up thine altar here, and dress
> it with such terrors as thou hast at thy command: for this is thy
> dominion! But of the loved, revered, and honoured head, thou canst
> not turn one hair to thy dread purposes, or make one feature odious.
> It is not that the hand is heavy and will fall down when released; it
> is not that the heart and pulse are still; but that the hand WAS open,
> generous, and true; the heart brave, warm, and tender; and the pulse
> a man's. Strike, Shadow, strike! And see his good deeds springing
> from the wound, to sow the world with life immortal!
>   No voice pronounced these words in Scrooge's ears, and yet he
> heard them when he looked upon the bed. He thought, if this man
> could be raised up now, what would be his foremost thoughts?
> Avarice, hard dealing, griping cares? They have brought him to a
> rich end, truly!
>   He lay, in the dark empty house, with not a man, a woman, or a
> child, to say that he was kind to me in this or that, and for the
> memory of one kind word I will be kind to him. (118)

The homiletic style of the apostrophe to Death affords its content the
status of holy writ or doctrine. That Scrooge hears the words comes, I
think, as a surprise, since they seem at first to belong wholly to the
narrator; but this reorientation works to locate them all the more firmly
as inviolable truth, making them a supernatural visitation, the workings

of uncalled illumination. These paragraphs concentrate the creed of *A Christmas Carol*, which preaches that there is neither Hell nor Heaven, only a life of bad deeds or of good, a reputation for the worse or for the better. Immortality is being remembered well. Fame is the spur.

This concept of 'immortal life' offers a way of coping with death in a secular society; a deserving name abides in the thoughts of others. It places the emphasis, however, squarely on the process of living, for which it sets the golden rule of feeling and charity, the hand 'open, generous, and true', the heart 'brave, warm, and tender'. When Scrooge, indeed, is forced to read his own name on the gravestone in the churchyard he trembles, not with a terror of mortality, but with the horror of having to identify with the man upon the bed: 'Am *I* the man who lay upon the bed?' (124). In making the connection he admits to a fate worse than death – a worthless life, without meaning except as a byword for unnaturalness, which is to be less than nothing.

The Valley of the Shadow of Death is thus Scrooge's Vale of Humiliation; but, brought cathartically low, he is ready to mend. The final movement of Stave Four brings to the fore the theme of personal transformation and the desire for a new life. Scrooge pleads for reassurance that he still 'may change these shadows you have shown me, by an altered life', and asks 'Why show me this, if I am past all hope?'. Simply to raise these questions signals a converted self, which is more directly expressed by his insistence that 'I am not the man I was. I will not be the man I must have been but for this intercourse' (126). Already Scrooge has laid claim to a potential for forging a different track, producing different outcomes:

> 'Men's courses will foreshadow certain ends, to which, if persevered in, they must lead,' said Scrooge. 'But if the courses be departed from, the ends will change. Say it is thus with what you show me!' (124)

What all these utterances, but especially the last-quoted, imply is that individuals have the power to reshape their lives – which is what the *Carol* wants us to believe. Yet Scrooge has only one alternative, a single choice of a worthy life and a life worth living: to participate in the social existence laid out for him, to which he has been at worst antagonistic and at best peripheral. While his formulation about 'Men's courses' turns around the soteriological idea of predestination and subjection to providential design, by suggesting effectual free will, his own course, his salvation, has in fact been predetermined from the first. When remonstrating that he cannot be 'past all hope' he appears to be half remembering the words of Marley's ghost, which had announced itself

as the harbinger of a 'chance and a hope', a 'hope [of shunning] the path
I tread' (63). The end is in the beginning; the proper path already traced.
What on the surface of the text is affirmed as growth, responsibility,
freedom of action, is underneath an engineering of consent.

*

'I am not the man I was.' No: but he is the man he was always meant to
be. Scrooge's *modus vivendi* in Stave Five is not distinct from that of his
former self; it is the opposite. He puts right his sins of omission,
rendering, in his own words, 'a great many back-payments' (131) – a
phrase that suggests the retrieval of a lost or absent true identity, as well
as, more obviously, indicating a turn-around from the ugly to the genial
aspect of *homo economicus*. He rewards the boy handsomely for
fetching the prize turkey and delivering it to the Cratchits, promises a
princely donation to charity, goes to dinner at his nephew's, and, last but
by no means least, increases his clerk's salary, buys him a second coal-
scuttle, and arranges to discuss over a bowl of mulled wine how he
might help him and his family:

> 'A merry Christmas, Bob!' said Scrooge, with an earnestness that
> could not be mistaken, as he clapped him on the back. 'A merrier
> Christmas, Bob, my good fellow, than I have given you, for many a
> year! I'll raise your salary, and endeavour to assist your struggling
> family, and we will discuss your affairs this very afternoon, over a
> Christmas bowl of smoking bishop, Bob! Make up the fires, and
> buy another coal-scuttle before you dot another i, Bob Cratchit!'
> (133)

When, as a prelude to all this, he throws open his window onto a 'clear,
bright, jovial, stirring cold . . . piping for the blood to dance to' (128),
the barriers between self and the world are symbolically cast aside; the
frozen currents of his previous 'secret, and self-contained, and solitary'
existence thaw into a bubbly vivacity; the ice melts, the flint creates
sparks, the oyster produces a pearl. Like the traditional convert Scrooge,
beneath a 'Heavenly sky' and to the sound of 'merry bells', puts on new
raiment, dressing himself ' "all in his best" ' (130) – not to hope for or
to enter the Celestial City but to step out gladly among men, women and
children in the London streets:[29]

> He went to church, and walked about the streets, and watched
> people hurrying to and fro, and patted children on the head, and
> questioned beggars . . . He had never dreamed that any walk – that
> anything – could give him so much happiness. (131)

All in all, it would be difficult to imagine a more colourful or exhilarating promotion for the Religion of Humanity. We find its earnest, graver, and telling equivalent, however, in Dorothea Brooke's awakening in George Eliot's *Middlemarch*, where, after a night of soul-trouble focussed on personal disappointment, the heroine, 'yearn[ing] towards the perfect Right' of her duty towards others, opens the curtains, glimpses in the 'pearly light' of dawn a man with a bundle and a mother with her child, and feels 'a part of that involuntary, palpitating life, and could neither look out on it from her luxurious shelter as a mere spectator, nor hide her eyes in selfish complaining'.[30] As part of the larger Victorian reconfiguration of values, Eliot and Dickens both rewrote conversion experience as release from egotism into empathy. In both, the active moral sense is made paramount.

For many later critics this is Dickens's most important bequest as an analyst of society. John Bowen, for example, discusses *A Christmas Carol* as a wide-awake attack upon the 'destructive selfishness' of capitalism, while Joseph Gold similarly stresses its advocacy of the 'human' as opposed to the monetary conception of worth.[31] There is obviously a case here for seeing Dickens as a certain type of committed radical. The 'siding with the oppressed against the oppressors' that George Orwell highlighted in the novels extends to tyranny of all kinds, including the economic despotism that Scrooge practises on the married couple who owe him money and secretly rejoice in reports of his demise. As Orwell argued in opposition to the strict Marxist viewpoint of the 1930s, though Dickens 'is not *in the accepted sense* a revolutionary writer' his plea for moral integrity, for a ' "change of heart" ' rather than of institutions, may suggest as valid a programme for improvement: ' "If men would behave decently the world would be decent" is not such a platitude as it sounds.'[32]

It is a fact nonetheless that *A Christmas Carol* upholds a system of social relations that is fundamentally conservative. This does not mean simply Dickens's reliance on standard New Testament ethics. He creates in his fable a *mythos* that underwrites an established order, urging adjustment where necessary, but not transformation, let alone overthrow. The narrator's summary sketch of Scrooge's translation into 'as good a master, and as good a man, as the good old city knew' (133), in the penultimate paragraph of the book, where 'city' must imply 'business quarter', projects an image of change from unacceptable introverted capitalist to an affable one. Scrooge may have been condemned for succumbing to the 'master-passion, Gain' (79), which crippled him emotionally and socially, but the *Carol* certainly approves of wealth creation providing the returns are spread around as he eventually disposes them, that is, with an even-handedness consisting, not by any means of equal shares, but of reasonable spending, regular give-aways and donations, and fair top-down management. On occasion, it is true, Dickens sanctions the progressive principle of upward mobility, for the Cratchits aspire to their son Peter becoming 'a man of business', while Bob later gets excited about meeting Scrooge's nephew because he 'shouldn't be at all surprised . . . if he got Peter a better situation' (98, 122). But this is, of course, movement within limits: not so much the idea of unfettered rising by merit – itself grotesquely demonized, we recall, in the career of Uriah Heep – as that of imitating one's betters and of patronage. Master Peter, into the bargain, cuts a jolly figure when dreaming of the 'particular investments' he will make when he starts earning (98). The society that is framed for recommendation in *A Christmas Carol* persistently aligns solidity with hierarchy, and good feelings, both of sympathy and pleasure, with work and financial success.

The pattern recurs at every level of the chain. The gratitude that the warehouse employees feel towards the beneficent and prosperous Fezziwig is echoed in the fact that Bob Cratchit, against all the odds, respects his boss. The miners who labour in the bowels of the earth and the rough sailors aboard ship bear out in their lowly spheres the dedication to 'patient industry' that Scrooge's betrothed – ever a mouthpiece of official wisdom – stipulates as the ticket to *admissible* 'worldly fortune' (80). And always the family is at once a microcosm of the greater unity and its chief bastion. Not only is the home, as we have seen, a source of mutual pleasure, it expressly enables contentment to triumph in the face of privation, as with the Cratchits:

> They were not a handsome family; they were not well dressed; their shoes were far from being water-proof; their clothes were scanty; and Peter might have known, and very likely did, the inside of a pawnbroker's. But they were happy, grateful, pleased with one another, and contented with the time. (99)

One example of the class distinctions that come often to the surface of the text is that Bob's daughter, Martha, works as a 'poor apprentice' to a milliner (98), while the daughter of the woman who might have been Scrooge's wife belongs entirely to the confines of the bourgeois drawing-room, which is itself carefully measured as to relative size and appearance, being 'not very large or handsome, but full of comfort' (81). The vertical arrangement that is thus revealed, however, is also cloaked in the cause of unification. Happiness is not the preserve solely of the well-to-do; and its quality, indeed, is the greater and more appealing, as particularly in the case of the Cratchits, in proportion to the obstacles that are overcome. Dickens does not go so far as to argue as Oliver Goldsmith does, through his spokesman Dr Primrose, that the poor on earth are fortunate and the rich ill-fated since the former will experience the joys of Heaven more intensely;[33] but there is a somewhat similar placatory manoeuvre at work.

Writing on *Oliver Twist*, Steven Connor reminds us of how in the nineteenth century 'truth and the knowledge of truth grew to depend upon narratives of growth, development and culmination, rather than upon classificatory patterns of relationship, difference and subordination'.[34] As Connor points out, Gillian Beer's account in *Darwin's Plots* of the wide-ranging influence of evolutionary theory is relevant here, as is Michel Foucault's characterization of the 'epistemic break' between the eighteenth and nineteenth centuries as a move from the Classical 'table' of correspondences which 'distributed across a permanent space the non-quantitative identities and differences that separated and united things' to the nineteenth-century narrative of History, which 'was to deploy, in a temporal series, the analogies that connect distinct organic structures to one another'.[35] *A Christmas Carol* conceives society very much on the old model of *discordia concors*, a fixed synchrony of separate but interdependent elements. We have already encountered Soame Jenyns's unreserved advocacy in the previous century of a God-given system of subordination in his *Free Enquiry into the Nature and Origin of Evil*:

> The universe is a system whose very essence consists in subordination; a scale of beings descending by insensible degrees . . . It would have been no . . . instance of God's wisdom to have created no beings but of the highest . . . It is, moreover, highly probable that there is such a connection between all ranks and orders by subordinate degrees that they mutually support each other's existence, and every one in its place is absolutely necessary towards sustaining the whole.[36]

Dickens continues this type of configuration, but he occludes the fact of inequality implicit in the notion of rank or degree, and removes God without sacrificing the assumption that things are *naturally* as they are, rather than man-made. He incorporates into the design the material concerns of an increasingly urban and commercial culture, not only setting value on work and money – 'business' and improvement through 'patient industry' (including the long-suffering Bob's and willing Martha's) – but also, conveniently for the status quo, proclaiming that disadvantage, as in the subsistence living of the Cratchits, can be transcended from within, or be alleviated by the better-off like Scrooge

– where we have the perfect reverberation of Jenyns's pronouncement that 'charity' is a duty by which 'God as it were demands our assistance to promote universal happiness'.[37]

Dickens was of course not alone in occupying such positions on society. A text by another who did so, the fashionable preacher Henry Liddon, canon of St Paul's, makes manifest motivations and strategic ends that are in the *Carol* undeclared. Much less sanguine about the mind-set of the underprivileged than is apparent in the accounts of the resilient and uncomplaining Cratchits, Liddon, in one of his sermons, tells his congregation that 'poverty' brings 'degradation of character in the home . . . and the loss of self-respect, and of all that loss implies, through the continued, unappeased, ever-increasing envy of the lot of others'.[38] These words of vigilant concern encompass the deleterious and unsettling effects of the straitened circumstances of working men in general, including humble clerks like Bob Cratchit; but Liddon's main subject is the mass of labouring poor who live in the 'dreariness and squalor' of 'the neglected quarters of a great town'. While the Cratchit formation in Dickens, if we may call it that, is a holding operation in the service of stability at one level of society, a reassuring of the lower middle or upper working class of their place and prospects within the scheme of things, it is also a line of forward defence against the greater menace of an expanding urban proletariat. The foreboding of civil unrest implicit in Liddon's reference to 'envy' is the polite counterpart of Dickens's stern warning of the threat being bred in the 'degradation' of 'wolfish' Ignorance and Want, the most haunting of the *Carol*'s Puritan-style cautionary spectacles, child-beasts emblematic of a wider alienation. 'This boy is Ignorance. This girl is Want. Beware them both, and all of their degree', cries the Spirit, 'stretching out its hand towards the city': 'but most of all beware this boy, for on his brow I see that written which is Doom, unless the writing be erased. Deny it! . . . And bide the end!' (108). The Apocalypse for Dickens is not the end of the world but the violent disintegration of society.

Peter Ackroyd's biography of the writer, which covers in detail his forays into the maelstrom of metropolitan 'Crime, Disease and Misery', shows that he put some hope in elementary education as a means of alleviating the rising tide of what he elsewhere referred to as 'taint and dirt and pestilence'.[39] This commitment to social reform, however, is not in any way at odds with his belief in a structure of subordination; the likes of Ignorance and Want belong (in the narrator's words) to no grade of 'wonderful creation' at all, but are 'a perversion of humanity', 'monsters . . . horrible and dread' (108), and as such they have the potential for disastrous *in*subordination, which must be averted. To reach down across the divide to the underclass, moreover, is to institutionalize the gap, even though it may be narrowed. Capitalism itself has been importantly defined as possessing 'a spirit that travels far and wide', giving and taking of the spirit as well as of material goods and resources;[40] but in so doing it continuously re-creates and confirms the distance between classes, as between races, nations, and other entities. The allegorical mode, as Dickens uses it here, is a means of setting a measured, that is a safe and negotiable, space: in the representations of Ignorance and Want the hordes that lie dangerously beyond the pale are drawn into the frame, are made symbolically visible, so that they may be contemplated, related to, and managed, the last of these because the pictures frighten, appal, and provoke a wise philanthropic response, where welfare projects are a small price to pay for preventing Armageddon, and for a quiet and more productive land.[41]

'Wise philanthropy' is one of Liddon's formulations, which he places alongside 'wise laws' on housing, holidays, and the hours of daily labour as measures needed to improve and unite the country.[42] The *Carol* never talks about employment or any other laws, though Scrooge's eventual more equitable treatment of Bob covers ground similar to that in Liddon's reference, and with similar sentiment. Dickens, it seems, would leave to the enlightened individual responsibilities which for Liddon required a framework of legislation. All the same, both thinkers recommend sensible and alert – 'wise' – liberality as the foundation of social discipline and order; and Liddon, like Dickens, makes the home, not the State, the royal institution of learning in this field of competence, for

> In the natural course of things, kindliness, courtesy, refinement, are the products of home life . . . [At] home the finer side of human nature has a chance of growing, as being sure of its nutriment and its welcome. At home a man . . . finds a field for the play of those affections in the exercise of which earthly happiness mainly consists.[43]

In Matthew Arnold's famous thesis the civilized 'culture' that was 'the most resolute enemy of anarchy' was vested in and trickled sparingly down from an intelligentsia educated, on the public school model, in finely tuned sensibilities and 'the best that has been thought and known'.[44] In contrast to this evident exclusiveness, Dickens and Liddon located it in the flow of quotidian relationships – the practical exercise from day to day of 'the finer side of human nature', within the four walls of the family home and in the larger arena. Nonetheless, the discourse of all three operates in the corporate interest of the nation, and of the

State, in ways that presuppose and lend strength to a class-based system. The *Carol* does this silently, but thereby the more subtly and effectively. What makes it so beautifully persuasive as an enculturation text is that it never lays any cards on the table, either by theorizing on issues of policy or by declaring allegiance to sectional interests. Arnold's *Culture and Anarchy* is written for a well-born liberal elite, a ruling class shaped and served by the code of Thomas Arnold's Rugby, defining itself in opposition to the 'barbarism' of the increasingly assertive Nonconformist tradition of commerce and trade; Liddon's fervent, intellectual sermon is written for a broader well-to-do audience of metropolitan churchgoers; *A Christmas Carol* is written for everyone.[45]

*

It has been said that 'Ideology, broadly speaking, is *meaning in the service of power*'.[46] On this basis the text of Scrooge's reclamation is unreservedly ideological. The power that it serves belongs overarchingly to the social system itself, though there are degrees of subsidiary power within that mechanism, some people getting more out of it and having more of a say in it than others. Brought in from the cold, responsibly circulating himself and his money, exhibiting always and encouraging everywhere 'the finer side of human nature', Scrooge is ultimately refashioned as a kingpin of communal life – like Tiny Tim, but at the top end of the scale, a binding agent and enabler within the narrative and in its symbolizing function vis-à-vis a confederacy of readers. He fills, as we know, the exemplary parts of 'good . . . friend', 'good . . . master', 'good . . . man' (134), and indeed combines these in his new attitude to the Cratchits, as is signalled by his addressing Bob familiarly by his first name and more formally as 'Bob Cratchit' in virtually the same breath (132) – closing yet keeping distance. To Tiny Tim, we are told, he becomes a 'second father'. Patriarchy is ever a *sine qua non* of the concept of successful community in the *Carol*. At the same time, however, described as 'one whose own heart laughed: and that was quite enough for him', Scrooge also develops a likeness to another Victorian star turn, the child – a character he has already taken on in his initial rejuvenation, when he cries 'I'm quite a baby . . . I'd rather be a baby. Hallo! Whoop! Hallo here!' (128). Childhood in Dickens is often associated with pain and oppression, as in the figure of the lonely young Scrooge and his reincarnation in David Copperfield, but presently we have the happy and innocent specimen, epitomizing the well-adjusted grown-up's surviving capacity for voracious and carefree enjoyment, which is very much a necessary gift in consumer culture. The rehabilitated Scrooge not only enacts the appropriate roles and relationships of a flourishing and orderly society, he mutates at last into a composite image of them, an icon within a larger bourgeois iconography.

John Leech's illustration in the first edition of the *Carol* of Scrooge serving hot punch to Bob draws out and reinforces this effect. Here, Scrooge appears as a cross between an august father figure and a blissful big baby well capable of making whoopee, while Bob, in accordance with his place in the scheme of things, resembles a good boy, eager and more than ever pleased with the time. The mix of 'liberal' and 'conservative' strains that we have so often noticed runs through the picture. Hierarchy is built into the detail and spatial structure of the scene, with Scrooge, dressed in a flowing robe, dishing out, liberally but in due measure, from a throne-like high chair and Bob, just below and off-centre, sitting expectantly and at attention on the edge of his seat, cup in hand and hat respectfully on lap. Garlands festoon the walls, giving nature's blessing; a candle burns, casting 'holy' light; a fire blazes on the 'altar' of the hearth. Scrooge and the event at which he presides shade allegorically into the S/spirit of Christmas, but a secular social arrangement is thereby put the more seductively on display, shrouded in ritual permanence and glow. It is a fitting gloss to the *Carol* as secularizing text, moreover, that the ceremony of humane and material exchange thus projected should subsume the core imagery of supernatural faith: Bob is in his way both father (man) and son (boy), Scrooge, in his, Father, Son (baby) *and* Spirit.

*

Not everyone likes the end of *A Christmas Carol*. Graham Holderness, for example, says of it categorically that 'the writer's imagination fails': Scrooge is allowed to slide into 'a rarefied limbo of Christmas sentiment and Christian charity, so abstract as to be empty of life and meaning'; his encounter with the three ghosts is 'far more "credible", far more "realistic", than this closing vision of a life of permanent goodness, . . . which scarcely resembles human life at all'.[47] In one respect, of course, this misses the point; the coda *A Christmas Carol* is not about the imaginative rendering of life at all, but the enciphering and 'selling' of a cultural dispensation – meaning in the service of power – and as such it, as it were, *signs off* the 'edifying' characterization that has gone before. On exit Scrooge is like a figure in an enjoyable cartoon, which is what Leech very cleverly builds on. On the other hand, Holderness does bring out a fairly obvious and important fact about the *Carol*, that it is

Fig. 1   'Scrooge entertains Bob Cratchit' by John Leech.

ultimately a work divided against itself. 'The End Of It', as Stave Five is entitled, is not the *Carol*'s single last word or sole enduring impression. There are dimensions of the text as a whole that fret at the rounded, celebratory conclusion, situating it as contrivance and a surrender of insight, and being themselves retrospectively highlighted by its evident narrowing of focus. Of these cross-grain factors, the most significant, of which we have had strong inklings already, concerns the conception of Scrooge; but there is something also in the treatment of society and humanity at large that demands comment. A good starting point is a passage we have looked at before.

In Stave One, we recall, Scrooge's nephew describes Christmas as 'the only time I know of . . . when men and women seem by one consent to open their shut-up hearts freely, and to think of people below them as if they really were fellow-passengers to the grave, and not another race of creatures bound on other journeys' (49). This can be read with alternative emphases, as either optimistic or pessimistic. Joseph Gold, a critic very much of the humanist persuasion, sees everything in the best light, taking from the *Carol* the message that 'It is Christmas all the time for the annual event is only ritual expression of ever-present spiritual possibility';[48] but possibility is one thing, actuality another and, though the positive values behind the nephew's statement are clear, we can hardly resist the implication that, if the yearly festival is 'the *only* time' when divisions are bridged, the show of fellow feeling is an exception that proves the rule of customary rift and bleak indifference. This negative thread persists in the *Carol*, pulling against not only the bluff closure of Stave Five and its confident salute to 'the good old world' (134) but the philosophy of collective well-being that is being woven throughout. Vice versa, the exaggerated good cheer of the final paragraphs of the book, and the recurrent pleading of the special healing spirit and merry time of Christmas that it rounds off, leave all the more exposed both the defects of human nature (conceded, we may note, in the nephew's reference to the 'shut-up hearts' of men and women) and the routine fault lines of class and inequality (pointedly caught in his own casual use of the word 'below'). Though the Cratchits are happy and get better off, for instance, there are still pawnbrokers, scanty meals, ragged clothes, and degrees of subservience. The miners who assemble at Christmas with their extended families are bound nonetheless to labour and a 'barren waste' (100). The sailors who exchange kind words 'on that day' (101) are subject all the same to the tensions of a tight, or a sinking, ship. That is to say, 'the good old world' remains, beneath the gloss, an imperfect and iniquitous one.

There is in the *Carol*, then, an effect whereby affirmative perspectives seem overdetermined and point up and are questioned by evidences of a grimmer and more troubling reality than they can accommodate or admit to. It puts a bourgeois culture successfully in place, and in alliance with it a post-religious Christian ontology; but, at certain points, it also supplies the wherewithal for challenging its own positions, and for deconstructing them as a wilful (mis)reading of humanity as essentially conforming to and best fulfilled in the already decided terms rendered palpable in Scrooge's converted self, the contented Cratchit family, and all the other paradigms of good conduct and being-in-the-world. In other words, the ideology of the *Carol* is made manifest, discussable, and controversial. That, at least, is one upshot of the presence of such unresolved issues as we have considered. There is, however, another, which is that they push the text beyond ideology and onto a broader philosophic plain. The point can be brought home by an incident near the conclusion of the narrative, where Scrooge is reported as giving little heed to the people who laughed at his altered personality, since

> he was wise enough to know that nothing ever happened on this globe, for good, at which some people did not have their fill of laughter in the outset; and knowing that such as these would be blind anyway, he thought it quite as well that they should wrinkle up their eyes in grins, as have the malady in less attractive forms. His own heart laughed and that was quite enough for him. (134)

This, I take it, is meant to support the status of Scrooge as *exemplum*, the idea that he is in the right, that he has found a superior outlook and enviable state of mind. Yet, on close reading, he cuts a rather ambiguous figure; though, as we have seen, a central force for good in his world, he now seems oddly out on a limb, strangely on the edge rather than in the thick of things. Perhaps he is the myopic one, a kind of holy fool wrapped in his own happy innocence and shielded from the ills and ill will – the 'malady' – abroad. But 'malady' there certainly is, whether it touches Scrooge or not. If on one level the *Carol* hails Scrooge and the reader for a particular culture of duty and fulfilment, on another it reveals the human condition as a matter of existing, of keeping going and doing the best we can, in a difficult, flawed, and often antagonistic world. This is the characteristic double vision of the Dickensian novel – ideology and experiential wisdom, the latter outreaching and detaching us from the former, making it a subject of debate.

More specifically of the protagonist himself, the impression grows in these later stages of the *Carol* that there are two Scrooges, the narrator's Scrooge, who plays his emblematic part in a plot whose ends are neatly tied, and a deeper, more complex Scrooge, whose make-up exceeds the demands of that plot, and who asks questions of it. One thing that is put under query is the very reliability of his new life, the certainty that it will last; for there is a point near the end of Stave Four when his own words invite us, if not actually to doubt his alteration, at least to set limits to it: 'I will honour Christmas in my heart, and *try to keep it all the year*' (126: italics mine). Resolutions are notoriously breakable: will Scrooge keep his? Will the change in him be constant or spasmodic? Will there be a relapse, a backsliding? This is another of the *Carol*'s untold stories, suppressed, like those of childhood trauma and secret or absent love, in favour of the narrative of enculturation, yet, also like them, inerasable, crying out for expression, and making the laughing-ever-after Scrooge of the 'End of It' look like a fairytale proposition.

This configuration of the two Scrooges has a precedent in Puritan conversion narrative, but the *Carol* finally produces a disjunction where, certainly in Bunyan, there had been indissoluble coexistence. For Bunyan conversion never did have a point of completion, after which there was a perfect reborn self, but was a never-ending process. In *Grace Abounding* he stresses how the 'old Adam' still lives on in him, forever threatening setbacks and reversion; conflict between the promptings of nature and of the spirit persist so far that even in the pulpit he has been so 'estranged' from the things he has been speaking that it was 'as if [his] head had been in a bag all the time of the *exercise*'.[49] Scrooge's transformation may be understood as similarly precarious – as perpetual '*try*[*ing*]' rather than permanent triumph. He goes on to declare at the close of Stave Four, 'I will live in the Past, the Present, and the Future. The Spirits of all Three shall strive within me. I will not shut out the lessons that they teach' (126). This utterance, powerfully accentuated by its verbatim repetition at the beginning of Stave Five, does keep faith with the parabolic theme of Scrooge's rescue from stagnation for a useful and rewarding existence; but it signifies neither rest nor completedness, whether of the one-dimensional Scrooge whose 'heart laughed; and that was quite enough' or that compound embodiment of roles to which he is simultaneously consigned, a bright figure within a tapestry of social relations. Nor is it in line with the regular conception of temporality as a sequence that assures us of order and significant continuity in our lives or, in Carlyle's words, that offers a patterning which allows the individual to 'unite himself in clear conscious relation . . . with the whole Future and the whole Past'.[50] Rather, it indicates an advance into unpredictable territory, where there lie both the treasure mines and the minefields of psychological experience; an unlocking of the several capacities by which we may live more fruitfully and bid to live better, the powers of memory, reflection, sensitivity, but also of the dark side, error, pain, the irredeemable. This is to say, of course, that in pointing forward here the text also looks back. Scrooge's pledge about how things will be recuperates and revalidates previous depths, the inward events already enacted, or in some cases unrealized. Lessons, and the learning of them, remain important, but the psychodrama of *A Christmas Carol* outdistances its socio-didactic purposes and resolution. The story of Scrooge bequeaths a richly textured account of being-in-the-world as a condition of striving, an infinite complexity of loss and gain, suffering and achievement, challenge and resourcefulness. 'Natural happiness' (to recall W.H. Mallock) is its end point but not its substance or centre.

In the final reckoning, however, though the *Carol* thus invites strong readings as experience text (as in Davis or Holderness) as opposed to culture text (as in Jaffe), the truth is that it is always both. The protagonist cannot choose the grounds of his striving, which takes place, not in an open or metaphysical realm, but within the bounds of social ideals and constraint. A possible analogy for the 'Past, Present and Future' passage is to be found in the thoughts of one of Bunyan's contemporaries on the other side of the Channel:

> Le moindre mouvement importe à toute la nature; la mer entière change pour une pierre. Ainsi, dans la grâce, la moindre action importe par ses suites à tout. Donc tout est important.
>
> En chaque action, it faut regarder, outre l'action, notre état présent, passé, futur, et les autres à quoi elle importe, le voir les liaisons de toutes ces choses. Et lors on sera bien retenu.

> (The slightest physical movement bears on all of nature; the entire sea is altered by a single stone. Similarly, in the spiritual realm, the least action entails consequences for everything else; everything therefore is important.
>
> In every action, our scrutiny must pass beyond the action itself to examine our present, past, and future states, the others it will affect, and how all these things are interconnected. And then we shall indeed be put under restraint.)[51]

Did Dickens know this passage from Pascal's *Pensées*? It seems probable. D.A. Miller, in his great study of the 'massive thematization of social discipline' in the nineteenth-century English novel, remarks that Pascal's first paragraph 'evokes the world of significant trifles related to one another in a minute causal network: the world to which the nineteenth-century novel gives solidity of specification'.[52] With regard to the *Carol*, however, it is the second paragraph that catches the eye, and not just on account of the reference to examining 'our present, past, and future states'. Pascal's statement at this point could serve as a succinct manifesto for a Religion of Humanity and for a belief in the interdependence of personal well-being and a concern for the well-being of others. Yet there is no skirting the fact that this outlook, this creed, entails a curtailment of freedom; to apply the virtues of prudence, caution and fellowship, weighing the consequences of our conduct for ourselves and for others, as Pascal and Dickens both insist we must do, is to embrace a programme of willing self-regulation – to be put 'under restraint'. The adage has it that in God's service lies perfect freedom, but it is so no longer when the deity is the Greater Good. As we have seen, the liberation of Scrooge in Stave Five – 'light as a feather . . . happy as an angel . . . merry as a school-boy . . . giddy as a drunken man' (127) – is an illusory surface, an adornment, as the use of the dazzling similes indicates: he has been redeemed so as to become a functionary of the social system. Here, of course, we encounter more plainly than ever the 'liberal subject' of recent theory, the term with which Miller alludes 'not just to the subject whose private life, mental and domestic, is felt [falsely] to provide inarguable evidence of his constitutive "freedom" but also to, broadly speaking, the political regime that sets store by this subject'.[53] To adopt Miller's designation of Victorian fiction at large, the point of A Christmas Carol as 'spiritual exercise' is to confirm novel-readers, as well as Scrooge himself, in their identity as 'liberal subjects'.

Then, as we have also seen, the Carol in its afterlife complicates and pressurizes this prospectus. Yet it does so finally not only because psychodrama can steal the show and get us as it were to default on our receptivity to ideological persuasion, or because ideology comes to the surface and parades itself as device, or because it becomes more generally, and all the more as time passes, an analysable element within an interpretable text – where, it must be reiterated, it might nevertheless be judged valuable. There is something else. Between what Pascal and Scrooge each says about past, present, and future there is after all a significant difference: the former talks of 'examin[ing]' them, the latter about them 'striv[ing] within' him and his 'liv[ing] in' them; the former's words imply a commitment to caring and self-control, the latter's an urge to give himself over to the currents within him and the influences from without and to exist – 'live' – in terms of them. Now, these forces, which will remain forever active, may produce, not conformity, but resistance to social and political restraint, a 'striving' *not* to be taken in and taken over. They may constitute the individual not as 'subject' but as misfit. So, does the Carol present any actual modelling of this counter-positioning? We think again of the gay – that is, homosexual – Scrooge, perhaps struggling to come out; of the Scrooge anguished with the pains of irrecoverable and unresolved loss; of the Scrooge of an uncertain future, the potential backslider, the possible apostate. For sure, such types and others like them take the larger stage of Dickens's novels.

We are brought here, moreover, to an odd fact. Why do those who have read the book, let alone those who have not, tend to think of Scrooge as the archetypal miser rather than as a man who was saved? The name is relevant, of course: 'Scrooge' hardly sounds like a kind heart or secular saint. Thinking further, however, we may reflect that the soteriology of bourgeois humanist culture produces and has need of its strong, memorable images of damnation like any other. Antisocial Scrooge – flinty, icy, humbug Scrooge – graphically embodies a reprobate condition that must, if we are to find salvation, be shunned for very life; he is 'Ignorance' to his own 'Christian', heart-hardened 'Man in the Iron Cage' to his own enlightened convert – scapegrace to his own worthier and integrated self. Yet the hold that the old Scrooge has upon the imagination may at the same time be seen otherwise than as the impress of the negative term. As socialized beings we can have no admiration for his self-enclosed existence, but we can have a respect, however sneaking, for the refusal to be incorporated, the desire for autonomy, that it represents, in however delinquent a form. With Scrooge *agonistes*, both before and after the inquisitorial Spirits come to teach him the error of his ways, we empathize because he is a relatively free spirit – because, as D.A. Miller helps us realize, we know the fundamentally mundane, unheroic, carceral future that lies in wait. This explains our subterranean delight in his unregenerate state. This is why it leaves so indelible a mark.

Freud can guide us a little onwards here, and coax us to a conclusion. It is wittily told in the final paragraph of the *Carol* that Scrooge had no more intercourse with Spirits but lived ever afterwards 'upon the Total Abstinence Principle' (133). His life in general, however, has come indubitably to be ruled by the Pleasure Principle – the pursuit of happiness for himself and for others. This is exactly the motivation Freud at first saw as governing actions and psychological drives, the objective being always in some manner 'an avoidance of unpleasure or a production of pleasure'; but the great revisionary speculations of *Beyond the Pleasure Principle*, extrapolated from evidences of '*an urge in organic life to restore an earlier state of things*', then proposed that '*the aim of all life is death*'. For a long time, perhaps, organisms were being readily created anew and died easily, until 'external influences altered in such a way as to oblige the still surviving substance to diverge more widely from its original course of life and to make ever more complicated *détours* before reaching its aim of death'. This of course runs counter to the positivist notion of life – whether on a universal or individual plane – as progressive development; the course between origins and ends comprises, not forwards growth but, as Freud says, 'circuitous paths to death, faithfully kept to by the conservative instincts'. The instincts of 'self-preservation' and 'self-assertion' serve the purpose of 'warding off any possible ways of returning to inorganic existence other than those which are immanent'. The organism wishes to die in the fashion proper to it, and which is built into it.[54]

What the pre-converted Scrooge wants to do is to take a short cut to death. Indeed, so cramped and stagnant is his life that it is already a form of 'inorganic existence'. The sights of the corpse upon the bed and of his grave are unveiled to him by the Ghost of the Future, but they not only prophesy his end but symbolize his present course. The Spirits, which may be considered regenerative forces within Scrooge himself, accuse him of wasting his life, that is of a kind of self-slaughtering, and, if we continue Freud's model, teach him to make the obligatory and apposite detour. However, when talking of the organism as having an 'immanent' sense of the direction it should take, of being programmed to complete and not break the circuit, Freud does not, in this work, think about what the determinants or content of the route might be. It has been apparent throughout our discussion of the *Carol* that the Spirits and their revelations cannot be taken simply as properties of the psyche, but represent specific cultural values and codes of conduct which have been or are being internalized in the mind of 'the subject'. As we have also witnessed in Scrooge's altered being and the surrounding topography of social relations, the culture for which Scrooge and the reader are thus conscripted, that combination of hierarchical capitalism and secular humanism, may, though no utopia, be estimated as much more for the better than for the worse in making life worth living against the background of an unsettled and difficult world. It still serves us well, though imperfectly. Whatever the advantages, however, their price is individual freedom: Scrooge's path is not of his own choosing; the Spirits who release him from mind-forged manacles also take possession of him. Hence, the abiding ambivalence of our response to his story. We rejoice in his rescue from the brink yet have an interest in his brinkmanship, are glad that he gets a life yet never relinquish a satisfaction with his desire to have a different one, or to have none. As outsider Scrooge strikes the chord of our deep-down, and impossible, wish to live and to die on our own terms.

Notes

1. Charles Dickens, *A Christmas Carol*, in *Charles Dickens: The Christmas Books*, Vol. 1, ed. Michael Slater (Harmondsworth: Penguin Books, 1971; repr. 1985), p. 69. All references are to this edition, and are hereafter given in the text.

2. Slater, ed. cit., p. xi. See John Lucas, *The Melancholy Man: A Study of Dickens's Novels* (London: Methuen, 1970), pp. 137–41; Joseph Gold, *Charles Dickens: Radical Moralist* (Toronto: Copp Clark, 1972), pp. 147–54. Lucas and Gold give standard liberal-humanist readings of the text, stressing Dickens's development of a scheme of moral values. William E. Morris, 'The Conversion of Scrooge: A Defense of That Good Man's Motivation', *Studies in Short Fiction*, 3 (1965), 46–55, mounts a helpful account of the various motifs of the *Carol*, and particularly of their reversal as a register of Scrooge's exemplary journey from dehumanized businessman to rounded human being. Elliot L. Gilbert, 'The Ceremony of Innocence: Charles Dickens' *A Christmas Carol*', *PMLA*, 90 (1975), 22–31, offering interesting parallels with the book of Job and other biblical materials, argues that Scrooge returns to a state of 'metaphysical innocence' that predates 'the character mechanisms that a man acquires through the process of living' (p. 24). Craig Buckwald, 'Stalking the Figurative Oyster: The Excursive Ideal in *A Christmas Carol*', *Studies in Short Fiction*, 27 (1990), 1–14, is a stimulating brief critical study of the work as a celebration of 'excursive sociality' (p. 14). Graham Holderness, 'Imagination in *A Christmas Carol*', *Etudes Anglaises*, 32 (1979), 28–45, focuses on the *Carol*'s expression, not least through the three spirits, of 'the transforming wisdom and regenerative moral power of the imagination' (p. 36). Audrey Jaffe's elegant and perceptive interpretation of the *Carol* as enculturation text, 'Spectacular Sympathy: Visuality and Ideology in Dickens's *A Christmas Carol*', *PMLA*, 109 (1994), 254–65, came to my attention after this chapter was first drafted. It has, however, been important in helping me to refine my ideas, though not always through agreement.

3. W.H. Mallock, *Is Life Worth Living?* (London: Chatto & Windus, 1880), pp. 76–7, 104, 111–12.

4. Mallock, pp. 19–20.

5. Bunyan's popularity with Victorian authors and readers forms the basis of Barry Qualls's enquiries in *The Secular Pilgrims of Victorian Fiction* (Cambridge: Cambridge University Press, 1982). Qualls has a chapter on Dickens ('Transmutations of Dickens' Emblematic Art', pp. 85–138) but nowhere mentions *A Christmas Carol*.

6. T.R. Wright, *Theology and Literature* (Oxford: Basil Blackwell, 1988), p. 111.

7. William Thackeray, 'A Box of Novels', *Fraser's Magazine*, 29 (February 1844), pp. 153–69; repr. in *Charles Dickens: The Critical Heritage*, ed. Philip Collins (London: Routledge & Kegan Paul, 1971), p. 149.

8. Jaffe, 'Spectacular Sympathy', p. 255. Sergei Eisenstein's theory is set out in 'Dickens, Griffith, and the Film Today', *Film Form* (New York: Harcourt, 1949), pp. 195–255.

9. John Bunyan, *Grace Abounding to the Chief of Sinners*, ed. Roger Sharrock (London: Oxford University Press, 1966), pp. 45ff.; *The Pilgrim's Progress*, ed. Roger Sharrock (Harmondsworth: Penguin Books, 1984), pp. 151–7.

10. Thomas Robert Malthus, *Essay on the Principle of Population*, 2nd edn (London, 1803), p. 531.
11. Alexander Pope, *Essay on Man*, Epistle IV, line 396.
12. Gold, *Charles Dickens: Radical Moralist*, p. 151.
13. *Pilgrim's Progress*, ed. Sharrock, pp. 66–7.
14. *Pilgrim's Progress*, p. 67.
15. In their meditations the Puritans proceeded in the belief that, since the Creation was specifically ordered by God, everything was charged with divine revelation; that, in the words of Isaac Ambrose, 'if [the heart] be sanctified, it ordinarily distils holy, sweet and useful Meditation out of all objects' (*Prima, Media & Ultima* (London, 1654), II, 68). Thus, the topics in the *Occasional Meditations* of the seventeenth-century divine Joseph Hall range from 'the change of weather' to 'the sight of a left-handed man' (3rd edn, London, 1633).
16. *Pilgrim's Progress*, p. 205.
17. Richard Baxter, *The Saints Everlasting Rest*, 4th edn (London, 1653), Part 4, p. 187.
18. *Grace Abounding*, ed. Sharrock, pp. 4–5. Dickens's interest in memory as a source of inspiration and instruction has perhaps a closer antecedent in Wordsworth's theory of 'spots of time' in *The Prelude*, 'Which with distinct pre-eminence retain / A vivifying Virtue, whence . . . / . . . our minds / Are nourished and invisibly repair'd': 'So feeling comes in aid / Of feeling, and diversity of strength / Attends us, if but once we have been strong' (*Prelude* 1805, XI. 258–60, 264–5; 326–9: ed. Ernest de Selincourt, 2nd edn rev. Helen Darbishire (Oxford: Clarendon Press, 1959)). Yet Wordsworth is himself in this adapting Puritan meditative practice: see my 'Wordsworth, Bunyan, and the Puritan Mind', *English Literary History*, 41 (1974), 212–34.
19. *Pilgrim's Progress*, pp. 41, 99.
20. Jaffe, 'Spectacular Sympathy', p. 257.
21. Doris Lessing, *Under My Skin* (London: HarperCollins, 1994), p. 218; Philip Davis, 'Why Do We Remember Forwards and Not Backwards?', in *Mortal Pages, Literary Lives: Studies in Nineteenth-Century Autobiography*, ed. Vincent Newey and Philip Shaw (Aldershot: Scolar Press, 1996), p. 83.
22. Davis, p. 83. John Foster wrote in 1805 of the idea 'of its being possible for a man to live back again in his infancy, through all the scenes of his life, and to give back from his mind and character, at each time and circumstance, as he repassed it, exactly what he took from it, and when he was there before' ('On a Man Writing Memoirs of Himself', *Essays in a Series of Letters* (London: Holdsworth and Ball, 1865), pp. 22–3).
23. Jaffe, 'Spectacular Sympathy', p. 258.
24. Jaffe (p. 258) appears to see the responses of the narrator and the father as conflated in the passage of wishful thinking about the girl. They are of course distinct, the narrator's actual and expressible feelings being in the father potential but taboo, unrealizable though at some level possibly real.
25. John Tosh, 'Home? It's Where the Heart Is', *Sunday Times*, 22 December 1996, section 3, p. 9.
26. Tosh, p. 9.
27. Though permeated by humour and sentimentality, these portrayals of family life are a fundamentally serious valorization of the commonplace as

miracle; a specialized version of humanized religion, with the prize of shared happiness at the core. They are manifestly shaped against the grain of the injunction in Luke 14. 26: 'If any man come to me, and hate not his father, and mother, and wife, and children, and brethren, and sisters, yea, and his own life also, he cannot be my disciple.' In this regard Dickens stands at an opposite pole from Bunyan, whose Christian begins his progress by running from his pleading wife and children with his fingers in his ears, and who, in *Grace Abounding*, records how, cast into prison for refusing to give up unlicensed preaching, 'the parting with my wife and poor children hath oft been . . . as the pulling of the flesh from my bones, . . . [but] I must do it' (*Pilgrim's Progress*, p. 41; *Grace Abounding*, p. 100). Yet in the second of these examples we do find a movingly inferred bonding that in the *Carol* is a fully realized tenet.

28. *Pilgrim's Progress*, pp. 150, 159–60.
29. For the convert's symbolic change of dress, see *Pilgrim's Progress*, p. 203.
30. George Eliot, *Middlemarch* (1871–72), ed. W.J. Harvey (Harmondsworth: Penguin Books, 1985), Ch. 80, p. 846. For a detailed discussion of this passage as signal manifestation of secularizing process, see my 'Dorothea's Awakening: A Note on *Middlemarch*', *Notes and Queries*, 229 (1984), 497–9.
31. John Bowen, 'The Transformation of Scrooge', *English Review*, 3:1 (September 1992), 38–40 (p. 40). In this Gold (pp. 153–4) takes his cue from Edgar Johnson, *Charles Dickens: His Tragedy and Triumph* (London: Gollancz, 1953). John Lucas (*Melancholy Man*, pp. 137–41) casts a helpful historical light on the 'theme of self' by developing the explanation of it as an attack on Utilitarianism.
32. 'Charles Dickens' (1940), repr. in George Orwell, '*Decline of the English Murder' and Other Essays* (Harmondsworth: Penguin Books, 1965), pp. 80–141 (pp. 97–98, 138).
33. Oliver Goldsmith, *The Vicar of Wakefield* (1766), ed. Stephen Coote (Harmondsworth: Penguin Books, 1986), Ch. 29, pp. 174–5.
34. Steven Connor, ' "They're All in One Story": Public and Private Narratives in *Oliver Twist*', *Dickensian*, 85 (1989), 3–16 (p. 5).
35. Gillian Beer, *Darwin's Plots: Evolutionary Narrative in Darwin, George Eliot and Nineteenth-Century Fiction* (London: Routledge & Kegan Paul, 1983); Michel Foucault, *The Order of Things: An Archaeology of the Human Sciences*, no translator given (London: Tavistock, 1970), pp. 218–19 (quoted in Connor, pp. 4–5).
36. Quoted from Jenyns in Samuel Johnson, 'Review of [Soame Jenyns], *A Free Enquiry*' (1757); *The Works of Samuel Johnson* (London, 1824), XI, 259–60.
37. *Works of Johnson*, XI, 271.
38. Henry Liddon, '[From] Sermon, 9 June 1876'; repr. in *Culture and Society in Britain 1850–1890: A Source Book of Contemporary Writings*, ed. J.M. Golby (Oxford: Oxford University Press, 1986), pp. 122–5 (p. 124).
39. Peter Ackroyd, *Dickens* (London: Minerva, 1991), pp. 427, 429 (quoting Dickens).
40. See Thomas Haskell, 'Capitalism and the Origins of the Humanitarian Sensibility', *American Historical Review*, 90 (1985), 339–61, 547–66.
41. This instance of the characteristic Dickensian blend of reformist tendency and socio-political defensiveness can again be seen to connect him, though

in a roundabout way, to eighteenth-century tradition. In *The Task* (IV. 374–428) William Cowper had praised the Olney cottagers, 'Poor, yet industrious, modest, quiet, neat', a 'meek and patient pair' who, unlike 'clam'rous importunity in rags', genuinely 'claim compassion' from those distributing public alms or private charity. The 'progeny' of this respectable family, 'well-trained' as they are, will soon find 'their hands, / And labour too'. Though Cowper's subjects are the rural poor, rather than the urban proletariat, he shares with Dickens an interest in social discipline and productiveness, in which responsible humanitarianism has a salient role, and he too corroborates class distinction while reaching out to those beneath. Cowper's 'meek and patient pair' have their most direct descendants in Dickens in such figures as the impoverished but independent and hard-working Betty Higden in *Our Mutual Friend*, who is given help to support herself by the charitable Mr Boffin and John Harmon.

42. Liddon, p. 124.
43. Liddon, pp. 122–3.
44. Matthew Arnold, *Culture and Anarchy* (1869), ed. J. Dover Wilson (Cambridge: Cambridge University Press, 1969), pp. 70, 204.
45. The two-sidedness we have discovered in the *Carol*, where social critique and conservative attitudes coexist, is more widely considered in D.A. Miller's seminal study *The Novel and the Police* (Berkeley: University of California Press, 1988), which, examining works by Dickens alongside other Victorian novels, argues that the manifest urge to reform institutions is ineluctably bound up with the form's undeclared emplacement of disciplinary codes. Thus, the treatment of delinquency in *Oliver Twist* is a sign of 'Dickens's progressive attitude' because he finds 'coercive system' where it was traditional only to find 'bad morals', but the text also draws a circle around the world of Fagin and the rest, holding 'the line of a cordon sanitaire' between that world and the privileged middle-class community (p. 5); or, in *Bleak House*, the recommendations of Dickens's 'vigorous reformism' are 'the weights . . . to preserve the family in its present balance', and the exposure of 'faultiness' in the domestic sphere implies, in Mr Bagnet's famous catchword, that 'Discipline must be maintained' (pp. 104–105). Miller's insight into this aspect of *Oliver Twist* is a major springboard for my own analysis of that novel.

Ambiguity is apparent on another level in the facts of, on the one hand, Dickens's desire, at the time of composing the *Carol*, to strike like 'a Sledge hammer' (*The Pilgrim Edition of the Letters of Charles Dickens*, ed. Madeline House et al. (Oxford: Clarendon Press, 1965–), III, 459) against the evils of child employment in the mines and factories, which he had discussed with the reformer Lord Ashley as early as 1840, and against the deprivations he had recently witnessed among the poorest sections of society when visiting Field Lane Ragged School as the agent of the philanthropist Miss Burdett-Coutts, and, on the other, his eager involvement in the elaborate processes of commercial book production and his preoccupation with getting maximum financial returns from the sales of his commodity. Peter Ackroyd points out that news of disappointing profits of only £130 from the first six thousand copies of the *Carol* brought Dickens near to hysteria: 'I really believed that I should never get up again, until I had passed through all the horrors of a fever . . . I shall be ruined past all mortal hope of redemption' (Ackroyd, p. 439). In this is further evidence that Dickens rejected the excesses of capitalism but not the system itself. For the background to the creation, marketing and reception of the *Carol*, see Ackroyd, pp. 429–37 and Grahame Smith, *Charles Dickens: A Literary Life* (Basingstoke: Macmillan, 1996), pp. 10–12.

46. John B. Thompson, *Ideology and Modern Culture* (Cambridge: Polity Press, 1990), p. 7.
47. Holderness, 'Imagination in *A Christmas Carol*', pp. 44–5.
48. Gold, p. 148.
49. *Grace Abounding*, p. 92.
50. 'On History', *Works of Carlyle*, ed. H.D. Traill (London, 1896–1901), XXVII, 88–9.
51. Blaise Pascal, *Pensées*, in *Oeuvres Complètes*, ed. J. Chevalier (Paris: Pléiade, 1969), p. 1296; quoted and translated in Miller, *Novel and the Police*, p. 32.
52. Miller, pp. ix, 32.
53. Miller, p. x.
54. Sigmund Freud, *Beyond the Pleasure Principle* (1920); repr. in *Freud: On Metapsychology*, ed. Angela Richards, The Pelican Freud Library, Volume XI (Harmondsworth: Penguin Books, 1984), pp. 275, 308, 311.

CHAPTER THREE

Oliver Twist

Hegemony and the Transgressive Imagination

Everyone knows *Oliver Twist* as a great work of social comment. The image of Oliver 'asking for more', popularized through illustration and film and stage adaptation, has become part of the staple iconography of protest against the inhumanity of humankind. A recent critic sees in the depiction of Oliver's oversize spoon rising at a forty-five degree angle from his groin towards the open mouth of the overseer in Cruikshank's original engraving a reference to deviant sexual practice.[1] Whether we accept this or not – and there is indeed no reason to think that children were less vulnerable in Victorian institutions than in our own – it is certain that the purpose of the early parts of the novel was an exposé of brutality involving physical and mental abuse. In this we are aware, of course, not only of oppression itself but of a challenge to the system that produces it. Oliver's erect spoon may also be read as an act of thrusting self-assertion. His confrontation with the poorhouse authorities – on this occasion the middle management – mirrors Dickens's robust indictment of a whole political philosophy and regime. Both Oliver and his creator are in their ways cocking a snook: the former desperately, bodily, in an involuntary gesture of want and defiance; the latter cerebrally, with a characteristic mix of calculated and rough deliberation.

This polemic is a natural starting-point for a study of *Oliver Twist*, as it was of Dickens's project in writing it. Such episodes as that we have briefly highlighted, or which have highlighted themselves, display Dickens's genius for catching life in a symbolic attitude and so generating a transhistorical level of meaning; but they are grounded none the less in a response to specific contemporary issues. Dickens never liked workhouses, and even when describing a relatively well-regulated example in *Household Words* (actually the one at Marylebone) lamented that a comparison with Pentonville prison revealed 'this dangerous, this monstrous pass, that the dishonest felon is, in respect of cleanliness, order, diet, and accommodation, better provided for, and taken care of, than the honest pauper'.[2] Yet he seems from this to have accepted the existence of pauperism and the necessity for some kind of public arrangement for containing it, no less than for incarcerating criminals. We may note the characteristic socio-political

Fig. 2   'Oliver asking for More' by George Cruikshank.

conservatism implicit in the general drift of Dickens's statement – where the poor are viewed circumspectly as a potential danger to the status quo and a pressing object for enlightened, wholesome provision – and, more markedly, in the categorizing, arm's-length literariness of 'honest pauper'. The more immediate point, however, is that the target of *Oliver Twist* was not so much root causes or phenomena as the particular measures brought in by the Poor Law Amendment Act of 1834, which *The Times* newspaper, in opposition to the government, had been vehemently attacking in a series of articles during the second half of 1836, just before the instalments which became the first four chapters of the novel appeared in *Bentley's Miscellany* for February and March 1837.

Dickens's critique is detailed, varied, and comprehensive. A major objective of the legislation had been to increase administrative efficiency by organizing the old local, single-parish units into larger divisions, or 'unions', superintended by specially appointed boards.[3] The board in charge of Oliver's workhouse is a scathing portrayal of faceless bureaucracy, not least in the shape of the vacuously despotic 'gentleman in the white waistcoat' whose repeated opinion of the boy is that he is sure to be 'hung' (59). This figure, at once ridiculous and sinister in his (necrophilic?) obsession with Oliver's demise, is a strange, shadowy focus for the mixture of absurdity, sadism and self-regard that, for Dickens, pervades the new order. He sees the same evils more obviously at work in the steps being taken to tighten the regimen for inmates to a degree where it becomes virtually unbearable; a policy which, along with a reduction in the payment of outdoor relief, was intended to deter welfare dependency and encourage the able-bodied to support themselves in the community.

This approach involved not only a near-starvation diet – the ubiquitous gruel of which Oliver does not have enough – but the enforced break-up of families, a point to which Dickens returns with a good dose of poetic justice at the end of the novel when reporting that, Mr and Mrs Bumble having become paupers 'in the very same workhouse in which they had once lorded it over others', the former's misery and degradation were so great that he had 'not even spirits to be thankful for being separated from his wife' (477). Orphans and other destitute children were, until the age of nine, 'farmed' to women on the outside, an arrangement inviting exploitation of the helpless by the weak, as in the case of Oliver's substitute parent, Mrs Mann, who proves herself a model participant in the financial scheme by top-slicing for her own needs the paltry weekly stipend of 'sevenpence-halfpenny' supplied for the upkeep of each of her 20 or 30 wards (48–9). Any pretence that the workhouse system might actually bear fruit in human or social terms is exploded by the directive Oliver gets from the board: ' "Well! You have come here to be educated, and taught a useful trade," said the red-faced gentleman in the high chair. "So you'll begin to pick oakum tomorrow morning at six o'clock," added the surly one in the white waistcoat' (54). Picking oakum was the production of a coarse fibre by undoing old rope. It was the main occupation of convicts.

The most hotly debated feature of the Act was that which made the *female* solely responsible for illegitimate offspring – another attempt to discourage calls upon the welfare bill. The stigma of lone parenthood was no doubt in Dickens's mind when making even the surgeon, a not unkindly man, categorize Oliver's mother, abandoned and dying, simply as one of the unmarried: 'The old story . . . no wedding-ring, I see. Ah! Good night!' (47). As we shall find, stories, old or new, are in the worlds of *Oliver Twist* a means by which identity is both given and circumscribed – or indeed withheld if by 'identity' we wish to understand the individual life of liberal-humanist tradition, whole, self-sufficient, and freely distributing meaning from its own centre. In the early chapters Dickens certainly writes from a humanist viewpoint. What preoccupies him is the way people are reduced to objects, currency, commodities, and relationships are determined by economic necessity or advantage. The wretched woman is treated as business to be dispatched by a doctor operating 'by contract' (45). Oliver, we are told, became an 'item' as soon as he was born – was dressed in 'old calico robes . . . and was badged and ticketed, and fell into his place at once – a parish child – the orphan of a workhouse' (47). His name, which Mr Bumble confers by his regular method of strict alphabetical sequence (51–2), is a mark not of his being but of general convenience. Later, just as Mrs Mann profiteers at the expense of the babies she is supposed to care for, many of whom die, so, on a reverse model, the board puts all its energy into striking the best bargain when negotiating to pay first Gamfield the sweep and then Sowerberry the undertaker to take Oliver off the parochial hands. The gentlemen take particular pleasure in knocking Gamfield down from five pounds to three pounds ten (62–3). In course of time Bumble himself, a true product of his environment, comes to approach matrimony in the same commercial spirit, assessing the attractions of the widow Corney by literally counting her teaspoons, weighing her sugar-tongs, and closely inspecting her silver milk-pot 'to ascertain that it was of the genuine metal' (223). Bumble's history often underscores serious themes through parody, and he actually laments that he has himself become an article of merchandise: 'I sold myself' (323) he declares when repenting at leisure the bad bargain he has made in trying the conjugal road to advancement.

These scenes are shaped by Dickens's fierce opposition to Utilitarian social theory, which comes bluntly to the fore in the sarcasm designating Mrs Mann a 'very great experimental philosopher' (48) and the board 'very sage, deep, philosophical men' (55). Dickens was convinced that a line of thought which elevated self-interest as the mainspring of human action was, though it paraded the upbeat slogan of 'the greatest happiness for the greatest number', bound to cause suffering at some level, as in the operation of the adjusted Poor Law, or, as in *A Christmas Carol* and *Hard Times*, the inflicting of psychological and moral damage on individuals and communities. The vein of rationalism Dickens has most firmly in his sights is that deriving from Malthus, whose *Essay on the Principle of Population*, many times reprinted and refined after first publication in 1798, argued that unchecked demographic expansion, and the consequent competition for resources, inevitably produced, by a law of reaction, the natural curbs of 'epidemics, wars, plague, and famine'. Malthus had attacked the old Poor Law on the grounds that parish assistance promoted 'vice and misery' by encouraging population growth among those least equipped to absorb it, and in the 1803 edition of the *Essay* this was supplemented with a call for preventive measures, including both the 'denial of sensual pleasures' and the avoidance of unsupportable marriage (however much these aims might, and in fact in this period did, sit uneasily together).[4] In denouncing the segregation of workhouse residents by sex, the low diet, injunctions against the 'sin' of childbearing outside wedlock, *Oliver Twist* is a direct assault on the practical application of these attitudes and ideas.

Dickens's relation to Malthus was, though, more complicated than blanket rejection. One interpreter shows how at certain points in *Oliver Twist* the novelist is very much in accord with the philosopher's view of existence as a battle for self-preservation, citing the description of how 'Oliver and Nature fought out the point between them' (45–6) – the issue being whether Oliver, a mere 'item of mortality', would expire at birth – and how the boy instinctively developed 'sense enough to make a feint' in order to avoid 'ill-usage' and in reward for his stratagem gets a much needed slice of bread and butter (52–3).[5] However committedly Dickens then modifies this bleak outlook by recognizing benevolence and, as he puts it in the Preface of 1841, 'the principle of Good' (33), he never sees the world as anything other than a difficult place. The amended Poor Law, in his opinion, only made things worse, not only by increasing hardship but by breeding a potentially explosive desperation in the deprived. When Oliver steps forward to say 'Please, sir, I want some more', the narrator calls him 'the small rebel', 'reckless with misery'. Though the tone is jocular, the implication of revolt is serious enough; and in the words 'I want', so different from the bland inscription to the Cruikshank picture of Oliver *'asking* for More' [italics mine], we catch the accents of an insistent demand, and one which injects into the apparent submissiveness of 'Please, sir' the possibility of an insolent formality. The whole scene is at once a parody of Malthus's grim account of nature and an acknowledgement of the force of his cautionary insights:

> Oliver Twist and his companions suffered the tortures of slow starvation for three months: at last they got so voracious and wild with hunger, that one boy, who was tall for his age, . . . hinted darkly to his companions, that unless he had another basin of gruel *per diem*, he was afraid he might some night happen to eat the boy who slept next him, who happened to be a weakly youth of tender age. He had a wild, hungry eye; and they implicitly believed him. (56)

As in Swift's *A Modest Proposal*, the preposterous reference to a literal cannibalism provokes an awareness of the devouring actually going on in a society where one person preys upon another or, in Malthusian terms, beats others to a share of the limited means of life and prosperity. Yet the paupers do not in the event fight among themselves. The energies of internecine competition are redirected outwards and upwards – like Oliver's projecting spoon in the Cruikshank engraving – into a conflict with authority, as lots are drawn and Oliver puts the unheard-of question as representative of his peers, who remain after all 'companions' with a common cause, maintaining group solidarity. A connection between reproductive capacity and food consumption was often emphasized in contemporary debate, as when the unidentified author 'Simplex', a Scottish Calvinist, condemned Malthus's doctrine of abstinence as immoral, given that 'the mutual propensity of the sexes is . . . as truly a part of the constitution of human nature as man's desire for food when hungry, or drink when thirsty'.[6] Dickens additionally underscores a third term, rebellion, which is made explicit in his preface to the cheap edition of 1850 when he calls for the rebuilding of London's slums lest 'those classes of the people which increase the fastest, must become so desperate . . . as to bear within themselves the certain seeds of ruin to the whole community'.[7] The word 'seeds' is no casual or dead metaphor. It articulates what was for Dickens a pressing biological truth. In these aspects of *Oliver Twist* we see the stirrings of that fear of disorder rising from below, and that answering concern with wise philanthropy and the larger fund of social checks and balances, which, as we know, were to find such urgent expression in the scenes surrounding the figures of the girl Want and the boy Ignorance on whose brow is written a presage of apocalyptic 'Doom' ten years later in *A Christmas Carol* – and which indeed were never to leave Dickens.[8]

Another significant prolepsis in these early chapters comes when Bumble, suddenly stepping out of his role as pompous and hard-hearted parish beadle, is moved by Oliver's anguish on the road to Sowerberry's:

> 'So lonely, sir! So very lonely!' cried the child. 'Everybody hates me. Oh! sir, don't, don't pray be cross with me!' The child beat his hand upon his heart; and looked in his companion's face, with tears of real agony.
>
> Mr Bumble regarded Oliver's piteous and helpless look with some astonishment for a few seconds; hemmed three or four times in a husky manner; and, after muttering something about 'that troublesome cough', bade Oliver dry his eyes and be a good boy; and, once more taking his hand, he walked on with him in silence. (73)

Dickens was no 'perfectibility' man, subscribing, as the main body of Malthus's opponents did, to William Godwin's irreducible belief in the benevolence of humankind and its progress to a utopian commonality;[9] but he did always set store by acts of sympathy and kindness as consoling and enabling witness in a dark and fallen world – a way of holding on to and cultivating the ideals of goodness and human worth. We shall encounter more elaborate examples in other novels, yet none sharper than the one before us. The event takes a special impact from the ingredient of surprise – the fact that Oliver's plight forces reactions of which we would never have thought Bumble capable. The beadle stifles his feelings and tries to cover them up, 'hemming' and mumbling about a cough, but the narrative subtly insinuates their irrepressible power in the gentle 'taking' (not grabbing) of the boy's hand and the subdued atmosphere of 'silence'. Bumble is the last person we would expect to be lost for words. In a twinkling he has been transformed from an exemplar of the worst in human nature – he has just rained down a torrent of 'intense malignity' on the sobbing, defenceless Oliver (72) – to a spectacle suggesting the best. The values Dickens is thus putting in the frame have more to do with impulse or active capability than with the abstract notion of Charity on which explicators of this novel sometimes concentrate,[10] and are underlined, with some irony, by the pride that the characteristically brutal Bumble takes in the parochial seal reproduced on the large brass buttons of his uniform, which portrays the Good Samaritan 'healing the sick and bruised man' (70). Bumble esteems ostentation and the signifiers of officialdom, but we – and on this occasion involuntarily he – know better.

The type of effect we have examined here, though rare in *Oliver Twist* itself, is a bedrock of the Dickensian 'secular scripture'. A counterpart of biblical exhortation, it functions to humanize perception through a recall to feeling and is one of the main reasons why we should still read Dickens. At the same time, however, it has a clear relation to ideological purposes and processes of culture formation. The scene from the parable of the Good Samaritan will reappear hanging on the wall of a room in the suburban house of Oliver's benefactor, Mr Brownlow, and there can be no doubt that goodness in Dickens is a middle-class virtue, whether it operates as a top-down palliative for disaffection, like rebuilding slums, or as a factor in the construction of a shared subjectivity, which is the case with the Bumble–Oliver episode in that it prompts readership participation in a refresher course in healthy emotional conduct modelled on the sensibility doctrines of Steele, Fielding or Goldsmith. Pointing in a similar direction, and cutting no less conspicuously against the grain of the satire on misguided authoritarianism than does Bumble's growing a heart, is the manner of Oliver's speech and behaviour, which can be extraordinarily genteel and sensitive for one supposed to have been so thoroughly neglected in his upbringing, or lack of it, and who was 'in a fair way of being reduced, for life, to a state of brutal stupidity and sullenness by the ill-usage he had received' (72). When he flees the scenes of his suffering, for example, his parting exchange with his friend Dick, with whom he had been many a time 'beaten and starved, and shut up', seems, magically, more the language of mutual good breeding and virtuous sentiment than of deprivation. It is as if they both know they are characters in a bourgeois adventure story or melodrama:

> 'I am running away. They beat and ill-use me, Dick; and I am going to seek my fortune, some long way off . . . How pale you are!'
> 'I heard the doctor tell them I was dying,' replied the child with a faint smile. 'I am very glad to see you, dear; but don't stop, don't stop!'
> 'Yes, yes, I will, to say good-b'ye to you,' replied Oliver. 'I shall see you again, Dick. I know I shall! You will be well and happy!' (96)

This artificial discourse can of course be explained as Dickens's accommodation with the expectations of his readers, to which he automatically sacrifices the imperatives of realism. However, if we now recall what has just happened at Sowerberry's, with some related passages, the matter becomes less straightforward. The text then seems not only to reflect cultural assumptions but to strive uneasily, though tenaciously, towards their elaboration.

Despite his constant bludgeoning at the tongues and sometimes hands of his fellow apprentice Noah Claypole, Charlotte the maid, and Mrs

Sowerberry, Oliver has it in him to erupt into violent self-affirmation when the insults go too far:

> A minute ago, the boy had looked the quiet, mild, dejected creature that harsh treatment had made him. But his spirit was roused at last; the cruel insult to his mother had set his blood on fire. His breast heaved; his attitude was erect; his eye bright and vivid; his whole person changed, as he stood glaring over the cowardly tormentor who now lay crouching at his feet. (88)

The reason for Oliver's fierce reaction – Noah's calling his mother a 'right-down bad 'un' – is significant. Though Dickens always maintained a strong interest in education and the influence of environment, he invests heavily in *Oliver Twist* in the idea of what is innately given, in genetics and genealogy. We have already learned that 'nature or inheritance had implanted a good sturdy spirit in Oliver's breast' (49), and that spirit now asserts itself in defence of his mother's honour. 'Nature' and 'inheritance' should not be taken as opposites of one another, but as alternatives standing together over against the concepts of nurture and acquired characteristics. In his defeat of Noah, Oliver cuts a figure of childish yet authentic heroism, his nobility showing in his heaving breast, his upright stance, his bright eye. In similar fashion, his likeness to his mother's portrait will later give clues to his true origins; and when Mr Brownlow suspects him of giving a false name and account of himself he has only to look at his face to know that 'it was impossible to doubt him . . . [for] there was truth in every one of its thin and sharpened lineaments' (130). Physiognomy is the outward sign of both pedigree and disposition, which are interdependent. Bumble, ever faithful to his name, thinks Oliver 'comes of a bad family' (94). This turns out to be not at all the case, although there are 'bad' tributaries that will have to be expunged or put right. Oliver's speech, which at the level of verisimilitude is simply incredible, is in keeping with his inborn and relatively high-born status, a mark of what he really is. In the light of our protagonist's as yet secret ancestry, Dickens is being perfectly consistent in mocking Noah for taking 'genealogy' (77) as a basis of his superiority over Oliver because he knew who *his* parents, a washerwoman and a drunken sailor, were.

This juncture in the presentation of Oliver initiates a pattern that is not only developed later in the novel in the unravelling of his paternity but runs throughout the length of Dickens's career and is still being adjusted and refined in the envisioning of a newly regenerate social order in *Our Mutual Friend*. The aristocratic conception of noble lineage is put to the service of formulating and endorsing the aspirations and authority of the middle classes.[11] The larger process involves not only writing out, or *into* the fictional text, a liturgy or code of practice specifying such qualities as the filial piety and courage that Oliver displays in his altercation with Noah – or indeed the generosity of spirit that for a moment so dramatically usurps the character of Bumble – but a justification of cultural dominance by reference to an overarching integrity and high-mindedness. In the Preface Dickens announces that his intention has been 'to show, in little Oliver, the principle of Good surviving through every adverse circumstance, and triumphing at last' (33). But the theme of goodness, in *Oliver Twist*, is not just a question of disinterested morality, however much we approve its ethos. It is not only Oliver who is intrinsically 'good'; so are Mr Brownlow and his housekeeper, Mrs Bedwin, who give him a home and sort out his patrimony, and so are the Maylies and their friends, who rescue him from criminals and care for him. In the old, rising middle-class ideology of Defoe's *Robinson Crusoe*, worth lies with the individual, resourceful, God-fearing, making his way; in *Oliver Twist*, as in aristocratic tradition but under a different hierarchical arrangement, it goes with rank.[12] Privilege is aligned with rectitude, and is thus legitimized. At the same time, moreover, its actual basis is occluded, as a possible alternative subtitle for this chapter could infer. 'Where do the Maylies get their money from?' We are never told – though they have a big house outside London, own lots of silver (which Bill Sikes tries to steal), employ a host of servants, and go on extended holidays in the country.

And what of the workhouse and its victims? These are consigned to the margins as the book moves to cultivate the centre – though we have yet in store some significant encounters with a metropolitan underclass. When Oliver returns to his birthplace in Chapter 51, it is to celebrate the 'pure, earnest, joyful reality' of his new life in contrast to 'the dreary prison of his youthful days', which itself stands unchanged and un-reformed, a curious monument with 'the same lean porter standing at the gate' (455–6). By this stage neither he nor the narrative in which he stars takes any interest in the institution or the plight of its inhabitants beyond their distant place in the history of his eventual affluence. Social conscience and complaint have evaporated in the chemistry of a concern with personal fulfilment within the nirvana of bourgeois plenitude.

Before we join Oliver in leaving that early dismal world behind, however, it is worth noting that it is not only those at the bottom of its pecking order that are under constraint. Indeed, they at least possess the freedom that comes from having nothing to lose, which Oliver himself exercises when he walks off to London. The other characters – Bumble, Mrs Mann, the Board, Noah Claypole – exist solely as creatures and functionaries of the system. Bumble is indivisible from his office and insignia of cocked hat, skirts, cane, and gold-laced cuff (50, 53, 72). Noah is a partial exception that proves the rule. A charity-boy, dressed in the despised uniform of coat, badge and leather breeches, he is so riddled with status anxiety that he spends all his energy swaggering and sadistically tormenting the one person beneath him, Oliver, whom he contemptuously calls 'Work'us' (76, 78). He has no certain place in a scheme that none the less entraps and defines him.

Does Dickens show us that society is everywhere so? Is the world of Brownlow and the Maylies in essence like that, or do mobility and independence come with power? Is the liberty of the individual ever anything more than an illusion? Does Oliver exchange one confinement for another? We shall see.

*

In the domain of Fagin and his associates, over against which the centres of middle-class authority are realized, money is visible, often discussed, and indeed something of an obsession. On his first morning in the thieves' den, Oliver secretly observes Fagin gloating over his hoard of treasure (107–108). Sikes is forever preoccupied with prising some 'blunt' from Fagin the fence, as well as from the well-to-do. Fagin sends out his boys and the young women, Nancy and Bet, with cash to spend, but makes clear that it is their duty to increase his stake should the opportunity arise (111).

With money goes work. Nancy, who wears a red gown and is said to frequent the 'stews' of London (138, 360), is a 'working girl' in a special sense;[13] but her exchange and mart, the body, is the basic form in a spectrum of activity that presents at the other extreme an evident sophistication. When the Artful Dodger and Charley Bates try to persuade Oliver to join their outfit, the talk is not only of making a living but of climbing the career ladder (182–5). We hear, for instance, of the Dodger's 'profession' and 'professional acquirements'; picking pockets is twice called a 'trade', and has its own set of guiding precepts, or 'catechism', in which, according to Fagin, the Dodger is wonderfully 'proficient'. Gain is paramount: 'What's the odds where it comes from?' the Dodger asks Oliver when showing him a handful of shillings and halfpence. There's even the chance to make a 'fortun' out of hand', of rising so far as to be able (in the mould of the legendary Whittington or Crusoe) 'to retire on your property and do the genteel'. Last but by no means least, success is synonymous with adventurous industry and self-reliance: 'Why, where's your spirit? Don't you take any pride out of yourself? Would you go and be dependent on your friends?'

This impression of a particular set of socio-economic tenets – individualism, aggressive commercialism, profit, the cash nexus, upwards mobility – is kept up throughout the novel in references to the criminal underworld. We witness, for instance, the backstreet emporium of petty larceny: 'a commercial colony of itself: . . . visited at early morning, and setting-in of dusk, by silent merchants, who traffic in dark back-parlours' (235). Or, just before the denouement, Fagin lectures his latest trainee, Mr Bolter (alias Noah Claypole), on the strength of their 'little community' which is driven by the forces of mutual self-interest – the principle of 'Number one for ever' (387–9). In all of this, of course, a negative light is cast on the subculture itself, the more so because the shadow of transportation and the noose falls on every cocksure at-testation, as when the care for 'number one' that is the foundation of Fagin's theory of collective responsibility comes down in the end to a fear of being turned in – the gallows being, on Fagin's own threatening assurance, the sure repayment for disloyalty which has provided an early terminus to 'many a bold fellow's career on the broad highway' (388). Vice versa, however, the constellation of values, the ideology of business and competitive enterprise, of simply 'getting on' or dramatically advancing one's station by effort and dexterity, is discredited by being cast in the form of criminality. Dickens, that is to say, rejects a foremost philosophy of modern times and how to exist beneficially in them.

Oliver's exchange of rags for riches is by the inverse route of recovering what is already his due – his inheritance. But before we examine the higher cultures and narratives that embody Dickens's preferred option for social standing and success, it should be stressed through one or two further examples how insistently he does undermine Fagin's microcosm. The appeal of this colourful small corner, which generations have felt, is continually compromised. This happens straightaway in the image of the 'old gentleman' with 'matted red hair', cooking sausages, toasting-fork in hand, with its evocations not only of apostasy (Jews don't eat pork) but of the devil himself (105).[14] Fagin, though associated with warmth, sustenance and refuge, then becomes the evil counsellor comparable to those of Bunyan's *Pilgrim's Progress*, of whom both the protagonist and the reader must be constantly wary. He applies one of the recurrent educative devices of Puritan mental journeying, the testimony of personal history and experience, to lead Oliver, not along the true path, but astray: 'the old man would tell them stories of robberies he had committed in his younger days: mixed up with so much that was droll and curious, that Oliver could not help laughing heartily . . . in spite of all his better feelings' (185). This, like learning to pick a pocket or two, is false nurturing, which will have its wholesome counterpart in the instruction Oliver receives at Mr Brownlow's and the Maylies' – whose parallel in Bunyan's allegory is the House Beautiful where Christian has discourse 'for the best improvement of time' with Piety, Prudence and Charity.[15]

On another occasion Fagin's instrument of tutelage – or attempted seduction – is a book:

> It was a history of the lives and trials of great criminals; and the pages were thumbed and soiled with use. Here, he read of dreadful crimes that made the blood run cold; of secret murders that had been committed by the lonely wayside; of bodies hidden from the eye of man in deep pits and wells. . . . The terrible descriptions were so real and vivid, that the sallow pages seemed to turn red with gore; and the words upon them, to be sounded in his ears, as if they were whispered, in hollow murmurs, by the spirits of the dead. (196–7)

This is the only text Fagin possesses, but it is a potent one. The well-thumbed, 'sallow' pages, running with blood, seem at once sinister and warmly compelling, weaving a spell of horror and fascination around the boy. But Oliver has a powerful text of his own. He prays. Asking 'Heaven to spare him from such deeds', he gradually 'grew more calm, and besought in a low and broken voice . . . that if any aid were to be raised up for a poor outcast boy who had never known the love of friends or kindred, it might come to him now, when, desolate and deserted, he stood alone in the midst of wickedness and guilt' (197). This too is reminiscent of *The Pilgrim's Progress*, where Christian regularly counters terror and temptation with prayer or verses from the Bible, as when in the Valley of the Shadow of Death, haunted by 'doleful voices and rushings' of fiends not unlike the 'hollow murmurs' of Oliver's verbal automotisms, he cries out, using the weapon called All-Prayer (with which he has been furnished at the House Beautiful), '*O Lord I beseech thee deliver my Soul*'; or when, shut up in misery in the castle of Giant Despair, like Oliver behind the 'rusty bars' of Fagin's fastness, and terrified with the 'bones and skulls' of the Giant's previous captives, as Oliver is by the images of the dead, he finds release by remembering the 'key of promise' in his bosom.[16] The theme of Oliver's incarceration is no less than the survival of his soul. All the same, the moral and spiritual drama is inscribed with sociological meaning. Scripture and religious discourse belong to the ideological centre and, no less than genteel speech, mark Oliver as being of that centre. Cruikshank saw this and took pains to emphasize the point; for in the relevant illustration the two pictures that look down upon Oliver in Mr Brownlow's house are the portrait of his mother (though no one has yet made any conscious connection), whom he has already dreamed of as a guardian angel coming down from heaven to comfort him (126), and the Good Samaritan (131). Even the relief nurse who sits overnight with Oliver carries a small Prayer Book with her (127).

Oliver's prayer laments, very precisely, lack of the love of 'friends and kindred'. Experiential religion and the inner turmoil that goes with it, which supply the background to Dickens's treatment of subjectivity in later novels, have no place in *Oliver Twist*, and within the value-system of the book religion itself is entirely subservient to the valorization of familial community. Fagin and the others constitute from the outset a negative configuration of the family. This is most obvious in the pretence Nancy and Bill use to kidnap Oliver in the street: ' "You see he knows me!" cried Nancy, appealing to the bystanders. "He can't help himself. Make him come home, there's good people, or he'll kill his dear mother and father, and break my heart!" ' (157). Nancy does in time fill the role of protective 'sister' towards Oliver; and indeed both she and Sikes, though in markedly different ways, become figures in a reverse texture, emerging from the morass of degradation in postures of honest and driven affirmation that complicates the meaning of the novel. For the moment, however, they are representatives of a vigorous but delinquent underside that implicitly promotes the perfect order of bourgeois civilization.

*

At the beginning of Chapter 14, Mrs Bedwin, Brownlow's housekeeper, spends some time with Oliver. The passage is worth quoting extensively since it brings out several leading features of the structure and *modus operandi* of Dickensian middle-class culture. Indeed, one of the mechanisms of that culture lies in the way casual and apparently inconsequential discourse and intercourse serves purposes of initiation and reinforcement. Learning never stops:

> As the old lady had been so kind to him in his illness . . . he listened attentively to a great many stories she told him, about an amiable and handsome daughter of hers, who was married to an amiable and handsome man, and lived in the country; and about a son, who was clerk to a merchant in the West Indies; and who was, also, such a good young man, and wrote such dutiful letters home four times a year, that it brought the tears into her eyes to talk about them. When the old lady had expatiated a long time . . . it was time to have tea. After tea she began to teach Oliver cribbage: which he

learnt as quickly as she could teach . . . until it was time for the invalid to have some warm wine and water. . . . They were happy days, those of Oliver's recovery. Everything was so quiet, and neat, and orderly; . . . it seemed like Heaven itself. (143)

Such in-text glossaries of key terms are not uncommon in Dickens and act as *aides-mémoire* for the reader, underpinning cultural bearings. A charitable cast ('kind'); good nature joined to good looks ('amiable and handsome'); familial virtue and cohesion (a married daughter, a 'good' and 'dutiful' son); sensitivity and feeling (the loving mother's 'tears'); narrative (Mrs Bedwin's 'stories') and writing (her son's 'letters'); mobility, to 'the country' and even abroad; rural connections; involvement in empire (a clerkship in the West Indies); play; food, in a proportion mixing prudence with a dash of ritual luxury (there is afternoon 'tea' as well as the medicinal 'wine and water'): all of this suggests an order that is humane and upright but also efficient at organizing itself, settled and self-contained yet spreading confidently outwards, practical without being averse to leisure and surplus possessions. We may compare the pocket-picking game at Fagin's with cribbage, which is harmless relaxation yet usefully teaches mental discipline and arithmetic. There is a reference to work and trade, but with such evocation of distance and the grand scale that we think of service and adventure rather than wealth creation or moneymaking, let alone colonialism or conditions on the West Indian plantations. Who would not crave a domesticity that is 'like Heaven'? – though there is a version of it later on that is even more blissful. Then, as the paragraph continues, we meet the outer weave of utility and display, as Oliver is clothed in a 'complete new suit, and new cap' that will both protect him and mark his change of status (where, we may recall, Bunyan's pilgrims put on fresh raiment as they enter *their* Celestial City). Finally, social hierarchy comes very starkly to the fore: Oliver, quick at picking up the philanthropic code of his new environment, asks a servant to sell his old clothes to 'a Jew' and to keep the money.

Stories and writing are perhaps the least easily graspable of the Bedwin clues to correct cultural disposition. They are, however, a principal connecting thread in the tapestry that unfolds. The first thing we notice is Brownlow's association with books. He is reading at a stall when the Dodger picks his pocket, starting the hue and cry that lands Oliver in court and subsequently in Brownlow's care. As soon as Oliver recovers from his illness, he is summoned to Brownlow's study, which is packed from floor to ceiling with 'such a great number of books . . . written to make the world wiser' (144). The ensuing interview makes plain that education in this domain will favour the intellect: 'How should you like to grow up a clever man, and write books, eh?' Yet there are signs that the old gentleman is not quite as unworldly as this question and his general *amateur* demeanour might suggest. His response to Oliver's expressed preference for being a book*seller* rather than a book-writer – 'Don't be afraid! We won't make an author of you, while there's an honest trade to be learnt, or brickmaking to turn to' – signals, behind the humorous play of adult condescension, a certain hauteur towards the realities of labour, which are beneath him but also, of course, a *sine qua non* of his superior way of life. Our impression is similarly modified by the information that the library contains conspicuous quartos 'with a good deal of gilding about the binding', and by Brownlow's own somewhat ambiguous remark that 'there *are* books of which the backs and covers are by far the best parts' (145), which implies both intellectual discrimination and pride of ownership. Though the sources of his wealth are undeclared, the fissures in the text show that he has plenty of it and takes pleasure in what it buys. We remember that his spectacles are 'gold' (114); and just after these exchanges Oliver is sent off with a five-pound note to pay for more books.

Respect for books and their wisdom, then, goes with, and of course helps to justify and protect, social privilege and the quiet enjoyment of material possessions. This is true also with regard to the Maylies, Oliver's other benefactors. When Mrs Maylie and Rose, her niece, take Oliver with them into the country, rural serenity provides the perfect context for learning, and the boy goes every morning to a venerable schoolmaster who teaches him 'to read better, and to write', and in the afternoon listens to the two ladies 'read' and 'talk of books' (291). He studies the Bible all week, and from time to time puts one of its recommendations into practice by finding a 'little commission of charity' to execute in the nearby village (292). Life with the Maylies basically repeats the regimen of life with Brownlow and Mrs Bedwin, except that the regular lessons and mention of playing cricket make it seem less preparatory and more a small-scale, homespun version of an Arnoldian public school education.

The Maylies, however, not only furnish Oliver with access to the power and discipline of texts but are themselves a text. This applies in particular to Rose, the epitome of chaste female beauty and dedication, 'in the lovely bloom and spring-time of womanhood' but with more than a tinge of the divine:

> Cast in so slight and exquisite a mould; so mild and gentle; so pure and beautiful; that earth seemed not her element, nor its rough creatures her fit companions. The very intelligence that shone in her deep blue eyes, and was stamped upon her noble head, seemed

scarcely of her age, or of the world; and yet the changing expression of sweetness and good humour, the thousand lights that played about her face, and left no shadow there; above all, the smile, the cheerful, happy smile, were made for Home, and fireside peace and happiness. (264)

This evokes the sanitized and sanctified body of classical art, especially of statuary (take, for instance, the phrase 'her noble head'), but as it were attenuated, virtually bodiless. The natural, the sacred and the social are conflated in a linguistic figuring of perfection. The name 'Rose' of course connotes Englishness as well as naturalness: Dickens's conception of this surpassing and unspoiled 'Angel in the House' adds a bright star to the national myth of hearth and home that only in our own generation has lost its ubiquitous force, and that can still be compelling. Reading this passage, it is impossible not to recall those words of the commentator in *Eliza Cook's Journal* on the purposes of popular literature, which frankly disclose the hegemonic project in which Dickens is participating in framing his accounts of domestic bliss and blissful presence:

to strengthen the bands of society by instruction, and to cement national union by social and domestic recreation. The love of families engendered by this potent, but quiet influence, extends and evolves itself into patriotism.[17]

Rose actually becomes a spokeswoman for the personal and societal advantages of 'love of families' when defending Oliver against the suggestion that he might have been a willing – 'voluntary' – associate of criminals:

'But even if he has been wicked,' pursued Rose, 'think how young he is; think that he may never have known a mother's love, or the comfort of a home; that ill-usage and blows, or the want of bread, may have driven him to herd with men who have forced him to guilt. Aunt, dear aunt, . . . as you love me, and know that I have never felt the want of parents in your goodness and affection, but . . . might have been equally helpless and unprotected with this poor child, have pity upon him before it is too late!' (268–9)

This is one of those places in Dickens where inflated speech rhythms and syntax – a kind of rhetorical seizure – signal his preoccupation with an issue, or with making a point, irrespective of (though not necessarily out of step with) characterization or story-line. Rose's disquisition reflects his interest in the busy contemporary debate between the champions of 'environmentalism', who held that behaviour, good or bad, was determined by conditions, and (according to J.S. Mill, overwhelmingly the greater number in the early decades of the century) the 'voluntarists', who argued for predisposition and the agency of free will.[18] Dickens, here and in *Oliver Twist* as a whole, steers a sensible middle course; he certainly believed in intrinsic wickedness (Monks, Oliver's evil half-brother, being, as we shall see, the prime example) but was in no doubt of the effects of circumstance. The latter viewpoint comes out forcefully in Chapter 32, where Oliver, in the bosom of non-sentient nature as well as of Rose and her aunt, is described as exchanging 'squalid crowds' and the company of 'wretched men' for a 'new existence' amidst 'green leaves' and 'sweet-smelling air'. He inhabits a pastoral idyll that echoes the same time-honoured antithesis between town and country as that sounded by the controversialists who, in the 1830s, condemning urbanization and industrialization, proclaimed that it would be better if society were 'distributed into families and hamlets, all over the country', that 'the more agricultural' people's occupations 'the more elevated the moral and religious feelings', and that 'the influences of rural life are more pure'.[19]

But what truly matters in the end is not so much the setting or the psychology of Oliver's experience as the ideal of domesticity into which he is initiated and inserted. The chapter comes to rest with the quiet but explicit affirmation that 'Oliver Twist had become completely domesticated with the old lady and her niece', through a perfect reciprocity between 'the purest and most amiable generosity' on the one side and 'warmest, soul-felt gratitude' on the other. Domesticity stabilizes and gives worth to Oliver's existence. It also overarches a proselytizing vision of a model organic community, tranquil, at ease with itself, in which the lowest orders respect, benefit from and mirror the attitudes of the higher, for the 'poor people' and 'labouring men' at whose houses Oliver called on errands of mercy were unfailingly 'neat and clean' and knelt 'so reverently in prayer' in the 'homely church' that 'it seemed a pleasure, not a tedious duty, their assembling there'. The 'quiet, and neat, and orderly' space behind Brownlow's closed doors, where 'everybody was kind and gentle' and the Christian ethic prevailed, which seemed like 'Heaven' to Oliver (143), thus reappears as the topography not only of the Maylies' country cottage but of optimal social organization.

This interlude contains one extended passage that does home in upon psychological process, where Dickens writes out of apparent acquaintance with Wordsworthian meditative tradition. In *Lyrical Ballads* Wordsworth had not only filled out a general prescription for well-being on the basis that in 'rustic life . . . the essential passions of the heart find a better soil in which they can attain their maturity' but had, in such pieces as 'It is the first mild day of March', proclaimed an evangelical faith in our capacity for finding grace in the presence of nature – 'And from the blessed power that rolls / About, below, above, / We'll frame the measure of our souls: / They shall be tuned to love.'[20] In Dickens the creed of renovation merges with the philosophy of the 'Immortality Ode': the 'new state of being' generated by contemplation of 'Nature's face' removes the base instincts of 'enmity and hatred' and stirs recollections of pre-existence, 'memories . . . not of this world, nor of its thoughts and hopes', a 'consciousness of . . . remote and distant time, which calls up solemn thoughts of distant times to come' (290).[21] Memory is a guarantee of transcendence and our share in it. What this underlines, however, is that in *Oliver Twist* it does not confer earthly identity or purpose; not even in the form of personal history, which in later Dickens can function very much to these ends, as it does in the genre of Puritan confession to which he, and Wordsworth, owed a large debt.[22] Being-in-the-world in this early novel is pre-eminently a matter of belonging to a network of relationships. We have seen this already within the confines, and the confinements, of the society of the workhouse parish. It is true also of middle-class society, and of society as a whole, though rank brings certain private, as well as collective, advantages.

The communal vision of *Oliver Twist* forms against the background of a definite, if fitful, sense of the problem, even futility, of trying to establish any stable presence in the world. Oliver is given the opportunity on several occasions to say who he is and what has happened to him, but these bear no real fruit. When he comes before Fang the magistrate he mutters his name and gets called 'Tom White', which then leads to Brownlow mistrusting him when he says he is 'Oliver Twist' (122, 130); and later at Brownlow's his attempt to tell his story is nipped in the bud by the arrival of Mr Grimshaw, who casts doubt on the whole enterprise of self-definition by sarcastically implying that what they will get from the boy in any case would be a fiction like those announced in the titles of novels – 'a full, true, and particular account of the life and adventures of Oliver Twist' (149). When he at last manages to unburden himself, to the Maylie household, of the 'catalogue of evils and calamities' visited upon him (270–71), it brings him emotional relief but decides nothing, since his new protectors have then to go to elaborate lengths to cover up his past and who he is lest the police should investigate him. What compounds the difficulty of founding an identity, moreover, is that others are always ready, through blindness or self-interest, to make up their own stories about you.

Bumble provides a good example of both motives. Responding to Brownlow's advertisement for information leading to the discovery of 'Oliver Twist' (truly a *missing person*) or throwing light on his 'previous history', the beadle expatiates on the foundling's 'low and vicious parentage', his 'treachery, ingratitude, and malice', and his cowardice in attacking the defenceless Noah and running away. We need not take the narrator's word for Bumble's wish that he had imparted a very different colouring to his little biography when he hears Brownlow say that he would have given treble the money for a favourable account of the boy, for that is exactly the tack Bumble subsequently takes in publicly expressing his long-standing love of the excellent Oliver after the latter has come into his own (174–6, 460).

One thing these ineffectual or untrustworthy stories have in common is that they are given (or sometimes fail to be given) by word of mouth – their 'oralcy'. This throws into relief the relative force and authority of the written which, though abstractly considered it has no claim to the status of absolute truth, can, the more so in palpably non-fictional generic modes, be true to all practical extents and purposes. Writing, in *Oliver Twist*, is an exclusive property of the middle class, which it provides with mechanisms both of internal organization and outward-looking control. At a simple but not insignificant level, letters – which Mrs Bedwin was proud to receive regularly from her dutiful son in the West Indies – are a means of social bonding as well as communication; and when Fagin's gang wish to make triumphant fun of Oliver after snatching him from Brownlow it is letter-writing, along with dress (his 'swell' togs) and household ritual and idiom (the custom of taking 'supper'), that is used in parody as the symbol of a rival culture: 'The Artful shall give you another suit, my dear, for fear you should spoil that Sunday one. Why didn't you write, my dear, to say you were coming? We'd have got something warm for supper' (163). If writing is thus an aid to cohesion, it is in other, equally important aspects an instrument of coercion. It can fix one's place in the order of things, autonomously, without the complications of choice or desire. It may do this benignly, bringing rewards, as in the charting of Oliver's descent which we shall consider in a moment. Or it may operate at a deadly stroke and with dire consequences. The latter case is indirectly exemplified in Oliver's narrow escape from having the indentures signed that would tie him for life, no doubt extremely brief, to the brutal Gamfield: searching for the inkstand, parchment before him, the 'half-blind and half-childish' magistrate notices instead the orphan's distressed look and dismisses the application (64–5).

Here, the doddery short-sightedness of officialdom provides a fair degree of humour, and works luckily to Oliver's advantage. In Mr Fang, who tries Oliver for stealing in London, myopia, though capable of yielding comic effects, is positively terrifying. Fang gives a new twist to the concept of blind justice, acting inconsistently, at random, without any real regard to the evidence: Oliver's fainting fit in court is taken as proof of guilt and a summary sentence of three months' hard labour is passed; when, subsequently, an eyewitness account of the boy's innocence is too clear-cut even for Fang to ignore the magistrate starts threatening Brownlow with prosecution for shoplifting (120–24). Yet in the final analysis everything turns out for the best in this episode too. The only paper evident in Fang's courtroom is a newspaper, which he reads in desultory fashion and casts casually aside. He seems to belong to an old-style, Fielding-like, bluff and bludgeoning, world, where things are done off the cuff and through spoken report and exchange, where they can go wrong but also happily right, where there is room for spectacular error but also for amazing turns of good fortune. A system relying on the written word, on the other hand, though not without room for kindness or sheer happenstance (as with Oliver's first magistrate), is both more predictable and harsher, disciplined but also disciplinarian. Of such a regime Brownlow and to a less conspicuous extent the Maylies and their friend, Mr Losberne the doctor, turn out to be skilful practitioners. In one hand Brownlow carries a book but in the other a cane (114, 125). Although he is what we call a nice man – the narrator tells us that his heart was 'large enough for any six ordinary old gentlemen of humane disposition' (129) – he becomes, when needs be, a determined class warrior wielding a sharp intelligence and a sharp pen.

Brownlow's greatest service to the interests of those around him is to produce the long and intricate master-text of Oliver's descent, which chronicles many strands of recent dynastic history and misadventure, reveals Brownlow to have been the close friend of Oliver's father, restores Oliver's patrimony, and finally proves Rose Maylie to be Oliver's aunt. His *magnum opus*, for all its coincidences, is distinctly other than fiction. He is a detective-researcher whose work takes him as far as the West Indies, involves interviews and agents, and entails the discovery, interpretation and reconstitution of documents. There are hunches, but nothing is arbitrary, everything verified. The most basic data are the talismanic clues connected with Oliver's mother and the background to his birth: the portrait hanging in Mrs Bedwin's room, which, in its resemblance to the child, first stirs Brownlow's curious intuition (128–9, 132); the locket and the ring with the inscription 'Agnes' upon it, which Monks casts into an underground stream as part of his plan to deprive his young half-brother of his inheritance (340–44).

The love tokens survive in the chain of evidence, in spite of Monks's efforts to suppress them, because they are traced on the memories of a line of witnesses going back to one who had attended Oliver's mother on her deathbed but, as if that were not enough, they are in due course authenticated by mention in a letter of penitence in which the father of Monks and Oliver, Edwin Leeford, had expressed to Agnes his devotion and his guilt at leading her into shame (457–8). This missive is one of a range of papers, from impromptu to highly formal, out of which the narrative is put together: at one end of the spectrum, the hasty notes Brownlow makes, rather like a policeman, during the secret meeting at which Nancy confirms the information she has already given to Rose about Monks's design in collusion with Fagin to destroy Oliver by turning him into a criminal (413); at the other, Edwin Leeford's last will and testament, which comes to light late in the novel, leaving the bulk of his estate, not to his first son, Edward Leeford (Monks's real name), offspring of an enforced and loathsome marriage and disposed to 'vice, malice, and premature bad passions', but to the coming love-child, provided that, if a boy, 'in his minority he should never have stained his name with any public act of dishonour, meanness, cowardice, or wrong' (458). In finally sorting things out, there is a particular reliance on the writing that is legally binding and cannot be gainsaid. When Brownlow confronts Monks with the necessity of fully confessing his schemes against Oliver he insists that the villain 'Set [his hand] to a statement of truth and facts, and repeat it before witnesses' (440). A signature puts the matter beyond question.

This is one of the areas of Dickens that does seem to reflect Foucault's 'epistemic break', where 'truth and the knowledge of truth grew to depend upon narratives of growth, development and culmination, rather than upon classificatory patterns of relationship, difference and subordination', and where an embrace of the principle of incremental process, the pursuit of ends, was inevitably linked to a desire to establish origins.[23] The expectation is that we shall find in Brownlow's narrative both the newly prevailing model of comprehension and more particularly the interest of an ambitious but uncertain middle class in finding a tradition of its own to mirror and rival grand aristocratic conceptions of blood line. Both things are there, but with manifest complications. Embedded in Brownlow's jigsaw is a radically prospective angle. That is to say, what matters, in a way, is not so much roots and branches, the groundedness and growth of the family tree, as purity of heart and mind; for the claims of the strictly legitimate heir, Monks, are subordinated on considerations of morality to those of the illegitimate but deserving Oliver. Yet investment in a fine nature is also good eugenics. Fitness of character is one with fitness of body and mind. Just as Oliver's integrity shows always on his countenance, so does Monks carry the disfigurement of an inbred viciousness: 'you, who from your cradle were gall and bitterness, . . . and in whom all evil passions, vice, and profligacy, festered, till they found a vent in a hideous disease which has made your face an index even to your mind' (439). Monks, whom Brownlow additionally describes as a 'most unnatural issue' (435), is bad blood that must be purged in the service of present health and future expectations. Ultimately, moreover, Brownlow's own position is consolidated alongside Oliver's. He adopts Oliver as his son (476), thus doubly securing their mutual welfare – that is, by affiliation *and* filiation.

These terms are from Edward Said who, in probing changes attendant upon the formation of the 'modern capitalist world-order' of the nineteenth and early twentieth centuries, with its 'atomizations', describes a shift from a 'filiative' to an 'affiliative' ordering of human relationships and structures of authority:

> Thus if a filial relationship was held together by natural bonds and natural forms of authority – involving obedience, fear, love, respect, and instinctual conflict – the new affiliative relationship changes these bonds into what seem to be transpersonal forms – such as guild consciousness, consensus, collegiality, professional respect, class, and the hegemony of a dominant culture. The filiative scheme belongs to the realms of nature and of 'life', whereas affiliation belongs exclusively to culture and society.[24]

That Oliver is integrated artificially and by law into the prospects of the Brownlow connection, which he in turn strengthens by his own background and links to the Maylie clan, yet is situated in the form of a natural relationship, as a 'son', shows the Dickensian ideology's resourcefulness in having it all ways. We have at once a strategic alliance of like-minded individuals and groups and one big happy family involving ties of blood and, now, adoption. The edifice of affiliation is underpinned by and itself regenerates the rootedness of filiation. The organic and the 'made' exist in supportive reciprocity.

A solidifying and enabling arrangement similar to those turning upon Oliver is enacted in the Maylie household in the marriage of Rose and Mrs Maylie's son, Harry, which cleanses the 'stain' (as Mrs Maylie and Rose both put it) that attaches to Rose because she, in parallel with Oliver, is of 'doubtful birth'. The taint is not so much eradicated as redeemed, however, since it continues to exist in the attitudes of 'cold and sordid people' who know not, or are unswayed by, Rose's sweetness, 'noble' nature and 'perfect sacrifice of self' (304–305, 317). Harry's love and admiration transcend the exigencies of convention and bear fruit in a union that is psychologically, physically and morally justified and wholesome. This exemplary fulfilment is placed in direct opposition to a new version of the worldly attainment which it is an underlying purpose of *Oliver Twist* to condemn. Dr Losberne, knowing the Maylie family, assumes that Harry is destined for eminence in the public arena: 'But of course they will get you into parliament at the election before Christmas. . . . Good training is always desirable, whether the race be for place, cup, or sweepstakes' (319). Far from entering the competition, Harry rejects all 'distinction among a bustling crowd' and pledges 'but a home – a heart and a home': 'power and patronage', 'relatives of influence and rank' are cast off as they have shrunk from him in his choice of Rose; 'but there are smiling fields and waving trees in England's richest country; and by one village church – mine, Rose, my own! – there stands a rustic dwelling which you can make me prouder of, than all the hopes I have renounced, measured a thousandfold. This is *my* rank and station now' (465). This manifesto and declaration of intent, delivered with a conclusive flourish, reiterates in summary peroration the ideology of domesticity, love, virtue, pastoralism, national pride (the reference to England is singularly prominent here), that is written into existence in *Oliver Twist* and is projected as the bright alternative to acquisitive materialism and self-interest.

It is at such points of conceptual review or concentration, however, that we are perhaps most conscious of what is being left out. Losberne's and Harry's words give an intriguing obscure glimpse of where the Maylies' wealth does come from. They are a power in the land, vaguely aristocratic maybe, carrying political clout, yet whether new money or old, gentry or business people, or something else, is not divulged or made subject to scrutiny. They are left quietly to their field of command. Shunning them, Harry becomes a clergyman, the most unworldly of professions. But even here there is a catch. How does he get the wherewithal? Curacies do not grow on trees (as we know from Jane Austen), and neither does the comfortable routine enjoyed by the couple in their rural living, where they are joined by Mrs Maylie and, as near neighbours, by Mr Brownlow, Mrs Bedwin, and Oliver, and later Mr Losberne. If these – or at least the leading lights, for the housekeeper Bedwin, the adopted child Oliver, and the wife Rose are dependants who must fit in, however happily and however corporate the decisions – have freedom of choice, to change career, to flee the urban rat race, to cultivate the advantages that come with altruism, it is because they have the money to do so. Though Harry renounces the chase for the glittering prizes, he and his friends by no means spurn the benefits either of a steady income or of surplus expenditure. They even erect a marble tablet in remembrance of Oliver's mother in the village church, a detail which Cruikshank features in the final illustration of the book: where Oliver had once stood spoon erect before the workhouse keeper, a defiant beggar, he now strikes a well-dressed but humble pose before the memorial, cap in hand and pointing respectfully downwards (478). This monument is in itself a conspicuous example of Dickens's aggression in cultural matters. His shrine is not to the great but to an unmarried mother, whose name is still simply the lone 'Agnes', uncompleted, and unmodified, by any designation either of family or of husband. But it is noticeable that the tribute to the voiceless outcast is put into the safe keeping of a set of affluent, thriving and contented middle-class characters, who dwell far away from the living dispossessed. This is an elite, and in both the gloss spread over it and the glossing over of its pecuniary base there is a politics at work.

The group comprises not only the nuclear 'fireside circle' of Rose and Harry and the 'merry prattle' of their children but the mother-in-law enjoying the fruits of 'a well-spent life', the good uncle and protective substitute father, the well-born orphan restored to his rightful circumstances, a kind housekeeper, two worthy ex-professionals (Losberne the doctor and Grimwig, his regular visitor, who trained as a lawyer), and the old Maylie servants who divide their attentions equally among the three adjoining establishments. In a late-twentieth-century context the assembly might be read with a different slant: a normative heterosexual relationship and family unit; the convenient living arrangement of a well-to-do elderly man and his widowed housekeeper, interestingly named Mrs Bedwin; two children adopted by lone parents, both illegitimate and from a background of broken homes (and one an English Rose); and a couple of confirmed bachelors who live apart but spend a lot of time together. But this subcurrent of meaning, though troubling narrow respectability, could make, in a way, for even greater inclusiveness – giving a kind of libertarian gallery of possible lifestyles. The narrator calls the gathering 'a little society' and it is just that, a microcosm of a larger set of social attitudes and existential priorities. Set beyond the tow of modern industrializing, commercial, urban society, it projects an ideal; not a utopia, but almost: a 'condition approach[ing] as nearly to one of perfect happiness as can ever be known in this changing world' (476). Too fantastical quite to identify with, it is nevertheless a beacon to steer by.

Steven Connor asserts that the ending of *Oliver Twist* is unsettled by the fact that the counter-design of Monks and Fagin, to criminalize Oliver, has not been assimilated.[25] Certainly, conviction is undermined to the degree that the effort Dickens takes in making complete the triumph of good, which includes Fagin's execution and Monks's death after being imprisoned for some fresh act of fraud (476), draws attention to closure as contrivance, as agenda discourse rather than reality or mimetic report; an effect accentuated by a reference in the final chapter to the process of writerly creation, 'the hand that traces these words . . . and would weave, for a little longer space, the thread of these adventures' (479). In the fates visited upon them Monks and Fagin are made entirely subservient to the official plot which is controlled above all by Brownlow (though with Fagin we shall ultimately have to consider a post-mortem effect that dramatically complicates our final assessment of *Oliver Twist*). And how these characters are treated tells us something important about the nature of the relations between Brownlow's demesne and society at large, which involve both distance and subtle interconnection. Fagin is subjected to due process of law. Monks, on the other hand, is dealt with all the more efficiently because he is not exposed to public judgement but is made to come to an out-of-court agreement, after which his own disease of profligacy, his 'old disorder' (476), wipes him out. Proceeding 'gently' out of fond recollections of his old friend, Monks's father, Brownlow exhibits his usual clean hands and clear conscience, but he acts nonetheless with 'severity and determination' (436) to put Oliver's house in order. The dispatching of Monks is a major example of the internal policing that, together with money, education (in the penultimate paragraph of the book Brownlow is still filling the head of his adopted child with 'stores of knowledge') and recourse to external institutions of influence and enforcement, helps to secure the bliss that apparently comes naturally to the deserving at the end of *Oliver Twist*. Fagin's arrest apart, the actual collaboration of state and solid citizen in the maintenance of law and order is nicely instanced by Brownlow's alacrity in adding 50 pounds of his own to the reward of a hundred put up by the Government for the capture of Sikes (440–41). Money can be a useful tool of social discipline, and Brownlow is ready to employ his combatively when the need arises. A similar point emerges when Mrs Maylie and Losberne pay Blathers and Duff, the detectives who investigate the break-in at Chertsey, a couple of guineas for services rendered (284).

But the relationship between the middle-class characters of *Oliver Twist* and the police is more complex than that simply of 'employers' and 'servants'. As the names Blathers and Duff suggest, the latter are stereotypes, if not quite of bungling incompetence, then at least of underdeveloped intelligence. Losberne makes this point by indicting their invariably one-dimensional reading of situations, their dangerously narrow insights: 'They never see, whether for good or bad, more than one side of any question; and that is, always, the one which first presents itself to them' (277). They are easily outwitted when Losberne and the rest agree that they must not divulge Oliver's part in the attempted robbery lest he be held a real criminal, rather than one forced against his will and true nature. There is, then, an element of tension, even opposition, between the two parties, as well as a distinction in terms of superior and inferior mentality. The police are necessary to the dominant culture (as when they assemble an army of 'spies' (440) to hunt down Sikes) but can be intrusive and must in some circumstances be held at bay while the communal good is managed from within. They stand, in a way, on the other side of a divide, or at least on the boundary of one, manning a cordon around the undesirables in society yet being also intertwined with them. This last aspect becomes apparent as soon as Blathers and Duff arrive at Chertsey, for their conversation is peppered with the slang of the underworld – 'gig', 'prad', 'blunt' (273, 279). When Blathers tells his hosts the story of Conkey Chickweed, the man who robbed himself and was found out, it may well be to insinuate that lies don't pay;[26] but the warning makes no impression, and the detail that really stands out is that Conkey at that time 'warn't one of the family' (279), suggesting that now he is an informer – the calling eventually taken up by Noah Claypole, who not only turns State's evidence against Fagin but gets his Charlotte to faint outside public houses on Sundays, buys brandy from the landlords to revive her, and next day pockets half the penalty imposed on them for illegal sales (477). The lines between crime and the agencies of its containment are blurred. Not so those that mark off the elite class. Losberne, Rose and Mrs Maylie practise deception only for the best of motives: 'The object is a good one, and that must be our excuse' (277). They occupy a merited and unassailable upper rung on the ladder. They are the wide-awake guardians of goodness and essential truth.

But the sovereign forces of *Oliver Twist* – the Dickens–Brownlow–Maylie axis – do not go entirely unchallenged. The most awkward questions are posed by the figures for different reasons farthest beyond the pale, the murderer Sikes and Fagin 'the Jew'. It is upon these characters, and also Nancy, that I wish to focus in the concluding part of my discussion, together with further aspects of the relationship between the upper and under worlds of the novel.

*

The geographic relation between the Maylies, Mr Brownlow and the criminals is concentrical. The Maylies live in the country, Mr Brownlow in the suburbs, Fagin, Sikes and Nancy deep in the city. The 'outer–inner' topography, however, is shot through with 'high' and 'low', the latter articulated most obviously in references to dirt and animals. As Oliver and the Dodger approach Fagin's den, they come to 'narrow' and 'muddy' streets, where 'the air was impregnated with odours':

> There were a good many small shops; but the only stock in trade appeared to be heaps of children, who, even at that time of night, were crawling in and out of doors, or screaming from the inside. The sole places that seemed to prosper amid the general blight of the place, were the public-houses; and in them, the lowest orders of Irish were wrangling with might and main. Covered ways and yards . . . disclosed little knots of houses, where drunken men and women were positively wallowing in filth; . . . great ill-looking fellows were cautiously emerging, bound, to all appearance, on no very well-disposed or harmless errands. (103)

Smithfield market, which Sikes and Oliver pass through on the house-breaking expedition to Chertsey, furnishes a livelier scene, though no cause for celebration:

> The ground was covered, nearly ankle-deep, with filth and mire. . . . Countrymen, butchers, drovers, hawkers, boys, thieves, idlers, and vagabonds of every low grade, were mingled together in a mass; the whistling of drovers, the barking of dogs, the bellowing and plunging of oxen, . . . the hideous and discordant din that resounded from every corner . . . and the unwashed, unshaven, squalid, and dirty figures constantly running to and fro . . . rendered it a stunning and bewildering scene, which quite confounded the senses. (203)

These passages are classic predictions of the modern idea of the inner city, cramped, degraded, dangerous, yet fascinating. Before looking at them more closely, we may recall for comparison the tenement Oliver visits with Sowerberry to collect a dead body, which is similarly 'crowded', 'dirty' and 'miserable', the houses being 'tenanted by people of the poorest class: . . . men and women who, with folded arms and bodies half doubled, occasionally skulked along'. Some properties, beyond repair, had become 'the nightly haunts of . . . houseless wretches', the rough boards wrenched aside 'to afford an aperture wide enough for the passage of a human body'. Outside, 'the very rats, which here and there lay putrefying, . . . were hideous with famine' (81). Extreme urban squalor is not restricted to the metropolis. The difference is, however, that in this description conditions are expressed as a social evil, a problem of poverty ('poorest class'), of homelessness ('houseless wretches'), of deprivation so great that even the rats starve to death. The reader is reminded that the inhabitants of this dismal place, though reduced to the lowest level of physical existence, hunched and emaciated 'bodies' lurking or squeezing through holes for shelter, are nonetheless 'human' and deserving of something more. These people are victims. There is no moral degradation; and indeed the reformist appeal to better feelings is extended in a portrait of a loving and tearful husband explaining how his wife had been destroyed by a system that had sent him to prison for begging in the streets as a last resort in trying to support her and her children. When he falls 'grovelling upon the floor' like a beast, it is because of what has been done to him (82).

The later episodes are not like this at all. A hint of what is to come surfaces in the early passage when the focus contracts to the dead woman's mother: '[her] face was wrinkled; her two remaining teeth protruded over her underlip; and her eyes were bright and piercing. Oliver was afraid to look at either her or the man. They seemed so like the rats he had seen outside' (82). Metonymic associations, rats as signifiers of neglect and putrefaction, an imposed situation for which the State is responsible, slide over into metaphor: the slum-dwellers resemble rats. In the London scenes the metaphoric displacement is more complete, built into the discourse itself. Children are 'heaps' of waste, or a horde of small animals 'crawling' around and 'screaming' by night; the drunks 'wallow' in filth like pigs. The mire of Smithfield accommodates a promiscuous riot of human, sub-human, and non-human forms: the countryman rubs shoulders with thieves and, at the very bottom of the pile, with vagabonds labelled 'low grade' as if they were livestock; the noises of men and animals merge in one huge cacophony; 'unwashed' and 'unshaven' forms rush indistinguishably across the canvas. If there seems an uppish detachment in the way humanity is observed here, even more worrying is the racism of the allusion to 'the lowest orders of Irish', who take their place naturally in the ranks of the irrational and degenerate (an attitude towards the western 'Celt' rife, it should be said, among Dickens's contemporaries, including Engels), and the similar biological thinking inscribed in the detail of the drunken poor '*positively*' sprawling in filth, seeking their predetermined level, driven from within, beyond help.[27]

In so far as it thus constitutes people or groups, 'others', in terms of bestiality and baseness, Dickens's text again reflects and reaffirms the superiority of the bourgeois subject. The low is the measure by which the ascendant culture positions itself. The reforming and reactionary stances that we have identified in the three passages represent not so much a split personality as twin aspects of the same sensibility. Sympathy for the deserving is as naturally rained downwards from a commanding height as is either neutral contemplation of irremediable inferiority or disapproval of self-willed depravity; and both attitudes legitimate the presupposed dominance. Moreover, as so often in Dickens, writing makes visible, from a safe distance, that which is hidden and feared – we may recall Oliver's terrified reaction to rats and the rat-like slum-dwellers alike – and in so doing renders it subject to regulation and control. Disease, vermin, drunkenness, even understandable desperation born of poverty, all, like crime, can be policed.

This last point is one of those developed by Peter Stallybrass and Allon White in their commanding study of principles of culture formation in England and western Europe from the Renaissance to the early twentieth century, which also highlights the persistent fascination among the governing classes, and not least the purveyors and consumer-recipients of Victorian bourgeois identity, with the grotesque, the marginal and the unclean, the 'Other', as objects of desire, even as they specify their own singularity against these categories of exclusion.[28] This dual motivation, the political imperative to reject and the imaginative urge to embrace, permeates the representation of the underworld in *Oliver Twist*, and the combination, offering as it were a twofold fulfilment, may well be a better explanation of the lasting appeal of these aspects of the novel than the customary straightforward citing of their richer aesthetic and sensuous life. We have already encountered lively parodies that yet promote earnest middle-class ideology in the fields of nurture and domesticity. There is in such events an element of the canivalesque, as the phenomenon is understood and applied in theories stemming from Bakhtin's elevation of 'carnival' as populist critique of prevalent hierarchies, but often, as in the work of Terry Eagleton and Roger Sales, qualifying that view by seeing carnival as 'a licensed affair' that underpins the establishment through rituals of 'permissible rupture'.[29] Barbara Babcock, in a book on anthropology and literature, gives a succinct appraisal of the kind of effect generally in question, which she terms 'symbolic inversion':

> All symbolic inversions define a culture's lineaments at the same time as they question the usefulness and the absoluteness of its ordering. . . . What is socially peripheral is often symbolically central, and if we ignore or minimize inversion and other forms of cultural negation, we often fail to understand the dynamics of symbolic processes generally.[30]

At one stage it is as if Fagin knows that he is performing in a drama of inversion, when, formally reading Oliver a 'long lecture' on the sin of ingratitude (again the theme of education), he (for once accorded the title 'Mr' as if he were a fatherly mentor) lays mischievous claim to the same good offices, the 'philanthropy', practised by Mr Brownlow. A young lad should not wilfully absent himself from 'the society of anxious friends', he pronounces, and should be thankful and obedient (as we are frequently told Oliver is to Mr Brownlow and the Maylies)[31] to the person who had 'taken Oliver in, and cherished him, when, without his timely aid, he might have perished with hunger' (177). Fagin has a point about what he has done for Oliver, which more or less mirrors Brownlow's interventions; but the difference lies, of course, in motives and outcome. There is no future in belonging to Fagin's community except thraldom and probably the noose, as we are immediately reminded by the wary old gentleman's anecdote for Oliver's benefit about the boy who was sadly but necessarily sacrificed to the hangman in order to protect his leader and a few select followers. Fagin's posture thus shifts from comic recalcitrance to ruthless cunning. Lest the reader should miss the put-down, the opening of the next chapter switches to another type of inversion. Fagin is not simply associated with filth, nor shown grovelling in it; he is a creature born of it, cold-blooded and predatory: 'As he glided stealthily along . . . the hideous old man seemed like some loathsome reptile, engendered in the slime and darkness through which he moved: crawled forth, by night, in search of some rich offal for a meal' (186). Reptiles are more exotic than pigs and more transfixive, but also more noisome. It is difficult to get lower than this.

With the Dodger and Charley Bates attention falls on the fantasy lives of the characters themselves rather than of the reader. They ape their betters and dream of being great men. This comes to a head when the Dodger is arrested for petty theft of a sneeze-box and booked for transportation. The affair is an immense let-down for Charley, not because his friend has been taken, but because a colleague of matchless promise will suffer an ignominious end and not achieve his expected place among the legendary criminals whose deeds, trials and last days were commemorated in the *Newgate Calendar*: 'Oh, why didn't he rob some rich old gentleman of all his walables, and go out *as* a gentleman, and not like a common prig, without no honour nor glory!' (390). Charley's disappointment is assuaged by the Dodger's performance in court, where he refuses to co-operate, turning the tables by asking the names of 'them two old files' on the bench, expressing annoyance at missing an appointment in the city, threatening the 'beaks' with an attorney delayed at breakfast in the House of Commons, and promising 'to make a parliamentary business of it; and then grinning in the officer's face, with great glee and self-approval' (396). In Charley's eyes, the Dodger thus wins for himself 'a glorious reputation'; but both are of course deluded. The Dodger acts as though he is in a carnival, an allowed jester, but the system simply and inexorably has its serious way with him, as he is dragged off to be 'locked up by himself in a little cell'. He is banished perhaps because his artfulness makes him a real danger to society; Charley, a naïve adolescent (as the *double entendre* in his other designation, 'Master Bates', might suggest), forever merrily thinking it is all 'a game . . . a regular game!' (391), is reclaimable and, deciding that honesty is the best policy, rises from farmer's drudge to grazier in Northamptonshire (477). It is worth noting, moreover, that the order mimicked in these episodes is not that of the novel's central ideology at all, but of the raffish gentleman (we think of 'decadents' like James Harthouse in *Hard Times*), of 'business', of the politically well-connected, of the pursuit of public fame – the very lifestyles rejected by Harry Maylie. The quiet heroism, realism and determination of the enlightened middle class remains untouched and, by contrast, the more solidly in place.

Though reaching but modest heights, Charley Bates is the one character to move from the wrong to the right side of the fence. Nancy tries to cross over but cannot. She is the symbolic reverse of Rose Maylie; the one chaste, ethereal, angelic, the other sensuous, earthy, tainted. Stallybrass and White comment upon the key figure of the prostitute in the social and psychic economy of the mid-nineteenth century, where the 'respectable' mission for reform, linked to fear of contamination, lodged ambivalently with a 'fascinated preoccupation with the carnival of the night, a landscape of darkness, drunkenness, noise and obscenity'.[32] There is in fact nothing of the latter subterranean absorption in Dickens, and indeed his single description of night-life tells emphatically of debilitation: 'women: some with the last lingering tinge of their early freshness fading as you looked; others with every mark and stamp of their sex utterly beaten out, and presenting but one loathsome blank of profligacy and crime' (237). The positive side of his own response adds instead a third term. In Nancy he humanizes the whore. This comes out even in reference to her physical being when, in a moment of rare frankness for this novel, we learn that on the eve of her journey to divulge Monks's plot to Rose, 'stooping over the bed, she kissed the robber's lips' (359), though it is important to register that the erotic element is linked to noble feelings of loyalty towards Sikes, which bind her to him whatever the cost – 'I am drawn back to him through every suffering and ill-usage; and I should be, I believe, if I knew that I was to die by his hand at last' (365). Oliver had been quick himself to detect the girl's 'better feelings', and the other main line of their development lies in her increasingly courageous defence of the child, stopping Fagin from beating him with a club being one thing (165), putting herself at risk from the whole gang by revealing their part in the abduction another. In the fraught aftermath of the attempted robbery at Chertsey, Nancy's love for Sikes clashes with her commitment to Oliver as, addressing Fagin, she hopes the boy 'is dead and out of harm's way, and out of yours', yet adds at once 'that is, if Bill comes to no harm' (241). At the same time, this grotesque wish for Oliver's blessed release arises from complicated emotions involving self-mistrust, self-disgust and desperate resentment at Fagin's power over her: it is 'no fault' of Fagin's if she is not always what he would have her be; when she says of Oliver 'I can't bear to have him about me. The sight of him turns me against myself, and all of you' (240) it is not only because she hates the cruelty she is implicated in and might be tempted to expose but because Oliver reminds her of her own abuse. More and more we see Nancy from the inside, in complex ways, with understanding. When, in a scene that wonderfully points the iron ring of segregation and the rigid distinctions existing *within* the lower strata, the servants at the hotel where she visits Rose treat her with 'virtuous disdain' – the housemaids remark that she is 'a disgrace to her sex' and strongly advocate that she be cast into the gutter (359) – we are on her side.

In his conception of Nancy, then, Dickens chivvies easy opinion and arouses sympathetic interest. Yet the qualities that he values in her belong to a recognizable and indisputably conservative frame. They are 'wifely' (towards Bill), 'sisterly'/'motherly' (towards Oliver), self-sacrificial (towards both). To these is added the moral uprightness of 'the sense of her own deep shame' (360), which, at the beginning of the interview with Rose, prompts her to an apologia: 'Thank Heaven upon your knees, dear lady, . . . that you were never in the midst of cold and hunger, and riot and drunkenness, and – and – something worse, than all – as I have been from my cradle' (360, 362). This effort at self-explanation both extends the process of Nancy's humanization and makes her at once sound judge and defence counsel in her own case. She confesses her unquestionable vices but insists that these should be seen as the result of corruption rather than of innate propensity. Her virtues are the traces of an essence; as the narrator puts it, 'something of the woman's original nature left in her still' (360). They derive from a fundamental womanliness, of which Rose is the unspoilt configuration.

For Nancy to become like Rose, her 'dear, sweet angel lady', would be, were it possible, a reversion to pure and proper type.

The white handkerchief Nancy begs from Rose in this episode symbolizes the unbreakable connection and unbridgeable distance between the two as the 'high' and 'low' of womankind, the immaculate and the unclean. It signifies most obviously Nancy's desire for something that she lacks, something of her better – or better self – which she wishes to possess but can have only at second hand, *in token form*. There are, however, distinct ambiguities that ruffle the text, dividing it against itself and disclosing larger conflicts of meaning. 'Worn' is one of the words describing the relation of the handkerchief to Rose, implying that her purity is not an essence at all, but a covering or attachment, an outward show – a construct in the service of an ideology. White, too, may be read as colourless, and the passing over of the handkerchief as a misappropriation, not *by* Nancy from below, but *of* her richness by an invasive anaemia, a lacework of etiolation. Rose subsequently transforms into a vehicle for a weightier onslaught in words which threatens to crush out of Nancy all the humanity Dickens has put in and to reduce her to an *exemplum* in a parable of sin and repentance: 'your evident contrition, and sense of shame; all lead me to believe you might yet be reclaimed. . . . Do hear my words, and let me save you yet, for better things. . . . It is never too late . . . for penitence and atonement.' The sheer, abrupt force of Nancy's devotion to Sikes resists the move thus to translate her: ' "It is," cried the girl, writhing in the agony of her mind; "I cannot leave him now! I could not be his death" ' (364). But not for long. When Sikes confronts her with his knowledge of (as he mistakenly sees it) her betrayal, she starts talking to him as if she were Rose, in the same semi-religious terminology of salvation: 'Let us both leave this dreadful place, and far apart lead better lives, and forget how we have lived, except in prayers. . . . It is never too late to repent' (422). Survival is made available to Nancy in the end only in terms of a language of conversion, which is subjection to abstract values wielded from the other side of the pale. As she lies dying, the blood symbolically draining from her body, she draws from her bosom the very handkerchief, holds it up to Heaven, and breathes 'one prayer for mercy to her Maker' (423). The white cloth is by one reckoning the sign of her having taken the right track, of her being 'saved'. By another, however, it is the flag of her surrender of life-affirming identity to life-denying code – though the drama of her being, as we have witnessed it throughout the novel, remains to cast its light and shade over this calculated conclusion.

The presentation of Nancy inaugurates a thematic tension between the self experientially projected and the self ideologically consumed that will, in one form or another, pervade the corpus of Dickens's writings. Bill Sikes is much more an instance of the former *per se*. He is neither converted, like Nancy, nor put on trial like Fagin. He is a low character who, against the odds, retains stature and an uncompromised independent life. In the long run, however, this does not mean that he subverts the hegemonic centre of *Oliver Twist* any more than does Nancy herself.

Sikes is afforded special standing from the first. His bestiality is decidedly top-scale, associated with animals that are feared and respected. While Fagin is a reptile in search of offal, Sikes is a wolf ready to tear the throats of his enemies (254). He is built like a bulldog, 'stoutly', with a 'bulky pair of legs, with large swelling calves' (136). His relations with his own dog, though no lesson on how to keep a pet, unite the two in a mutual exercise of rage, upon one another – he kicks the dog, the dog bites back – and upon the world, both bearing the marks of frequent injury. Where Fagin robs his colleagues, including Sikes, Sikes robs the wealthy. It has been interestingly argued that every time he hits his dog 'he represents the underclass' [*sic*] frustration with its disempowerment – its inability to express itself in terms other than violence to itself';[33] but in his invasions of middle-class territory, including that of the Maylies, there seem to be healthier, or at least understandable, surges of extrovert class antagonism. In what he does and in what he is – are wolves not in some respects superior to men? – Sikes puts the conventional boundaries of *super* and *sub* under severe pressure. He is a threat to the thought categories on which the established order rests, a lot more so than Nancy in whom the seeds of conformity have never ceased to live.

In the crime, flight and end of Sikes is lodged Dickens's transgressive imagination – that side of his creativity that operates at the extreme and opposite pole from the orthodox fable of 'Good surviving through every adverse circumstance' that is privileged in the author's Preface. *Oliver Twist* becomes in these segments a sophisticated version of the *Newgate Calendar* or the history of great criminals with which Fagin tries to seduce Oliver. Around Sikes they weave a fascination unbreached by socio-political strategy or moral preoccupation.

The descriptive writing of the opening of Chapter 48, 'The Flight of Sikes', is not only the product but an allegory of a particular kind of creative process, bright Gothic, strangely exultant, intent, compulsive, impure. The sun's rays, suggestive of the Apollonian light of revelation, stream into the room where the murdered woman lies to show, not the foulness of the deed, but the soft-wet horror of mutilation, 'such flesh, and so much blood'. The eyes of the corpse, 'glaring upward', become a lens through which to contemplate the exquisitely offensive 'reflection of the pool of gore that quivered and danced in the sunlight on the ceiling' (423). The bloodstains were 'dispersed about the room', marking it selectively, screen-like, with the quiet but telling traces of a violent frenzy. 'The very feet of the dog were bloody.' Sikes tries to cover the body from view, but sight is overtaken by the greater tyranny of imagination as he envisions the eyes staring at *him*. This puts in the coil that will gradually twist, for it is the *idée fixe* that accompanies Sikes right up to the point of his own death.

Once we leave the scene of the murder the pattern changes, no longer a synchrony of arresting images, but still unprogressive, a meandering 'to and fro, and up and down, and round and round, and still linger[ing] about the same spot'. The literal protagonist on the road merges with the writer struggling to find a way forward in the troubled aftermath of wrongdoing, seeking 'a good place' after 'a strange perversity' (425). Dickens's immediate crime has been to indulge a genius for low writing, dealing out the gross stimulants of a populist genre. Before that, however, in the killing of Nancy, he has robbed the rational, upright overworld of its prize. Sikes's assault intervenes at the instant of the woman's dissolution into doctrine, as she incants the formula for redemption she has absorbed from Rose and Mr Brownlow. It is the primitive resurrection of the body, reclaiming her for the conflation of sex and violence that has all along been the mark of their relationship as, fast in her embrace, he beats her with his pistol upon the 'upturned face that almost touched his own' and, having cleft her with a 'deep gash', follows up with the climactic stroke of a heavy club (422–3). Dickens goes with the full flow of a furious affront to the culture of disembodied high-mindedness, profaning in Sikes's act of reckless self-assertion the ideology of his own central narrative.

When the story of Sikes's journey does move on, the proto-filmic technique continues but is conducted with immense poetic intelligence. A series of tableaux unfolds his inner states through a combination of broad strokes and incidental detail. The murderer's guilty conscience is brought to distinctive life in Sikes's paranoid sense of being under suspicion from everyone he meets, even 'the very children at the doors' at Hendon, and in the finely paced set-piece of his encounter in the public house at Hatfield with the pedlar hawking an infallible mixture for removing every imaginable stain – including blood (425–7). (The catalogue of real places through which Sikes passes – not only Hendon and Hatfield but also Hampstead, Highgate and many more – intensifies the phantasmagorical atmosphere that suffuses the journey.) Spots of the mind are not so easily removed as the blemish the mountebank tries to set about on Sikes's hat, and the perspective then moves more incisively inwards to explore the haunting of Sikes by the ghost of Nancy. At the fever pitch of his torment he throws himself on his back upon the road: 'At his head it stood, silent, erect, and still – a living gravestone, with its epitaph in blood' (428). The body and the tomb, a pulsing physicality and hard, cold deathliness, merge in the apparition; but the 'it' is not only Nancy's corpse, and the nightmare fantasy expresses a confusion of terror and erotic desire consistent with the energies at play during the murder itself.

This detail is also interesting for another reason. It reminds us of those wayside figures that confront Christian in *The Pilgrim's Progress*, which are sometimes demons out to destroy him, sometimes spectacles of pilgrims or others (like the pillar of salt that was Lot's wife) who have met a premature end. The whole of this part of Sikes's travels, and especially his immersion in the crowd fighting a conflagration, recalls Christian's passage through the Valley of the Shadow of Death.[34] The 'dread and awe' that he feels; the spectre stalking him, so that he could 'hear its garments rustling, . . . and every breath of wind came laden with that last low cry'; the semblance of 'some fearful thing' everywhere around him; 'figures tearing to and fro', the 'roar of voices . . . sheets of flame . . . driving clouds of smoke': these echo the 'howling and yelling, . . . dreadful', 'flame and smoke', the 'rushings too and fro', the 'frightful sight' and 'hideous noises' that assail Christian in the Valley, where 'fiends' make track to drag him into the mouth of Hell. There seems to be a parallel, too, in the way Christian emerges unscathed from the danger and confusion, 'morning being come', and Sikes, finding relief from himself in the frantic activity of combating the fire, 'bore a charmed life, and had neither scratch nor bruise, nor weariness nor thought, till morning dawned again' (430). Yet the differences speak more loudly than the similarities. Christian holds on against fiendish raids by remembering 'how he had already vanquished many a danger', fights back through that other most potent weapon of the Puritan pilgrim, the biblical text, and is finally rescued by God ('*He hath turned the shadow of death into the morning*'). Sikes, on the other hand, is a man 'flying from memory' that tortures him (430), has no texts, and is pursued by an avenging Providence: 'Let no man talk of murderers escaping justice, and hint that Providence must sleep. There were twenty score of violent deaths in one long minute of that agony of fear' (428). His destiny is the reverse of Christian's deliverance. The only light that shines upon him is that of the ghastly, glaring eyes, 'light in themselves, but giving light to nothing' (428). When day dawns, 'there returned, with tenfold force, the dreadful consciousness of his crime' (430).

Although Sikes is surely of the damned, however, he invites little or no condemnation. His very status as the antitype of Bunyan's hero yields a mythic aura, and aids his entry into the folk imagination as a figure beyond simple approval or disapproval, though not of course fundamental questions of right and wrong. His predicament is treated much less as a lesson in the punitive workings of self-conscious guilt than as a psychodrama of anguish, torture, madness; an isolation so vivid and extreme that it cannot but attract sympathy. Our mixed feelings about Sikes are brought out forcibly in the amazing brief episode in which, resolving to return to London and fearing his dog might give him away, he tries to drown the animal with a heavy stone tied in a handkerchief: 'The dog wagged his tail, but moved not. Sikes made a running noose and called him again. The dog advanced, retreated, paused an instant, turned, and scoured away at hardest speed' (432). We are glad the dog escapes, not least because of the knowing look he directs 'into his master's face' while the matter-of-fact preparations are in the making. But Sikes too is a hunted creature. A part of us doesn't want him to be caught either.

Sikes is indeed allowed to evade the hangman's noose, as the dog has avoided his. As the police close in on him in the derelict building on Jacob's Island, he cries out to the crowd below, 'Do your worst! I'll cheat you yet!' (449). He does 'cheat' expectations to the extent that he is not taken alive – which is what is planned for him by a man on a horse, presumably a senior officer, who promises a twenty guineas reward for his capture, and by 'an old gentleman' who puts up fifty pounds, and might well be that less than conspicuous guardian of public order, Mr Brownlow (449, 451). Sikes hangs himself from a rooftop chimney, his intention having been to lower himself by rope into the muddy ditch that surrounds the Island. There is in this setting another evocation of Bunyan's Valley of the Shadow of Death, which is skirted on one side by 'a very deep ditch' into which the blind have ever led the blind and on the other by a bottomless 'quag'. The 'filthiest, the strangest, the most extraordinary' of many such localities hidden in the city, Jacob's Island is a modern hell, a ghetto of lost souls, breeding place of destitution and refuge of the iniquitous (442–3). Rising literally and figuratively above this landscape of 'filth. rot, and garbage', Sikes loses his footing:

> the murderer, looking behind him on the roof, threw his arms above his head, and uttered a yell of terror.
> 'The eyes again!' he cried in an unearthly screech.
> Staggering as if struck by lightning, he lost his balance and tumbled over the parapet. The noose was on his neck. It ran up with his weight, tight as a bowstring, and swift as the arrow it speeds. He fell for five-and-thirty feet. There was a sudden jerk, a terrific

convulsion of the limbs; and there he hung, with the open knife clenched in his stiffening hand. (453)

But this is not the last thing, and what follows is a real *coup de roman*. Enter a dog:

> A dog, which had lain concealed till now, ran backwards and forwards on the parapet with a dismal howl, and collecting himself for a spring, jumped for the dead man's shoulders. Missing his aim, he fell into the ditch, turning completely over as he went; and striking his head against a stone, dashed out his brains.

We have noticed likenesses between Sikes and his dog. Here we are aware of the difference. Whether we see it as frenzied instinct or blind loyalty, the dog's leap after his master reaffirms the latter's humanity. Sikes is not an animal but a 'man', which is what Dickens markedly starts to call him a paragraph or two earlier when describing how he stands alone against 'the ferocity of the crowd' (451).

Sikes's is a transcendent end; not sublime, certainly ironic in the act of self-destruction, yet extraordinary nevertheless, and on a relatively grand scale. He doesn't manage to steal the Maylies' silver but he does steal the show. One of the novel's interpreters argues that in it murder proves 'a great uniter' in a world where everyone has hitherto led separate and self-centred lives; that because of it 'society develops the cohesion and point that it lacked before'.[35] But in truth, the unity of the crowd that pursues Sikes on Jacob's Island is that of a mindless mob, 'as though the whole city had poured its population out to curse him' (450). In so far as there is a cohesive force it is represented by the squad of officers and by the authority figures of the man on horseback and the wealthy old gentleman who keep cropping up, trying to harness the currents of mass hysteria, and who enjoy a freedom of action and movement in keeping with their place in society but also relative to the obligation to serve it (the horse being an especially telling detail, indicative at once of comparative mobility and magisterial rank). The manner of Sikes's death, like that of his fractious and insurgent life, defies both the crowd and the system. Triggered by a returning consciousness of Nancy's gaze – 'The eyes again!' – it is situated as a psychological event or as an interposition of Providence, or both. It is poetic justice, not human justice.

In the final analysis, however, the pull of the story of Sikes creates ambiguity in the novel but not fracture. Its 'fit' with the ideological core may be approached through the question of the cohesion existing or being produced at a third level – that of the community of Dickens's readers. In his Preface Dickens defended himself at some length against objections that had been made to the 'coarse and shocking circumstance' of his having portrayed 'criminal and degraded' characters, and did so by insisting that 'stern truth' must be told and that there was a moral lesson to be had from contemplating such 'horrors' (33–5). In retrospect this seems an exercise in irrelevance; for something altogether subtler is going on, both in the text and in the relation between text and reader. The problem of Sikes's appeal gets less the more appealing he becomes, and it ultimately dissolves in an aesthetic experience. The transcendent is pre-eminently reassuring and consumable – which is why, perhaps, Hardy, wishing to shock his public into a recognition of injustice, does not allow Tess to die magnificently on the altar at Stonehenge but has her mundanely arrested by the police and executed. Dickens's treatment of his murderer does not subvert, though it may face against and outrun, and for a time disrupt, the novel's central narrative and values. To recall Stallybrass and White, imaginative transgression can supplement cultural conviction. The Sikes episodes of *Oliver Twist* feed *and* refine the bourgeois fascination with 'otherness', until in their climax they evacuate the body itself, which is the nub of that allure, of both its offensiveness and coarse attractions. The 'lifeless', empty 'dangling body' of the dead Sikes is a ritualistic display of the middle-class erasure of bodily function, although the symbolic attitude in which he is caught at the instant of dying stores in extreme, orgasmic, form the preoccupation that is being expunged – the 'sudden jerk', the 'terrific convulsion of the limbs', 'the open knife clenched in his stiffening hand' (453).

Sikes is the first of many ambivalent outsiders and reprobates among Dickens's characters. If there is a problem left over from *Oliver Twist* for the modern reader, however, it is not Sikes but Fagin. This may seem surprising, since on the surface the fence merely gets his just deserts; but the way payment is exacted yields troublesome results.

There is a moment in Chapter 52 when sympathy could swing towards the prisoner in the condemned cell as he cries out in plaintive terror, 'What right have they to butcher me?' (472). This apart, the trend is all downwards to humiliation. 'Butcher' is an apt term. The animal imagery has been insistently kept up; the reptile grows the fangs of a 'dog' or 'rat' (417), for example, and an onlooker's account of the fracas following Fagin's arrest pictures him as a fox or other quarry at bay: 'I can see the people jumping up . . . and snarling with their teeth and making at him' (445). This makes a telling contrast with Sikes. Whereas for him the populace become something between excited spectators and impassioned supporting cast in a spectacular adventure, for Fagin they provide a savage band of willing executioners, themselves animals, 'snarling', 'making at' their cornered prey. The police are, ironically, Fagin's 'dearest friends' in saving him from the mob; but they preserve him – again in sharp contradistinction to Sikes – so that he can undergo the more formal but no less ruthless retribution of the State.

During the trial scene itself there are one or two interludes which bring to the surface the sluggish flow of Fagin's distracted consciousness – his sight of the young sketch-artist casually sharpening his pencil point, his ruminations on the judge's costume, its cost, how he put it on – but these arouse our detached curiosity rather than empathy. Mostly, the narrative is gauged to stress the revulsion of the onlookers. Sikes puts a show on, Fagin is put on show. There is atmosphere but little or no suspense, since everyone has already decided the outcome. The people peer at the accused from all sides, 'some applying glasses to their eyes, and others whispering to their neighbours with looks expressive of abhorrence', while not a single face, even among the women, showed 'any feeling but one of all-absorbing interest that he should be condemned' (466). A 'peal of joy' goes up from the gathering outside at the news that the prisoner was to die; and all 'assailed him with opprobrious names, and screeched and hissed' (468). Perhaps it is because it is thus presented as a play, with the prescribed audience response to the villain right down to the proverbial hissing, that we do not take seriously the deadly implications of what is happening or relate them to a possible real-life situation. Here art breeds insensitivity.

Fagin is then shown cursing even the 'venerable men of his own persuasion' who wish to pray with him in his cell. Oliver and Mr Brownlow come visiting, not in this case out of charity but on business, the latter being typically concerned to strengthen his party's position by recovering from Fagin written evidence, 'some papers', that would help to wrap up the matter of Oliver's inheritance, and being coolly alert, too, to the chance to discipline and arm Oliver by teaching him a lesson in the inexorable laws of crime and punishment – 'as this child has seen him in the full career of his success and villainy, I think it as well – even at the cost of some pain and fear – that he should see him now' (471–2). This offers a further occasion for abasement, for Fagin, almost farcically, tries to get Oliver to smuggle him out. The turnkey asks of Fagin, 'Are you a man?' The answer comes in the negative, as the animal references are carried through to the very end. The last we hear of Fagin, this 'snared beast' (472), is a howling 'cry upon cry that penetrated even those massive walls' (474).

Why does this relentless downgrading and dehumanization matter? Why should we linger over it? For one thing, as John Sutherland explains,[36] it is by no means clear that Fagin is in fact guilty of a capital offence. Yet the question of how just or unjust the sentence technically is can only be a secondary consideration. Even if we accept that his egging on of Sikes against Nancy in Chapter 47 does make him an accessory before the fact – which one of the gang indicates would, if proved, qualify him to swing (445) – this would not in itself justify the denigration he gets from Dickens, who after all views the definite murderer, Sikes, with equivocation. The inescapable truth is that Fagin's fate in the novel is bound up with the fact of his Jewishness. There is about Sikes something of the bulldog breed, whether British or English; in his sturdy ferocity and independence, his strength and determination not to give in or take things lying down, something of a celebration of national characteristics. Though not part of the dominant culture within the book, he is a positive element in its overarching one. Fagin is irredeemably alien, the more threatening because of his mental, as opposed to physical, resource and (to recall solid citizen Brownlow's word) his undeniable 'success'. Fagin is an anathema in which traditional associations of 'the Jew' merge with Dickens's specific concern to deprecate a culture founded on materialism and self-help, and, a natural extension of this, a rebellious attitude which pushes the law of competition so far as to sanction the dispossession of the privileged – a point nicely underscored by the detail of the corrupter of youth teaching his pupils not only to pick handkerchiefs out of pockets but to unpick the owners' marks out of handkerchiefs (109). There can be no doubt Dickens was intent upon emphasizing the stereotype and provoking standard reactions. Fagin is introduced, for example, as 'a very old shrivelled Jew, whose villainous-looking and repulsive face was obscured by a quantity of matted red hair' (105); and in the earlier editions the designation 'the Jew' is laid on thick and fast, not least in the later reaches of Chapter 52, which was until 1867 entitled 'The Jew's Last Night Alive'. At the beginning of the chapter there is a shift which, whether deliberate or not, marks Fagin off from the humanity of Dickens's audience and from their humane consideration: 'all looks were fixed upon one man – the Jew'; on second thoughts not a 'man' but something else, 'the Jew'. A similar effect occurs when the warder's question, 'Are you a man?', is followed by ' "I shan't be one long," said the Jew, looking up with a face retaining no human expression'. In the 1867 edition this second reference was changed – to 'he replied' – but not the first.[37] Sociological polemic – the critique of utilitarian ideology – seems beside the point here. Whatever Dickens's intentions, and in spite of his revisions, 'the Jew' as the worthless, detested, subhuman Other is a major focal point in *Oliver Twist* for aggregating identity, cultural and nationalistic, in the reading classes.

Support for this argument comes from the representation of the fence Ikey Solomon, reputedly the real-life prototype for Fagin, by Phiz (Hablot Browne) in the *New Newgate Calendar* (1841). Entitled 'Doing a Jew', the illustration shows Solomon, who is clutching a box of ill-gotten gains, having his beard pulled by a Bill Sikes lookalike, while a terrier tears at the Jew's coat and ordinary men, children and a woman look on with amusement, and, in one instance, active complicity.[38] This may actually reflect Browne's understanding of the metatextual relation between Fagin and Sikes in *Oliver Twist*, which he would certainly have read. In any case, both Dickens and Browne express the pandemic anti-Semitism of their time, when a range of legal restrictions on the occupations, ownership rights and public offices allowable for Jews persisted in spite of calls for liberalization following passage of the Catholic Emancipation Act in 1829. A proposed parliamentary bill of repeal produced a rash of opposition, from cartoon campaigns picturing bloated and bejewelled Jews to Sir Robert Peel's defence of exclusion on the grounds that 'the Jew is not a degraded subject of the state' but is 'regarded in the light of an alien, . . . a foreigner'.[39] Against this background, it is not difficult to comprehend Dickens's letter of rather hurt surprise when his friend, Mrs Eliza Davis, made a point of de-ploring the 'great wrong' he had done her people in his depiction of Fagin, though his swift profession of wholly 'friendly' feelings towards them and enclosure of a contribution to a Jewish charity suggest that the point struck home and was well taken.[40] Soon after, Dickens restored the balance as novelist with the portrait of the thoroughly 'good' Jew, Mr Riah, in *Our Mutual Friend*, and then in the 1867 edition of *Oliver Twist* carefully eliminated the bulk of the references to Fagin as 'the Jew'. But no amount of change and restitution can erase the original stance.

Dickens's response to Mrs Davis's misgivings contains an arresting line of defence. Fagin, he insists, 'is called a "Jew," not because of his religion, but because of his race'.[41] Needless to say, we cannot but be put off by the assumption – however much it accords with the biological theory of Dickens's age – that 'race' supplies acceptable grounds for type specification, though religion does not. When Fagin, his execution approaching, has visions of 'strong and vigorous men' reduced by the hangman 'to dangling heaps of clothes' (469) it is hard not to think, by transference, of the 'heaps of clothes' that feature in the most forbidding landscape of twentieth-century history – of 'the Jew' denied all identity right down to and including the body, as in a sense Fagin is, and left only in the trace of a salvageable and disposable commodity, itself eerily of the kind in which 'the Jew' had characteristically dealt for a living. In a famous essay, Steven Marcus gives an elaborate psychoanalytical interpretation of the conception of Fagin, which he tracks to Dickens's repressed but potently creative memories of his experiences as a child labourer at Warren's Blacking Factory, where he had known someone called 'Fagin'. Fagin of the novel relates, in a long arc, to both the suffering of the young boy and the audacious resilience, especially as an entertainer and storyteller, with which he had countered the bleakness. Marcus weaves a brilliant fiction that is itself, in one aspect at least, evasive of the facts: Fagin's Jewishness, for him, 'turns out to be not merely minor but almost fortuitous'.[42] The afterlife of *Oliver Twist* must accommodate a sterner truth than this.

Notes

1. Richard Dellamora, 'Pure Oliver: or, Representation Without Agency', in *Dickens Refigured: Bodies, Desires and Other Histories*, ed. John Schad (Manchester: Manchester University Press, 1996), pp. 58–60. See Charles Dickens, *Oliver Twist*, ed. Peter Fairclough, with an Introduction by Angus Wilson (Harmondsworth: Penguin Books, 1966; repr. 1985), pp. 56–8. References throughout are to this edition, which is hereafter cited in the text.
2. Charles Dickens, 'A Walk in a Workhouse', *Household Words*, 25 May 1850; repr. in *Dickens' Journalism, Volume II: 'The Amusements of the People' and Other Papers: Reports, Essays and Reviews 1834–51*, ed. Michael Slater (London: J.M. Dent, 1996), pp. 234–41 (pp. 237–8).
3. A succinct account of the main measures of the Act of 1834 and Dickens's response to them is given in Appendix A of *Oliver Twist*, ed. Fairclough, pp. 481–5. See also, Monroe Engel, *The Maturity of Dickens* (Cambridge, MA: Harvard University Press, 1967), pp. 48–59. Norman McCord, *British History 1815–1906* (Oxford: Oxford University Press, 1991; repr. 1995), pp. 190–96 offers a historical outline.
4. T.R. Malthus, *An Essay on the Principle of Population* (1798), ed. Geoffrey Gilbert (Oxford: Oxford University Press, 1993); *Essay*, 2nd edn (London, 1803): passim. Michael Mason, *The Making of Victorian Sexuality* (Oxford: Oxford University Press, 1994; pb. edn 1995), pp. 258–83 gives a relevant account of the *Essay* and its context, including Malthus's attitude to the Poor Law, the important revisions he introduced in 1803, and the contemporary debate about how far the postponement of marriage might defer or simply problematize the fulfilment of sexual needs. See also Dellamora, 'Pure Oliver', pp. 62–4.
5. S.J. Newman, *Dickens At Play* (Basingstoke: Macmillan, 1981), pp. 41–3.
6. 'Simplex', *An Enquiry into the Constitution, Government, and Practices of the Churches of Christ* (Edinburgh, 1808), p. 228.
7. *Oliver Twist*, ed. Steven Connor (London: Dent, 1994), pp. xli–xlii.
8. See *A Christmas Carol*, in *Charles Dickens: The Christmas Books*, Vol. 1, ed. Michael Slater (Harmondsworth: Penguin Books, 1971; repr. 1985), p. 108.

9. Godwin's *Of Population* (1820) is relevant here, as well as the better-known *Enquiry Concerning Political Justice* (1793): see the discussion of the controversy between Malthus and Godwin, and their respective supporters, in Mason, *The Making of Victorian Sexuality*, pp. 263–9, 272–80. The early appeal of Godwin's benevolence for Dickens, which did persist in the branch of his thinking that valued charity and the spirit of Good, is covered by William J. Palmer, *Dickens and New Historicism* (Basingstoke: Macmillan, 1997), pp. 24–47 passim, 120–21.

10. The obvious example is Dennis Walder, *Dickens and Religion* (London: George Allen & Unwin, 1981), pp. 42–65, which takes the consistent view that 'the fundamental aim of *Oliver Twist* is to reveal the sufferings of the unknown poor' (p. 65).

11. A similar point is made by Catherine Waters, *Dickens and the Politics of the Family* (Cambridge: Cambridge University Press, 1997), p. 31. The traditional grounding of aristocratic authority in notions of lineage is an underlying theme in Michael McKeon, *The Origins of the English Novel, 1600–1740* (Baltimore: Johns Hopkins University Press, 1987): see, for example, pp. 419–20.

12. For a study of the 'progressive ideology' of Defoe's novel, see McKeon, pp. 315–37.

13. Not until the Preface to the Third Edition (1841), when complaints about the novel's 'coarse' elements had been made, did Dickens actually call Nancy 'a prostitute' (ed. Fairclough, p. 33).

14. See Lauriat Lane, 'The Devil in *Oliver Twist*', *Dickensian*, 52 (1956), 133.

15. Christian and his companions in *The Pilgrim's Progress* constantly enlighten and encourage one another, and themselves, by recollecting the past, as when, on first meeting, Christian and Faithful formally exchange accounts of spiritual trials they have undergone (John Bunyan, *The Pilgrim's Progress*, ed. Roger Sharrock (Harmondsworth: Penguin Books, 1984), pp. 103–10). For the House Beautiful, see pp. 78–89 (p. 80).

16. *Pilgrim's Progress*, pp. 87, 97, 156. Just before the Valley, Christian defeats the demon Apollyon *literally* with a text: ' "*Rejoice not against me, O mine enemy! when I fall I shall arise*," and with that [Christian] gave him a deadly thrust' (p. 94).

17. *Eliza Cook's Journal*, 1 (1849), 2.

18. See Mason, pp. 241–59. Mill, recalling his father's conviction of 'the formation of all human character by circumstances . . . and the consequent unlimited possibility of improving the moral and intellectual condition of mankind by education', comments that of all James Mill's doctrines 'none was more important than this, or needs more to be insisted on; unfortunately there is none which is more contradictory to the prevailing tendencies of speculation, both in his time and since' (*Autobiography of John Stuart Mill* (commenced 1853, published 1873), with a foreword by Asa Briggs (New York: New American Library, 1964), p. 91).

19. *Moral Reformer*, 1 (1831), 8; G. Calvert Holland, *An Inquiry into the Moral, Social, and Intellectual Conditions of the Industrious Classes of Sheffield* (London, 1839), p. 25; Mrs D.L. Child, *The History of the Condition of Women* (London, 1835), II, 205.

20. Wordsworth, Preface to *Lyrical Ballads*, in *Poetical Works of William Wordsworth*, ed. Ernest de Selincourt and Helen Darbishire, 5 vols

(Oxford: Clarendon Press, 1940–49; rev. edn 1952–4), II, 386; 'It is the first mild day of March' ('To my Sister'), ll. 33–6, *Poetical Works*, IV, 60.

21. Dickens's long theorizing paragraph as a whole looks back beyond Wordsworth's poem to the didactic-descriptive tradition of religious meditation on nature of which Young, in *Night Thoughts* (1742–44), and Cowper were the most popular and influential exponents. His emphasis on both sensuous 'pleasure' and psychological 'peace', on the restorative effects of nature upon 'pain-worn' and 'jaded' city-dwellers, on rebirth (the 'new state of being'), on nature's power to 'purify our thoughts', and on the granting on earth of 'a foretaste of heaven' all have clear and developed parallels in Cowper's *The Task* (1785), Books I, V and VI. See my account of Cowper's pursuit of 'contemplation as a means of grace', in *Cowper's Poetry: A Critical Study and Reassessment* (Liverpool: Liverpool University Press, 1982), pp. 16–34, 127–64. Wordsworth's 'Tintern Abbey', itself much indebted to Cowper, may also be in Dickens's mind.

22. See pp. 24–6 and 57 note 18 above.

23. Steven Connor, ' "They're All in One Story": Public and Private Narratives in *Oliver Twist*', *Dickensian*, 85 (1989), 4–5, 12–13.

24. Edward W. Said, *The World, The Text, and The Critic* (London: Faber & Faber, 1984; Vintage edn 1991), pp. 19–20.

25. Connor, ' "They're All in One Story" ', p. 15.

26. See Connor, pp. 11–12.

27. Engels, writing in a tradition of colonial discourse going back to the sixteenth century, places the Irish in a category of the subhuman nomad, and makes an easy association between such savages and swine: 'the Irishman allows the pig to share his own living quarters. . . . The Irishman lives and sleeps with the pig, the children play with the pig, ride on its back, and roll about in the filth with it' (*The Condition of the Working Class in England* (1845), trans. W.O. Henderson and W.H. Chaloner (Oxford: Basil Blackwell, 1971), p. 106). Engels's attempt to purify the English proletariat consigned what he saw as residual, or rather in this case invasive, riff-raff to a permanent level of bestiality. The currency of such attitudes is sharply demonstrated by Henry Mayhew's report of the sewer worker who described the sewers which Irish labourers had helped to build as packed with rats 'fighting and squeaking . . . like a parcel of drunken Irishmen' (quoted in L. Wright, *Clean and Decent* (New York: Viking Press, 1960), p. 155). Mason, p. 245, comments on the steady advance of the 'biological' interpretation of behaviour, which, though most striking in the late-nineteenth-century 'eugenicist' school, was quite explicit from Herbert Spencer, William Farr and others in the middle years of the century.

28. Peter Stallybrass and Allon White, *The Politics and Poetics of Transgression* (London: Methuen. 1986), pp. 2–26, 133–40, 191–202.

29. Terry Eagleton, *Walter Benjamin: Towards a Revolutionary Criticism* (London: Verso, 1981), p. 148 (quoted). Roger Sales, in *English Literature in History 1780–1830: Pastoral and Politics* (London: Hutchinson, 1983), focusses expansively upon the ambivalence of rites of reversal, which could be 'a vehicle for social protest and the method for disciplining that protest' (p. 169).

    An upbeat assessment of the positive power of the carnivalesque is given by Dominick La Capra, who writes of Bakhtin's basic conviction . . . that the context of folk culture and festive popular celebration 'reveal the deepest meaning of the historical process'. The festive, carnivalesque attitude shapes time to its own image as a destructive, regenerative force that opens the dialectic at both ends and supplements it with the ambivalent power of laughter. (*Rethinking Intellectual History* (Ithaca: Cornell University Press, 1983), pp. 304–305)

This is quoted by Palmer, *Dickens and New Historicism*, p. 170–71, as a possible description of Dickens's own attitude and effects. But Palmer's account of *Oliver Twist* (pp. 118–24) actually does anything but show 'a destructive, regenerative force' at work, opening up dynamic processes of change and questioning. Rather, he sees the novel in flatly conventional, one-dimensional terms as an adaptation of the themes of George Lillo's play *The London Merchant* with the objective of upholding the Godwinian concept of perfectibility and natural benevolence (through the portrayal of Brownlow and the protection of Oliver from corruption) and, in the treatment of Fagin, framing 'a moral lesson' about the wages of sin.

30. Barbara Babcock, *The Reversible World: Symbolic Inversion in Art and History* (Ithaca, NY: Cornell University Press, 1978), p. 32.
31. Oliver's early response to Mr Brownlow's kindness – 'Very happy, sir, . . . and very grateful indeed, sir, for your goodness to me' (130) – is repeated on many occasions. After his recovery from his injury at Chertsey, his main concern is to find some way of showing the Maylies 'the love and duty with which his breast was full', and that he 'was eager to serve them with his whole heart and soul' (285).
32. Stallybrass and White, p. 137.
33. Palmer, *Dickens and New Historicism*, p. 8.
34. *Pilgrim's Progress*, pp. 95–100.
35. John Bayley, '*Oliver Twist*: "Things As They Really Are" ', in *Dickens and the Twentieth Century*, ed. John Gross and Gabriel Pearson (London: Routledge & Kegan Paul, 1962), p. 59.
36. John Sutherland, 'Why Is Fagin Hanged and Why Isn't Pip Prosecuted?', *Can Jane Eyre Be Happy?: More Puzzles in Classic Fiction* (Oxford: Oxford University Press, 1997), pp. 54–60.
37. In deference to a Jewish friend (see note 40 below) Dickens removed most of the references to Fagin as 'the Jew' from the new edition issued by Chapman and Hall in 1867. These excisions are described and discussed by Harry Stone, 'Dickens and the Jews', *Victorian Studies*, 2 (1959), 223–53; repr. in *Oliver Twist*, ed. Fred Kaplan (New York: W.W. Norton & Co., 1993), pp. 448–54 (pp. 452–3). Modern editions, including that from which I have quoted throughout this chapter, have usually followed 1867; but Kaplan's Norton edition and Kathleen Tillotson's Clarendon edition (Oxford, 1966) and its World's Classics offshoot (1982) are based on the first one-volume edition of 1846.
38. Camden Pelham, *The Chronicles of Crime; or, The New Newgate Calendar* (London: Miles & Co., 1887), facing page 241: see Robert Tracy, ' "The Old Story" and Inside Stories: Modish Fiction and Fictional Modes in *Oliver Twist*', *Dickens Studies Annual*, 17 (1988), 17 and note 17; also Dellamora, p. 66–8.
39. Stone, 'Dickens and the Jews', pp. 449–50.

40. Letter to Eliza Davis, 10 July 1863; repr. in *Oliver Twist*, ed. Kaplan, p. 378.
41. Ibid.
42. Steven Marcus, 'Who Is Fagin?', *Dickens: From Pickwick to Dombey* (London: Chatto & Windus, 1965), pp. 358–78 (p. 378).

CHAPTER FOUR

David Copperfield

Selving and Social Modelling

In 1848 Dickens finished a new Christmas story, reminiscent of *A Christmas Carol* but more abstract and schematic. A virtual allegory of thoughts about the importance of memory, *The Haunted Man* develops ideas intrinsic to the form and content of *David Copperfield*, which was begun at Devonshire Terrace, London in February 1849 and finished at Broadstairs in October 1850.

Redlaw, a research chemist, shut up in the cold walls of an ancient institute and in the echoes of his own gloomy past, is visited one night by a phantom that is the projection of his dark side and grants him his deepest wish – to be relieved of his memory.[1] As part of the bargain, moreover, it is arranged that the people with whom he henceforth comes into contact will also have their memories erased. This gift, like the Midas touch, becomes of course a terrible curse. Redlaw soon realizes that he has been charged with poison for his own mind and for the minds of others: 'Where I felt interest, compassion, sympathy, I am turning into stone. Selfishness and ingratitude spring up in my blighting footsteps' (304). Ultimately, he and the rest are restored through the healing influence of a young woman, Milly, who has a special power of attracting and radiating love, and who is referred to as 'an angel' (350).

Memory, Dickens insists, is a *sine qua non* of any life beyond the merely mechanical or the brutish. The amnesiac Redlaw is damaged, obliterated, on his own account. When the capacity to remember fades, identity itself slips away: 'He looked confusedly upon his hands and limbs, as if to be assured of his identity . . . for there was a strangeness and terror upon him, as if he . . . were lost' (271). Ironically, he appeals for reassurance to bodily substance where the problem is inward lack. One of the victims of his baleful spell cries out 'Give me back myself!', to which Redlaw responds 'Give me back *my*self!' (304–305). There can be no self without memory – and, vice versa, the self exists through memory.

Yet selfhood in Dickens can never for long be considered apart from the question of relations with the external world. One interesting aspect of *The Haunted Man* is its adaptation of the Romantic sense of the interdependence of inner well-being and responsiveness to nature, which has a place in *David Copperfield* in the account of David's recovery on

the Continent after the death of his wife, Dora. The blankness that visits
Redlaw is manifest in his failure to be moved in the presence of universal
beauty, for 'the moon induced him to look up at the Heavens, where he
saw her in her glory, surrounded by a host of stars he still knew by the
names . . . science has appended to them; but where he saw nothing else
he had been wont to see, felt nothing he had been wont to feel, in
looking up there, on a bright night' (309). This recalls Wordsworth's
'Immortality Ode' and Coleridge's 'Dejection', the latter with its ritual
lament, 'Those stars . . . / Yon crescent Moon . . . / I see them all so
excellently fair, / I see, not feel, how beautiful they are'.[2] Redlaw's
dereliction is more a close variant than a repetition of the earlier model
of faded reciprocity, since it results not so much from the falling off of
an innate spiritualizing capacity, Wordsworth's 'vision splendid' and
Coleridge's 'Imagination', as from a bereavement of acquired
impressions.[3] In both cases, however, feeling is elevated above
understanding; a distinction is drawn between two kinds of knowing,
the intellectual – what Coleridge in the 'Ode' calls 'abstruse research'[4] –
and the intuitive or experiential. This superior order of insight, this way
of connecting, is equally to the fore in the field of human relationships.
Milly, the central redemptive presence, who tends the infirm and
comforts the afflicted, whose aura of simple affection causes the little
children 'to throng about her, and caress her' (342), is its epitome. On
another level, as Barry Westburg points out, the family is everywhere a
prime casualty of Redlaw's plague of oblivion because 'the sentimental
ties' that have built up to link husband and wife in the midst of common
suffering have been dissolved, and fathers disown their sons, and sons
revile their fathers.[5]

What perhaps most stands out in the mnemonic theory of *The
Haunted Man*, however, and most obviously predicts *David
Copperfield*, is an insistence that individuals should acknowledge and
embrace, rather than try to flee from, their painful experiences, which
for Redlaw include the death of a beloved sister, the loss of his
sweetheart to his best friend, and, in a striking anticipation of the novel,
a stranger's early filling of his father's place. Distresses are integral parts
of the accrued psychic formation, which the phantom, tempting Redlaw
with the promise that his consciousness will be beneficially wiped clean,
describes as an 'intertwisted chain of feelings and associations, each in
its turn dependent on, and nourished by, the banished recollections'
(270). Redlaw himself comes to see that the whole person, indeed the
person *per se*, is constituted by a mixture of the good and the bad that
it is irresponsible to tamper with: 'In the material world, as I have long
taught, nothing can be spared; no step or atom in the wondrous

structure could be lost, without a blank being made in the great universe. I know, now, that is the same with good and evil, happiness and sorrow, in the memories of men' (322). Yet it is a principal message of *The Haunted Man*, as it is of *David Copperfield*, that the 'evil' is to be not just accepted but learned from. Milly tells the student she rescues from death's door – as Agnes will inform David – that 'adversity is a good teacher' (302). The story, here taking a lead from Scrooge's destiny, upholds that this is so not only because suffering breeds fortitude or greater thankfulness for blessings but also because it is a prerequisite for sympathizing fully with others in their ordeals and aspirations. Redlaw cries out, 'I have lost my memory of sorrow, wrong, and trouble, . . . and with that I have lost all man would remember' (344); his regeneration, which consists especially in his reconciliation with his bitter rival, now fallen, and protectiveness towards that man's unfortunate son (no other than Milly's ailing student), would not have been possible without the sensitizing currents of a profound hurt within himself. The anguish that had originally driven Redlaw to want to escape his past becomes at last the springs of his renewal.

The Haunted Man may be considered a serious contribution to Victorian discourse on the structure of mind and personality. It has a particular affinity with, and could have been influenced by, the 'palimpsest' modelling which in Thomas De Quincey's seminal definition of 1845 emphasized the 'everlasting layers of ideas, images, feelings [that] have fallen upon [the] brain' so as to form a diverse but unified fund of mental resources and activity, and which in the evolutionary approach of Herbert Spencer and others became the basis of a fully-fledged physiological account of memory as the generator of acquired habits and reflex actions.[6] A similar conception had been earlier available to Dickens in Wordsworth's organicist approach, with its topography of 'Invisible workmanship that reconciles / Discordant elements, and makes them move / In one society', and the 'passions that build up our human Soul' are intertwined

> With life and nature, purifying thus
> The elements of feeling and of thought,
> And sanctifying, by such discipline,
> Both pain and fear, until we recognize
> A grandeur in the beatings of the heart.[7]

Such thinking about the make-up, growth and balance of the psyche is fundamental to *David Copperfield*, particularly within the overlying theme of David's journey to a 'disciplined . . . heart' (903). As first-person *Bildungsroman* and semi-autobiographical fiction, however, it faces also in another direction, of which in the mid-century Frances Power Cobbe was an original and forceful expositor. Cobbe challenges the 'storehouse' notion of mind, seeing memories not as a stable, if expanding and dynamic, accretion but as constantly falling away and being replaced and modified:

> Memory is neither an impression made, once for all, like an engraving on a tablet, nor yet safe for an hour from obliteration or modification, after being formed. Rather is memory a finger-mark traced on shifting sand, ever exposed to obliteration when left unrenewed; and if renewed, then modified, and made, not the same, but a fresh and different mark.[8]

Recollection is not accurate report but reconstruction, substitution, selection, elision, even mendacity. Cobbe's metaphor of the 'mark' suggests of course writing. *David Copperfield* is about the 'writtenness' of the self and its history – selving as in part given expression (for there is still the basic input from experience and the determinants, conscious or unconscious, that we cannot help) and in part worked-for invention.

For Barry Westburg, who deals informatively with the confessional genre in Dickens, the focus on subjectivity in *David Copperfield* means that there is little or no interest in 'cultural truths'.[9] On the contrary, though the novel does not parade supervisory social comment as the *Carol* does – or indeed the end of *The Haunted Man* where a monstrous waif redolent of Ignorance and Want is philanthropically integrated into an atmosphere of co-operation, harmony and love – David's own development and its outcomes, and the wider landscapes in which they are set, offer *exempla* of how to be and how to behave. David is the hero of his own life, but the heroism he represents is neither free of cultural presuppositions nor without force in promulgating specific values. As Julian Jaynes remarks in a study of the emergence of the idea of the self in modernity, 'The advantage of an idea of your self is to help you know what you can or can't do or should or should not do.'[10]

The text of David Copperfield's self-construction, then, is also, as surely as any other of Dickens's works, the text of the protagonist's and the reader's enculturation. In discussing these interconnected movements I shall take as my focal points David's relations with other figures in his life-history, mainly but not exclusively Steerforth, Uriah Heep, Dora, and Agnes. These characters, like those of *Oliver Twist*, in one dimension comprise a typology of roles and functions, and resistances and dysfunction, that delineates and promotes Dickens's preferred social order; but they are all in some degree, too, projections of David's unfolding and labouring consciousness, which is to say questions and answers, problems and supports, along the course of his progress to a distinct version of maturity and individuation.

But no quest for identity or a sense of purpose is ever plain sailing. The narrative of David's own is shadowed by figurings of the threat and the fear of getting stuck, of toppling into the morass of morbid arrestment, though these are so set back in perspective as to signal the solidity of his advance, his outstripping of precariousness and peril. There is most obviously the story of Mr Dick's writer's block, which involves a severe malfunctioning of the memory. In a treatise on cerebral disorder, Forbes Benignus Winslow described in 1860 a species of disturbance 'which consists in the patient remembering everything except himself. He has, as it were, forgotten his own existence, and when he speaks of himself, it is in the third person.'[11] The impasse whereby Mr Dick cannot get on with his memorial of himself because it is always being invaded by the subject of King Charles's head is an intriguing variation of this condition, with both lesion and obsessive fantasy; the continuous usurpation and breakdown of his attempt to have a history of his own is a mirroring of the – to him literal – scenario wherein those about the King 'made that mistake of putting some of the trouble out of his head, after it was taken off, into mine' (258). Aunt Betsey, who looks after Mr Dick by mostly leaving him to his own devices, may take the optimistic view and consider it good that he should be kept employed by copious ink and paper, and that he should have found an indirect discharge for his agitation in his 'allegorical way of expressing it' (261); but his state is hardly something to be desired by Copperfield the autobiographer and well-known author, any more than is the fate of the pages which are regularly dispatched by kite, with only the most random expectation of a readership. Mr Dick is Copperfield's potential Charles's head – but also the sign that he is ahead of the danger.

Another simulacrum of the mad double is the lunatic who inhabits David's old room at Blunderstone Rookery. David mentions him twice, during an excursion to the grave of his father and mother and at the time of Barkis's funeral:

> The garden had run wild, and half the windows of the house were shut up. It was occupied, but only by a poor lunatic gentleman, and the people who took care of him. He was always sitting at my little window, looking out into the churchyard; and I wondered whether his rambling thoughts ever went upon any of the fancies that used to occupy mine. (378)

> The mad gentleman looked on, out of my little window . . . (508)

This is what Copperfield might have been, caught in a premature end, passive, cut off in a stream of inchoate thoughts. An interesting loop is created between David and the insane gentleman by the phrase 'took care of him', which reiterates the placard tied to David's back at Creakle's school – *'Take care of him. He bites'* (130). The young boy, having sunk his teeth into his stepfather, had hanging over him the stigma of aberrancy, of committal to the ranks of the 'mad' and untrainable, who must be set apart, supervised, and treated guardedly. This terrible prospect is now behind him. The 'fancies' that had visited David were of the sleeping dead and their being raised (62, 92); at the present moment of writing the ghosts of the past still haunt his mind but are effectively laid at rest. (The ambiguity of the expression, 'take care of', exposes the thin lines between, or the conflation of, protectiveness, rejection, and penal surveillance in the treatment of abnormality; and these shades of meaning throw perfectly into relief the attractiveness of Steerforth's unequivocal – though not necessarily unself-interested – promise of succour at Creakle's: 'Good night, young Copperfield, . . . I'll take care of you' (140).)

Lawrence Frank makes the point that the second mention of the lunatic occurs just before David recounts Steerforth's seduction of Emily and that in being able to face up to memories of that dread event – 'It is no worse, because I write of it. It would be no better, if I stopped my most unwilling hand' (509) – he shows his transcendence of any such disruption as is figured in Mr Dick's habits of repression and displacement.[12] Few interpreters thus note that *David Copperfield* inscribes and is written from the viewpoint of a goal achieved – a hard-won adult and authorial wisdom. Towards the end of the novel, David reports how Agnes had urged him on to share the gains of his endurance of 'calamities': 'as they had taught me, would I teach others' (888). *The Prelude* had traced the path of 'Love of Nature Leading to Love of Man',[13] but it was in *Lyrical Ballads* that Wordsworth spread the fruits of this consummation. In *David Copperfield* we are aware from the first of the novelist of humankind, of the product of the evolution that is being chronicled. This does not mean there is no psychodrama at the primary, first-person level of the text; for identity can never be entirely stable or secure, or without its subterranean reaches. There are skeletons, or King Charles's heads, always ready to rise up and give combat, of which Uriah Heep, another of David's doubles, is chief. But it is important to recognize that *David Copperfield* offers all along subtle and assured examples of the Dickensian secular scripture. I would like to take one from early in the book. Its subject, hardly promising in itself, is a schoolboy's insolence towards an impoverished teacher. Our previous instance we might have titled 'Bumble's Tear'. This can be 'The Taunting of Mr Mell'.

The Taunting of Mr Mell

There is a conversation between Steerforth and David just after they have spent the evening with the Peggottys at the boathouse on Yarmouth sands, in which Steerforth exhibits his customary hauteur towards those beneath him on the social scale. Little Emily, who is about to get married to Ham Peggotty, has made an immediate impression:

> 'A most engaging little Beauty!' said Steerforth, taking my arm. 'Well! It's a quaint place, and they are quaint company, and it's quite a new sensation to mix with them.'
> 'How fortunate we are, too,' I returned, 'to have arrived to witness their happiness in that intended marriage! I never saw people so happy. How delightful to see it, and to be made the sharers in their honest joy, as we have been!'
> 'That's rather a chuckle-headed fellow for the girl; isn't he?' said Steerforth.
> He had been so hearty with him, and with them all, that I felt a shock at this cold reply. But turning quickly upon him, and seeing a laugh in his eyes, I answered, much relieved:
> 'Ah, Steerforth! It's well for you to joke about the poor! . . . When I see how perfectly you understand them, how exquisitely you can enter into happiness like this plain fisherman's, . . . I know that there is not a joy or sorrow, not an emotion, of such people, that can be indifferent to you. And I admire and love you for it, Steerforth, twenty times the more!'
> He stopped, and, looking in my face, said, 'Daisy, I believe you are in earnest, and are good. I wish we all were!' (376–7)

If Steerforth treats Emily and the rest as (to use John Lucas's word)[14] a 'connoisseur' would a set of picturesque objects (apparent in the phrase 'little Beauty', which might be used of a prized animal, as well as in the relatively new coinage 'quaint', meaning 'old-fashioned'), David's own response is in its way hardly less formulaic and detached. Enthusiastically naïve where his friend is nonchalantly experienced, David, in his stilted language ('How delightful . . . to be made the sharers in their honest joy', 'this plain fisherman'), seems to be imagining a conventional literary pastoral. We certainly respect the earnestness and honesty in David which Steerforth's closing statement highlights, and see these qualities as proper to the emergent novelist (his phrase 'enter into' suggests the famous Keatsian gift of 'negative capability'), but we also understand that there is another level of knowing and reporting the world than he yet possesses, going deeper, working harder as revelation and comment.

This other order is amply displayed in Chapter 7, the drama of the public humiliation of the poor schoolmaster, Mr Mell, at Creakle's Academy (148–55). During the charged confrontation between downtrodden usher and privileged pupil, not only does Steerforth contemptuously and contemptibly mock Mell's low origins before the assembled class – 'You are always a beggar, you know' – he happily seizes the occasion to use the confidence David had let slip about his pauperized mother to turn the knife – 'If he's not a beggar himself, his near relation's one'. This is a strong example of Steerforth's ruthless disregard for the feelings of others, but even more shocking is his perfunctory refusal of Mell's very existence: 'I don't give myself the trouble of thinking at all about you.' The searing exposé of aggressive self-centredness, veering into the larger theme of class antagonism, is immediately reinforced but also modified by a shift in focus to the reactions of other participants in the scene, among them David's own:

> He glanced at me, and Mr Mell's hand gently patted me upon the shoulder. I looked up with a flush upon my face and remorse in my heart, but Mr Mell's eyes were fixed on Steerforth. He continued to pat me kindly on shoulder, but he looked at him. (152)

David's discomfort and regret at having, if inadvertently, supplied Steerforth with his cruellest weapon is a welcome confirmation of expectations, for we have already been informed of David's anxiety lest his friend should make use of 'such a secret' (147). What brings us to attention is Mell's reassuring touch upon the boy's shoulder, an action he repeats as he leaves the room after Creakle has dismissed him, which speaks more loudly of his kindliness than any words. (Touching is important in *David Copperfield*; and it is because David remembers his mother's story of how she once sensed Betsey's 'no ungentle hand' upon her hair (53) that he subsequently throws himself on his aunt's mercy at Dover.) Though he loses the battle for place and position, Mell triumphs in his humanity. The same goes for Tommy Traddles who, at the cost of isolation from his classmates and a sound beating at the hands of Creakle, insists that Mell has been 'ill-used' – an insight born of the desolation within Traddles himself that is expressed in his habit of drawing skeletons. Effects come thick and fast: Steerforth's quick announcement that he intends of course to write home for some money to be sent to Mell, an act suspended between troubled defensiveness, self-justification, and a strategic reasserting of authority; the fact that the whole company were 'glad' to see Traddles so put down, where the

Steerforth and Mr. Mell.

Fig. 3 'Steerforth and Mr. Mell' by Hablot K. Browne ('Phiz').

apparently simple word implies all the pressure of relief from an uneasy conscience, no less than the group's exultant participation in the victory of its (ironically) 'noble' and 'unselfish' leader. There is in all of this a profound lesson, for David and for the reader, in the best, the worst, and the undecidable in human nature.

When Peggotty describes to David his mother's death, she pinpoints a core value of *David Copperfield*, as also of *The Haunted Man*: 'Daybreak had come, and the sun was rising, when she said to me, how kind and considerate Mr Copperfield had always been to her, . . . and [that he had] told her, when she doubted herself, that a loving heart was better and stronger than wisdom' (186). Usually, we are asked to appreciate the virtue of 'a loving heart' less directly than this, as in the sign of Mr Mell's capacity for taking account of David's emotions even in the heat of bitter conflict, or later, surprisingly, in David stepfather's behaviour in the days before Clara's funeral, when he 'would open [a book] and look at it as if he were reading, but would remain for a whole hour without turning the leaf, and then put it down and walk to and fro . . . the only restless thing, except the clocks, in the whole motionless house' (183). The bereaved Murdstone's incapacitating sorrow, which Peggotty detects and names though the maltreated David cannot (188), humanizes even this man of flint, if only for a stretch – as Bumble's single tear for the distraught Oliver on the road from the workhouse had humanized that man of straw. The secular scripture never allows us to rest upon our prejudices. The sudden reorientation of feeling is one of its most potent devices.

By Beauty and By Fear: or, 'Here's lookin' at you, kid'

The kind of reading Dickens fosters in such episodes is outgoing and at once sensitively engaged and thoughtfully judicious. Reading of a very different sort has a significant place in David's account of his early life, and is a convenient starting point for a consideration of Dickens's distinctive handling of the child's psychology and the theme of personal development and self-formation. David recollects how, after his mother had remarried and the Murdstones had taken over, he would sit for hours greedily devouring his father's small collection of books, *Tom Jones*, *Gil Blas*, *Robinson Crusoe*, the *Arabian Nights* and the rest, 'reading as if for life' (105–106). Martha Nussbaum celebrates this passage because 'it tells us clearly how powerful novel-reading is in and for life, how surely it forms the life of fantasy';[15] but, as the mention of 'fantasy' indicates, we should remember that we are dealing with one species of novel and one species of reading. Literature here is vicarious adventure and romance, a way of escaping the world rather than discovering or evaluating it. David's little room overlooking the churchyard, which repeats the empty classroom of the abandoned Scrooge's school, becomes the 'blessed' site, not of change or transformation, but of holding on. Playing roles, projecting fabulous places and events onto his mundane environment, the boy 'consoled' himself under his 'troubles': 'I have been Tom Jones . . . for a week together. I have sustained my own idea of Roderick Random for a month at a stretch. . . . This was my only and my constant comfort.' Where there are gains – 'They kept alive my fancy, and my hope of something beyond that place and time' – these serve to keep open the way ahead, not to point direction.

The activity described in this passage, which we may term autoimagining or auto-satisfaction, is a therapy to be thankful for but also in itself a condition of immaturity. It beats the blank withdrawal of the lunatic old gentleman (of whom we are of course reminded by the location), yet is similarly an introversion that must be outrun. An important psychological polarity, it has parallels elsewhere in David's experience, and particularly in his relations with Steerforth, who is necessary to him but only ever a false, or partial, model of fulfilment. First, however, it is worth asking what it is that David needs to find relief from among his books. What are his 'troubles'?

The atmosphere of the opening chapters of *David Copperfield* is remarkably thick with violence. The discourse on death by drowning occasioned by David's infant caul, an object popularly supposed to preserve the owner against such a fate, will find tragic extension later in the novel. Then comes Aunt Betsey's buffeting of Ham, when she 'shook him, rumpled his hair, . . . and otherwise tousled and maltreated him' as they wait for Clara's child to be born (59). There is much of the farcical about this assault, though it is darkly linked to Betsey's unfortunate history in marriage and antipathy towards the male sex. On first appearance Miss Murdstone, too, cuts something of a comic figure, the 'metallic lady' with her appendages of steel purse and hard black boxes initialled in brass nails, the prude who is convinced that the servants have hidden a man somewhere in the house (97, 98). But there is nothing funny about the regime under which David and his mother suffer once the Murdstones have got control, which David, looking back, calls a 'tyranny' (99). When Clara is induced to hand over her keys to her sister-in-law they change from the appurtenances of housekeeping to those of the prison; and David finds himself under constant surveillance, a 'guarded captive', struggling hopelessly at his lessons under the unnervingly 'watchful' Murdstone gaze (102, 107). Mental cruelty is backed up by corporal punishment as Murdstone introduces his 'lithe and limber cane' into the proceedings, which in turn leads to David's reaction and an explosion of mutual and savage fury: 'I caught the hand with which he held me in my mouth, between my teeth, and bit it through. . . . He beat me then, as if he would have beaten me to death' (108).

David Copperfield, like William Wordsworth, 'grew up / Foster'd alike by beauty and by fear'.[16] These parts are the fear. The Murdstone system of education and child-management, which is founded on the 'grand quality' of 'firmness' (99), is counter-productive, breeding alienation, just as Creakle's sadism at the school David is sent to for correction – 'his delight in cutting at the boys, which was like the satisfaction of a craving appetite' – dries up all currents of intellectual improvement and, still worse, brutalizes his wards, making them 'miserable little dogs' defensively collaborating in his abuse of his victims, 'laugh[ing], with our visages as white as ashes' (141–2). Yet David learns nonetheless from his darkest hours. His very defiance of Murdstone is an affirmation of independence, after which he surprisingly discovers something about himself: 'I crawled up from the floor, and saw my face in the glass, so swollen, red, and ugly that it almost frightened me. My stripes were sore and stiff, . . . but they were nothing to the guilt I felt' (108). In David's shock at the disfigurements of degradation, and in his shame, however misplaced, we perceive his incipient power to discriminate between an unworthy and a worthy self, to know his vulnerability but also the possibility of being and doing better. *David Copperfield* proceeds on the premise that in the life of a hero everything counts, and the developmental model is never long out of view. Even at Creakle's, David 'pick[s] up some crumbs of knowledge'; and the evils of that place prepare him for enthusiastic commitment to the 'good' alternative, the 'sound system' of Dr Strong's school to which Aunt Betsey later sends him, 'very gravely and decorously ordered', depending largely upon the boys looking after their collective interests under the guiding principles of honour and good faith (146, 293–4). 'We all felt that we had a part in the management of the place, and in sustaining its character and dignity.' Institutions run better like that, and have a more secure future.[17] The attractions of best bourgeois social practice are kept faithfully in sight too.

The beauty by which David is fostered is various. In a memorable example Peggotty's secret attentiveness during David's incarceration in his room after the biting episode – they each kiss the keyhole, defiantly turning the barrier between them into a channel of communication –

intensifies the sway and the appeal of the devoted servant's loyal attachment: 'She did not replace my mother, no one could do that; but she came into a vacancy in my heart, which closed upon her' (111). This is significant not only for the prestige it brings to direct and open affection but also for the light it throws on David's relation to his mother. Whatever David may say about his heart closing around her, Peggotty claims always a substantial presence in her own right, separate and apart. She is solidly physical yet supremely unsexual, one of her regular performances being to burst the buttons on her dress very unseductively in the plump exertion of hugging David. David's mother, on the other hand, exists in the head, an image, an erotic charge. She is realized through details of the body and posture, with more than a hint of fetishism. David's memory of his first awareness of her pictures 'her pretty hair and youthful shape' (61); in his account of their last parting, as the life drains from her, she is at the garden-gate alone 'and not a hair of her head, nor a fold of her dress, was stirred, as she looked intently at me, holding up her child' – a form he then dreams of, a silent presence near his bed at school (174–5). In between come recollections of 'watch[ing] her winding her bright curls round her fingers, and straitening her waist' (65), of how, as he left for Yarmouth prior to her marriage to Murdstone, he 'felt her heart beat' as she embraced him, and of the intimacy with which she 'lifted up her face to mine' (76). Clara is an object of desire for David no less than she is for Murdstone, who banters with his friends about 'the pretty little widow' (72) but shows deadly earnest in courting her attentions. The text is frank in referring to the 'uneasy jealousy' that drives the action of David's near and distant recoil from the insistent suitor for whom his mother responsively 'plucked' a blossom 'and gave it into his hand' (with obvious evocation of Eve's temptation and the Fall), and whose hand David refused to take lest it 'should touch my mother's in touching me' (67–9).

It is hardly surprising that 'touch' should figure largely in definitions of love relationships. More noteworthy in these expressions of David's inner life is the prominence of the eye as an organ of pleasure and attachment, which is no doubt why, from David's point of view, though certainly not from his mother's or necessarily ours, Murdstone has a villainous 'shallow black' one with a 'cast', suggestive of threatening and unhealthy energies. The erotopoeic satisfactions of looking and being looked at will be fulfilled for David in his union with Dora, Clara's sensuous incarnation, and these are then absorbed and superseded in his more – though not exclusively – spiritual bonding with Agnes, who recalls the other pole of femininity, the iconic conception of the madonna, unearthly and inviolable, which he takes with him from the occasion of his mother's final farewell. Before this, however, there is Steerforth, whom David also loves.

To understand fully the relationship between these two, which has puzzled and divided commentators,[18] we must note another aspect of the importance of being seen. It guarantees existence and potentially guides it. David's continuing anxiety about himself on this score is brought out by his preoccupation with his posthumous birth, his father's 'eyes [having] closed upon . . . this world' six months before his opened: 'There is something strange to me, even now, in the reflection that he never saw me' (50). It unsettles him, even as an adult, to contemplate himself without anyone to situate him in the world, to give him identity.

Steerforth supplies the authority of the father, or the older brother, David never had – 'I'll take care of you.' There is a leadership vacuum in David's life, which Steerforth fills. But the situation is more complicated than that. 'You belong to my bedroom, I find', Steerforth informs David at their first meeting (137). This arrangement means midnight feasts (with David's money and food parcels, let it be said), mysterious, covert, presided over by the magical Steerforth casting a strange light akin to the blue glare of the phosphorus match he periodically applies, graphically remembered by David with a feeling of 'solemnity and awe' (138). Steerforth is a master of revels, and not at all a mentor in the needful arts of discipline and getting on. And there is something else:

> I thought of him very much after I went to bed, and raised myself, I recollect, to look at him where he lay in the moonlight, with his handsome face turned up, and his head reclining easily on his arm. He was a person of great power in my eyes; that was, of course, the reason of my mind running on him. No veiled future dimly glanced upon him in the moonbeams. There was no shadowy picture of his footsteps, in the garden that I dreamed of walking in all night. (140)

The homoeroticism is all the more evident here for being displaced as hero worship, and becomes a truly open secret in the light of David's being so often associated with the feminine by Steerforth himself, who predicts from the new boy's looks what his sister would be like ('pretty, timid, little, bright-eyed'), casts him in the role of the Sultana Scheherazade during interminable bouts of storytelling, and later on renames him 'Daisy'. David talks of 'being cherished as a kind of plaything' (145), and when summarizing Steerforth's powers of 'enchantment' links his inexplicable capacity to weave a 'spell' with more palpable attractions – 'his carriage, his animal spirits, his delightful voice, his handsome face and figure' (157). This is, problematically for David's development, the end-stopped image of the mother laid on the presumed site of masculine mobilizing and shaping force.

This adolescent bonding persists into David's future and provides a way of answering the vexed question of why he stays loyal to Steerforth despite the latter's serial transgressions, which culminate in what David actually terms, in strong language, 'his pollution of an honest home' (516) in running off with Little Emily. Love disregards all – is above issues of morality. At their last meeting, just before Steerforth's great offence, his ominous wish always to be thought of 'at my best' is met by David's 'You have no best to me, Steerforth, . . . and no worst. You are always equally loved, and cherished in my heart'; and at this point we see that the ties stretch right down to the time of the present narration, as his lost friend materializes in the circuit of David's emotion-infused memory: 'I was up with the dull dawn, and, having dressed as quietly as I could, looked into his room. He was fast asleep; lying, easily, with his head upon his arm, as I had often seen him lie at school' (497–8). The chain of attachment is even more vividly reinscribed in the scene when, years later, the body of Steerforth, washed up on the beach, appears in the same pose:

> But, he led me to the shore. And on that part of it where she and I had looked for shells, two children – on that part of it where some lighter fragments of the old boat, blown down last night, had been scattered by the wind – among the ruins of the home he had wronged – I saw him lying with his head upon his arm, as I had often seen him lie at school. (866)

David's memory of Emily, with whom he was once infatuated, is flat, void of charm; not so that of the sleeping Steerforth. We perceive in the syntax of this passage that the violation of the Peggotty home exists in David's recollections as a parenthesis while the image of Steerforth is their unspoken first term and their end point. When, at the opening of the next chapter, he talks of being unable to condemn Steerforth 'now . . . looking on this sight' he not only refers to the body in the landscape but also confesses, and celebrates, the lure of the picture within. The dead Steerforth is alive to David still and has power to enthral and to excite him.[19]

These examples of David's Steerforth-fixation return us to the question of art and the artist, in that they postulate a connection between erotic fascination and imaginative creation. Steerforth, moreover, has himself been associated from the start with writing and with fiction. He makes his first appearance as an inscription on the door at Salem House – 'one boy – a certain J. Steerforth – who cut his name very deep and very often' (131) – and organizes David's regular story-telling sessions. We are told that he 'is such a speaker that he can win anybody over' (196); that he 'could always pass from one subject to another with a carelessness and lightness' (349); that he possessed 'a natural gift of adapting himself to whomsoever he pleased' (367); and that he was able to 'become anything he liked at any moment' (402). He captivates even his mother's bitter companion, Rosa Dartle, with the 'influence of his delightful art' (495). 'Aren't these all traits of a good novelist?' asks Martha Nussbaum, with an expectation of agreement.[20] Abstractly considered, perhaps so; but in context they are diabolic attributes, suggesting a cunning and deceit reminiscent of the arts of Milton's Satan: smooth rhetoric, lack of principle, clever role-playing, the tendency to manipulate.[21] On the larger scale, he not only orchestrates a scene in which the innocuous Mr Mell is humiliated, he creates a family tragedy which sees one man, Ham, killed, and another, Dan Peggotty, driven virtually insane. On Rosa Dartle he has placed his mark with a hammer: the scar that cuts through her lips and throbs and colours when she is passionate; a synecdoche of sexual wound, fierce resentment, and smouldering desire, which is the combination on show when at one meeting she reacts to Steerforth's playful embrace by flying violently at him and from him. This is no orphean tamer of the wild beasts but one that mutilates and arouses.

Steerforth is the antitype of the 'good' author, if from an author we expect constructive designs. David is not conscious of the catalogue of objections, which are implied rather than stated in his text, but he does go along with them inasmuch as he sets strict limits to his allegiance to what Steerforth represents. For David, Steerforth is implicated in a particular field of creativity, which he describes as that 'within me that was romantic and dreamy' (146). David keeps faith with this side of himself, while putting his future in trust elsewhere, ultimately with Steerforth's rival, Agnes, who openly warns David against the 'bad Angel' (426) in his life. We shall come to David and Agnes in due course, yet the contrast between her and Steerforth is always apparent. She too, for example, is linked to books early on, but these are texts of instruction, as she helps David with his homework: 'when I brought down my books, [she] looked into them, and showed me what she knew of them . . . and what was the best way to learn and understand them' (288). 'Modest, orderly' intelligence, 'goodness, peace, and truth' (288–9), are Agnes's unchanging bounty. Steerforth's characteristic symbolic pose is the sinuous and horizontal line, sleeping head on outstretched arm, passive, aesthetic, alluring, self-justifying. Agnes's is 'pointing upward, . . . ever leading to something better' (916), signalling aspiration, onwards endeavour, and the moral sense. The one image reflects the compulsion to rest and to repeat, the other to press higher and further.

The discrimination between kinds of authorship built into the David–Steerforth–Agnes relationship is clearly part of a whole ideological schema which at the historical level can be understood as Dickens's salute to Romantic sensibility – or that of the second generation, specifically the Byronic (aristocratic) phase – and his situating of it so as to promote a Victorian (middle-class) mental and social discipline. Similar ideas and cultural issues are taken up later by another writer, the philosopher and sociologist Georg Simmel, whose essay on 'The Adventure' throws interesting light on Dickens through both parallels and differences.

Simmel defines the phenomenon of the adventure as something quintessential to existence but discontinuous from the mainstream of a life:

> More precisely, the most general form of adventure is its dropping out of the continuity of life. 'Wholeness of life', after all, refers to the fact that a consistent process runs through the individual components of life, however crassly and irreconcilably distinct they may be. What we call an adventure stands in contrast to that interlocking of life-links, to that feeling that those countercurrents, turnings, and knots still, after all, spin forth a continuous thread. An adventure is certainly a part of our existence, directly contiguous with other parts which precede and follow it; at the same time, however, in its deeper meaning, it occurs outside the usual continuity of this life.[22]

Steerforth is David's adventure, of the essence but not of the telos, or the overall direction that his life takes. This does not, however, make David the adventurer: he can cherish Steerforth, store away his image for occasional contemplation, and move generally and purposefully on. The adventurer, in the likeness of Simmel's characterization, is Steerforth himself: 'the ahistorical individual, . . . who lives in the present'; the man who 'believes in nothing'; the 'gambler' in whom activity and passivity are tightened into 'a coexistence of conquest, which owes everything only to [his] own strength and presence of mind, and complete self-abandonment to the powers and accidents of the world, which can delight us but in the same breath can also destroy us'.[23] Steerforth is very much the gambler. His mother names him such when, resentful of his flight with low-born Emily, she talks of him as one who 'can stake his all upon the lightest object' (531). David, looking back, knows now that his friend's treatment of the Peggotty family and Emily herself was all 'a brilliant game, played for the excitement of the moment, . . . [and] in a mere wasteful careless course of winning what was worthless to him, and next minute thrown away' (368). It is the experience that matters, not its content or the prize. Steerforth proclaims the point himself when, in patently Byronic mood,[24] he reiterates his motto – 'Ride on! Rough-shod if need be, smooth-shod if that will do, but ride on! Ride on over all obstacles, and win the race!' – and to David's reasonable question, 'What race', answers simply 'The race that one has started in' (488). For this gentleman of fortune Little Emily is in a sense the perfect partner. She like him is an inveterate risk-taker, mysteriously drawn even as a child to court danger, walking proleptically 'much too near the brink of a sort of old jetty . . . and I was afraid of her falling over' (86). At the same time she displays that attribute of the adventurer which is the (feminine) counterpart of Steerforth's (masculine) scepticism: in her entrenched 'glorious vision' of being 'a lady' (85, 363, 513) she is a dreamer, the fantasist who, as Simmel puts it, embraces 'the incalculable element in life in the way we ordinarily treat only what we think calculable', and for whom 'the unlikely is likely'.[25]

The compulsion to gamble is a common trait among the characters of *David Copperfield*. Micawber, for example, has it, spending above his means, and waiting for something to turn up. Heep has it, ever pitching for the main chance. Aunt Betsey speculated on love when she married a man 'younger than herself' and 'very handsome', lost (she was soon 'beaten' in two senses of the word), and has been paying ever since, literally because she is being blackmailed for him to keep away, psychologically because, her 'own old wrongs working within her', she rails not only against the opposite sex but also against Peggotty on the occasion of her marriage, when she issues a curse in terms that suggest a very strange case of sexual frustration: 'I only hope . . . that her husband is one of those Poker husbands who abound in the newspapers, and will beat her well with one' (51, 55, 253). (Betsey does keep a 'Mr Dick' in her cottage, but all he does, so far as we know, is jingle his pocket money.) Aunt Betsey's luck ran well and truly out when she made her wager. Not so for David. It is his destiny to surmount the consequences of impulse. When Steerforth goes astray, he can take his winnings and tuck them aside – or rather inside – as a distillation, a dream, 'self-sufficient . . . and held together by an inner core' like a work of art,[26] to which he can fondly return, leaving his progress on the path of maturation unruffled, and indeed accentuated by contrast between the codes of pleasure and earnestness.

Yet Steerforth is not David's great adventure. To that distinction Dora has better claims. In his relationship with his eventual 'child-wife' (711)

David calculates blindly on the incalculable, stepping with Simmel's traveller 'into the mist, as if the road will lead us on, no matter what'. This is the erotic in pure (if with hindsight superficial) form, the love affair as exploit *par excellence*, where the internally necessary dissipates all reason and conquest conjoins with grace. But Dora must then yield to Agnes, in whose ambit are vested the qualities both of the adventure and of that which succeeds it in Simmel's scheme, the 'objectivity and retrospective reflectiveness' of maturity. Though Simmel's essay is academic, a free flow of philosophic thought on a topic of life, it does in effect place value upon the spirit of adventure relative to all else, and in doing so privileges youth over age, which it presents as a flattening, a falling off. The adventure is for him properly available only to the young. (There is nothing more distasteful or ridiculous, he points out, than the elderly roué.) What Simmel thus keeps asunder and places as incompatible opposites – and at another point dubs 'the romantic and the historical spirit of life'[27] – Dickens seeks to combine in his depiction of the alliance of David and his second wife, with obvious relevance to the need for practical social ideals.

Before David gets his Agnes, however, he has to negotiate the formidable hazard of Uriah Heep, who is his rival not only for Agnes's hand but for the role of hero, and is basic to the ideological shape of the book.

Heep, David, and Heep Again

Steerforth aside, we are twice faced with displays of flagrant social prejudice by characters in *David Copperfield*. One is when Steerforth's mother offers to pay off Mr Peggotty for his niece's 'ruin' but will hear nothing of marriage because Steerforth would thereby 'disgrace himself': 'You cannot fail to know that she is far below him' (529). The other is Rosa Dartle's extraordinary denunciation of the contrite Emily, on whom she pours not only blame but vicious contempt, addressing her as 'a thing' and an 'earth-worm' and then launching into bitterly sarcastic approval of such 'a worthy cause . . . of grief in a house where she wouldn't have been admitted as a kitchen-girl'. Emily is a 'piece of pollution, picked up from the water-side' (786–8). In Rosa we see the inverse of Rose Maylie, damning with abhorrence where the latter, in her approach to Nancy, had dispensed hope of redemption; but both insist on the distance between 'high' and 'low', the more so no doubt because neither, the lady's companion nor the adopted daughter, is naturally secure in her position – that is, simply born to it. Rosa applies the familiar motifs of bestiality, or worse ('earth-worm'), and contamination – she later says she cannot breathe freely the 'sickly' air that Emily moves in (790) – to put Emily in her place with a venom that should disgust and alienate us. Even here, however, it is not easy to take sides. There seems more to Rosa's vituperative energy than to Emily's prostrate regret for the pain she has caused and protestation that she 'believed . . . trusted . . . loved' Steerforth (788). Emily, never a paragon of good sense or sound instincts, is compromised in our judgement, as Mr Peggotty is in his way by his strangely intimate and obsessive relationship with his 'little puss', when 'patting her with his great hand' and 'taking up her curls' (195). Moreover, the attitudes of Rosa and Mrs Steerforth are explicable in terms of psychic aberration – Rosa's erotomania, which puts her in envy of the fallen Emily, and Mrs Steerforth's 'wilful spirit' (531) – rather than as unadulterated expressions of class-determined hatred and haughtiness. Dickens's moral criticism and psychological analysis leave the social structure basically unquestioned.

And so it is with the presentation of Steerforth. The usual ideological factor, whatever else, is at work in David's being given feelings of 'sorrow' towards his friend but no 'angry thoughts' or 'reproaches' (517). Goodness matters, but so does blood. Steerforth may be seen to err but cannot be scorned. Conversely, Ham Peggotty can, as in Steerforth's own reference to this 'chuckle-headed fellow', a remark about which John Lucas entertains the interesting speculation that 'Dickens displaces on to Steerforth doubts [regarding Ham's limitations] he can't allow his hero to entertain'.[28] There again, Ham *is*, as his name suggests, a simple and ungainly soul and, like Mr Peggotty (and Joe Gargery after him), knows his place, cap-on-head or cap-in-hand (which is both men's automatic gesture of respect when visiting their betters).[29] He is no threat to anybody, and for that reason it is easy enough for us to share Lucas's indignation at his being slighted by Steerforth. A sterner test of our capacity for taking issue with Dickens's vision of the social order lies with the case of Uriah Heep. He is a redoubtable climber who causes David, and his creator, a great deal of trouble, and who is ruthlessly – though, as we shall see, not altogether conclusively – put down. Of all Dickens's characters, Heep most strikingly inscribes his commitment to a fixed structure of subordination. As Steerforth the gentleman stands somehow above the taints of vice, so in Uriah Heep, the ambitious charity boy, they are relentlessly emblazoned.

Uriah Heep surely has no rival in literature as an article of denigration. All ugliness and slime, he is described variously as a snail, a fish, a frog, a vulture, a fox, a bat, a malevolent baboon, and a devil

(290, 293, 440, 443–4, 636–7, 471, 580, 636–7). Particular emphasis is placed on his face, which is said to be 'cadaverous' (275, 431), 'older' than its years (275), 'pale' (278), 'flabby and lead-coloured' (638), and 'clammy' (816), and to have 'sleepless' and 'shadowless' eyes (278, 431); on his 'long, lank, skeleton' hand (275), which is also 'clammy', 'lank' again (290), 'skeleton' again (312), 'damp and cold' (437), 'grisly' (439), 'damp' (442, 638), 'lean' (816); and on his habit of contorting himself, in 'the writhing . . . and snaky twistings of his throat and body' (292), his 'snaky undulation' (437), and the way he 'serpentined and corkscrewed' like an 'eel' (579).[30] This looks like unique Dickensian caricature. But a comparable terminology crops up in another discourse of the period, non-fictional, earnestly matter-of-fact:

> They get thin, pale, or irritable, and their features become haggard. We notice the sunken eye, the long, cadaverous looking countenance, the downcast look . . . These . . . have a dank, moist, cold hand, very characteristic of great vital exhaustion; their sleep is short, and most complete marasmus [wasting of the body] comes on; . . . nervous symptoms set in, such as spasmodic contraction, or partial or entire convulsive movements . . . . The frame is stunted and weak, the muscles undeveloped, the eye is sunken and heavy, the complexion is sallow, pasty, . . . the hands are damp and cold, and the skin moist.

This is the physician William Acton writing in 1857 on the effects of masturbation, and quoting from the English translation, published in 1847, of a popular treatise by the influential French doctor, Claude François Lallemand.[31] Whether or not Dickens drew directly on Lallemand's work, which the date of David Copperfield and the similarities in vocabulary make entirely possible, there can be no doubt that Heep is to be considered a devotee of the solitary vice. The point is several times colourfully flagged. In Uriah thoughts of Agnes Wickfield tend to be accompanied by the same telling gestures. Trying to get David to share his secret excitement that Agnes is so 'beautiful', for instance, he 'began wiping the palms of his hands' and 'gave himself a jerk, like a convulsive fish' (440). Again, mentioning 'the beautiful, namely, Miss Agnes', he 'jerked himself about' uncontrollably – in a no less symptomatic manner than he had just previously adopted in greeting David by 'lifting [his] hand up and down like a pump handle' (579). When he refers to Agnes as a pear to be 'plucked' at the right time – for 'it'll ripen yet!' – he does it with another 'jerk' (644–5). Agnes is Uriah's recurrent fantasy.

It is plain from these episodes, however, that the trouble with Uriah is not the passiveness and enervation, so perilous to national well-being, that the medical establishment customarily cited, under the head of 'spermatorrhoea', as the dire consequence of self-abuse, or indeed of any over-expenditure of semen.[32] (Paradoxically, and as Acton noted, the perversion was ubiquitously encouraged by the very institutions designed to form rational male subjectivity and the leaders of the nation – the private schools.)[33] Uriah represents a different kind of peril. Though he keeps himself to himself – 'hugging himself' (637) is another of his habits – he is, once he gets going, no debilitated drop-out but a disruptive force. His offensive in pursuing Agnes, where sexual energy reaches outwards, is of a piece with his plan for 'emerging from my lowly station' (441). David condemns the former as 'odious passions' (817) and the latter as the 'scheme' of a 'rascal' (441). When Micawber eventually uncovers Uriah's manoeuvres to supplant Mr Wickfield he talks of the scoundrel's 'discharge of his infernal business' (820), thus associating work at getting on with ejaculation and defecation, with an ingredient of devilishness thrown in. Uriah, with his famous strategic 'umbleness', is a grotesque demonization – and criminalization – of the creed of upwards mobility. Like Fagin and the Dodger, yet more zealously, he is given a language of self-help and success in order to discredit them. To David he says, for example, referring to his partnership in Wickfield's law firm, 'I am very umble to the present moment, Master Copperfield, but I've got a little power!' (639). Rising in the world is, by implication, really about the usurpation and exercise of power. At other times, the arraignment is made explicitly:

> It was not that he had lost his good looks, or his old bearing of a gentleman – for that he had not – but the thing that struck me most, was, that with evidences of his native superiority still upon him, he should submit himself to that crawling impersonation of meanness, Uriah Heep. The reversal of the two natures, in their relative positions, Uriah's of power and Mr Wickfield's of dependence, was a sight more painful to me than I can express. If I had seen an Ape taking command of a Man, I should hardly have thought it a more degrading spectacle. (578)

Wickfield the well-to-do solicitor, who has degenerated into a helpless alcoholic, is still the 'Man', Uriah the industrious clerk, good at the job, is the 'Ape' – genetically inferior. Uriah is stamped with a decadence that is not fecklessness or a fall from grace, as in his natural superiors such as Steerforth or Wickfield himself, but the result of origins. And the impression is driven ever deeper. Much later in the process of Wickfield's decline and Uriah's rise to dominance the narrative designates the former 'the broken gentleman' and the latter a 'baboon' (640, 637). The text has often linked Uriah to rudimentary forms of life but he now becomes something pointedly less than human, recognizably lower on the evolutionary scale.

Yet, if Dickens is ready to use evolution against Uriah in this way, it is not a concept he likes when it means changing places or the survival of the fittest. His thinking is very much in line with that of T.H. Huxley, who, though believing in the reality of 'cosmic process', repudiated the gladiatorial version of existence and insisted that human culture could not be explained by extrapolating from biological mechanisms:

> The practice of that which is ethically best – what we call goodness or virtue – involves a course of conduct which, in all respects, is opposed to that which leads to success in the cosmic struggle for existence. In place of ruthless self-assertion it demands self-restraint; in place of thrusting aside, or treading down, all competitors, it requires that the individual shall not merely respect, but shall help his fellows; its influence is directed, not so much to the survival of the fittest, as to the fitting of as many as possible to survive. . . . Laws and moral precepts are directed to the end of curbing the cosmic process and reminding the individual of his duty to the community.[34]

In creating Uriah Heep Dickens was combating the application of natural laws to the conduct of life. It is interesting to note Huxley's reference to 'community', for in *David Copperfield*, as elsewhere, Dickens too has the collective good at heart. His treatment of the would-be parvenu reflects a widespread fear of ethnic degeneration that finds direct expression in writers such as Charles Turner Thackrah, who saw 'business' and 'commercial life' as the source of illness and insanity because they placed men in a state of 'excitement . . . partial, irregular and excessive', and Henry Maudsley, who attributed to the modern gospel of 'money-getting', 'wealth' and 'social rank' the evils of 'madness or ruinous vice', of 'cunning and duplicity, and an extreme selfishness of nature – a nature not having the capacity of a true moral conception or altruistic feeling'.[35] A serious point lurks behind Micawber's pompous announcement that what he has done in exposing the self-seeking and deceitful Heep was done 'For England, home, and Beauty' (826).

The problem is, however, that although the ethical imperative is primary for Dickens, his novel is not altogether secure in its own moral position. The remark about having 'got a little power' rounds off a passage of autobiography, a sort of apologia, which throws a surprising light on Uriah, giving access to reasons for his behaviour:

> Father and me was both brought up at a public, sort of charitable establishment. They taught us a deal of umbleness – not much else that I know of, from morning to night. We was to be umble to this

person, and umble to that; and to pull off our caps here, and to make bows there; and always to know our place, and abase ourselves before our betters. And we had such a lot of betters! Father got the monitor-medal by being umble. So did I. Father got made a sexton by being umble. He had the character, among the gentlefolks, of being such a well-behaved man, that they were determined to bring him in. 'Be umble, Uriah,' says father to me, 'and you'll get on. It was what was always being dinned into you and me at school; it's what goes down best.'

It was the first time it had ever occurred to me, that this detestable cant of false humility might have originated out of the Heep family. I had seen the harvest, but had never thought of the seed . . . I had never doubted his meanness, his craft and malice; but I fully comprehended now, for the first time, what a base, un-relenting, and revengeful spirit, must have been engendered by this early, and this long, suppression. (639)

At least David perceives that Uriah's actions were not without ex-planation, a motiveless malignity. But his claims to full comprehension are hardly justified when his language – 'detestable cant . . . meanness . . . revengeful spirit' – is everywhere that of indignant condemnation, rather than of understanding. He fails to treat Uriah as the three-dimensional character that the evidence, if only for an interval, presents. Moreover, when he does achieve an insight into causes he uses terms – 'originated out of', 'seed', 'engendered' – that suggest some *predetermined and unalterable* process. Baseness runs in the family; conditioning seems to have become unconditional. It is perhaps unclear whether the early and long 'suppression' refers to the influence of school or family, or both, but, whatever the answer, nowhere does David impugn the system that produced Heep father and son, nor contemplate grounds either for reforming it or for exculpating Uriah.

This passage discloses limitations in David's viewpoint and per-sonality which are never resolved in the novel, and which Dickens never deprecates. And further questions are posed by Uriah's own resistance, and resilience, in the face of attack. *He* forgives David when David strikes him out of rage at being drawn into the discovery of Annie Strong's apparent infidelity towards her husband, the kindly and vulnerable Doctor. *He* refuses to quarrel at all in this seething encounter where the blow to Uriah's cheek serves only to bind David more intimately to his adversary, the physical marks which leave the skin 'a deeper red' being mirrored in the more searing wound of David's 'slow fire' of torment for having somehow made a false move and come off second best (686–7) – the disfigurement of Uriah's face reflecting that of David's mind and emotions. Amazingly, when he is finally exposed as a swindler Uriah accuses David of the very misdeeds for which we are supposed to reject Uriah: he calls him an 'upstart' and one who has always been 'against' him (828); he charges him with being 'proud' and being driven by 'envy' of another's 'rise' (816); and most disturbingly, he alleges hypocrisy, asking David, 'You think it justifiable . . . you who pride yourself so much on your honour and all the rest of it, to sneak about my place, eavesdropping with my clerk? If it had been *me*, I shouldn't have wondered; for I don't make myself out a gentleman . . . but being *you*!' (817). Is there not something in what Uriah says? Is not decadence lifting the veil, however slightly, from self-proclaimed rectitude?

The point is driven home when Uriah again raises the awkward issue of his schooling, against which he now brings the charge of programmatic, and none too subtle, indoctrination, for he was taught 'from nine o'clock to eleven, that labour was a curse' (presumably in religious instruction lessons) and (in sessions inculcating civic duty) 'from eleven o'clock to one, that it was a blessing and a cheerfulness, and a dignity, and I don't know what all'. 'You preach, about as consistent as they did' is Uriah's scathing verdict on David's pronouncement on his enemy's comeuppance, the style of which suggests that private schools and charity schools have certain lofty languages in common: 'It may be profitable to you to reflect, in future, that there never were greed and cunning in the world yet, that did not do too much, and overreach themselves' (829). Never is David more clearly implicated, as proponent and beneficiary, in the system that Uriah Heep defies, and that renders him corrupt and ripe for punishment. In effect David is telling Uriah to be humble, and that the only 'profit' lies in being satisfied with one's allotted portion. To ask for more is to ask for trouble. During the unmasking scene Micawber – who himself bucks the system by his pecuniary improvidence but here takes an allowable initiative in serving it as an undercover agent – catches Uriah's knuckles with a ruler and 'disable[s] his right hand' (819), thus putting a curb no doubt on both his self-abuse and his abuse of others, the latter having depended on the forgery of documents, which is the only creative writing he, in contrast to David, has at his command. But there is no blocking out Uriah's voice and intelligence, or making them entirely misdirected or void of compelling truth.

The novel's official 'plot' (itself an ambiguous word, which Uriah applies (816) to the elaborate moves to defeat him) sets up, within its account of David's progress, a model of personal development and social adjustment defined as virtuous endeavour and selfless fulfilment, with nothing in it of strategy, worldliness, or competitive bearing. When, at the beginning of Chapter 42, he reflects at length upon the advances he has made in his life, David attributes them to the 'golden rules' of 'punctuality, order and diligence', 'sincere earnestness', and sees struggle and misdoing, not as involving others, but as solitary conflict, 'a war within his breast' where the neglect of talents or the waste of opportunities are continually checked by 'steady, plain, hard-working qualities'. This ethos, which is a version of traditional Protestant ideals,[36] is then augmented by Agnes's letter to David after he has left England following the deaths of Dora, Steerforth and Ham, which values adversity, and the ability to surmount it, in specifically non-material terms, as a source of inner strength: 'As endurance of my childish days had done its part to make me what I was, so greater calamities would nerve me on, to be yet better than I was' (888). We hear later that his writing is a 'vocation', not a profession. The success of his novels prompts him to the virtue of 'modesty'; self-interest, the market, money, do not feature at all: 'They [his fictions] express themselves, and I leave them to themselves' (758), in splendid isolation. Uriah's 'counterplot' (816) does nothing to decentre the philosophy of being that is thus communicated through David, and is, on the contrary, the aberration by which the privileged norm is legitimized; but it does unsettle its grip by querying its impartiality and by implying concealment, a mask to be lifted.

There remains much to said about the nature and indeed about the positive force of the central ideology of *David Copperfield*. Before widening and turning the angles of approach to the theme of David's maturation, however, we must stay a little longer with Uriah Heep, who unexpectedly pops up again near the end of the book.

The strange episode of Uriah's appearance in gaol for financial fraud and conspiracy, where David improbably bumps into him while on a fact-finding visit with Traddles, may be explained as a late tactic, on Dickens's part, for shutting him up and putting him where he belongs once and for all. Dickens does not analyse the underlying and overarching system here either. He is seemingly in favour of prisons, though, judging by some brusque satire, not of an experimental regime that consults inmates about the standards of food they are getting and thinks it can make 'sincere and lasting converts and penitents' (921) out of convicted criminals.[37] In a sense, Uriah's imprisonment is his true destiny. The house of correction continues the charity school in which he and his parent were brought up to be 'umble' and well-behaved. It is important to note, moreover, that the magistrate in charge of the new reforming code is none other than Creakle, once headmaster, not of Uriah's modest place of instruction, but of David's and Steerforth's higher, if itself flawed, establishment for the middle classes. School and prison are society's interconnected mechanisms for structuring and managing its human components: for making them fit and fitting, and, if necessary, keeping the misfits out of circulation.[38]

Yet even in prison Uriah is a source of discomfiture. Not that he is a direct threat to the system; far from challenging the rules, he plays the game to perfection, an exemplary inmate 'changed' and safe from 'sin', proclaiming to those who come to view him that 'It would be better for everybody, if they got took up, and was brought here' (928). In any case the warders who routinely patrol the place are always alert to possible deceit – they 'knew pretty well what all this stir was worth' (929) – and thus provide a fail-safe device should artful co-operation go beyond an acceptable mark and become troublesome. Creakle and his band of official tourists may be fooled, but the veteran footsoldiers are not. Uriah's situation raises uncomfortable questions precisely because it makes evident to the reader the network of social regulation and enforcement that normally avoids inspection, or is taken for granted.

At the same time, David is provoked into declaring hidden motivation and suppositions in himself when Uriah dredges up the memories most calculated to throw him off balance – the blow David had long ago landed on his face and the answering offer of forgiveness, which is now renewed. The point is not only that Uriah still refuses to be kept down or to let David off the hook of his own violent inclinations but that he draws from him at this very point a revealing condemnation, shared only with Traddles and addressed privily to the reader, of the two 'hypocritical knaves' (Steerforth's old servant, Littimer, is also in gaol for stealing from an employer) who 'knew [the] market-value' of their professed contrition 'in the immediate service it would do them when they were expatriated', and of their 'rotten hollow, painfully-suggestive piece of business' (930). The language here denounces both David's enemies and the whole capitalist order of 'market-value' and 'business', which is linked to an assumption of corrupt and corrupting practices; but it also again betrays an underlying partisan stance on David's part, and on Dickens's. It is tempting to define their position straight-forwardly as, to adapt Raymond Williams's formulation, the separation of virtue from the practical world that is a feature of the later phases of Puritanism and still later of Romanticism.[39] But there is more to it than that. Through the hero of *David Copperfield* Dickens channels an ideology that does negotiate effectively, and aggressively, with and within the world but cloaks the realities of social and economic stationing in an idealism of goodness and patient privacy. Audrey Jaffe remarks that 'Uriah embodies qualities that David refuses to acknowledge in himself – in particular, social ambition'.[40] This is true but insufficient. The conception of Uriah also casts a deconstructive light back upon David and the values he represents.

David, Dora, Agnes

Uriah is in fact the displacement of a whole set of impulses David cannot or will not recognize in himself. Mark Spilka's formulation that *David Copperfield* is a 'projective novel, in which surface life reflects the inner self' attracts a special import in this regard, beyond Spilka's own sense of how David's 'feelings fuse with outward action, and his selection of events advances inward meaning'.[41] Uriah is at once the expression and suppression of psycho-biological drives. There is a telling moment in this regard when, on the day he first goes to Mr Wickfield's, David, in a mood of *bonhomie*, approaches Uriah and gives him his hand:

> But oh, what a clammy hand his was! as ghostly to the touch as to the sight! I rubbed mine afterwards, to warm it, *and to rub his off*. (281)

The final phrase, where the italics are Dickens's, raises interesting possibilities. If masturbation is a figure of social transgression, David's reflex action symbolizes a desire both to rid himself of a guilty association with the vice and to perpetrate it by touching, 'rub[bing] . . . off', Uriah – expresses, that is, both the urge towards a secret, subversive life and an overlying will to self-regulation. When David then retired to his room, the 'uncomfortable hand . . . was still cold and wet upon [his] memory' and, fancying Uriah's face looking at him from one of the beam-ends outside the window, he took steps to 'shut him out in a hurry' (282). He carries the trace and the horror of infraction everywhere with him, and it is a constant battle to keep them in check. At the beginning of the next chapter the nature of the conflict within the young David is highlighted by his meeting with his new master, Dr Strong: 'he gave me his hand; which I didn't know what to do with, as it did nothing for itself' (282). Whatever difficulty there might be in the Doctor's married life with the youthful Annie, an assumption of which must surely be supposed to have encouraged David, Uriah and others in their suspicions of an affair between Annie and the profligate yet virile Jack Maldon, he is a figure well beyond the issue of guilt and con- formity, potency and restraint, that troubles David – the good old lovable Doctor, inoffensive and unoffending.

It is from the beginning a concern to David whether he 'liked Uriah or detested him' (311); and the mixture of attraction and repulsion reaches an eerie climax when, with Uriah asleep on the floor in the next room in his lodgings, David dreams of running him through the body with a 'red hot' poker, and, waking up, cannot help going to look at him over and over again 'lying on his back, with his legs extending to I don't know where, stoppages in his nose, and his mouth open like a post-office' (443). This adds orifices, penetration and involuntary noises to the impression of gross physicality already woven around Uriah through references to his limp, slimy or sinewy parts. We cannot but read the image as the reverse of David's fascination with the classic beauty of Steerforth: as the notation of a jumble of homoerotic and homophobic energies in the narrator-hero; an intense ambivalence involving compulsion towards and recoil from the male body as object of desire. Steerforth and Heep, whom David elsewhere gets muddled in his dreams,[42] are interdependent polarities of his own sexually-driven fantasy life – loci of, on the one hand, idealization and a refined pleasure and, on the other, a base and ugly arousal.

But there is something else going on in the sequence of which this event is a part. Agnes Wickfield, too, has found a place in David's developing inner life. It is Uriah's confession of his 'pure affection' for Agnes, and his 'love [of] the ground [she] walks on', that first prompts David to think of applying the red-hot poker. The putative instrument of assault, or the thought of using it,

> went from me with a shock, like a ball fired from a rifle: but the image of Agnes, outraged by so much as a thought of this red-headed animal's, remained in my mind when I looked at him . . . He seemed to swell and grow before my eyes; the room seemed full of the echoes of his voice; and the strange feeling . . . that all this had occurred before, at some indefinite time, and that I knew what he was going to say next, took possession of me. (441)

That David says he is made 'giddy' by thus imagining Agnes being violated enforces our sense that Uriah has become the distorted reflection of his own repressed longing for her. David's first encounter with Agnes had clearly brought some emotional confusion: 'I love little Em'ly, and I don't love Agnes – no, not at all in that way – but I feel that there are goodness, peace, and truth, wherever Agnes is; and that the soft light of the coloured window in the church, seen long ago, falls on her always, and on me when I am near her' (289). This protests too much the innocence and platonic virtue of the attraction, as, it could be argued, does David's reiteration of Agnes's status as his 'sister' (325, 326, 430), as well as his 'good Angel' (426). His words concede the pressure of that way of loving that is being ruled out. Stanley Friedman considers the *déjà vu* experience sparked off in David by thoughts of

Uriah's designs on Agnes in the light of psychoanalytic theories of stress management and self-correction; the threat of his rival and of his own unruly sexual feelings are checked by being distanced, set back in time and mind-space, while David could also be wishing for a 'second chance' with Agnes that will allow him to recuperate the physical responses he has denied and so – presumably as husband – be her true protector.[43] This last point in particular is interesting, and we will return to it in due course.

The more obvious interpretation of the passage, however, is that Uriah is the exteriorization of David's buried instincts. Freud, in 'Creative Writers and Day-Dreaming', proposes that the 'psychological novel' owes its distinctive nature to 'the inclination of the modern writer to split up his ego, by self-observation, into many part-egos, and, in consequence, to personify the conflicting currents of his own mental life'.[44] But Uriah is a special type of 'part-ego': when David becomes strangely aware of 'what he was going to say next' it is because Uriah is his primitive double – Hyde to his Jekyll. In another essay, 'The Uncanny', Freud makes reference to Otto Rank's account of the double as at once 'an assurance of immortality' and 'a harbinger of death'.[45] Uriah Heep seems decidedly the second. In fighting him off David is battling for the life of his worthier self.

Of Uriah and his mother David says, 'They did just what they liked with me; and wormed things out of me that I had no desire to tell' (314); and when Uriah attempts to claim David publicly as a sharer in his suspicions about Annie Strong, David is unable to conceal his feelings, the 'confession of [his] old misgivings' being 'too plainly written on [his] face to be overlooked': 'I could not undo that. Say what I would, I could not unsay it' (683). Uriah himself is both the form of David's secrets and a potential usurpation. In forcing David to confess what he wishes to keep hidden Uriah makes him an actor in a drama of his making – or a character in a narrative he is devising. Many times David suffers helplessness, even paralysis, in his company: when, early on, Uriah's eyes, the 'two red suns', defeat all attempts to avoid them and 'always attracted me back again' (278); when, as David strikes him, the two stand motionless, locked hand in hand for a seeming eternity, and when, as Uriah chides David in the aftermath, the latter concedes that 'He knew me better than myself' (686–7). In these moments David seems to come to the very point of subjection, even obliteration. Once he appears actually to have been displaced; for, revisiting the Wickfields' house after a protracted absence, he learns that 'He sleeps in your old room' (571). Fending off Uriah is crucial to David's selving, and a close run thing – though there is, as we shall see later on, one respect in which his enemy does positively serve his future, something of value that in the long run David must transfer over from him.

Even in the midst of this intense psychodrama a socio-political position is being promulgated. When Uriah talks of his 'pure affection' for Agnes and of worshipping the ground she walks on, he is aping a traditional language of courtly love which in David's earnestly Victorian version is the encrypting of a class code. David's sublimation of his feelings, which at their most refined and refining transform Agnes into that celestial beauty of a 'stained glass window' (280, 570), is the mark of a true gentleman, middling compared with the high-born Steerforth but impeccably upright. This brings us to the theme of regulation and self-regulation that is a crucial thread in the making and meaning of David's development.

It has been shown that one way in which *David Copperfield* serves the time's needs is to offer a 'theodicy' bringing consolation, or at least acceptance, in the face of the precariousness of life and the certainty of death.[46] So many of the situations in the book tell of the limits of human control over events, onwards from Aunt Betsey's inability to dictate the sex of Clara Copperfield's baby, through the tragicomical picture of Barkis's 'tortures' as he crawls from his deathbed to rummage in the camouflaged treasure chest in which he has carried around his money and valuables, to the sheer fact of mortality registered in the unexpected demise of a whole succession of characters, including Clara, Steerforth, Ham, and Dora. Over against the stress of misfortune and incapacity, however, is placed the compensatory rationale of submission to the divine plan – which Aunt Betsey in one of the many examples calls 'the mysterious dispensations of Providence' – or else an elegiac stance that embraces loss as an inevitable consequence of nature's laws and rhythms, an attitude memorably illustrated in Mr Peggotty's disquisition, as Barkis's ends approaches, on how 'along the coast' life ebbs and flows with the tide (506).[47]

This metaphysical wisdom is an important element in Dickens's resourcing and guidance of thought processes in his readers. Another example of the survival of religious discourse in popularized form in his work, it is both culturally produced and productive of culture. It is not this, however, that most stands out or is most sustained in the regulatory design of *David Copperfield*, but rather its reflection, reinforcement, and refinement of apparatuses for structuring individual and collective identity at a less philosophical and more socially practical level. Though this fundamental aspect of the novel is centred in David himself and a specific class experience, it has a wider application in its generation of conduct models and value preferences.

The institutions that operate to shape David from without, or bid to do so, we have already touched upon. Creakle's violent determination to 'have a thing done' (135) at Salem House is counter-productive, though David does in spite of it pick up crumbs of learning and lessons in humanity such as that instilled by the harassment of Mr Mell. At Strong's academy, by contrast, where the Doctor keeps absent-mindedly out of the way, engrossed in the Greek lexicon he is endlessly compiling, David is left to the immediately beneficial effects of a 'sound system', at once competitive and co-operative, in whose smooth running the boys have a major role and a definite stake, and which supplies a ready framework for making advances, both inwardly and upwards through the school into the world, by dint of 'honour and good faith' in appli-cation and the observance of rules. This place, headed by the 'kindest' and least 'worldly' of men (294), amply fulfils the certainly not unworldly or unself-interested objectives of Aunt Betsey in entering David there – to make him both 'happy and useful' (277).

In these adverse and benign learning situations alike, external influences serve educative processes whose real business is done at the level of the individual and on the inside, though, as in the case of Dr Strong's school, the local effects may then feed back by a very prompt circuit into the larger social structure, reinforcing it. The supervisory regimen of the academy, and to an extent of the law, is importantly replicated in the home after David arrives at Dover in flight from the drudgery of Murdstone and Grinby's London warehouse. If Murdstone, at the Rookery, had resembled Creakle, Aunt Betsey herself seems hardly more promising when, as David approaches, she cuts an aggressive figure, 'making a distant chop in the air with her knife', 'march[ing]' across her garden in military style (247). With Betsey, however, strictness is tempered by kindness (as we are at once reminded by David's softly touching her, no doubt again remembering his mother's story of his great-aunt's fleeting caress), and has a purpose. She dispenses discipline with businesslike care and deliberation, as her bedraggled nephew is 'collared', plied with restoratives, consulted about, washed, fed, and put to bed. David is thereafter conscious of being 'under close scrutiny', and when the Murdstones come to claim him he is 'fenced . . . in with a chair, as if it were a prison or a bar of justice' while his future is being decided (256, 264). But this is a protective custody decidedly in his favour, and very much for the future good of kith and kin; David is not being taken out of circulation but set on a correct course for being put effectually into it. The Murdstones defeated, Betsey gives him new clothes and a new name for a 'new life' (271). David is being caught for the thriving middle class, and to set the seal on his reintegration into his proper sphere and line of prospects he is stamped with familiar devices of bourgeois self-definition and power, that is, dress, money, lineage and the written word: '[the] clothes, which were purchased for me that afternoon, were marked "Trotwood Copperfield", in her own handwriting, and in indelible ink, . . . and it was settled that all the other clothes which were ordered to be made for me . . . should be marked in the same way' (271). As with Oliver, though in shorter span, the secular pilgrim takes on the accessories of his class-specific conversion – or rather confirmation of election.

The young David's 'education' (273) is continuous, and depends as much upon routine intercourse and environment as upon formal pedagogy. Repressive methods are repeatedly condemned. In her interview with the Murdstones Aunt Betsey denounces the destructiveness of their egotism and mental cruelty towards David's mother – 'you must begin to train her, must you? begin to break her, like a poor caged bird, and wear her deluded life away, in teaching her to sing *your* notes' – and Murdstone himself admits that his comparable mode of 'bringing [David] up', which was 'to correct his vices', had proved ineffectual (266, 270). Betsey's subtler approach is to spare the rod and through gentle guidance get David to make her tune his own. There are several occasions on which she offers advice. 'Be a credit to yourself, to me, and Mr Dick, and Heaven be with you', she tells him; 'Never . . . be mean in anything, never be false; never be cruel. Avoid these three vices, Trot, and I can always be hopeful of you.' The policy of placing obligation and responsibility upon the subject works no less well here than at Dr Strong's, for David, with gratitude and esteem, swears not to 'abuse her kindness or forget her admonition' (280). Later, we see Betsey's related skill in leading her ward down the right path through casual approval: 'I am very well persuaded that whatever you do, Trot, will always be natural and rational' (331). The individual is made to interiorize the necessary virtues, not through bludgeoning confrontation, but a training based on compliance, the negotiation of positions, and the pressing of mutual self-interest. That, Dickens perceives and demonstrates, is the successful middle-class way. 'All is agreed and understood between us', announces Betsey to her Trot (407).

To the catalogue of personality strengths compiled in these exchanges – naturalness, reasonableness, honesty, respect for others, and so on – we must add one other. David is told, or rather 'trusted', by Aunt Betsey to be 'firm and self-reliant' (415). Self-reliance is of course a signal Protestant virtue. It does not, however, mean only fending for oneself and making good but being able, like Scrooge, to learn from experience and to grow inwardly. This aspect of David's development entails above all his conquest of his own 'undisciplined heart'.[48] The quotation is one of three that make a deep impression on him from Annie Strong's public pledge of love for her husband, the Doctor, whose interest had saved her from the error of a rash union with her cousin Maldon: 'The first mistaken impulse of my undisciplined heart'; 'There can be no disparity in marriage like unsuitability of mind and purpose'; 'My love was founded on a rock' (729–33). David ponders these words at first hearing and they later frequently recur to him. Designated in his narrative as bearing 'some particular interest, or some strange application that I could not divine' (729), they are the equivalent of the texts, often enigmatic yet always potent and full of relevance, that take root in the consciousness of the Puritan autobiographers in their spiritual struggles, such as the biblical verses and heaven-sent (or demonic) voices that had resided within Bunyan during the prolonged battle of the scriptures in *Grace Abounding*, where the phrase about the 'arms of grace' being open ultimately prevails over that about Esau selling his birthright and being unable to repent.[49] They are something given, a leading, but the way ahead that they signpost must nonetheless be worked for. Indeed, the nature of their coming signals one of the difficulties: the individual is subject always to a field of force where, for better or for worse, the unpredictable may happen.

Gwendolyn Needham, in her seminal article, points out that David's journey to a disciplined heart takes place against a backdrop of various characters who hardly start out or who fall by the wayside. Steerforth is a good example since, in a rare moment of self-deprecation, he confesses that, with a sure hand to direct him and a grip on himself, he might have been other than he irredeemably is: 'David, I wish to God I had had a judicious father these last twenty years! . . . I wish with all my soul I had been better guided . . . I wish with all my soul I could guide myself better!' (380). Little Em'ly, who never regains speech or presence *in propria persona* after her return in shame to England, has become transfixed at the point of her inability to resolve the contradictions in her feelings, reduced (like Lot's wife) from human being to a sentence: ' "When I leave my dear home . . . it will be never to come back, unless he brings me back a lady. This [the letter she is leaving for Ham] will be found at night, many hours after, *instead of me*. Oh, if you knew how my heart is torn" ' (513: italics mine). Through Aunt Betsey we learn how David's father had possessed a dreamy romantic nature and a predilection for 'wax dolls'; his mother is 'a simple affectionate Baby' who becomes an 'unhappy, misdirected baby' and 'benighted innocent' for falling under Murdstone's spell (53–4, 269). In urging David to cultivate a 'strength of character' that his parents 'might both have been

. . . better for' she lets out her fears for his inheritance of an overactive sensibility and a too pliant disposition, a falling short in 'practical ideas of life' (53, 332).

For her part, however, Aunt Betsey is proof that people can change and improve. To David she presents herself as an *exemplum*. On the outside her clothes and accessories, long skirt and shirt-collar, chin-straps, wristbands and gentleman's watch, that unsex her from ankle to head, and her eccentric behaviour in hopelessly banning her pretty servants from consorting with men, are the vestigial marks of her reaction to suffering at the hands of a violent husband; but on the inside time and contact with David have wrought a worthy transformation:

> 'It's in vain, Trot, to recall the past, unless it works some influence upon the present. . . . Only be a loving child to me in my age, and bear with my whims and fancies; and you will do more for an old woman whose prime of life was not so happy or conciliating as it might have been, than ever that old woman did for you.' (407)

More directly, she confesses to having been 'a wayward sort of a woman' who has 'judged harshly of other people's mistakes . . . because [she] had bitter reason to judge harshly of [her] own' (705). Such sentiments indicate in a sense an *un*disciplining of the heart, a more relaxed outlook on life; but the point so far as David and the book's concept of maturation are concerned is that steadfast and flexible self-knowledge, a concern for other lives, a capacity for learning from the past, are the form of an ordered personality.

No episode in David's life is a greater or more formative test of character than his relationship with Dora. In its courtship days, however, the adventure rules, there being no considerations of profit or loss but only of immediate satisfaction. The distracted lover, David, is caught in a whirl of romantic images: 'the girlish, bright-eyed lovely Dora . . . form . . . face . . . enchanting manner'; 'a fairy, a Sylph'; 'white clip bonnet and a dress of celestial blue'; 'straw hat, blue ribbons, and a quantity of curls'; the 'idea' of Dora, the 'star of Dora' (450–51, 456, 534, 542). He was 'wandering in a garden of Eden all the while, with Dora' (452) – and had no sense at that time that Eden could be the site of a fall. Death, in the shape of Mr Spenlow's sudden collapse, does nothing to deter his pursuit of the prize, which must be gained at all costs. His aunt's bankruptcy serves only to make him redouble his efforts, and to cast himself in the role, if not of the chivalric knight, certainly of the determined lower-class hero taking his 'woodman's axe . . . [and] cutting at those trees in the forest of difficulty' until he came to Dora: 'Great was the labour; priceless the reward. Dora was the reward, and Dora must be won' (582).

For all its vibrancy and magic, it is clear from the beginning that David's experience of Dora is a mis-taking. This is no random error, however, but psychologically determined. It comes as no surprise to learn that *David Copperfield* was among Sigmund Freud's favourite books,[50] for onto Dora David projects his desire for his mother. He lets slip in the present narrative the feelings and motives of the past encounter, without ever quite knowing he is doing so. Dora's tresses – 'such curls' (455) – repeat Clara's 'bright curls' (65); her girlish form duplicates Clara's 'youthful shape' (61). Both women are allied with flowers. Dora is David's 'Little Blossom', but a more vital association comes in his recollection of the time they once retreated to the greenhouse: 'It contained quite a show of beautiful geraniums. We loitered along in front of them, and Dora often stopped to admire this one or that one, and Dora, laughing, held up the dog childishly, to smell the flowers' (456). It had been a geranium that Clara had plucked for Murdstone the second time David, jealous and disturbed, had seen him at the Rookery. Does not the later memory stick the more sweetly because it records an intimacy that is, at least in part, a recompense for a childhood slight and separation? It is as though it stores the unspoken statement, 'It's my turn now'. Yet another bridge is built with the past at this time by the incredible coincidence of Miss Murdstone's resurfacing as Dora's chaperon. She explains that she was acquainted with David in his 'childish days', and 'should not have known him now' (451). But *we* recognize a connection: in his response to Dora there is a strong element of the 'childish' still.

This is love founded, not on a rock, but on an illusion. Aunt Betsey sees this and tries to alert David to the dangers of the liaison: his subjection to a 'fancy'; the soft-centredness of the relationship, in which the ingredient of compatibility amounts to no more than that of 'two pretty pieces of confectionery' (564). 'Blind, blind, blind!' she murmurs, before inferring that what David needs is not the attachment of a 'poor Baby' like his mother but 'deep, downright earnestness . . . to sustain him and improve him' (565). David's myopia consists of course not only in his impetuous commitment to Dora but his failure to appreciate that Agnes would make him the better wife; and this point is underscored just afterwards when close on his thoughts of the 'calm seraphic eyes' of the 'sister of his boyhood' comes an echo of Aunt Betsey's words from a beggar in the street, 'Blind! Blind! Blind!' (581–2). One long-term benefit of David's marriage to Dora is that it prepares him for marriage to Agnes. Before that happy outcome, however, he suffers.

It is not long after the dizzy whirl of the wedding that disillusionment begins to creep in. David awakens from the dream of love to the weird reality of routine cohabitation: 'I would lean back in my chair, and think how queer it was that there we were, alone together as a matter of course – nobody's business any more – all the romance of our engagement put away upon a shelf, to rust – no one to please but one another – one another to please for life' (701). This evocation of the eerie shock of felt isolation, anticlimax and partnership as lifelong challenge is a strong example of the insight and pathos that Dickens can bring to the treatment of marriage and the getting of wisdom. Closeness does not banish difference or difficulty but brings them frighteningly to life. The adventurer discovers that actions have consequences. Vague inklings of the problem that Dora might become in his life have been present to David from the first. He notices, for example, that everyone regards her as a 'pretty toy or plaything', a 'pet child', much as she views her lapdog Jip (669), the pretty, spoilt animal that is the extension and doubling of her own nature (669). More ominous still is her insistence on his occupying her level, as she addresses *him* 'as if I were a doll, I used to think' (608).

Always he felt she was 'a little impracticable' (604); but in the fully-fledged domestic context this shortcoming – which is another way in which she replicates his mother, who, as Aunt Betsey put it, never had 'any practical ideas of life' (53) – is magnified severalfold. The story of the household disasters that beset David and Dora – his request for cheap fish that turns into her purchase of an inordinately expensive salmon, half-opened oysters and undercooked mutton, account books splashed with ink and used to play games with Jip, a female servant found drunk under the boiler, a page whose thieving necessitates charges and prosecution – are presented as a bitter-sweet comedy. But David is quite capable of coming to the edge of tragic despair when things seem to have gone too far, as in his comments to Dora after she has fainted saying goodbye to the young criminal on the eve of his being transported: 'The fact is . . . there is contagion in us. We infect everyone about us' (761). The impression is that Dora is too shallow to know what she is doing, or to feel David's outburst as the cruel accusation it might otherwise be.

Whatever Dora's personality, however, David cannot be absolved from the obligation of trying to make the marriage work. His appeal to Aunt Betsey for help brings a brusque admonition, for self-reliance is as much an imperative here as in public and professional life: 'But remember, my dear, your future is between you two. No one can assist you; you are to work it out for yourselves' (706). All the same, it is one thing to appreciate the duty of taking up the burdens of ill-conceived life-choices and quite another to move productively on. David resolves to 'form' Dora's mind, only to discover that it was 'already formed' and to feel the shame and the futility of putting her under restraint, acting as 'a trap, a pitfall', a 'spider to Dora's fly' (762–3). As in other situations, the strict and self-centred approach brings negative returns; but in this case there is no subtler alternative than simply to make the best of things: nothing else than for David to adapt himself to his wife, 'to share with her what I could, and be happy; to bear on my own shoulders what I must, and be happy still' (766).

This attitude of acceptance is a landmark in David's progress to a disciplined heart. It comes as a breakthrough at a time of crisis akin to the period of soul-trouble that familiarly precedes conversion in Puritan spiritual testimony. In *Grace Abounding*, John Bunyan, his soul seized upon by accusatory texts from holy scripture, had felt that 'the very stones in the street, and tiles upon the houses, did bend themselves against me', crying out against his commission of some unpardonable sin;[51] and so, in a similar turmoil of disorientation, David, wrestling with the torments of his own more commonplace misdemeanour, finds the words of Mrs Strong – 'The first mistaken impulse of an undisciplined heart', 'There can be no disparity in marriage, like unsuitability of mind and purpose' – again present to his mind: 'I awoke with them, often in the night; I remember to have read them, in dreams, inscribed upon the walls of houses' (766).

Squaring up thereafter to his lot made David's second year 'much happier' than his first and, 'what was better still, made Dora's life all sunshine' (766). These words, however, bring home to us another dimension of David's narrative – the fact that he places Dora in a partial light. His text, whose meanings are more than his conscious intentions, reveals both the limits of his perspectives, which are subjective, and aspects of Dora's own character that are never directly acknowledged. David underestimates the part Dora plays, and has always played, in stabilizing their relationship. Their marriage is saved from disaster because they reach an understanding, an unspoken negotiated settlement. What makes the account of their life together so moving, and in certain respects so inspirational, is that Dora, though the junior partner, applies herself in her virtually helpless way to keeping the ship afloat. 'Child-wife', for example, is not simply the judgement David or others put upon her but the name she gives herself, defensively yet knowingly, creating a buffer against the disappointment her intuition tells her all along will be inevitable: 'When you are going to be angry with me, say to yourself, "it's only my child-wife!" . . . When you miss what I should like to be, and I think can never be, say, "still my foolish child-wife loves me!" ' (711).

We see that behind the superficial impression that she makes upon the world and that the world makes of her, Dora does after all have an interior life – that is, needs, motives and tactics for the support of her marriage and, which is the same thing, for her own survival. And there is then the episode in which, having blotted her account-book and messed up her bills until (in David's words) they looked 'more like curl-papers than anything else' (712), she takes up regular position holding David's pens for him as he writes his book, or copying a page or two of manuscript: 'The preparations she made for this great work, the aprons she put on, the bibs she borrowed from the kitchen to keep off the ink, the time she took . . . and the way in which she would bring it to me, like a school-copy, and then, when I praised it, clasp me round the neck, are touching recollections to me' (715).

Some modern readers and critics will no doubt be offended by Dora's subservience to her husband – the way she becomes, willingly at that, a slightly comic servant of his creative and productive endeavours, going through the motions of being useful, grateful for his affectionate approval. But the picture is more complex than that. For one thing, as we shall see, this kind of relationship is by no means an ideal one for David himself, or for Dickens. More immediately, however, it is difficult for us, when interpreting such passages, to distinguish, on Dora's side, between deference, self-defence, and courage. There is an important insight in David's later remark that 'Dora held the pens; and we both felt that our shares were adjusted as the case required' (766); both parties do what they can to make an imperfect situation liveable.

A subtler example of this demanding art of keeping faith emerges just before Dora dies:

> 'I have begun to think I was not fit to be a wife.'
> I try to stay my tears, and to reply, 'Oh, Dora love, as fit as I to be a husband!'
> 'I don't know,' with the old shake of her curls. 'Perhaps! But if I had been more fit to be married I might have made you more so, too. Besides you are very clever, and I never was.' (837)

Death creates special conditions of course (we note that Dora begins to speak of herself in the past tense); but the exchange we witness here is a version of what has gone before, not something entirely new. For all the frankness of a near-parting confession, there is, as previously, that strong element of accommodation resting upon leaving some things unsaid. The two communicate in part through being reticent. Philip Davis draws attention to the 'natural decorum' which prevents David from saying 'Yes, Dora, I too began to fear that you were not fit', and by which he knows just as surely that the response 'Oh no Dora, you were most fit to be my wife' would be no good either. 'He could not tell a lie at such a moment nor could he make a reply that was all too obviously a placebo.'[52] Instead of blaming one another, the two concede doubts about themselves: intimacy is bound up with hesitancy, and they are able at last to share the fact that they were too young, together: 'But, as years went on, my dear boy would have wearied of his child-wife . . . He would have been more and more sensible of what was wanting in his home. She wouldn't have improved. It is better as it is' (837).

Davis rightly takes this conversation as an example of what Thomas Hood had in mind when he saw Dickens as a saving grace in an age of (in Hood's own phrase) 'cold calculating utilitarianism'.[53] It is the kind of writing by which Dickens 'was able to warm the human heart' in the way Hood inferred in his praise of the young novelist whose 'drift is natural, along with the great human currents, and not against them'.[54] Whatever the force of the portrayal of the David–Dora relationship as affective wisdom, however, whatever its power in giving access to the timeless drama of human vulnerability and strength, this does not mean that we cannot, on another level, detect David's hand and mind significantly at work in it. As he struggled in the past, no less than Dora, and together with her, to bring stability to his life, so in the present he strives to establish value and progression in the larger history of which his first marriage was a part. Writing is for David the medium of positive self- and world-creation against a background of abiding uncertainty. Audrey Jaffe sees this when arguing that in reaction to a fear of being objectified such as haunts him when he is forced to wear the placard announcing 'He bites' – he 'always fancied that someone was reading it' and began 'to have a dread of myself, as a kind of wild boy' (131) – he seizes mobility and control by making other people characters in *his* book.[55] He had coped with his early passive isolation, at least provisionally, by inhabiting his favourite roles from the fictions he had come upon in his father's small library and by putting the Murdstones, who had him forever under their watchful gaze, 'into all the bad ones' (106).

This strategy for taking command, involving mechanisms both of therapeutic defence and assertiveness, is apparent across the whole novel of *David Copperfield*. It is plainly there, for example, in the incident where Murdstone and his cronies make fun of David as the 'sharp' 'Brooks of Sheffield' but he in the long run has the last laugh through sharply telling the story and thus using them as his stooges.

Jaffe calls this 'revenge via narrative'. Other motives operate in the important aftermath to the episode, when the young David is put subtly on the offensive by the old, as, returning home, the boy lets slip to his mother how the men had talked of her as 'Bewitching' and as 'The pretty little widow' and she, through her excited and flattered response, is situated the more firmly in the frame as a lovable, shallow, 'girlish' figure (74). The narrator asks at this point, 'Can I say she ever changed, when my remembrance brings her back to life, thus only?' The reflection underlines how imagination captures and perpetuates cherished moments; but it also reminds us that in *David Copperfield* other characters are fixed stars in the constellation of David's evolving life, and are reference points by which he steers his course. His mother and her continuation, Dora, assume an ultimate fixedness, *rigor mortis*, while he moves on to Agnes. Agnes is the end-point of the destiny into which he is shaping his life, or rather a teleological axis from which light and serenity project forwards upon his future; and whatever his successes in coming to terms with Dora, there is always a lurking, unavoidable shadow of disappointment and of something better beyond:

> I did feel, sometimes, for a little while, that I could have wished my wife had been my counsellor; had had more character and purpose, to sustain me and improve me by; had been endowed with power to fill up the void which somewhere seemed to be about me . . . . (713)

> What I missed, I still regarded – always regarded – as something that had been a dream of my youthful fancy; that was incapable of realization . . . But that it would have been better for me if my wife could have helped me more, and shared the many thoughts in which I had no partner; and that this might have been; I knew.
> . . . When I thought of the airy dreams of youth that are incapable of realization, I thought of the better state preceding manhood that I had outgrown; and then the contented days with Agnes, in the dear old house, arose before me, like spectres of the dead, that might have some renewal in another world, but never more could be reanimated here. (765–6)

The difference between these passages lies in David's dawning awareness that the absence in his life is due not simply to Dora's shortcomings but to the fact that Agnes is not there, although, as yet, he has no hopes for a return to his true home. Ultimately, not only does Dora's death clear a space for her predestined successor, she is made an instrument of approval in the scheme of David's salvation when, on her deathbed, admitting that she would have 'tried and disappointed' him as time went by, she sends for Agnes – whom, we learn later, she charges to 'occupy

[the] vacant place' (939). It is an element of our resilience that we structure our 'reality' in accordance with our wishes, as David does here.

The union of David and Agnes is one of the places in Dickens where psychodrama and didacticism, the novel of the self and the novel of ideology, notably converge. It not only makes the hero's existence complete but, in sociocultural terms, represents a model life-arrangement, just as the relations of David and Dora have shown how to make the best of a flawed one. If in the first association there had been 'contagion' to bear (761), the second is wholly a prescription for personal well-being and the collective good. Before the plot fully matures, however, David, in exile, goes through a preparatory cleansing of the mind and spirit. This sojourn abroad following the deaths of Dora, Steerforth and Ham, moreover, is foreshadowed by an earlier trial, when his stepfather had sent him to work at Murdstone and Grinby's warehouse. Both episodes conform, in their different ways, to that segment of the traditional myth of the hero during which the protagonist undergoes an ordeal in the wilderness or some other place apart where he gathers special knowledge that will prove valuable to him on his return to the civilized world.[56]

David's time as a 'little labouring hind', described in Chapter 11, initiates or advances several threads in the folds of his heroic identity. The folk-hero familiarly has a 'helper'.[57] In the young David's case this is Micawber, who makes his debut in the novel as the boy's impecunious but friendly landlord. Yet the most obvious motif is that of learning to bear up single-handedly. 'I led the same secretly unhappy life; but I led it in the same lonely, self-reliant manner' is David's comment on a routine where, a 'shabby child' toiling among 'common men and boys', or else prowling the streets, he had 'no consolation, no assistance'. He was alone but held on; and the resistance he developed has future applications, as in due course he directly acknowledges when facing the challenge of his aunt's financial ruin by 'turn[ing] the painful discipline of my younger days to account, by going to work with a resolute and steady heart' (582). There are, too, gains beyond this basic power of survival. The humiliation of a life of drudgery alongside Mealy Potatoes and other dregs of humanity intensifies, even as it threatens to crush, David's self-esteem. Thus, he felt the 'shame' of his position; and it was a misery to believe that 'what I had learned, and thought, and delighted in, and raised my fancy and my emulation up by, would pass away from me, little by little' (210). We hear how, fearing contempt, he quickly became 'at least . . . as skilful' as the other boys; and how his 'conduct and manner' were sufficiently different from theirs to put him on a special footing, so that the men spoke of him as 'the little gent' (218).

The retrospective angle makes clear what is incipiently present to the child's consciousness: that he is set apart by birth, talent, and training – three things that usually go together in Dickens.

Overarching this conviction of singularity and personal merit is the idea of election, or divine dispensation; for, like one of his favourite heroes from fiction, Robinson Crusoe, David succeeds not only by his own efforts but through the help of Providence: 'I know that, but for the mercy of God, I might easily have been, for any care that was taken of me, a little robber or a little vagabond' (216).[58] Yet the sense of calling in David's narrative is not so much religious as to do with his vocation as novelist. He recollects, for example, that in the midst of a near-crushing agony he managed to keep alive his gift for story-telling, entertaining his superiors at the warehouse with 'some results of the old readings' that had brought him succour at Salem House (218). Adversity at the same time worked positively to sensitize his powers of observation and imagination as, in mysterious places, riverside or debtors' prison, he took an interest in the life around him – 'made stories for myself, out of the streets, and out of men and women' (224). Looking back, David then discovers himself as an object of contemplation: 'When I tread the old ground, I do not wonder that I seem to see and pity, going on before me, an innocent romantic boy, making his imaginative world out of such strange experiences and sordid things!' (225). Pitiable though he may be, the child is father of the man: there is both change and continuity of identity; and the past is at once the source and the material of the creative self.

Learning through pain; self-reliance and providential design; the making of the artist; social standing: all these themes are repeated in the course of David's travels on the Continent, except perhaps the last, although even that is assumed in the likeness of his journey to the gentleman's Grand Tour among the 'abiding places of History and Fancy' (886). Mention of his 'pilgrimage' and of the 'burden' of his despondency remind us once more of *The Pilgrim's Progress*, but the precursors here are much more Byron and Wordsworth than Bunyan. David's addresses to a grand but sympathetic Nature in the form of the 'awful solitudes' of Switzerland – 'great Nature spoke to me', 'I sought out Nature, never sought in vain' (887, 889) – recall the hard-driving rhetoric of Canto III of *Childe Harold's Pilgrimage*, where the Childe, 'unfit / . . . to herd with Man', holds converse, in 'mutual language' of the soul, with the 'wonder-works' of Nature; and there is a general similarity, also, in the respective concepts of inner desolation, with shared references to being wounded, to emptiness and the desert waste, and to restlessness.[59]

As in the treatment of Steerforth, however, the Byronic aesthetic, the heroism of apartness and passion, is conjured with yet set aside. The closer comparisons lie with Wordsworth's *Prelude*, which was published as Dickens was working on the later stages of *David Copperfield*,[60] and which predicts important aspects of the schema of David's recovery, that is both the pattern of its psychology and the values it upholds. Whereas Byron (having in the course of Canto III dropped the persona of Harold) renounces the world of men and women – 'I have not loved the world, nor the world me, – / But let us part fair foes'[61] – David edges his way back to it, concentrating in the drama of his collapse and restoration the same movement that unfolds in Wordsworth's spiritual history, the path 'Through Nature to the Love of Human Kind'.[62]

Suggestive parallels emerge if we remember certain central passages from *The Prelude*: Wordsworth's tribute to Dorothy, 'beloved Sister', who helped him, through 'sudden admonition', to maintain connection with his 'true self' during his breakdown in the aftermath of the French Revolution, and 'preserved [him] still / A Poet'; the further thanksgiving to this 'Sister of my soul' for softening the 'over-sternness' of his imagination – his fondness for 'that beauty, which . . . / Hath terror in it' – and opening his heart to 'tenderness' and 'regard for common things'; his general celebration of the qualities of 'female softness . . . humble cares . . . delicate desires . . . Mild interests' which he sees as having been nurtured in him by 'Nature's self' and 'all varieties of human love', as well as by Dorothy's influence.[63] For David, too, the sublime is something to be left behind (though not in itself rejected) in favour of the beautiful and the humane. He says, 'I had found sublimity and wonder in the dread heights and precipices . . . but as yet, they had taught me nothing else' (887). It is during a descent amidst 'beauty and tranquillity' that the oppression of despair starts to loosen its grip, and in a valley of picturesque 'serenity', dotted with wooden cottages and echoing with the distant song of shepherds, that it finally breaks up, and he begins to 'weep as I had not wept yet, since Dora died!' Agnes is his Dorothy, fountain of wisdom and 'sisterly affection'.

Her letter of encouragement and consolation, which he auspiciously finds waiting for him at this moment, is not presented to us verbatim but through David's selective report, so that we get a sense both of her role as helper and his awakening determination to move on. The Puritan ethos and its meditative practices here loom large: the earnest frugality of spirit that distils real advantage from seeming detriment, as David writes out Agnes's prompting that he should 'turn affliction to good' (888); the appeal to evidences of past experience as support and spur, notable in that elegant formulation of grounds for seeing pain as profit,

'As the endurance of my childish days had done its part to make me what I was, so greater calamities would nerve me on, to be yet better than I was'; the insistence that, when all is said and done, the outcome of human affairs is nevertheless in the hands of God, as Agnes has affirmed in 'commend[ing]' David to His care and David in turn recognizes by uttering 'thank Heaven' (886) when thinking of his deliverance (and Wordsworth, too, had thought fit to underscore in late revisions by interpolating 'Thanks to the bounteous Giver of all good' as preface to his commemoration of his sister's redemptive agency[64]).

Vocation is central to identity-definition in this chapter. The true self that David rediscovers becomes more and more explicitly the creative writer, and renewal, when it arrives, consists of his being able 'to resume [the] pen', after which he goes from strength to strength, first composing a story that he gets published at home (through Traddles) to great acclaim and then beginning another 'in my old ardent way, on a new fancy, which took strong possession of me' (889). This phase of his history reiterates in a short span the shape of Wordsworthian authorial maturation and artistic mission, but only to peel off and settle at last on different ground. The Dickensian post-Romantic scripture is at once linked to its origins and tracked through one of its distinctive spheres, character-formation, to another, wedlock and the home. The one piece of advice in Agnes's letter that we have not yet noted is the hope that David will be an example to others – 'as they [various calamities] had taught me, would I teach others' (888). It is the role of the novelist to instruct. The particular lesson suggested by Agnes's reported words seems to be that human worth and capacity are as apparent on the dark side of experience as on the bright; which is exactly the message to be derived, on one level, from the present chapter of *David Copperfield*, the events of which have the effect, in David's own phrases, of 'making me more self-denying, more resolved, more conscious of myself, and my defects and errors' (891) – of improving his 'undisciplined heart'.

There is, however, another model of creativity taking shape in the same pages. This is not quite the feminization of imagination that Wordsworth espouses in theory and David in turn moves towards when leaving the masculine sublime for the gentler contours of his valley refuge; nor simply its humanization, though this is a step of the first importance that is achieved when David lets into his breast a 'human interest' which brings him as many friends in the Swiss valley 'as in Yarmouth' – a detail that connects the awakening of energies in this episode with the democratic art and purposes already displayed in the novel of *David Copperfield*. Rather, we have imagination domesticized. Within the chapter Agnes is viewed as much as ever by David as a chaste and sacred presence in his life – he uses the term 'sisterly affection' twice (once with reference to her letter, once in subsequent free reflection) and in the course of a single sentence designates her 'sacred', 'friend' and 'sister' (890) – but he begins also to think of her in a new way, as a wife and love-partner. He grows conscious of the fact that Agnes has been the cause and the potential remedy of that 'old unhappy loss or want of something' in his life, and that in his blindness he has thrown away 'the treasure of her love' (890). Marriage and romantic attachment become the focal point of fictional creation, whether David's or Dickens's, and this novel's concluding repository of value.[65]

Agnes has not had a good press. She has been seen as lifeless and too good to be true; in George Orwell's famous quip, 'the real legless angel of Victorian romance'.[66] Even a critic who takes her relatively seriously is worried: 'In a novel populated by sharply realized characters, she stands out as an emblematic figure whose meaning lies beyond her merely human qualities, which are unquestionably vague.'[67] Of course she *is* an emblem, both within David's mind and the novel as a source book of social and ontological values. Yet, despite the critical consensus, she does also have physical being and presence, though for a long time David cannot perceive it. We have already considered how David's revulsion towards Uriah Heep's sexual predatoriness may reflect his own subconscious desire for Agnes; but there have also been times in the past when Agnes herself has manifested traces of erotic feeling, as in the 'blush' (a standard nineteenth-century signifier of arousal)[68] that meets David's talk about people falling in love (333), or her flirtatious reaction to his remark that he never thinks of her other than as his 'good angel' ('Agnes answered with her pleasant laugh, that one good Angel (meaning Dora) was enough' (576)), or the animation, the 'bright change in her attentive face', that greets his sudden appearance (630). One of the things David learns is to reciprocate this aspect of Agnes's nature. Thus, on first glimpsing him after his return from Switzerland 'she stopped and laid her hand upon her bosom' – perhaps from sheer surprise or perhaps in subconscious invitation, but certainly not pointing upwards to heaven – and he 'caught her in his arms' (912). When they finally declare their love he embraces her, 'Closer in my arms, nearer to my heart, her trembling hand upon my shoulder, her sweet eyes shining through her tears, on mine' (936).

However melodramatic, this intimacy is a crucial element in the final form of the David–Agnes relationship, which brings together the spheres of body and soul, with Agnes as it were a combination of the essence of Nancy and Rose Maylie, and a subsuming of Dora's passionate temper within a wider conception of wifeliness. The spiritual side of Agnes becomes, if anything, more conspicuous in these later stages of the novel, with references to such features as her 'angel-face', to the 'religious care' and 'veneration' with which David views her, and to those divine offices of mediation and influence that are symbolized at the close by her 'shining . . . light' and 'pointing upward' (913–17, 950). This is Agnes the 'secular Madonna'.[69] But we are also meant to see her as a 'flesh-and-blood' woman.

This balance of the spiritual and the physical is of course part and parcel of the ideal texture of the David–Agnes relationship – its status as one of Dickens's models to live by – and connects with that other perfect synthesis of which we were put in mind by Georg Simmel's 'The Adventure'. Hard upon his declaration of love, David goes over the recent steps in his reasoning which have brought him to this point, calling them his striving for 'better knowledge of myself and of her' (936). Such reflection shows how far David has come from what he now terms, self-critically, the 'headlong passion' for Dora for which he has paid his 'forfeit' (903); best love is thought out, deferred – disciplined. The attitude thus expressed is the 'historical spirit' characterized by Simmel, over against the 'romantic spirit', as being 'in its objectivity and retrospectiveness . . . devoted to contemplating a substance of life out of which immediacy has disappeared';[70] though Dickens, in contrast to Simmel's presumption of the mutual exclusiveness of the two states, insists upon their co-presence. With David and Agnes the steady 'historical' frame of mind and the excitement of the 'romantic' come together.

The elevation of heterosexual partnership as a cultural ideal is nowhere more apparent than at those moments when David's memories are projected in graphic scenarios with celebratory commentary or 'talkover'. Here is the immediate aftermath of the lovers' opening of their hearts:

> O, we were happy, we were happy! . . .
>
> We walked, that winter evening, in the fields together; and the blessed calm within us seemed to be partaken by the frosty air. The early stars began to shine while we were lingering on, and looking up to them, we thanked our GOD for having guided us to this tranquillity.
>
> We stood together in the same old-fashioned window at night, when the moon was shining; Agnes with her quiet eyes raised up to it; I following her glance. Long miles of road then opened out before my mind; and, toiling on, I saw a ragged way-worn boy, forsaken and neglected, who should come to call even the heart now beating against mine, his own. (937)

It had been common for Puritan converts to walk in the fields during or after their entry into a conscious state of grace,[71] and the words 'blessed calm' and the thanksgiving for God's guidance leave us in no doubt that, in Dickens, fulfilment in love is being upvalued as a quasi-religious experience and is a secular displacement of the old consummation. The idea of transcendence is being tied to, and made available through, ordinary emotional circumstance; love is both rapture and a divine gift. We are aware also, as we read the passage, of David's active mind, of a structuring from within out of personal motives. Two of the details we have met before. The 'ragged, way-worn boy' recalls the 'shabby child' of Murdstone and Grinby's, whose preservation from a life of crime and beggary the adult David had attributed to 'the mercy of God' (216). To this early dispensation David now adds the boon of Agnes herself, her 'heart . . . beating' against his own; travelling back, he reviews a road to the present that suggests his happiness was preordained. But this heart then returns us to the occasion of David's first departure from Blunderstone for Yarmouth: 'I felt her heart beat against mine' (76). If in Dora David had united with the pretty child in his mother, in Agnes he comes into possession of her deeper sensuous being, makes it his 'own'. While the first of these mnemonic events displays a purposive mechanism for endowing the individual life with privilege, for making it a destiny, in the other an inadvertent repetition signals both the persistence and laying to rest of a troublesome desire. Sometimes the force of a collective creed can be compromised by its being specified to individual circumstance, personalized, but this is not the case here for David, in the fullness of his happiness, is the exemplar of the new faith of Eros and Hymen. Love is a many-splendoured thing. Marriage is made in heaven.

The implications of David's text being a subjective construct, however, are wider than this, and we must return to them later. Certainly, it is only on occasion that the account of the relationship with Agnes breaks free from the limits of his consciousness to become, as in the scenario we have just considered, spectacular, and specular, persuasion for unmediated public consumption. Ordinarily, it remains under control of his point of view; Agnes, no less than others though more equal than any, is a character in *his* book. She complements him but on his terms. What he most cherishes about her on his return from Switzerland, for example, is that she supplies him with an anchor amidst the shifting currents – or, as he puts it at a time of particular stress, the 'quicksands' (891) – of his mental life. This really is love founded on a rock; and the solidity is provided not only by Agnes herself but also by the place with which she is inextricably connected, the house at

Canterbury. David's impressions of it after his arrival back in England are worth quoting at length. It is not only in rational analysis that he displays Simmel's 'historical spirit' but in processes of contemplative recollection:

> The well-remembered ground was soon traversed, and I came into the quiet streets, where every stone was a boy's book to me. I went on foot to the old house, and went away with a heart too full to enter. I returned; and looking, as I passed, through the low window of the turret-room where first Uriah Heep, and afterwards Mr Micawber, had been wont to sit, saw that it was a little parlour now, and that there was no office. Otherwise the staid old house was, as to its cleanliness and order, still just as it had been when I first saw it. I requested the new maid who admitted me, to tell Miss Wickfield that a gentleman who waited on her from a friend abroad, was there; and I was shown up the grave old staircase (cautioned of the steps I knew so well), into the unchanged drawing-room. The books that Agnes and I had read together, were on their shelves; and the desk where I had laboured at my lessons, many a night, stood yet at the same old corner of the table. All the little changes that had crept in when the Heeps were there, were changed again. Everything was as it used to be, in the happy time.
>
> I stood in a window, and looked across the ancient street at the opposite houses, recalling how I had watched them on wet afternoons . . . The feeling with which I used to watch the tramps, as they . . . limped past, with their bundles drooping over their shoulders at the ends of sticks, came freshly back to me; fraught, as then, with the smell of damp earth, and wet leaves and briar, and the sensation of the very airs that blew upon me in my own toilsome journey. (911)

The home that Agnes built, and has restored, equips David with sure and vital links between his present and his past. It is the reverse of Miss Havisham's Satis House; the latter a sepulchre of perished hopes, resentment, and living death, this a shrine and a haven for the mind in search of rootedness yet intent on growth. David registers change at the margins – the 'new maid' – but rediscovers and can centrally affirm that continuity in life which is essential to a secure identity. The 'staid old' house itself, its parts (the stairs he 'knew so well', the 'unchanged' drawing-room), and the objects it contains (books, desk and table) serve, like Peggotty's work-box and the Crocodile Book that make regular appearances right up to the last chapter, as reassuring constants by which David stabilizes and orients his existence. The threat of terminal dislocation of his progress, in the form of the Heeps' near-victorious bid to supplant him and usurp his story, is recalled only to be consigned to the annals of perils negotiated; though the demons cannot be forgotten, their defeat is confirmed by iteration, in the landscape of memory, of the erasure of the traces of their influence upon the territory they once occupied.[72]

The second of the two quoted paragraphs then underlines how vocation is an inextricable thread in the tapestry of continuity and change. Looking out upon the world from his window, as he had done when reading for very life as a child and later when 'speculat[ing] about the people who appeared' on wet afternoons (911), the David who revisits Canterbury is in line with his former incipiently creative self, including the wandering street-observer of Murdstone and Grinby days. And so is David the novelist-narrator, product and chronicler of the past, for he brings to life the very sensations that had come to him in those interrelated bygone times, when he had watched the tramps with their bundles and when he had been on his 'own toilsome journey'. Here the evocation of *The Pilgrim's Progress* is telling in a special way. The side-by-side images of common humanity with its burdens and the toiling boy who is David project with particular clarity the twin features of Dickensian scripture – writing the self and reading the human lot.

Of Agnes herself, once they are reunited, David says 'What she had always been to me, she still was; wholly unaltered' (931). Constancy is a major, if not the exclusive, quality of her character, displayed in her unwavering care for her ailing father – the performance of 'filial duty' which David so admires (915) – as well as in her loyalty towards David himself. There is, however, another sense in which she remains 'unaltered'. She is placed, from the start, in fixed roles. She first appears as Wickfield's 'little housekeeper, his daughter Agnes': 'She had a little basket-trifle hanging at her side, with keys in it; and she looked as staid and as discreet a housekeeper as the old house could have' (279–80). Years later the keys are still there. 'Even this . . . seems to jingle a kind of old tune!' she says to David shortly before he proposes (913). The point of this remark seems to be that Agnes wishes to remind the man she loves of their earlier happy times together. Nonetheless, the keys are the insignia of an office for which she is always destined – which she ineluctably *is*. Though David comes to view her in a changed light, as spouse rather than sister or friend, she already as a girl inhabits the position into which she must thus grow – not like Dora a 'child-wife', arrested in adolescence, but a woman before her time, a wifely child. And this situation of being marked out for certain functions vis-à-vis David obviously extends beyond the duties of housekeeper to those of monitor and counsellor, enacted respectively, for example, in her warning against Steerforth, his 'bad Angel', after his night of dissipation, and in the letter that rouses him from depression in Switzerland. That Agnes is conceived from David's viewpoint and for the sake of his well-being is brought out by the fact that her agency as the voice of discipline and support echoes the providential interventions, the cautions and leadings, of the religio-confessional discourse in which, to a significant extent, he casts his history.

The disciplined David tells Agnes, 'There is no alloy of self in what I feel for you' (935); and indeed we may contrast the relative give-and-take, the balance, of their relationship with the self-centredness of his passion for Dora, the all-consuming nature of which is interestingly flagged in his remark about their first meal together, 'I dined off Dora, entirely' (452). Yet, as we have seen, there is more of self in his dealings with Agnes than he knows, or cares to admit, in that he situates her according to his needs and authority. In doing this David channels and produces an ideology. In the contemporary context, that Agnes is located within the drama of David's mind makes her and the relations between the two not less but more effective as social and regulatory exempla, as standards to follow, because they are presented as lived experience and gain, a practical cornucopia, rather than as authorial (that is, Dickens's) ideas or beliefs.

In assessing the situation retrospectively, however, we cannot help but have mixed feelings. The ideology is, for want of other terms, gendered and patriarchal, though not entirely unprogressive. The catalogue of Agnes's attributes is at once a canon of cardinal virtues and an inventory of limitations. To her interrelated roles of dutiful daughter and faithful loving wife is added the profession of school-keeper, an office that emphatically extends the reach of her social standing and usefulness but whose circumscription lies in its being an extension of domestic and motherly roles. This is an advance for the middle-class woman, which is also to say, less positively, as good as it gets. It is decidedly more than is achieved by the other female characters in *David Copperfield*, who invariably throw into relief Agnes's eminence. Sophy, Traddles's 'dearest girl', who wonderfully 'manages' his home, which is also his workplace, with her 'punctuality, domestic knowledge, economy, and . . . cheerfulness' (919), comes near the mark; but what fits the well-meaning yet unfocussed Traddles will not quite do for the earnest and creative Copperfield, and where Sophy acts as her lawyer husband's copyist, Agnes teaches school and performs as David's advisor and muse. Martha, the prostitute, endorses the driven norm, which is in Agnes, by obscenely deviating from it and then vulgarly conforming to it, for she settles down happily ever after with a farm-labourer in the Australian Bush. With Emily, it is underpinned by a fate that is both encouragement and warning; although she never marries, she does take up a life of 'doing good', helping the sick and the needy – but only after she has assumed the marks of punishment and penance for her transgression, 'kiender worn, . . . a pritty head, leaning a little down; a quiet voice and way – timid a'most' (942). If we imagine Agnes as the centrepiece of the proverbial stained glass window, then the domesticated Martha and the meek Emily would be icons tucked somewhere in the corners, each with an inscription like 'Woman saved from sin – much improved'.

The ideological position centred in Agnes is reinforced thus by parallel and by contrast, by accounts of the right and the wrong, and of the aberrant reclaimed, or, in the case of 'dark, withered' Rosa Dartle, who is obsessed with Steerforth even beyond his death ('I loved him better than you ever did', she taunts his grieving mother (948)), insanely persisting. Upgrading Agnes involves downgrading and, even in her, circumscribing female identity. Yet, as always with Dickens, the last word must be that the ideology is vulnerable to subversion. That which is manifestly fashioned begs scrutiny – a construction waiting to be, in due course, deconstructed. More than this, however, the 'lives' through which it parasitically projects and legitimizes itself have it in them to answer back. When we think of Emily and Martha as transgressors restored it is difficult to avoid an uncomfortable sense of patriarchal overdetermination of 'normality', whether by David or Dickens. Rosa, on the other hand, though condemned to the paralysis of erotomania, at least retains the force of her sexuality, leaving a question about women's constitution.

Even a character as peripheral to the action as Mrs Gummidge raises awkward issues. To begin with, she seems simply a comic version of the man-sick woman, the 'lone lorn' widow pining for the 'old 'un' and dependent on the support of the good Mr Peggotty. When, on the way to Australia, she is made an offer of marriage by the ship's cook, she reacts by nearly killing her suitor with a bucket; but the reason for this can hardly be a continuing attachment to her long-lost spouse, for we learn from Mr Peggotty that 'thinking of the old 'un is a thing she never done' since she left England (943). Mrs Gummidge has changed, and the most plausible explanation of her physical assault on the unfortunate cook is that it is an assertion of independence; or the symptom of a desire for independence, since we also gather from Mr Peggotty that she is as reliant as ever on her place in his household, having become 'the willingest, the trewest, the honestest-helping woman'. Mr Peggotty's words mark him as the most thoroughgoing of patriarchs, taking a positive glee in the widow's new-found compliance to routine expectations of subservience and loyalty. But that is his view. Beneath the surface of her behaviour may lie something else, perhaps a resentment continuous with her assault upon her would-be second husband, perhaps a quiet satisfaction with her single state. Who can tell?

Most unsettling, however, is that Agnes herself exceeds the mould in which she is wrapped. She lets out clues to another story, another mode of being and of being understood. At one point we meet with a strangely uncharacteristic outburst, as, weeping bitterly, she works up a tirade of self-laceration: 'Oh, Trotwood! . . . I almost feel as if I had been papa's enemy, instead of his loving child.' She expresses horror at how much he has renounced in his devotion to her, 'and how his anxious thoughts of me have shadowed his life, and weakened his strength and energy'. If only she could make restitution for the harm she has done him: 'If I could ever set this right! If I could ever work out his restoration, as I have innocently been the cause of his decline!' (430). How are we to account for such guilt? Peter Gay, in a deft psychoanalytical move, points to the fact that, as Agnes had told David in the early days, her mother had died just after childbirth, and the daughter 'could not help reading her father's affection for her, then, as the severest of reproaches'.[73] Agnes blames herself for the death of her father's paragon of a wife, for his insatiable grief, and for her own very presence on which he is fixated at the expense of all other interests and his entire well-being.

We can interpret Wickfield's paternal fondness then as an involuntary sadism, and Agnes as having internalized (in Gay's word) a 'slander'. This reading is supported by Wickfield's later recantation, in which he concedes his neurosis and its deleterious effects: 'My natural grief for my child's mother turned to disease; my natural love for my child turned to disease. . . . I have brought misery on what I dearly love' (642). He emerges here as another figuring, like the mad gentleman who takes over David's room, of the dangers of psychic arrestment; but we have also a tale of patriarchal domination *in extremis*, of which David's imposition of roles upon Agnes is the milder, even benign, form, yet a form nonetheless. There is a case for seeing the apparently serene Agnes as oddly resembling Uriah Heep – that is, screwed up by familial pressures and social restrictions. On this reckoning, Gay convincingly accounts her goodness and her reserve, her patience and her fortitude, 'symptoms', 'defenses against an ever renewed inner hurt . . . [for] being very good was a way of denying that she was very bad'. Or should we rather celebrate them as evidence of the capacity of the human being for snatching stability, purpose and worth from the teeth of oppression and potential ruin? Either way, *David Copperfield* inscribes for Agnes a life other and more complex than that predicated on David's needs for a refuge, a best friend, a counsellor, a wifely attendant – and for the soothing radiance of a stained glass window. She claims an independent spot from which her own position and those of others can be evaluated.[74]

Again the Dickensian scripture puts into relief and under question its own ideological core, and insists that we perceive truth and values from various, sometimes conflicting, angles. I wish to return finally to another area of this multivalency – the theme of vocation, profession, and social mobility.

Rising Down Under

References to David's vocation come thick and fast as the novel draws to a close. Just before describing his excursion with Traddles to Creakle's new-model prison, for example, he talks about the self-sufficient life of the artist, with its 'delights, anxieties, and triumphs', and of his honest, passionate dedication: 'I truly devoted myself to it with my strongest earnestness, and bestowed upon it every energy of my soul' (917). This is authorship as profound and upright pursuit; and to these virtuous characteristics can be added the one Agnes has previously identified – the 'power of doing good' (915). Yet there is another way of looking at David's occupation, which Betsey introduces in response to her nephew's grateful sense that it has 'its own charms': ' "Ah! I see!" said my aunt. "Ambition, love of approbation, sympathy, and much more I suppose? Well: go along with you!" ' (932). This teasing evocation of worldly motives and self-regard (the 'sympathy' in question is, I take it, one which is being sought) David simply ignores. His reaction could be explained perhaps as that of an idealistic young man with no concept of pride or acquisitive ends. But the situation is, as we already know, more complex than that: the theme of the hero's calling in *David Copperfield* – his selfless cultivation of his gifts – posits a divide between value and the practical world that is both a context for deprecation of the business ethic and the idea of rising by merit and a mechanism for masking realities of hierarchy, authority and wealth in society. We have seen how, after the tour of Creakle's gaol, the novel's conservative ideology is simultaneously expressed and exposed to critique by David's extravagant condemnation of Uriah Heep's commitment to 'market value' and the 'business' of getting on (930), and how it is also contested from without by Uriah's dogged determination not to vacate tamely the field of running battle. The same undermining of the core emerges in Aunt Betsey's virtual charge of hypocrisy, and obliquely but no less tellingly in David's account, at the beginning of the penultimate chapter, of the good life he has come to enjoy:

> I had advanced in fame and fortune, my domestic joy was perfect, I had been married ten happy years. Agnes and I were sitting by the fire, in our house in London, one night in spring, and three of our children were playing in the room, when I was told that a stranger wished to see me. (939)

David's happiness has a threefold base: not only the joys of wedlock and domesticity but those of 'fame and fortune', standing and prosperity. To claim that the latter includes material success does not altogether depend on an emphatic reading of the word 'fortune', for we learn that the Copperfields now have a London residence, either in addition to or instead of the house in Canterbury, which we might have expected the unaffected couple could never have faced leaving. The Copperfields' rise in the world and their right to the other rewards of David's labours are taken for granted. Indeed, their affluence is not seen as worldly or laboured for at all, but rather as the benefaction of minor providential power – 'fame and fortune'. While in this the hard facts of gain and possession are glossed over and made innocent by the generalizing terminology, so is *David's* getting on credited with the form of a positive 'advance'. Though he paints the idyllic picture in good faith, there is at bottom, and in the light of the novel's antagonism towards procurement in the field of well-being, more than a hint of the disingenuous about it.

Downgrading of business and the commercial spirit pervades *David Copperfield*, albeit less overtly than elsewhere in Dickens. Mr Omer the undertaker and Mr Chillip the doctor are exceptional and come off well, not only because of their kindly and cheerful dispositions but because they deal with the body in aspects of its natural condition and requirements. Miss Mowcher's hairdressing and manicuring circuit, on the other hand, becomes, like Uriah Heep's apprenticeship, a setting for shady dealing in the lives and problems of others; her dwarfish stature and trading in false appearances match the deformity of her prying and spying in search of female prey for Steerforth and his like – until, that is, Dickens was obliged to turn the portrait around under threat of legal action by the 'original', Mrs Jane Seymour.[75] Murdstone and Grinby's warehouse is the scene of the most soul-destroying experiences; and Murdstone himself is all the more disreputable for carrying the profit principle into the very heart of relationships, being on the prowl for marriageable 'money' as well as 'beauty' (539). Duplicity exists even in the professions; for Mr Spenlow, who it is that thus underscores Murdstone's reputation for venality, uses the fiction of his partner

Jorkins's ferocity to deceive anyone making a call on his own financial, or even human, resources.

At one point, in David's closing report on the fate of Dora's old friend, Julia Mills, even colonialism comes into view. About this form of cut-throat economic activity, however, Dickens appears to have no real qualms. The concern is neither with opportunity nor opportunism, or with issues of imperial expansion, or questions of morality, but with lifestyle, the luxury and excess which have arisen from Julia's husband's success in the Indian trade. The 'black man' that carries cards and letters to Julia on a golden salver back in England and the 'copper-coloured woman' that serves her tiffin are neither happy nor ill-gotten gains, neither lucky captives nor oppressed victims; they are simply trappings that go with the vulgar display of Julia's stately home and sumptuous dinners. Disliking how she is 'steeped in money to the throat', Dickens's hero preferred her when she was poor – metaphorically in the 'Desert of Sahara'. He seems to have forgotten how much *he* hated indigence and life at the bottom of the pile; but we are left, all the same, with the impression, not that poverty is a noble thing, but that affluence gathered from overseas is, like David's and Agnes's from a different source, allowable so long as it is not flaunted. It is never wealth *per se* that is under question, but how and by whom it is acquired, and how it is 'worn'. The fault of Julia and her spouse is not that they have a fortune, but that it, and their habits of consumption, are overly visible and unsatisfactorily managed.

The subtlest indictment of the ideology of business and upwards mobility in *David Copperfield* is in the treatment of Mr Micawber. In him it is not condemned but made fun of. A man of 'talent' eager for the 'battle of the world', he has plans for going into various lines – coal, corn, brewing, banking – none of which get off the ground (478). He is forever waiting, laughably, for something to 'turn up', a loud take-off of the figure of the driven go-getter like Uriah Heep who makes it secret policy to twist every opening ruthlessly to advantage.[76] When Micawber does find a position which, as Mrs Micawber puts it, gives promise of a 'rise . . . to the top of the tree', 'a commanding station' (595–6), his expectations are as fantastical as ever, for the ladder of preferment on which he has stepped is none other than that of Heep's partnership with Wickfield, the toppling of which he will in due course be instrumental in bringing about. Heep and Micawber share the fate of getting nowhere at a steady pace, misguided dreamers unable to literalize their hopes of self-advancement;[77] but whereas the former is a threat to the established social order and has to be checked, the latter is a lovable rogue who ultimately serves the status quo. Even then, however, the conservative

Dickens does enter firm measures against Micawber as required, by putting him in gaol when he transgresses too far his own wonderfully sound theory of socio-economic conduct – 'Annual income twenty pounds, annual expenditure nineteen and six, result happiness' (231). It is as irresponsible to flout the rules of exchange value as to court the anarchy of meritocratic free enterprise; bills have to be paid. Dickens disowns but cannot ignore *homo economicus*; this troublesome figure, especially in the form of the upstart, whether menace like Heep or feckless irritant like Micawber, must be constantly kept in its place.

Yet, granted a last-minute reprieve, Micawber is after all transformed into a positive model of honest endeavour and rising talent. He can look back, in the penultimate chapter, on a 'successful career', has reached a position from which 'bettering himself' hardly seems possible, and is a pillar of the community, 'the ornament of our town' (944). He has even become a magistrate. There are three points to be made here, however. Firstly, all of this happens in Australia. It is acceptable for Julia Mills's husband to exploit the situation in India, but his nabob mentality then only puts a blot on the English landscape. Better for the expatriate to build abroad. The mobility that would unsettle structures of authority and class in England can have a welcome pay-off in a virgin colony on the far side of the 'ocean of enterprise' (840), where it operates to replicate, but does not touch, the existing order in the old country. Secondly, Dickens uses the twist in the tale of Micawber to reinforce the book's central values of dutiful hard work and upright good behaviour. When first considering emigration, Mrs Micawber asks Aunt Betsey if circumstances in the antipodes are such as to provide a man of her husband's abilities with 'a fair chance of rising in the social scale' and 'a reasonable opening for his talents to develop themselves' (833). To this Betsey replies, 'No better opening anywhere . . . for a man who conducts himself well, and is industrious'; and so Australia will provide for Micawber 'a legitimate sphere of action'. 'Fair', 'reasonable', 'legitimate': the words validate and make exemplary the brief history which takes Micawber from hard labour in the Bush, 'bald head . . . perspiring in the sun' (944), to the respected heights of Port Middlebay middle-class society, and which in fact reiterates the 'golden rules' of David's own success, built as that was on 'steady, plain, hard-working qualities'. That David and Micawber both end up as writers is another interesting repetition; but this brings us to the third item, which is that, whatever the parallels, a distinct hierarchy is nonetheless preserved, with on the one hand the famous humanist English author and on the other the émigré newspaper correspondent, who actually contributes a piece in the *Port Middlebay Times* in praise of his old friend's 'Eagle course' and the 'delight', 'entertainment' and 'instruction' he disseminates far and wide (945). There is in this the affirmation of national precedence as well as that of imaginative literature over journalism. From the distant bounds of empire comes tribute to the intellectual and moral leadership of the motherland, of which the novel *David Copperfield* is a conduit.

When all is said, however, this episode too gives mixed signals. In cloning the social structures of England – and Mr, now Dr, Mell, for example, is also there, with a large family and apparently running Colonial Salem-House Grammar School – Australia puts itself in a position to shift, sometime in the future, from a relationship of sub-servience to one of equality or rivalry, even ascendancy. By chron-icling the dynamism and aspirations of the immigrants, seeing the seeds of a vigorous new nation rather than the detritus of an overblown penal colony, Dickens aids that process which we have come to think of as the empire striking back.[78] Moreover, one of the energies he registers is a certain adeptness at subterfuge, for it dawns on us that the anonymous article in the *Port Middlebay Times* celebrating the qualities and achievements of Wilkins Micawber, his family, and his associates is by Wilkins Micawber himself. Perhaps Micawber's new-found straightness is more apparent than real, and he is, with a warier tread than the manifestly reprobate Uriah Heep ever mastered, carving a route for his self-interest, putting a spin on things, weaving a political spell. David Copperfield is not the only one to author himself in the service of power. Virtue, frankness, loyalty may be everyman's declared standard – including Heep's – but the real world is by and large a battlefield of dishonest forces vying for supremacy. This message, which in *David Copperfield* is mostly present as an undercurrent, becomes alarmingly clear in *Great Expectations*.

Notes

1. Charles Dickens, *The Haunted Man*, in *The Christmas Books*, Vol. 2, ed. Michael Slater (Harmondsworth: Penguin Books, 1971; repr. 1985), p. 246. References throughout are to this edition; hereafter cited in the text. For *David Copperfield* all references are to Charles Dickens, *The Personal History of David Copperfield*, ed. Trevor Blount (Harmondsworth: Penguin Books, 1966; repr. 1985).
2. Wordsworth, 'Immortality Ode', ll. 12–18, in *Poetical Works*, ed. Ernest de Selincourt and Helen Darbishire (Oxford: Clarendon Press, 2nd edn 1952–54), IV, 278; Coleridge, 'Dejection: an Ode', ll. 33–8, in *The Portable Coleridge*, ed. I.A. Richards (New York: Viking Press, 1950), p. 170.
3. 'Immortality Ode', l. 74; 'Dejection: an Ode', l. 86.
4. 'Dejection', l. 89. See also Wordsworth's celebrated opposition between 'the

lore which Nature brings' and the 'meddling intellect' which 'Mis-shapes the beauteous forms of things: – / We murder to dissect': 'The Tables Turned', ll. 25–8, *Poetical Works*, IV, 57.

5. Barry Westburg, *The Confessional Fictions of Charles Dickens* (Dekalb: Northern Illinois University Press, 1977), p. 58. I am indebted to this fine study for drawing my attention to the importance of the theme of memory in *The Haunted Man* and to connections with *David Copperfield*.

6. Thomas De Quincey, 'Suspira de Profundis', *Blackwood's Edinburgh Magazine*, 57 (June 1845), 742–3. For the relevant ideas in Herbert Spencer and his contemporaries, see the commentary and collection of documents in *Embodied Selves: An Anthology of Psychological Texts 1830–1890*, ed. Jenny Bourne Taylor and Sally Shuttleworth (Oxford: Clarendon Press, 1998), especially pp. 68–9, 72, and (which reprint sections of Spencer's *Principles of Psychology* (1855)) 83–7, 157–60.

7. Wordsworth, *The Prelude* 1805, I. 437–41; ed. Ernest de Selincourt and Helen Darbishire (Oxford: Clarendon Press, 2nd edn 1959), p. 26. *The Prelude* did not appear until the same year as the one-volume *David Copperfield*, 1850; but the present lines had been published separately on several previous occasions, including the 1815 edition of *Poems*. See also note 60 below.

8. Frances Power Cobbe, 'The Fallacies of Memory', *Hours of Work and Play* (London: N. Trübner & Co., 1867), p. 103. This essay had first come out in the American periodical the *Galaxy* in May 1866. Cobbe's emphasis on memory as construction rather than simple recognition was taken up in particular by William Benjamin Carpenter, who, when considering recollection as the basis of our sense of 'personal identity', observes:

> Though we are accustomed to speak of memory as if it consisted in an *exact* reproduction of past states of Consciousness, yet experience is continually showing us that this reproduction is very often *inexact*, through the modification which the 'trace' has undergone in the interval. Sometimes the trace has been partially obliterated; and what remains may serve to give a very erroneous (because imperfect) view of the occurrence. And where it is one in which our own Feelings are interested, we are extremely apt to lose sight of what goes against them, so that the representation given by Memory is altogether one-sided. (*Principles of Mental Physiology* (1874), 2nd edn (London: Henry S. King, 1875); repr. in Taylor and Shuttleworth, pp. 154–7 (pp. 156–7))

9. Westburg, *Confessional Fictions*, p. xiii.

10. Julian Jaynes, *The Origin of Consciousness in the Breakdown of the Bicameral Mind* (Harmondsworth: Allen Lane, The Penguin Press, 1979; rev. edn 1993), p. 458.

11. Forbes Benignus Winslow, *On Obscure Diseases of the Brain and Disorders of the Mind* (1860), 4th edn (London: John Churchill, 1868), p. 277.

12. Lawrence Frank, *Charles Dickens and the Romantic Self* (Lincoln, NE.: University of Nebraska Press, 1984), pp. 78–9.

13. The title of Book VIII of Wordsworth's poem.

14. John Lucas, *Charles Dickens: The Major Novels* (Harmondsworth: Penguin Books, 1992), p. 57.

15. Martha C. Nussbaum, 'Steerforth's Arm: Love and the Moral Point of View', *Love's Knowledge: Essays on Philosophy and Literature* (New York: Oxford University Press, 1990), pp. 335–64 (p. 354).

16. Wordsworth, *The Prelude* 1805, I. 305–306.

17. George Orwell talks of the 'woolly vagueness' of Dickens's description of Dr Strong's school, which shows the novelist's 'utter lack of any educational theory'; Strong's is 'simply Salem House with the vices left out and a good deal of "old grey stones" atmosphere thrown in': Dickens 'can imagine the moral atmosphere of a good school, but nothing more' ('Charles Dickens', *'Decline of the English Murder' and Other Essays* (Harmondsworth: Penguin Books, 1965), p. 96). On the contrary, Dickens depicts and sanctions a specific programme of inculcation and training that serves definite purposes in perpetuating social power. The writing is not, as Orwell believes (p. 97), void of precise 'political doctrine'.

18. In 'Steerforth's Arm' Martha Nussbaum summarizes the cons and then mounts a scintillating case for seeing Steerforth in a positive light. The weight of numbers lies still, however, with Steerforth's detractors, where John Lucas, who views him as a dangerous 'class snob' (*Charles Dickens*, p. 51), supplies a committed representative.

19. In addition to the extended discussion in Nussbaum, the erotic charge of the David–Steerforth relationship is given incisive consideration by D.A. Miller, *The Novel and the Police* (Berkeley, CA: University of California Press, 1988), pp. 188–99.

   Linda M. Shires, 'Literary Careers, Death, and the Body Politics of *David Copperfield*', in *Dickens Refigured*, ed. John Schad (Manchester: Manchester University Press, 1996), pp. 117–35, comments on the way both Steerforth and Uriah Heep are 'implicated with David in homo-eroticism' (p. 132). Eve Kosofsky Sedgwick, though she can be no less stimulating than Nussbaum, sacrifices the depth of this particular Dickens text to her schematic interest in the narrative of male socialization when stating that 'David's infatuation with his friend . . . is *simply* part of David's education': 'Homophobia, Misogyny, and Capital: The Example of *Our Mutual Friend*', in *Charles Dickens*, ed. Steven Connor (London: Longman, 1996), pp. 178–96 (p. 192: italics mine); repr. from Sedgwick, *Between Men: English Literature and Male Homosocial Desire* (New York: Columbia University Press, 1985), pp. 163–79.

20. Nussbaum, pp. 356–7.

21. For the satanic features of Steerforth and other characters in Dickens, see my 'Dickensian Decadents', in *Romancing Decay: Ideas of Decadence in European Culture*, ed. Michael St John (Aldershot: Ashgate, 1999), pp. 64–82.

22. 'The Adventure', in *Georg Simmel, 1858–1918: A Collection of Essays, with Translations and a Bibliography*, ed. Kurt H. Wolff (Columbus, OH: Ohio State University Press, 1959), pp. 243–58 (p. 243); translated by David Kettler from 'Das Abenteuer', *Philosophische Kultur: Gesammelte Essays* (1911), 2nd edn (Leipzig: Alfred Kröner, 1919).

23. Simmel, pp. 245, 249–50.

24. Compare the imagery of reckless 'riding' at the beginning of canto III of *Childe Harold's Pilgrimage* (Lord Byron, *Complete Poetical Works*, ed. Jerome J. McGann, 7 vols (Oxford: Clarendon Press, 1980–93), II, 77):

> And the waves bound beneath me as a steed
> That knows his rider. Welcome, to their roar!
> Swift be their guidance, wheresoe'er it lead! . . .
> Still must I on; for I am as a weed,
> Flung from the rock, on Ocean's foam, to sail
> Where'er the surge may sweep, or tempest's breath prevail.
>
> (stanza 2)

The association with ocean storm – the force which finally engulfs Steerforth – further connects Dickens's character with the Byronic hero.

25. Simmel, pp. 249–50.
26. Simmel, p. 245.
27. Simmel, pp. 249, 254–5.
28. Lucas, *Charles Dickens*, p. 57.
29. See *David Copperfield*, ed. Blount, pp. 155, 529.
30. For further examples, see *David Copperfield*, pp. 311, 312, 436, 437, 637.
31. William Acton, *The Function and Disorders of the Reproductive Organs in Childhood, Youth, Adult Age, and Advanced Life Considered in their Physiological, Social and Moral Relations* (1847), 4th edn (London: John Churchill, 1865); repr. in Taylor and Shuttleworth, pp. 209–14 (pp. 211, 213). Acton is quoting from Claude François Lallemand, *A Practical Treatise on the Causes, Symptoms, and Treatment of Spermatorrhoea*, trans. and ed. Henry J. McDougall (1847). Lallemand's work was first published in France, 1836–42.
32. See Acton, in Taylor and Shuttleworth, pp. 212–14. George Drysdale, in *Elements of Social Science, or, Physical, Sexual and Natural Religion* (1854), though a maverick figure in arguing openly for the benefits of sexual intercourse outside marriage, was clear about the evils of excessive activity and of self-abuse, the latter of which he conceived as afflicting all levels of society and as a problem of utmost public concern:

> I come now to consider one of the most serious and frequent causes of disease in youth; one which ruins more constitutions than enters into the conceptions of the uninstructed. Its evil effects . . . are found in all ranks of society; and there are few rocks, on which the health of more individuals is wrecked. The unfortunate habit . . . grows on the young man, and if he be not diverted from it, may gradually master his powers of mind and become irresistible. . . . Were [natural sexual expression] readily available without the danger of disease and the degradation of illicit intercourse, masturbation would rarely if ever be resorted to, and one of the most fearful and prevalent causes of disease, moral and physical, eradicated. (13th edn (London: Truelove, 1873); repr. in Taylor and Shuttleworth, pp. 217–22 (pp. 221–2))

Drysdale's plea for the introduction of a programme of sex education and permissiveness among the young proposes in practice, of course, not less but more regulation.

33. Acton, in Taylor and Shuttleworth, p. 211. See also Drysdale: 'The . . . habit of solitary indulgence or masturbation, is frequently contracted at schools

or elsewhere, and often adopted more out of sport or ignorance of the consequences it may lead to, than from any more serious purpose' (Taylor and Shuttleworth, p. 221).

34. T.H. Huxley, *Evolution and Ethics* (London: Macmillan, 1893), p. 33.

35. Charles Turner Thackrah, *The Effects of Arts, Trades and Professions, and of Civic States and Habits of Living: With Suggestions for Removal of Many of the Agents which Produce Disease, and Shorten the Duration of Life* (1831), 2nd edn (London: Longman, 1832); repr. in Taylor and Shuttleworth, pp. 293–4 (p. 294). Henry Maudsley, *The Physiology and Pathology of Mind* (London: Macmillan, 1867); repr. in Taylor and Shuttleworth, pp. 297–300 (pp. 299–300).

36. The same ideals are set out in William Cowper's *The Task* (1785), the popular voice of strict Evangelical tradition and a poem very widely read in the nineteenth century. The manifesto of the contemplative man whose 'warfare is within' at the end of Book VI (lines 906–1024) is especially relevant to David's emphasis upon 'the war within his breast' (672), though even Cowper the recluse is keen, like David, to claim that he has a useful place in the world, if no 'public praise', because he sets a 'fair example'.

37. The present chapter of *David Copperfield* extends Dickens's satiric attack on the Separate System of solitary confinement in use at the new, purpose-built Pentonville Prison, which attracted his scathing attention in the leading article 'Pet Prisoners' in *Household Words*, 27 April 1850 (repr. in *Dickens' Journalism, Volume II: 'The Amusements of the People' and Other Papers: 1834–51*, ed. Michael Slater (London: J.M. Dent, 1996), pp. 215–27). In this piece he concentrates on contrasting the comfortable lodgings of the prisoners with the hardships of the honest poor at home or in workhouses, and on the way the prisoners were encouraged to profess moral and spiritual reformation.

38. For the seminal account of this theme in *David Copperfield*, see Miller, *The Novel and the Police*, pp. 217–20 especially.

39. Raymond Williams, *The Country and the City* (St Albans: Paladin Books, 1973), p. 84.

40. Audrey Jaffe, *Vanishing Points: Dickens, Narrative, and the Subject of Omniscience* (Berkeley, CA: University of California Press, 1991), p. 127.

41. Mark Spilka, '*David Copperfield* as Psychological Fiction', *Critical Quarterly*, 1 (1959), 292.

42. Felicity Hughes makes this point but gives no examples: see her 'Narrative Complexity in *David Copperfield*', *English Literary History*, 41 (1974), 89–105 (p. 102). Perhaps she is thinking simply of David's preoccupation with both characters' outstretched bodies. There is a stranger configuration, however, when, soon after meeting Uriah, David dreams of him launching Mr Peggotty's house under a black ensign and carrying off little Em'ly and himself to the Spanish Main, to be drowned (293). We may read this as a vague premonition of the disaster that will befall the Peggottys' happy home, which happens at the hands, not of Heep, but of Steerforth, who metaphorically drowns Em'ly and literally dies at sea. Yet the account is of course retrospective, and can therefore be seen as David's deep-level displacing of the refined villainy of the friend whom he loved with the blatant piratical offensiveness of his diabolical enemy. For certain, these two men share a hold on David's imagination much stronger than any exercised by Agnes or even Dora.

43. Stanley Friedman, 'Dickens' Mid-Victorian Theodicy: *David Copperfield*', *Dickens Studies Annual*, 7 (1977), 128–50 (pp. 137–8). Felicity Hughes (pp. 103–105) sees the same passage as a reflection of Dickens's interest in mesmerism, thus underlining the theme of compulsion, or the loss of freedom of will; but Friedman's emphasis on psychological determinism takes us farther.

44. Sigmund Freud, 'Creative Writers and Day-Dreaming' (1908), in *Freud: Art and Literature*, ed. Albert Dickson, Pelican Freud Library, Vol. XIV (Harmondsworth: Penguin Books, 1985), p. 138.

45. Freud, 'The "Uncanny"' (1919), *Freud: Art and Literature*, ed. Dickson, p. 357.

46. See especially Friedman, 'Dickens' Mid-Victorian Theodicy', passim; also William J. Palmer, *Dickens and the New Historicism* (Basingstoke: Macmillan, 1997), pp. 70–81, which offers an account of shipwrecks in *David Copperfield* as metaphors for the apocalyptic forces of nature, history and fate.

47. See Friedman, pp. 143, 146–9.

48. The classic account of this theme is Gwendolyn Needham, 'The Undisciplined Heart of David Copperfield', *Nineteenth-Century Fiction*, 9 (1954), 81–107.

49. Thus Bunyan longs for respite from the relentless tug of war between the conflicting texts that have entered his mind:

> And I remember one day, as I was in diverse frames of Spirit, and considering that these frames were still according to the nature of the several Scriptures that came into my mind; if this of grace, then I was quiet; but if this of *Esau*, then tormented. Lord, thought I, if both these Scriptures would meet in my heart at once, I wonder which of them would get the better of me. . . . Well, so they did indeed; they boulted both upon me at a time, and did work and struggle strangely in me for a while; at last, that about *Esau's* birthright began to wax weak, and withdraw, and vanish; and this about the sufficiency of Grace prevailed. (*Grace Abounding to the Chief of Sinners*, ed. Roger Sharrock (London: Oxford University Press, 1966), pp. 68–9)

50. See Ernest Jones, *The Life and Works of Sigmund Freud*, ed. and abridged by Lionel Trilling and Steven Marcus (Harmondsworth: Penguin Books, 1964), p. 166.

51. *Grace Abounding*, pp. 58–61 (pp. 60–61).

52. Philip Davis, *Memory and Writing from Wordsworth to Lawrence* (Liverpool: Liverpool University Press, 1983), p. 197.

53. Davis, p. 196; quoting from *The Works of Thomas Hood*, edited by his son and daughter, 11 vols (London, 1882–4), IX, 103.

54. *Memorials of Thomas Hood*, edited by his daughter, 2 vols (London, 1860), II, 41.

55. Jaffe, *Vanishing Points*, pp. 112–28 (p. 119).

56. I draw here upon the description of the life-path of the archetypal hero by Joseph Campbell in *The Hero with a Thousand Faces* (1949; 2nd edn, Princeton, NJ: Princeton University Press, 1968). The Murdstone and Grinby episode is an early 'rites of passage' and learning experience, while

the period abroad conforms to the pattern of the more mature stage of isolation, adventure, self-examination, and return, followed by fame and the exercise of new-found power to bestow benefits on one's fellow human beings. Campbell says emphatically of the hero's journey, for example, that 'fundamentally it is inward – into the depths where obscure resistances are overcome, and long lost, forgotten powers are revivified, to be made available for the transformation of the world' (p. 29). A succinct résumé of Campbell's exposition of the myth is given, in relation to another nineteenth-century writer, in Frank J. Sulloway, *Freud, Biologist of the Mind: Beyond the Psychoanalytic Legend* (1979; London: Fontana Paperbacks, 1980), pp. 446–8.

57. See Sulloway, p. 447.

58. Friedman (p. 143) notes the emphasis in both *Robinson Crusoe* and *David Copperfield* on 'the need for self-help and the importance of providential care', and on 'the idea of the ultimate value of adversity', quoting Crusoe's exclamation, 'How mercifully can our great Creator treat his Creatures, even in those Conditions in which they seem'd to be overwhelm'd in Destruction. How can he sweeten the bitterest Providences, and give us Cause to praise him for Dungeons and Prisons' (citing Daniel Defoe, *Robinson Crusoe*, ed. Michael Shinagel (New York: W.W. Norton, 1975), p. 116). But these are basic commonplaces of the tradition of Puritan spiritual autobiography.

59. Byron, *Childe Harold's Pilgrimage*, III, stanzas 10, 12–13 (quoted). David talks of the 'wound' with which he has to strive, of 'a ruined blank and waste' lying around him, and of moving 'restlessly from place to place' (885–7), while Byron's 'self-exiled' hero is 'Wrung with the wounds which kill not', is 'Restless and worn', and leaves 'a sterile track' behind (stanzas 16, 8, 15, 3).

60. *The Prelude* was published in July 1850; the eighteen monthly parts of *David Copperfield* appeared from 1 May 1849 to 1 November 1850. Chapter 58, 'Absence', was mostly written in October (see *David Copperfield*, ed. Nina Burgis (Oxford: Clarendon Press, 1981), p. xlix), and could therefore have been directly influenced by Wordsworth's poem.

61. *Childe Harold*, III, stanza 114.

62. Thus *The Prelude* 1805, VIII. 586–8; but the 1850 version takes the same tack, with the poet telling how he came to settle creatively on the subject of 'human passions' (VIII. 423–6).

63. *Prelude* 1850, XI. 333–48, XIV. 232–66, XIV. 218–31.

64. *Prelude* 1850, XI. 334.

65. Interestingly, Wordsworth anticipated Dickens in thus valorizing the matrimonial union, for in the major revisions of *The Prelude* during the period 1816–19 he introduced a tribute to his wife alongside that to his sister (1850, XIV. 266–75). Wordsworth's praises – 'inmate of the heart' yet also 'spirit' and 'essence of pervading light' – offer exactly the combination of earthly–emotional and ethereal–moral qualities developed by Dickens in David's Agnes.

66. Orwell, 'Charles Dickens', p. 139. More recently, Michael Slater incants a litany of common criticisms, from 'nullity' to 'religious ikon, an inert figure', and concludes that 'the disastrously *voulu* nature of the presentation of Agnes remains a rock ahead, even for the most ardent Dickensians': see *Dickens and Women* (London: J.M. Dent, 1983), pp. 100, 161, 250–53, 372.

67. Robert R. Garnett, 'Why Not Sophy? Desire and Agnes in *David Copperfield*', *Dickens Quarterly*, 14 (1997), 212–31 (p. 215).

68. Regularly so in Jane Austen's love-relationships, for example. Elizabeth Bennet in *Pride and Prejudice* is much prone to this language of the body, as is noted by Tony Tanner in his introduction to the novel, where we are reminded that Norman O. Brown, following Freud, views blushing as 'a sort of mild erection of the head' (*Pride and Prejudice*, ed. Tony Tanner (Harmondsworth: Penguin Books, 1972; repr. 1985), p. 35).

69. Slater, *Dickens and Women*, p. 251.

70. Simmel, p. 254.

71. See, for instance, Bunyan's exulting at the promise of his salvation in *Grace Abounding*, which happened as he was 'passing in the field' (ed. Sharrock, p. 74). The miraculous confirmation of Wordsworth's calling as Poet, itself a reframing of orthodox conversion experience, takes place in 'open field', where, with 'heart . . . full', 'vows . . . made', 'bond . . . given', he walks on in 'thankful blessedness' (*Prelude* 1850, IV. 320–38).

72. This is exactly the case in the relation between the guided tour of the Second Part of *The Pilgrim's Progress* and the life-and-death struggle of the First Part.

73. Peter Gay, *The Bourgeois Experience, Victoria to Freud: Volume IV: The Naked Heart* (London: HarperCollins, 1996), pp. 274–5.

74. It is in chapter 16 that Agnes tells David, 'Mama has been dead ever since I was born' (286). There come at the same time other telling clues to the nature of the relationship between father and daughter. Agnes has her mother's looks, as we learn from a portrait on the wall, and her father is so 'fond' of her that he couldn't 'spare [her] to go anywhere else'; but since Agnes is the one who offers these pieces of information, it is clear that, consciously or unconsciously, she co-operates in playing, even perhaps constructs, her substitute role. Her position as at least co-author of the continuing Wickfield familial drama is further suggested when, on the same occasion, she names herself by function in remarking that 'His housekeeper must be in his house, you know'. In thus assuming a non-personal identity Agnes is at once subject to external controls, which she has interiorized, and exercising a self-saving control by mentally organizing the situation around her and her place in it. This is a special case of a condition shared, not only manifestly by David and Uriah, but in some measure by most of the characters of *David Copperfield*.

75. For the circumstances of this revision, see Blount, Introduction to *David Copperfield*, pp. 22–3.

76. We may take Micawber's speech in chapter 27:

> 'You find us, Copperfield,' said Mr Micawber, with one eye on Traddles, 'at present established, on what may be designated a small and unassuming scale; but you are aware that I have, in the course of my career, surmounted difficulties, and conquered obstacles. You are no stranger to the fact, that there have been periods of my life, when it has been requisite that I should pause, until certain expected events should turn up; when it has been necessary that I should fall back, before making what I trust I shall not be accused of presumption in terming – a spring. The present is one of those momentous stages in the life

of man. You find me, fallen back, *for* a spring; and I have every reason to believe that a vigorous leap will shortly be the result.' (468–9)

The reference to surmounting difficulties and conquering obstacles shows Micawber's outlook as a comic expression of David's own creed of endeavour – a carnivalesque mirroring that enforces the authority of the official ideology. Micawber is like a music-hall comedian (a quality not lost on W.C. Fields in the famous David O. Selznick film adaptation) doing a loud take-off of an aspect of the hero himself, which, by contrast, underlines the genuineness of the latter's own 'career' and the authenticity of his high status, while also keeping the very facts of this 'career' and status out of view, helping to render them something taken for granted. David and Traddles are an audience who laugh at and stand comfortably above and beyond the idea of seizing the moment in the service of self-advancement, though both are at bottom engaged in such a project through the professions of writing and the law. These effects, of course, are one with the force of Micawber as a portrait generally satirizing the manifest form that this project takes in Uriah Heep. In relation to the book's defence of an established order, Micawber and Heep are both 'grotesques', the one benignly incompetent at making inroads, the other villainously proficient. As I argue later, however, at the end of the novel Micawber emerges as the greater threat to the superiority vested in David, because his challenge is more politically adept and strategically positioned, and itself an undeclared opposition.

77. A classic instance of desire realized comes in Robinson Crusoe's fulfilment of the wildest dreams of possession, power and status:

> My island was now peopled, and I thought myself very rich in subjects; and it was a merry reflection, which I frequently made, how like a king I looked. First of all, the whole country was my own mere property, so that I had an undoubted right of dominion. Secondly, my people were perfectly subjected. I was absolute lord and lawgiver; they all owed their lives to me, and were ready to lay down their lives, if there had been occasion of it, for me. (Daniel Defoe, *Robinson Crusoe*, ed. Harvey Swados (New York: New American Library, 1961), p. 236)

The ambitions of a Heep or a Micawber are comparatively modest, but in the same progressive tradition as those of Defoe's hero.

78. Dickens in fact thought a fair amount about Australia, as a land both of drawbacks and of promise, and once had a slight idea of going to settle there. It is a place of redemption and maturation (for prostitutes and for convicts, as well as the Micawbers of this world who need a jolt) – but also, as Magwitch puts it in spite of growing rich there, 'flat'. See *The Oxford Reader's Companion to Dickens*, ed. Paul Schlicke (Oxford: Oxford University Press, 1999), pp. 26–7.

CHAPTER FIVE

Great Expectations

Pip Pirrip's Gospel for Modern Man

In a secluded spot in the garden of Satis House, during his second visit to Miss Havisham, Pip has a fight with Herbert Pocket. The contest provides an occasion for the portrayal of erotic contact and exchange, both hetero- and homo-sexual.[1] Pip's reward for winning is the opportunity to kiss Estella, the unseen observer, whose evident arousal complicates her image as the proverbial ice-maiden, for 'there was a bright flush upon her face, as though something had happened to delight her . . . [and] she stepped back into the passage, and beckoned me. "Come here"' (93).[2] The sensory charge of the male–male encounter is also strong. Stripping plays a part, as Herbert undresses for combat, 'pulling off, not only his jacket and waistcoat, but his shirt too' (91–2). Yet this formal routine, which is described as 'light-hearted, business-like, and bloodthirsty', is perhaps less of a tease than Pip's uneasy preoccupation with particulars of his antagonist's physique: 'Although he did not look very healthy – having pimples on his face, and a break-ing out at his mouth – these dreadful preparations quite appalled me. . . . [He] was a young gentleman in a grey suit (when not denuded for battle), with his elbows, knees, wrists, and heels, considerably in advance of the rest of him as to development.' This fascination with the repulsive and ungainly, the mixture of disgust and enthralment, recalls David's curious attachment to Uriah Heep.

Pip goes so far as to imagine Herbert sizing him up in return, and as having a somewhat suspect motive, 'eyeing my anatomy as if he were minutely choosing his bone'. My concern here, however, is not so much with the homoeroticism in Dickens's fiction as with his relation to a larger subject of which this theme is an element – the ethos of the public school. When Herbert challenges Pip to 'Come and fight' he acts like one who has been reading *Tom Brown's Schooldays*, or who attends an institution like Dr Arnold's Rugby. Herbert in fact is never named in this part of *Great Expectations*, but appears only, and repeatedly, as the 'pale young gentleman'. He is depicted as 'inky' and having been 'at his books', and is placed among 'the studious youth of England' (90, 93). Thomas Hughes's fictionalized account of Arnold's character-building system, published in 1857, just three years before Dickens's novel, devotes a long chapter to 'The Fight' between Brown and Williams, where we meet the same rituals and appendages as those foregrounded in Dickens's scene – choosing the ground, sponge and water, throwing up the former in defeat, stripping off (in Hughes's description) 'jacket, waistcoat, and braces, . . . thirsting for the fray'.[3] Tom keeps his shirt on, but (in spite of a flat denial by the book's latest editor)[4] there is ample occasion for the thrill of looking and touching: the close physical detail, including Williams being 'feeblish' 'down below' and Tom 'good all over, straight, hard, and springy'; the friend's 'tremble' of 'excitement' when Tom sits on his knee between rounds (*Tom Brown's Schooldays*, 290–91). In the absence of anyone else, Herbert seconds both himself and Pip. Although the Queensbury Rules in boxing were not formulated until 1867, conventions are already firmly in place in Tom Brown's sporting world, and Herbert in his turn is a stickler for them: ' "Laws of the game!" said he. Here, he skipped from his left leg on to his right. "Regular rules!" Here, he skipped from his right leg on to his left. "Come to the ground, and go through the preliminaries!" Here, he dodged backwards and forwards, and did all sorts of things while I looked helplessly at him' (91).

At the end of the chapter on 'The Fight' Hughes makes his didactic point. Fighting, if it is regulated, improves body and mind; there is no exercise 'so good for the temper and for the muscles' (*TBS*, 301), where 'temper' suggests powers of judgement as well as resilience and determination. Like other organized sports ('Learn to box . . . as you learn to play cricket and football'), if controversially (Hughes enters a contemptuous aside on the 'cant and twaddle' of current opposition), it contributes a fundamental dimension to that educational practice applied by Arnold and popularized by Hughes which attracted the designation of 'Muscular Christianity'. The manner of Dickens's episode marks him, of course, not as a proponent of the Arnold–Hughes method, but as its parodist. Herbert's comical war dance and the queer counterparts of Hughes's ingenuous corporal images show this clearly. Similarly, more than a hint of the ridiculous is cast upon one of Hughes's sternest precepts, which is to fight to the bitter end, and 'don't give in while you can stand and see'. Herbert's stiff upper lip brings only a farcical procession of 'bloody nose', 'face . . . foreshortened', 'black eye', and heavy bruising. Hughes's assumptions, moreover, are undermined in another, very dramatic, fashion. The blacksmith's boy gives the 'young gentleman' a sound beating. Suppositions about class superiority take a severe knock.

Yet scepticism and subversion are by no means the whole story about Dickens's attitude to the ideology presented in *Tom Brown's Schooldays*. Herbert Pocket proves after all one of the 'good' characters in his novel; if his muscular side is weak, the Christian turns out to be strong. And Pip's words seem wholly genuine when he reports that, in their tussle, his opponent's 'spirit inspired me with great respect' (92). For Thomas Arnold, character-formation in teaching morals and ardent integrity was the supreme task, more important than the cultivation of strictly intellectual success: 'If there be one thing on earth which is truly admirable', he wrote, 'it is to see God's wisdom blessing an inferiority of natural powers, where they have been honestly, truly, and zealously cultivated.'[5] In the course of *Great Expectations* Dickens manifestly favours such uprightness, not only in Herbert, and in Joe Gargery (whose 'natural powers' are markedly inferior), but in Pip himself, who must learn courage and Christian virtue in the aftermath of the return of the convict who has been his unknown benefactor – and, interestingly, must also, in trying to achieve Magwitch's escape by sea, use a great deal of the muscle he has developed when training on the river during his time under tutelage at Matthew Pocket's, whose regime, from what we see of it, follows the familiar theory of *mens sana in corpore sano*. Pip is in a positive sense Tom Brown's double, in that they share a journey to the discovery of 'manfulness and thoughtfulness, as every high-couraged and well-principled boy must' (*TBS*, 255). Tom's breakthrough in selfless awareness when he realizes his obligation to take protective care of the vulnerable younger boy, Arthur, from whose example he gains in turn a conviction of the value of openness and frank endeavour (in two major crises involving a public confession of religious principles and rejection of the deceit of using cribs in studying the classics),[6] has its complement in Pip's recognition of his duty to Magwitch, 'the hunted wounded shackled creature who held my hand in his, . . . and who had felt affectionately, gratefully, and generously, towards me with great constancy through a series of years' (446).

In both novels the spirit of humanism is set over against indifference and the lure of material wealth. One of the masters tells Tom that his aim in future life should be 'doing good . . . in the world': 'Keep the latter before you as your one object, and you will be right, whether you make a living or not; but if you dwell on the other, you'll very likely drop into mere money-making, and let the world take care of itself for good or evil' (*TBS*, 363). This calls to mind, not only the critique of money culture throughout *Great Expectations*, but also the emphasis placed upon Pip's altruism in secretly supplying the means to start up Herbert's career – an action recognized as 'good' by other characters (296, 396) and wept over by Pip himself as the one way in which his 'expectations had done good to somebody' (298). (That this disinterested deed –

which is to buy Herbert into a mercantile concern – entails investing in a self-interested capitalist system is an irony to which I will return later.)

Doubles, though, are nothing if not duplicitous, threatening death or distortion even as they promise continuity.[7] Pip Pirrip stands in certain respects opposite Tom Brown. His low origins make a difference. It is not the case, however, that Pip has to battle through life while Tom, well-born, enjoys easy going. Indeed, for Thomas Hughes fighting is the inescapable condition of being in the world:

> From the cradle to the grave, fighting, rightly understood, is the business, the real highest, honestest business of every son of man. Every one who is worth his salt has his enemies, who must be beaten, be they evil thoughts and habits in himself, or spiritual wickedness in high places, or Russians, or Border-ruffians, or Bill, Tom, or Harry, who will not let him live his life in quiet till he has thrashed them. (*TBS*, 282)[8]

Pip's existence too, as we shall see, is a constant struggle against demons and shortcomings within and adversaries without. The distinction is that Hughes's protagonist has institutions to shape his purposes, frameworks of belief in which to persevere and excel, shared goals to pursue. So, what objectives does this passage on the 'highest, honestest business' evoke? Spiritual health and Christian principles are plainly in view, as is personal freedom, the right to live in peace; but other, more practical motives emerge in the reference to foreign foes and, I think, to 'Bill, Tom, or Harry'. Fighting 'for the School-house flag' (*TBS*, 300), as Tom proudly puts it, is a preparation for defending the Empire, as against the Russians in the Crimean War, which had just ended when *Tom Brown's Schooldays* came out, or on the borders of British India where the drawn-out Sikh Wars had erupted a few years earlier, and the great Mutiny of 1857–58 was brewing. Elsewhere in the book, Rugby under Arnold is offered as the perfect model of how imperial local government should be conducted; it is perhaps, says the 'young master', the 'only little corner of the British Empire which is thoroughly, wisely, and strongly ruled just now' (*TBS*, 355).

Along with this spotlighting of the national interest goes an implicit call to the cause of class solidarity and survival. The proverbial 'Bill, Tom, or Harry' that interfere in one's life and must be trounced signify no doubt the school bully and those like him, yet they also evoke an image of the proletariat, the urban underclass which, in an earlier and direct allusion, are depicted in their 'smoky hole, . . . a very nest of Chartism and Atheism' (*TBS*, 239). Status anxiety and aggression are at the same time the unspoken imperative behind the emphasis on organized games. If fighting teaches you to stick up for yourself, football and cricket, which occupy much of the narrative of *Tom Brown's Schooldays*, instil group cohesion. As Tom comes famously to realize, cricket is 'more than a game. It's an institution', and the master then goes on to acclaim its merit in encouraging 'discipline and reliance on one another' (*TBS*, 355). The political motives and underlying tensions operating here reflect those of the wider context, where the middle decades of the century saw the increasing prominence of amateur-dominated county clubs ('gentlemen') as against city sides and professional travelling elevens ('players') amid elite fears generated by change in the wake of the 1832 Reform Act and by the heated debates that led to the further franchise extension of 1867.[9]

The process of social exclusion and division apparent in cricket was initiated in other sports in the 1860s, including rowing. Pip, as we know, takes a boat on the Thames during his education at Matthew Pocket's. This is part of entering the field of privilege – of becoming a gentleman. The difficulty of accomplishing the transition, however, is made immediately apparent when the expert ferryman whom Pip hires to increase the elegance of his style compliments him, much to his consternation, on having 'the arm of a blacksmith' (195); the gap between Pip's past and present, his real and putative selves, is maintained by both his ineluctable self-consciousness – he was on this occasion mightily 'confused' – and by outward signs. Thus Pip plays outsider to Thomas Hughes's insider; caught between two worlds; lacking solid ground for his energies and aspirations to take root and flourish. Just before Tom Brown goes off to school, his father, the Squire, outlines his hopes: 'If he'll only turn out a brave, helpful, truth-telling Englishman, and a gentleman and a Christian, that's all I want' (*TBS*, 74). All these positives are present in the account of Pip's life; the trouble is that they are not in his case, or for Dickens, the components of a vital or coherent culture, but – like Pip's schooling – something artificial, second-hand, up for grabs. Beside Tom, who is the embodiment of a set of collective ideals, Pip is the existentialist hero, or anti-hero, of modern tradition, going places but ultimately getting nowhere, enduring in a world of forms bereft of meaning.

We shall find many instances in *Great Expectations* of hollow creeds, including Christianity. For the moment I would like to mention just one other. Pip, in the image of many a scion of Rugby, ends up as a servant of the Empire, working out East for Clarriker and Co., the commercial House in which he had earlier found Herbert a place. As he explains to the reader, 'We were not in a grand way of business, but we had a good name, and worked for our profits, and did very well' (480). There is no glory or sense of mission in this, only a story of diligence and solid success. Imperialism is of course as much in force in the background of Dickens's novel as in that of Hughes's. The modest pretensions of Pip's firm, the regard for probity and fair trading, his accent on honest endeavour, cloak and justify what is fundamentally – and in the light of the word 'profit' manifestly – an exercise in power and self-interest. All the same, the contrast between Hughes and Dickens, the dissolution of patriotic and high moral sentiment into the idea of making a decent living, signals the extent of the latter's retreat from a promulgatory or didactic stance. Where there were transcendent ambitions lurks the worldly-wise individual, hanging on, getting along, making the best of things; not the life that illustrates Truth, but the life that embodies truth. The point can be underlined by the enemies Tom and Pip must chiefly resist. With Tom it is Flashman, who represents the old dispensation, a misrule much like that which pits the ruthless and all-powerful Steerforth against the well-meaning Mr Mell at Creakle's Academy; with Pip it is Orlick, the 'double' that is the projection of the dark side of his own personality.

*

That Dickens puts no faith in institutions in *Great Expectations*, that he invests in them no hopes for the future of the nation or of humankind, does not mean, however, that there are none present. The early chapters are full of references to structures of regulation: the gibbet on the marshes 'which had once held a pirate'; the Hulks or prison-ships, from which Pip's convict has escaped and for which Pip fears himself destined for stealing food from the pantry; the soldiers who requisition Joe's labour 'in the name of the King'; handcuffs, muskets (7, 14–15, 30–31). Though the precise details are set back in time, within an action covering the pre-Victorian decades of the nineteenth century, when a 'King' reigned, we are nonetheless aware of an abiding instrumentation of punishment and control, of chains, the gallows and the gaol, the army and the gun. Later on, in contrast to the old-style public cautionary symbolism and triumphal display of state retribution centred in the gibbet (if the pirate had been, as is likely, a foreigner, then this would be an interesting but isolated case of outward-looking interdiction), we shall encounter the subtler system of the contemporary law, of which Jaggers and Wemmick are adroit functionaries, with its blend of bullying and reliance upon mechanisms of self-discipline through internalized guilt, terror, and cringing compliance.

In *Great Expectations* the individual is made subject to networks of restraint that are almost invariably forms of oppression – the family is something of an exception – and never, as for Thomas Hughes, depositories of wisdom or garners of human potential. A good example from Pip's childhood is when he is frogmarched by Pumblechook – a kind of avuncular coercion – to the magistrate's court to be 'bound out of hand' as apprentice to Joe (104–105). Pip is 'bound' in two respects, both to the job and to the rules governing his indentures, transgression of which would be a serious civil offence, as Pumblechook fiendishly reminds him when reeling off the vagaries – gambling, drinking, keeping bad company – for which henceforth he would be 'liable to imprisonment' (106). The connection between profession and constraint is nicely suggested by the black comedy of Pip's being mistaken by an onlooker for a criminal and handed a tract ornamented with a woodcut of 'a malevolent young man fitted up with a perfect sausage-shop of fetters', and entitled 'TO BE READ IN MY CELL'. In a sense Pip is already in chains.

We are all prisoners. This insight of Dickens's makes *Great Expectations* a disturbing analysis of society, of which we shall discover much more in due course. Even at the beginning, however, where we are asked to focus upon the single life in a primitive setting, the open marshes, the social context cannot be kept out. 'I called myself Pip, and came to be called Pip' (3). Names are a means by which individuals are inserted in the communal order, as we may recall from Bumble's naming of the orphans in the workhouse in *Oliver Twist*, which reinforces the process of their being 'badged and ticketed' (*OT*, 47, 51–2). Bumble's method, which is to move sequentially through the letters of the alphabet as the occasion arises, is, in human terms, arbitrary, labelling each child as an item in an impersonal system. It is not like that with Pip, who is designated patrilineally, after the father who was 'Philip Pirrip'. Yet this groundedness does not make his existence secure, any more than his reinvention of himself, as 'Pip', brings freedom. Pip's identity is always at the mercy of others and of circumstance.

Several times during the novel he is renamed. Joe, for example, shifts confusedly between 'Pip' and 'Sir' throughout the scene in which he visits his former 'playfeller' after the latter has become 'a gentleman' (222–4); and at the point where Pip moves from one sphere – the village and the forge – to another – his shabby-genteel lodgings in London – Herbert baptizes him 'Handel', thus registering his entry into the ambit of a new, polite culture but also suggesting that his links with his old station persist beneath the polished surface, for the rationale behind the nomenclature is that there is 'a charming piece of music by Handel, called the Harmonious Blacksmith' (178). These episodes sound the important theme of split personality, being caught between incompatible worlds.

There is, however, a still more extreme danger. The convict in the churchyard threatens to 'eat' Pip alive and then frightens him with an imaginary 'young man' who will 'get . . . at his heart, and at his liver', who, unbeknownst, will 'softly creep and creep his way to him and tear him open' (4, 6); and it is in a sense an act of consumption that Magwitch (now 'Provis') subsequently practises on Pip, secretly taking his life, making him 'my boy', becoming his 'second father' (316, 320). The appropriation is always on the cards: one of the first things Magwitch says to Pip is, 'Tell us your name!' (4). Not only is identity shown to be unstable and subject to being torn apart, it is open to annexation. In his seminal discussion of 'plotting' in *Great Expectations*, Peter Brooks points out that 'Pip', which sounds like a beginning, 'a seed', is in fact a palindrome and as such concentrates the core movement of the book, 'unarrested shuttling back and forth', constant traversing of the space between origins and inconclusive ends.[10] We may elaborate the point by noting that 'Pirrip', against which 'Pip' defines himself, is also a palindrome, so that in bidding for independence from one set of limits Pip finds another, tighter confinement – a pattern of irony that is repeated when he exchanges the forge for his 'great expectations'. What is certainly clear is that the entrapment Brooks pinpoints is important but not the only kind inscribed in Pip's situation.

The problem most urgently represented in the time of Pip's 'expectations' is that of the place-less person. Difficulties of manners are superficial and easily managed, though they occasion some humorous touches in Chapter 22 in the account of Herbert's discreet schooling of Pip in the proper handling of knives, spoons and wineglasses. Those of rootlessness go unyieldingly deep, as is shown by the very different comic episode in which Pip, on his return to the old provincial town early in his career as a novice gentleman, is baited by the shopkeeper's assistant, Trabb's boy, who, in his most telling tactic, draws alongside him wearing a blue bag in the fashion of a fine great-coat, and 'pulled up his shirt-collar, twined his side-hair, stuck an arm akimbo, and smirked extravagantly by, wriggling his elbows and body, and drawling to his attendants, "Don't know yah, don't know yah, pon my soul don't know yah!"' (246). Clothes, posture, speech, are ever signifiers of class, and had been the focus of an earlier wounding in Estella's biting remark at Satis House: 'He calls the knaves, Jacks, this boy! . . . And what coarse hands he has. And what thick boots' (60). Accomplishments the lack of which had once brought Pip contempt, and self-contempt, have become on the other side of the fence weapons to be used against him. The injury inflicted on Pip by Trabb's boy arises from a mimicry – 'Don't know yah' – which makes him out to be a snob. But his pain is also that of the exile, of being an outcast – no longer 'known' – where he had previously belonged; a point that is underscored by the description of his being chased out of town by his crowing opponent, and 'so to speak, ejected by it into the open country' (246). Pip's further quandary at this point is that, having lost one home, he has not found another; leaving the past behind, being in 'open country', brings, not the expected release or room for advance, but the distress of unsettlement, and of being stuck in a vacuum. On returning to London, he says to Herbert 'I was a blacksmith's boy but yesterday; I am – what shall I say I am – to-day?' (248). Identity, or the lack of it, is a two-sided matter of definition – of being known by others and of being able to know oneself.

This episode also reminds us, however, that individuals are not entirely powerless in the circumstances of their being, or non-being. The self can be written into existence. *Great Expectations* is the richest and most complex of Dickens's versions of Puritan spiritual autobiography, and lays bare the mechanisms and purposes of the form. Pip the narrator shapes the past in the service of present needs. His recollection of the scene of his humiliation is in certain respects a confession, reflecting a sense of guilt and error that is elsewhere plainly expressed, as it is in his reference just afterwards to the 'penitential codfish and barrel of oysters' (246) which he sent to Joe to salve his conscience for not visiting him (where the wryly ironic 'penitential' projects a satirical image of his old phoney self). Against this background, Trabb's boy appears as the agent of reckoning in a parable of pride going before a fall. Yet, in so far as the relation of the incident comes to constitute an act of self-affirmation, this remorse is not at all the line it develops. It slides, rather, into a revenge fantasy and sermon of abomination, with Trabb's boy becoming, not the angel of retribution, but the devil of mindless scurrility – 'an invulnerable and dodging serpent, who, when chased into a corner, flew out again between his captor's legs', but whom, on second thoughts, Pip can get back at by informing Trabb the tailor that he will lose business if he continues to employ an assistant who 'excited Loathing in every respectable mind' (246). Is it not Pip who is devilish, or at least has something of the recalcitrant serpent in him?

It has been argued, by Jack Rawlins, that Pip's history is of a sad 'recantation of the self', where the protagonist has to sacrifice his desires – 'to love grandly . . . to aspire . . . to dream' – to the mores of his society: 'the older Pip, by thinking in terms of goodness, misses his own greatness.'[11] There is a lot of truth in this; Pip does comply, as we shall see, with the expectations of the world in which he moves and has his being, in the fields not only of morality but also of economic, class and gender relations. Yet to postulate a conclusive change – 'The poetic Pip dies then, survived by a clerk'[12] – is misleading. *Great Expectations* presents us with nothing so simple as a stable ego, even where the figure in question is the relatively empty and bounded one of Clarriker's unassuming clerk. It reveals, rather, a divided self and a self ever in a state of turmoil and inner conflict. We have seen how in the account of Trabb's boy's offensive the impulse to exemplary penance, expressed through a ventriloquism of self-mockery, is jostled in Pip by the urge to claim both a moral and social superiority, which brands the boy an 'unlimited miscreant' (245) and actually uses a conformist stance, in the appeal to 'every respectable mind', to press the advantage home. 'The invulnerable and dodging serpent', psychologically understood, seems to be the agency at once of self-censorship, Pip's desire to be 'good', and of self-assertion, his desire to be on top. This duality – which reproduces the irrepressible propinquity in Puritan representations of the self between the spiritual and the natural sides, the persistence of 'the old Adam' after conversion and unto death[13] – is, moreover, only one of a conglomeration of psychic tensions in Pip's make-up.

Another, reminding us this time of the traditional Protestant distrust of fictionality,[14] is the duplicity of imagination. It may act, on the one hand, as a healthy source of self-defence, as when Pip stills the relentless enquiries of Mrs Joe and Mr Pumblechook concerning his first visit to Miss Havisham's by inventing a story about that lady sitting in 'a black velvet coach' being handed cake and wine on a gold plate by her niece, while he sat up behind and four dogs fought over veal cutlets out of a 'silver basket' (67–8); but, on the other, and more often, it may deceive and hold the mind dangerously in thrall, as it does with Mrs Joe's and Pumblechook's obsessive dreams of material wealth and advancement, which makes them vulnerable to Pip's ruse, or, more seriously, in the case of Pip's own fantasy of upwards mobility and romance, the false plot in which the 'Witch' with her crutch-headed stick becomes the fairy godmother who 'was going to make [his] fortune', in a story where he would 'do all the shining deeds of the young Knight . . . and marry the Princess' (85, 133, 231).

Continuing psychological complexity, and not progressive simplification, is the paramount theme of *Great Expectations*. Just after the Trabb's boy debacle, Herbert Pocket describes Pip, to his puzzled face, as 'a good fellow', but then qualifies this straightforward sketch by adding, 'with impetuosity and hesitation, boldness and diffidence, action and dreaming, curiously mixed in him' (248). This complicated brew never thins out; the 'good fellow' never subsumes the driven or inadequate one. I wish now to examine the curious mixture more closely in major aspects of the novel: the *Bildungsroman* trail, which pursues an agenda of positivist self-formation centred in an ethics of guilt and redemption, and in movements from blindness to seeing; society, the field of force that subjects Pip to its own purposes, as it does others, yet which also allows him, on its terms and as a provisional saving grace, to assume authority positions; the masquerade of Pip's 'doubles', the pre-eminent form of psychic tension and unconscious motive, swirling across the daylight narrative of development, denying coherence; and his romantic love for Estella, the issue with which the book ends, the strongest, though not the sole, expression of unresolved impulse.

*

That *Great Expectations* is a *Bildungsroman,* or education novel, is apparent from the start, as the adult Pip looks back on his earliest attempts to connect with and make sense of the world, the infant imagining his family's likenesses from the inscriptions on their tombstones, then one day the sudden sense of the real 'identity of things', the graves whose occupants are 'dead and buried', the wilderness, the 'small bundle of shivers' that was Pip (3–4). Already the narrator is himself an enigma. Does his Malthusian, or proto-Darwinian, aside on his five little brothers having given up 'trying to get a living, exceedingly early in that universal struggle' (3) signal disillusionment with the ordeal of existence, or wise passiveness in the face of it, or careless scepticism? What has Pip learned, and what has he become, and how? Time will tell.

At the end of Chapter 1, as often in Dickens, there are echoes of the great *Bildungsroman* of modern times, *The Prelude.* Wordsworth had described himself as 'Fostered alike by beauty and by fear'; but the beacon and the gibbet rising from Pip's marshes take us to that part of the poem dealing with the particular species of the latter named as 'visionary dreariness', the child's feelings of being lost and belonging to another time and place, his intimations of immortality.[15] Pip's experience and upbringing, altogether unsublime, are dominated by cruder fears in an atmosphere of violence: horror at the thought of the convict's young man who will tear out his liver; Mrs Joe's rampaging and liberal application of 'Tickler' as she raises him 'by hand'; the verbal brutality meted out by Pumblechook and the rest at the Christmas table, where Pip is arraigned as 'a world of trouble', the squeaker 'more detestable' than a pig (17). The young Pip acts out of 'terror', as his older self stresses in a short paragraph that repeats the word seven times (15). That is why he steals the pork pie and brandy for a starving fugitive, not the goodness of his heart; and that is why he dreads detection. In the scene where Magwitch is returned to the Hulks and pretends to the onlookers that it was he who had taken food from the blacksmith's pantry, there is a telling contrast between Joe Gargery's expression of forgiving sympathy for a 'poor miserable fellow-creatur' and Pip's own evidently self-interested, and no doubt relieved, silence (40).

Joe's stance here is important, however, since it represents a position to which Pip must travel. Pip's life is configured within the narrative as a journey to conscience and a sense of true and humane values. At the beginning of the very next chapter, the narrator, with the benefit of enlightened hindsight, judges his conduct in not telling Joe the whole truth about the robbery as an instance of his then being 'too cowardly to do what I knew to be right', though he tempers this self-reproof with the explanation that he held back because he was afraid of losing the good opinion of Joe, whom he 'loved' (41). The admission of mis-demeanour, with or without qualification, is a strong element in Pip's account of his personal history. We have seen already at one level of the Trabb's boy episode an oblique confession of the sin of pride, for which Pip had been taught a lesson. Elsewhere he offers himself deliberately as a cautionary spectacle. Thus, he recounts how just before leaving for London to take up his expectations he had asked Biddy to spare no chance of improving Joe 'in his learning and manners' in case he should wish to elevate him to 'a higher sphere'; to which Biddy, out of respect for Joe, had replied that 'He may be too proud to let any one take him out of a place that he is competent to fill, and fills well'; which in turn had prompted Pip to accuse her of being 'envious, . . . and grudging' at his rise in fortune, and of showing 'a bad side of human nature' (148–9).

Exactly the same charge – 'This really is a very bad side of human nature' – is again flung at Biddy several chapters later when she implies that Pip should care more for Joe, who 'never complained . . . but ever did his duty in his way of life, with a strong hand, a quiet tongue, and a gentle heart' (284). It is clear where the 'bad side of human nature' really lies; and the point is made explicit through a running commentary of direct self-deprecation: Pip's painful memory that 'I was ashamed of the dear good fellow – I *know* I was ashamed of him', his reference to the 'gallon of condescension' he poured upon those around him, his deeming that he was a 'self-swindler' in thinking he *would* ever visit the forge (101, 147, 225). Pip's regret over his treatment of Joe is one with his condemnation of the whole era of his 'great expectations', which in retrospect he terms 'those wretched hankerings after money and gentility . . . all those ill-regulated aspirations' (236). Using a religious language, he turns his experience into a moral tale where wealth brings only misery; his hatred 'beyond expression' of the chambers where he and Herbert lived, his shame at the 'lavish habits' that led Herbert's 'easy nature' astray and 'corrupted [his] simplicity', his inability to endure the sight of the perverse and symbolically named manservant, the 'Avenger', he calls his 'period of repentance' (272, 275). This constitutes perhaps the most devastating indictment of materialism and social climbing in Dickens.

The mature Pip's advances in perception, however, involve the recognition not only of error in himself but of goodness in others. Joe Gargery is crucial in this regard. He stands, in Pip's vision, for the better side of human nature. Biddy, as we have just seen, wraps Joe in a constellation of virtues – capable in his allotted sphere, uncomplaining, 'a strong hand, a quiet tongue, and a gentle heart'. This impression of a model existence is amply reinforced by Joe's own words. When Jaggers asks him to name his sum for annulling Pip's apprenticeship, for example, he instinctively asserts the claims of human attachment: 'But if you think as money – can make compensation to me – fur the loss of the little child – what come to the forge – and ever the best of friends! – ' (141). The fiasco of his visit to Pip's London lodgings (which significantly Pip would have paid anything to prevent) is redeemed by the 'simple dignity' of his acceptance of the gulf that has opened up between himself and his erstwhile ward and companion, on whom he finally bestows a blessing:

> 'Pip, dear old chap, life is made of ever so many partings welded together, as I may say, and one man's a blacksmith, and one's a whitesmith, and one's a goldsmith, and one's a coppersmith. Diwisions among such must come, and must be met as they come. If there's been any fault at all to-day, it's mine. You and me is not two figures to be together in London; nor anywhere else but what is private, and beknown, and understood among friends. . . . I'm wrong in these clothes. I'm wrong out of the forge, the kitchen, or off th'meshes. You won't find so much fault in me if you think of me in my forge dress, with my hammer in my hand, or even my pipe. . . . And so GOD bless you, dear old Pip, old chap, GOD bless you!' (224)

If this reads like the set speech of someone playing a part, that is because Joe is being situated by Pip at the heart of his life story and the moral scheme it affords. Accordingly, Pip himself never misses an opportunity to point either Joe's merits or his present capacity to appreciate them. He still feels how the touch of 'dear good faithful tender Joe' upon his shoulder, in its combination of 'strength with gentleness', had been like 'the rustle of an angel's wing' (141). At the London parting, the fashion of Joe's dress could no more come in the way of his integrity 'than it could come in its way in Heaven' (224–5). The Joe who nurses Pip back from his near-fatal illness is – 'God bless him!' – 'this gentle Christian man' (463).

These passages of course raise important general issues. One of these is the theme of what makes a gentleman, which much preoccupied Dickens and his contemporaries, and to which the conception of Joe as a low-born exemplar brings a deeply interesting turn. The other, which is connected, is the question of the ideological orientation of the novel. Joe's dutiful tolerance of 'diwisions' and hierarchy, and of his place in the scheme of things, clearly reflects Dickens's familiar conservatism in matters of social organization.[16] Does the good Joe's embrace of the status quo, or at least fruitful conformity, from within the lower echelons render it a more secure and sympathetic proposition, or do we see him, rather, as being strategically sacrificed for socio-political ends and in the service of a structure of subordination? Does Joe bring credit to the system, or is he a kind of Uncle Tom, settling unsettlingly for small mercies?

Answers on such overarching concerns will come later. For the moment, Joe is more specifically a moral compass and instrument of self-definition in a spiritual autobiography which, in the manner of the old Puritan confessors, brings shape and meaning to the individual life and instruction to others. Pip's path to expiation and right-mindedness culminates in his return to the forge to beg forgiveness of Joe and Biddy, which is granted with an appeal to Heaven: ' "O dear old Pip, old chap," said Joe. "God knows as I forgive you, if I have anythink to forgive!" '; ' "Amen! And God knows I do!" echoed Biddy' (480). The air is thick with religious and moral sentiment in this part of the book. Pip talks, for instance, of his 'remorseful thoughts', of his intention to press his 'penitent remonstrance' with Joe, of the blunders of his 'errant heart' (470, 472). The illness during which Joe tends him unbeknownst is cast in the form of an identity crisis – he was 'a brick in the house-wall', 'a steel beam of a vast engine' (462)[17] – from which he awakes a new man. As he toils home to make reparation, infirmity of body is attended by inner strength; for 'my limbs were weak, but with a sense of increasing relief as I drew nearer to them, and a sense of leaving arrogance and untruthfulness further and further behind' (477). Pip's progress becomes Pip's redemption.

But only up to a point. The final lesson of Pip's penitential return seems to be that you are never more at risk than when you think yourself saved. Life kicks him in the head against the grain of his intentions. Before examining this resolution, or rather irresolution, however, we may usefully consider the other major narrative of personal develop-ment in Pip's story, his changing relations with Magwitch.

*

Peter Brooks's brilliant reading of the scene of Magwitch's return in the light of Freudian theory comprehends it as 'a painful forcing through of layers of repression, an analogue of analytic work'.[18] Earlier Pip reports that, when, journeying by coach back to his town, he had come upon the convict who long ago had been Magwitch's secret envoy and bearer of a gift of money, he had trembled with an 'undefined and vague . . . dread, much exceeding the mere apprehension of a painful or dis- agreeable recognition'. The great fear 'took no distinctness of shape, and . . . was the revival for a few minutes of the terror of childhood' (230). What this depicts is the pressure of an experience that is buried to conscious memory, 'forgotten', but not dead, and is chafing the barrier of psychic resistance. Pip knows that his distress is more than can be attributed to his recognizing the emissary convict but cannot locate its true source, since it is precisely that which has been shut out, repressed. In his fancy he saw the boat waiting at the slime-washed stairs to take this convict to the prison-ship lying out on the black water, without at all associating the picture with the originating event, the meeting with Magwitch. This is one of the moments in the text where repetition works to indicate that Pip cannot remember and ensures, at the same time, that the reader cannot forget. When Magwitch reappears, in Chapter 39, Pip can resist the past no longer:

> Even yet, I could not recall a single feature, but I knew him! If the wind and the rain had driven away all the intervening years, had scattered all the intervening objects, had swept us to the churchyard where we first stood face to face on such different levels, I could not have known my convict more distinctly than I knew him now, as he sat in the chair before the fire. No need to take a file from his pocket and show it to me; no need to take the handkerchief from his neck and twist it round his head; no need to hug himself with both his arms, and take a shivering turn across the room, looking back at me for recognition. I knew him before he gave me one of these aids, though, a moment before, I had not been conscious of remotely suspecting his identity. (315–16)

As Brooks points out, the scene 'replays' numerous details of the churchyard drama, the 'praeterition on which the passage is constructed – "no need . . . no need" – mark[ing] the gradual retrieval of the past as its involuntary repetition'.[19] What Pip calls 'that chance intercourse . . . of long ago' has become (in Freudian terminology) the 'primal scene' that is ineradicable and must be re-enacted in the present. Though the convict's actions are described, his taking a file from his pocket and so on, the emphasis is truly all on mental process. Everything is on Pip's inside, as is suggested by the detail of the convict 'looking back at [him] for recognition', inviting recollection from within, and rendering the dumb show itself a mirroring of the imagery of Pip's consciousness. That the convict 'take[s] a shivering turn' reminds us of 'the small bundle of shivers' (4) that was Pip, thus further conflating the two figures. One element of the mime has striking symbolic force in the context of Pip's life and destiny. The file that the revenant takes out and shows him signifies the phallus; Pip's trauma in the churchyard had involved initiation into the force of raw masculine power (he had stood 'face to face' with Magwitch but 'on such different levels'), but he is on the edge of discovering the more devastating dark secret that the convict has played the paternal role in his existence. Shortly, Magwitch's words will put plainly what has been dawning on Pip: 'Look'ee here, Pip. I'm your second father. You're my son' (320).

Freud opens his report of 1914 on psychoanalytic practice, entitled in the English translation 'Remembering, Repeating and Working-Through', by looking back to his and his associate Josef Breuer's early simple faith in 'remembering and abreacting', whereby the patient was induced to recall the moment when repression took place and to 'reproduce the mental processes involved in that situation, in order to direct their discharge along the path of conscious activity'.[20] This is the cathartic method that is the stuff of Hollywood movies (Hitchcock's *Spellbound* comes to mind) and of popular conceptions of psycho-analysis.[21] The analogue to what happens in *Great Expectations*, how-ever, is not this but the more mature Freudian technique of 'working-through' where, over a long, arduous and possibly interminable period, the subject is helped to engage with and redispose the materials that have been brought to light, and indeed may continue to surface, so as to be able to control and come to terms with them. This Freud refers to as 'the "abreacting" of . . . quotas of affect', and he is careful to emphasize not just the immediate curative gains but the extended incremental benefits of the work in hand, the battle with oneself being on 'solid ground out of which things of value . . . for future life have to be derived'.[22]

When the truth about Magwitch's agency in his life dawns on him, Pip, far from finding release, is thrown into disarray, even to the point of physical distress: 'All the truth of my position came flashing on me; and its disappointments, dangers, disgraces, consequences of all kinds, rushed in in such a multitude that I was borne down by them and had to struggle for every breath I drew' (319). A second-order resistance is then set up, not to recall of the past but to Magwitch himself. As often in Dickens, abhorrence comes out in configurations of bestiality: Pip shrinks from his benefactor as from 'some terrible beast'; he recoils from his touch 'as if he had been a snake'; he looks with an insurmountable aversion upon the 'hungry old dog' (320, 331). At the same time, all attempts to cover up Magwitch's identity inevitably fail for Pip. The better he dressed him, 'the more he looked like the slouching figure on the marshes', and he appeared to drag his leg 'as if there were still a weight of iron on it' (337). 'From head to foot there was Convict in the very grain of the man.' Pip reads Magwitch in accordance with the deposits and demands of his mental life. Anxiety, and something too of cultural conditioning in matters of decorum and contamination, clothe this other in forms indicative both of rejection and of dread, of Pip's aggressive-defensive impulses, whether we consider the imagery of hideous and violent animals or that of an undisguisable criminality.

This is mind-jerk reaction rather than 'working-through', at worst impasse, at best a holding operation. In the longer term, however, Pip achieves vis-à-vis Magwitch, as we noted early in this chapter, the positive ability to look beyond appearances to the person beneath; as Pip comes to recognize the simple dignity that makes irrelevant the fashion of Joe's dress so, after the failed attempt to flee the country, does he lose all his repugnance towards Magwitch, and 'in the hunted wounded shackled creature . . . only saw a man . . . who had felt affectionately, gratefully, and generously, towards me with great constancy' (446). In a distinct readjustment of the projected images, the animal becomes 'a man', the delinquent an exemplar of centrally human qualities. Seeing productively, Pip sets about repaying the virtues of affection, gratitude, generosity and constancy actively and in kind.

This new self holds evident sway in the account of Magwitch's trial and its aftermath, where Pip, stripped of pretension, keeps public faith with the one who had cared for him, becoming in turn his supporter, symbolically 'holding the hand that he stretched forth' from the dock (456). These scenes are moving on one level because they capture very exactly the impersonality and summary nature of the justice system, there being precisely 'two-and-thirty' men and women put together before the judge to receive the sentence of death, while indifferent placemen and self-important officials lord it with 'great chains and nosegays', and a gallery full of people looks on curiously like 'a large theatrical audience' (456–7). In keeping with his improved character, Pip's sympathy (as no doubt Dickens's) goes all to the two-and-thirty condemned, whom he brings suddenly into the frame, not as animals to be herded to the slaughter or an entertaining show, or as a mere statistic, but as human beings with a spectrum of emotions, 'some defiant, some stricken with terror, some sobbing and weeping, some covering their faces, some staring gloomily about'. Magwitch, who had been repellent, is now granted the dignity of quietly answering back in the face of earthly authority by invoking the greater Power above, and of re-enforcing the narrator's insight into the divine scheme where all are ultimately equal:

> The sun was striking in at the great windows of the court, through the glittering drops of rain upon the glass, and it made a broad shaft of light between the two-and-thirty and the Judge, linking both together, and perhaps reminding some of the audience, how both were passing on, with absolute equality, to the greater Judgement that knoweth all things and cannot err. Rising for a moment, a distant speck of face in this way of light, the prisoner said, 'My Lord, I have received my sentence of Death from the Almighty, but I bow to yours,' and sat down again. (458)

Pip, it seems, has got not only goodness but religion. And these two strains then persist in the adjacent deathbed scene in the prison hospital, where Pip gently tends Magwitch like a son ('dear boy' is the dying refrain), consoles him by revealing that his child, Estella, lives and is the object of his love, and at the last confers a blessing:

> I thought of the two men who went up into the Temple to pray, and I knew there were no better words that I could say beside his bed, than 'O Lord, be merciful to him, a sinner!' (460)

Insisting that *Great Expectations* be read as moral fable and enlightened social comment, Q.D. Leavis links the courtroom and deathbed scenes with the Vanity Fair episode of *The Pilgrim's Progress*; and certainly the connection, which is real, underscores both the value that the novel does place on Pip's changed relationship with Magwitch, which echoes Christian's steadfast loyalty towards Faithful when the latter stands trial and suffers a martyr's death, and the criticism meted out to the heartless spectators who strut, 'putting their dresses right' (458), as they might at church or elsewhere, and treat the Sessions as an amusement.[23] There is, moreover, an equally obvious link with Bunyan's text which Q.D. Leavis does not notice: that is, the theme of God's overriding plot, which makes nonsense of the pride of the people of Vanity Fair, for no sooner is Faithful dispatched at the stake than a chariot and a couple of horses come to carry him up through the clouds the nearest way to the Celestial City.[24] Bunyan guides the reader to comprehend, not by nature, which is blind, but by the light of Faith and the Spirit; and so does *Great Expectations* at a point where it is hardly possible to distinguish Dickens from his narrator, as the sun streams through the windows symbolically joining judge and prisoners under the dominion of a 'greater Judgement that knoweth all things and cannot err' (458) – although it should be noted that Bunyan's is a radical didacticism, ridiculing secular authority, its 'rightness', while Dickens, conservatively, does not fundamentally question either the legal process itself or the social hierarchies it depends upon and confirms, but rather legitimizes the inequalities of this world by privileging a transcendent order of justice. Yet, spiritual reading is not sustainable in *Great Expectations* beyond the isolated moment, and is overtaken by psychological reading. Palpably set within the ambit of Pip's individual consciousness, even religious discourse functions as an instrument of self-definition, or indeed of self-empowerment.

To help us understand this, we may return to an episode where Pip is bereft of control over himself. Receiving from his friend Wemmick the missive, 'DON'T GO HOME' (lest he be discovered with Provis), Pip spends a night in the Hummums lodging-house in Covent Garden, a place aptly named from the Turkish for 'sweating' since, sleepless, he suffers there a welter of nightmare sensations. He imagines flies and grubs tumbling down upon him from the canopy over his bed, but by far the most persistent horror is that of the threat of language. He is hemmed in by sounds, the closet 'whispered', the fireplace 'sighed', the washing-stand 'ticked', a guitar-string played in the chest of drawers; and, most alarmingly of all, he becomes transfixed by words, as the 'eyes' cast on the wall by the rush-light 'acquired a new expression, and in every one of those staring rounds I saw written, "DON'T GO HOME"' (366–7). The phrase 'new expression' catches perfectly the supersession of specular by linguistic menace. Pip is then literally *sentenced* to torture by words, being compelled to go repeatedly through the act of conjugation, where language is purely given system and forms, without application, without meaning:

> 'Don't go home' . . . became a vast shadowy verb which I had to conjugate. Imperative mood, present tense: Do not thou go home, let him not go home, let us not go home, do not ye or you go home, let not them go home. Then, potentially: I may not and I cannot go home . . . until I felt that I was going distracted, and rolled over on the pillow, and looked at the staring rounds upon the wall again. (368)

And so on, presumably; back again to stage one. The recitation reminds us of education, which is supposed to make us free; but in truth we are never immune to impositions, of which the network of language constitutes a major intensity. R.B. Onians, in his classic book on *The Origins of European Thought*, shows that in common parlance the action of words is formulated as a beating or constriction: 'the blows of fate, the chains or bonds of destiny', and so on; and 'where human life is seen as ordered by a larger design, this design is conceived as a form of speech (e.g. a prophecy, a sentence), which is imposed with violence upon the subject'.[25] This is exactly the case with Pip at the Hummums, where the message 'DON'T GO HOME' stands for the whole dreadful fate that has been visited upon him. There are elsewhere in the narrative, moreover, similar convergences of terms designating physical affliction, adverse destiny, and the force of language. Pip, we remember, talks about being 'borne down' upon and 'struggling for . . . breath' under the weight of the 'consequences' he cogitates will arise from the fact of who his real benefactor is (319). Just before his account of Magwitch's return, he likens the forthcoming events to the 'Eastern story' of how the Sultan Misnar's enemies were destroyed by a trap involving miles of rope, an axe, and a slab of stone descending through the ceiling; that is, to an elaborate plot or, as he goes on to say, 'work': 'the work, far and near, . . . had been accomplished; and in an instant the blow was struck, and the roof of my stronghold dropped upon me' (312).

What happens in the chapters describing the trial and death of Magwitch is that Pip turns the tables on language, scripting a plot in which he is the self-controlled and controlling presence, or voice, and fountain of wisdom. Where Magwitch had been Pip's hideous 'father' (in a kind of reversal of the *Frankenstein* story), Pip now becomes guardian and kind keeper. The monster in Pip's life is not only humanized but tamed into submission and, in a passage we have so far not considered, is condensed to an exemplum of humility and contrition; though he seemingly pondered to himself the question 'whether he might have been a better man under better circumstances . . . he never justified himself by a hint tending that way, or tried to bend the past out of its eternal shape. . . . As to all the rest, he was humble and contrite, and I never knew him complain' (456).

Pip most certainly 'bends' things in sacrifice to his personal needs. In his utterance of that final prayer for Magwitch – 'O Lord, be merciful to him, a sinner' – we detect him in the act of thus appropriating the Bible. In Christ's parable of the Pharisee and the publican (Luke 18. 10–14), 'The Pharisee stood and prayed thus with himself, God, I thank thee, that I am not as other men are, extortioners, unjust, adulterers, or even as this publican . . . And the publican, standing afar off, would not lift up so much as his eyes unto heaven, but smote upon his breast, saying, God be merciful to me a sinner.' Julian Moynahan was the first to spot Pip's Pharisaic rewording of the text and took this to mean that he had not, after all, learned from his experience.[26]

Moynahan of course has a point; Pip's pronouncement smacks of self-righteousness and the sin of pride. But there are subtler needs and processes at work, and ones that signal a whole change of ethos in the contemporary milieu. The biblical passage is the very same that had come to Tom Brown when, taking a cue from the newcomer Arthur, he had summoned the courage to pray openly in the dorm: 'God be merciful to me a sinner', Tom falls to repeating over and over again (*TBS*, 228). In the orthodox world of Thomas Hughes the torch burns for frankness and humility, an honest, unsophisticated, exemplary embrace of inviolable truth; in Pip's, on the other hand, truth is blurred and innocence has dissolved. Is Pip's memory of the New Testament playing tricks with him, or is he knowingly wearing a mask? Whichever the case, he has undoubtedly learned *something*, which is prowess in applying, deliberately or not, strategies of self-affirmation; not even sacred truth, the Bible itself, is safe from misreading where the obduracy and survival of the ego are concerned. Then, however, we must look beyond simple criticism of Pip to the fact that no one is perfect and that *Great Expectations* is the revelation of an ineluctable dividedness, where worthy and unworthy selves intertwine, and of the endlessness of the task of working-through. The same impression of ambiguity prevails where Pip tells Magwitch about Estella and his love for her. Is this purely an outgoing act of comforting a dying man, or does it signal the persistence in Pip of troublesome erotic phantasy – of other psychic material to fall by or deal with?

*

The survival of the ego is very much at stake in what is perhaps the most remarkable of all the episodes *en route* to Pip's penitent return to the forge – the encounter with Orlick in the sluice-house near the limekiln. In the course of 'Remembering, Repeating and Working-Through' Freud also introduces the phenomenon of 'acting out', where the patient compulsively repeats repressed material in displaced or symbolic form, 'reproduc[ing] it not as a memory but as an action'.[27] Freud's own illustrations are restricted to the psychoanalytic situation so that, for instance, the subject 'does not remember having been intensely ashamed of certain sexual activities and afraid of their being found out . . . but he makes it clear that he is ashamed of the treatment on which he is now embarked and tries to keep it secret from everybody'. But the idea relates more widely to mental life and can be connected with the functioning of the 'double'. Like Apollyon's relation to Christian in *The Pilgrim's Progress*, which Dickens clearly has somewhere in mind, Orlick embodies in general the shadow side of the hero's psyche, the dark impulses that he does not consciously recognize in himself.[28] The combat at the sluice-house brings climactically to the surface – 'acts out' – both these deep currents and a sense of guilt associated with them. It is another, but peculiarly concentrated, drama of indirect confession, self-accusation, and expiation.

There are suggestions in the text that the events at the sluice-house never take place 'in reality' at all, but in Pip's mind, as dream-work. Pip receives a letter drawing him into a rendezvous, but when he wants to refer to it again it has disappeared, as if it had not existed. Then, at the opening of Chapter 53, he finds himself in a hauntingly familiar landscape, afraid yet compelled by something deep down to go on, which is back into the shadows of the past, the 'old Battery', the 'distant Hulks', the 'blank horizon', the marshes. In the sluice-house, the first thing Pip comprehends is being caught in a 'strong running noose' thrown over his head from behind (422–3). This obviously symbolizes feelings of guilt. But how, in his heart of hearts, has Pip transgressed? A clue comes quickly in another symbolic reference, this time to his injured arm which, having hurt before, now, under Orlick's onslaught, felt as if it were 'being boiled'. Though Pip's arm had been burnt in the effort to save Miss Havisham from the flames, its present gross affliction is symptomatic, not of an act of mercy, but of some buried apprehension of criminality. It was with his right hand that Pip had stolen the pork pie, had floored Herbert Pocket, and (thinking again of William A. Cohen's not easily refuted thesis) had probably masturbated; but the offence actually at work is a wish rather than a deed, for the 'suppressed voice' that is Orlick (423), and that suggests the voice of conscience, breaks out accusing Pip of the maiming and murder of Mrs Joe:

> 'Wolf!' . . . 'Old Orlick's a going to tell you somethink. It was you as did for your shrew sister.'
> 'It was you, villain,' said I.
> 'I tell you it was your doing – I tell you it was done through you,' he retorted . . . 'I come upon her from behind, as I come upon you to-night. *I* giv' it her. I left her for dead . . . But it warn't Old Orlick as did it; it was you. You was favoured, and he was bullied and beat. Old Orlick bullied and beat, eh? Now you pays for it. You done it; now you pays for it.' (426)

Pip had not battered his sister, but there are several hints elsewhere that he had wanted to and felt somehow responsible. At the time of the assault, he tells us, 'I was at first disposed to believe that *I* must have had some hand in the attack', and, a convict's leg-iron having been found at the scene, was much troubled by the thought that he 'had provided the weapon, however undesignedly' (120–21). The resentment that permeates the early pages of the autobiography – 'I was always treated as if I had insisted on being born, in opposition to the dictates of reason, religion, and morality' (23) – never passes off, and even at Mrs Joe's funeral Pip observes that 'I could scarcely have recalled my sister with much tenderness' (278). On this latter occasion Pip is nonetheless seized by 'violent indignation' against the assailant who had made his sister suffer, be it 'Orlick, or anyone else'. But that is the daylight Pip; the night-time Pip circles back upon himself and flushes out his own subterranean desire – 'You done it; now you pays for it'. Orlick's habit of speaking of himself as if he were someone else – 'But it warn't Old Orlick as did it' – suggests he is not an articulating first-person presence but a medium in and through which Pip's shadowy underside is expressed.

The episode not only thus elaborates the matter of Pip's attitude to his sister but raises that of his relationship with Biddy. Orlick charges him with coming between him and 'a woman I liked', by giving him 'a bad name' to her (424). 'Liked', with Orlick, has sinister implications, and reminds us of Biddy's fear of his lecherous attention, which she had once reported to Pip, saying 'I am afraid he likes me', causing Pip to feel 'hot as if it were an outrage on myself' (132). Orlick's attack on Mrs Joe, too, has sexual connotations – 'I came upon her from behind, . . . *I* giv' it her' – and he represents basic instincts which, as the heated sense of outrage suggests, in Pip are evidently kept in. This suppression, of course, can be viewed as very much to Pip's credit, and the showdown at the sluice-house brings to light not only the devil within – secret thoughts and demonic potential – but also a resistance to it. As in Christian's fight with Apollyon, which takes place in the Valley of Humiliation, the worthier self is brought low – Orlick sits 'gloating' over Pip and 'goad[s]' him (425–6) – but ultimately prevails. Called 'wolf' again and again, Pip is all but subsumed under the head of predatory nature; and a similar extinction of the better side looms when Orlick threatens to consume him – '"I'm a going to have your life"' . . . his mouth water[ing] for me' – or more enigmatically explains his object as that of supplanting him, ' "Because I mean to do it all myself. One keeps a secret better than two" ' (424–5). But Pip holds on, opposing to these sinister possibilities a simple determination to build a good name, not to be 'misremembered after death' (425), and (the clearest link with Bunyan's Christian) a 'prayer' to Heaven 'humbly beseeching pardon' (426, 429).

Yet neither is the episode, in the end, a straightforward fable of the triumph of good over bad, the upright over the base. That the battle is so closely run points not so much the strength as the precariousness of the self; and, as we shall see in a moment, the victory is never entirely satisfactory. There is, however, an even more radical flaw in the fabric of Pip's positivist narrative. The effect of one strand of Orlick's diatribe is to leave us unable ever again to take Pip and his text at face value, and enforces an uncomfortable demand to read against the grain of their perspectives.

Here, we should note that it is not only Pip's interference in his pursuit of Biddy that Orlick drags up. Pip had also vowed (in a conversation with Biddy) to use his money to drive him out of the country; he had got him dismissed from his job at Miss Havisham's: 'You was always in Old Orlick's way ever since you was a child' (425). The complaint of having been 'bullied and beat', while Pip was 'favoured', harks back in particular to the episode, in Chapter 15, of Orlick's fury at being excluded from a special half-day holiday at the forge and the thrashing he had received from Joe after quarrelling with Mrs Joe. Orlick calls Pip 'a liar', for claiming that he was not responsible for doing him 'harm'; and most startlingly of all, he brands him a crook, utterly contemptible beside his new companions and masters, Compeyson and his associates: 'Some of 'em writes my letters when I wants 'em wrote – do you mind? – writes my letters, wolf! They writes fifty hands; they're not like sneaking you, as writes but one' (427) – a taunt Orlick so relishes that he soon after gives it a reprise, saying of his allies that 'Perhaps it's them that writes fifty hands, and that's not like sneaking you as writes but one' (428).

Surely all of this is preposterous, coming from the likes of Orlick, himself a bully and a beater, and one who consorts with fraudsters. Or is it? Why shouldn't there be a view according to Dolge Orlick? Nothing he says about the way he has been treated is, on the evidence, untrue; and it is worth noting, when judging him resentful at being denied privileges at the forge, that Joe at least had been ready to concede his journeyman's merit – 'You stick to your work as well as most men' (114). Pip *does* lie when excusing himself from any responsibility for harming Orlick, not least in the light of his spontaneous, and quite ruthless, decision to get Jaggers to have him sacked from his post at Satis House. There would seem to be a surprisingly accurate hit in the charge of 'sneaking you'; there is not necessarily any more probity, and may be less openness, in the practice of one hand than in forging several, though, into the bargain, in constructing his story Pip does in fact craft even more than fifty.

In these exchanges Orlick ceases to be an aspect of Pip's psychological life and becomes an outside interrogator lifting the lid on the hero-autobiographer's self-interest and egocentricity. A familiar position is being reflected: Orlick is one of those would-be climbers that the conservative Dickens finds dangerous and objectionable, like Uriah Heep but more lowly born, cruder, and sometimes slouching on the edge of being a shocking parody of social ambition. More than this, however, Pip, from his place in the pecking order, is revealed as being as antagonistic towards Orlick as Orlick is to him – a point underlined by a reversal of detail from Bunyan, for, whereas Christian defeats Apollyon with the cry of ' "*Rejoice not against me, O mine enemy*" ', it is Orlick who addresses Pip, twice, as 'Oh you enemy' (424–5).[29] More than in any other novel of Dickens, existence is conceived of as competition and the hero is drawn blatantly into the contest for survival and for power. In this setting words become untrustworthy – the means not only of self-fashioning but of fabrication for personal ends. In the gospel of modern man it is never certain where truth and integrity lie.

The primitive Orlick must lose so that the civilized Pip, guile and all, can go on. Yet there is something amiss in the winner's legacy. Not only does the authority of the core narrative become decentred under pressure from rival accounting, the hero makes no advance in fullness or force of character, and, on the contrary, emerges relatively attenuated. Pip escapes from the sluice-house, not through his own efforts, but by the lucky intervention of Herbert, Startop, and, of all people, Trabb's boy, suggesting that the crisis is staved off from without rather than resolved from within. He has encountered his darker impulses and has left them behind, but has not reached a settlement or integrated them into his personality; they have been 'acted out' but not 'worked through'. A day or so later, in a moment reminiscent of the high points of the Puritan conversion or learning process, Pip wakes up to a beautiful sunrise, where 'millions of sparkles' burst out upon the river, and 'From me too, a veil seemed to be drawn, and I felt strong and well' (433); but this proves a false dawn, a transient regeneration.[30] When he awakens from his second illness – the one Joe nurses him through – it is as a child, needful and passive: 'I was like a child in his hands'; and when the carriage arrives to take him for a ride, 'Joe wrapped me up . . . and put me in, as if I were still the small helpless creature to whom he had so abundantly given of the wealth of his great nature' (466–7). Pip's life seems to have come full circle, and we are back with the 'small bundle of shivers' (4) that he was at setting out.

His dependency can of course be understood at this point as the consequence of his illness, but the physical condition then shades into a mental one, so that when he determines to return to 'the good old forge' it is with the hope that he can 'relieve [his] mind and heart' and be received 'like a forgiven child' (472). Biddy, whom he plans to marry, he sees likewise not so much as a partner as a support: 'And now, dear Biddy, if you can tell me that you will go through the world with me, you will surely make it a better world for me, and me a better man for it, and I will try to make it a better world for you.' The outcome of this *Bildungsroman* is, ironically, regression to a state of infantile want. Pip's motives in going back, as they emerge in these passages, call in question, moreover, the earlier emphasis on the development of a moral and humane sensibility; in the end, the desire to repent and acknowledge the goodness in others is bound up with, and indeed subservient to, the drive for self-preservation and the assuaging of personal pain; making reparation is really a salving of Pip's own wounds.

A measure of the deficiency in Pip's character is provided here by the contrasting way in which Joe deals with the guilt *he* so surprisingly expresses to his convalescing charge. Raising the matter of 'Tickler', the stick with which Mrs Joe had beaten her ward, Joe explains his reluctance to intervene as being due, not to any concern for himself, but to the fact that his direct opposition only meant that 'she dropped into you the heavier for it', and goes on to raise a hypothetical question about tolerating harm in the service of a greater good: ' "Where is the good as you are doing? I grant you I see the 'arm," says the man, "but I don't see the good. I call upon you, theerfore, to pint out the good." ' (469). This, of course, is Joe's way of getting reassurance, and he tells Pip afterwards that he had also shared his worry with Biddy, who had eased his mind by concurring that 'J. Gargery's power to part you and Tickler in sunders, were not fully equal to his inclinations'. It comes as a shock to the reader, I think, to learn that the apparently placid and innocent Joe has been troubled for years by a secret anxiety and fear of having done, though perforce, the wrong thing; nobody is immune to the complications of living or of the psyche. (Perhaps he should simply have put a stop to Mrs Joe's rampaging – which is what Orlick says *he* would do during the quarrel at the forge, and afterwards uncompromisingly does. But things are not so black-and-white for ordinary people, and early in the book Joe had told Pip, for example, that he put up with a great deal from his wife because he recalled the horror of his own father's violence towards his mother.) At the same time, however, we admire the way he copes with his difficulty, admitting it, bringing it into the open, consulting Biddy, talking it over with Pip himself, postulating an outside view, putting himself in a text and interpreting it – that is, thoroughly working it through. The character we think of as one of Dickens's big babies – 'a foolish, dear fellow' (8) is Pip's introduction of him – turns out to be as wisely grown-up in managing himself as in judging others, whereas Pip reverts to adolescent craving for care and attention. If Orlick is Pip's dark underside, Joe is his superior counterpart in the process of self-regulation and (a point on which there will be more to be said) in relationships.

Pip's idea of 'go[ing] through the world' with Biddy is a self-indulgent fantasy, as if he knew the end of *David Copperfield* and wanted to be like David with Agnes, but without having earned the right by learning the lessons of adversity, as David does through loss and exile, and without that commitment of sexual energy which David discovers in himself (and which in Pip is, as we shall see, bound unproductively elsewhere). Reality refuses to accord with Pip's expectations, in this as in other respects; the day he arrives at the forge is that of Joe's and Biddy's wedding. Circumstance makes cruel nonsense of his hopes for the future and his attempt to reverse past mistakes. Yet it is not just the tragic, or grimly comic, lack of fit between the external shape of things and the plots we construct for ourselves that is brought into focus. We are also asked to consider what kind of salvation is available to us, and how it should be sought. Pip is looking for an easy ride, and there is none. He wants his life changed for him, but such things don't happen, unless your name is Ebenezer Scrooge, and even then you have to go through purgatory. The message of Pip's character and situation in this segment of the novel, as inversely of those of David or Joe, who succeed where he fails, is that redemption of one's life must be worked for, and consists, not of transformation, but of getting along.

But Pip does, after all, salvage something from the pieces of his broken existence. After the initial shock, he comes to terms with Joe's and Biddy's arrangement, wishes them well, asks their forgiveness for past conduct, and then sells up and goes abroad to join Herbert. His white-collar job at Clarriker's, the small-scale trading House which 'had a good name, . . . and did very well' (480), where he rises to be third in the Firm, represents solid but modest success – getting along through application but without grandeur and seemingly without great difficulties. It is a version of the work ethic that emerges in *A Christmas Carol* and *David Copperfield*, but is in a minor and much lower key; a peripheral affair and mildly interesting set of facts about a character, it contrasts vividly with the model of social organization implicitly celebrated in Scrooge's benevolent economic paternalism, which has its base at the heart of the nation in 'the good old city' (*Christmas Carol*, 134), and with the cultural idealism expressed in David's middle-class values and achievements. We are left in Pip's case, not with an ideology, but with a form of existence. Even Pip's writing is a relatively subjective and private affair in that, though his confessions may contain lessons for others, it is never granted the status of an account of how to live, as

David's novels are, and indeed is never considered at all as a vocation or in terms of any public function.

Yet, Dickens does not close the book of Pip Pirrip without assuming one of his other favourite affirmative stances. After eleven years away, Pip returns to the forge in the final chapter to discover a happy family scene:

> There, smoking his pipe in the old place by the kitchen firelight, as hale and as strong as ever though a little grey, sat Joe; and there, fenced into a corner with Joe's leg, and sitting on my own little stool looking at the fire, was – I again!
>
> 'We giv' him the name of Pip for your sake, dear old chap,' said Joe, delighted when I took another stool by the child's side (but I did *not* rumple his hair), 'and we hoped he might grow a little bit like you, and we think he do.'
>
> I thought so too, and I took him out for a walk next morning, and we talked immensely, understanding one another to perfection. (481)

As David Trotter points out, the dysfunctional family of the beginning of the novel has been reconstituted.[31] There had been the unhappy Joe and Mrs Joe, without children of their own; the orphaned Pip, with no true home; and Pumblechook, who had appointed himself Pip's patron only to abuse him with words and sometimes hands. At the end, Joe is as much an image of constancy as ever; the 'pleasant and wholesome and sweet-tempered' (125), and fruitful, Biddy has replaced the unco-operative, frustrated and violent Mrs Joe; her son has taken Pip's place, and Pip Pumblechook's, an adoptive uncle determined to be the benign opposite of his forerunner, and *not* ruffle his nephew's hair. As a finishing touch, Biddy then appears with an infant girl on her lap, a pose that neatly ensures gender balance and differentiation. In all of this, to use Trotter's phrase, the family is undoubtedly 'the medium of social and moral understanding'. It is quite another thing, however, to ask how far the picture represents, like the family groups foregrounded in the endings of *Oliver Twist* and *A Christmas Carol*, a value bank of overriding importance, an investment of prescriptive hope for the stability and well-being of the nation. The answer begins to become apparent, I think, as soon as we reflect upon the detail of Pip's taking his young namesake off for a walk, in the churchyard where the book opens, and their 'talk[ing] immensely' and 'understanding one another to perfection'. Whereas Tiny Tim, who also has a stool by the fireside, is a permanent miracle agent that binds the exemplary Cratchits more intimately together and 'uncle' Scrooge more closely to them, little Pip is removed from the frame of familial accord and put in the landscape

of a wider and uncertain world. Will this double – 'I again!' – repeat Pip
Pirrip's troubled history or tread a different track? In either case, he is
born a hostage to fortune. The novel soon outruns the seeming closure
of the symbolic family setting for the indeterminate realm of individual
experience.[32] This focus then presses onwards and backwards, for the
last scene of *Great Expectations*, to a Pip made permanently lonely by
his unfulfilled desire for Estella; but this, like fuller assessment of the
status of the idyll of the forge, is best understood in the light of further
consideration of the book's analysis of society.

*

> Mr. Carlyle, Mr. Ruskin, the Aesthetes, are all wrong about the
> nineteenth century. It is not the age of money-bags and cant, soot,
> hubbub, and ugliness. It is the age of great expectation and
> unwearied striving after better things.[33]

Robin Gilmour quotes this passage from an essay of 1882 by Frederic
Harrison, leading adherent of the Positivist movement and Comte's
Religion of Humanity, when seeking to argue that *Great Expectations*
partakes of a contemporary 'sense of hopefulness and promise, even
idealism' about 'improvement, both personal and social', with Dickens
implying a contrast between the dynamic urban society of his own day
and the cultural poverty of the earlier more rural society which Pip
endeavours to rise above in his pursuit of gentility.[34] What Gilmour
omits to mention, or fails to see, however, is the scepticism in Harrison's
voice, and his deep anxiety about the dangers attendant on the advances
that have been made 'in our material and external life'. In the next
sentence of the above-quoted paragraph Harrison questions the narrow
creed of progress, asking of the age, 'Still, is it the Millennium foretold
by the prophets, by civil engineers and railway kings?'; and his essay
becomes increasingly preoccupied with the 'risks', 'drawbacks' and
'evils' of a situation of unprecedented expansion of 'material acqui-
sitions'. Proclaiming the value of 'spiritual life over material life', he
warns his readers that to multiply 'the appliances of human life' does not
increase 'the powers of thought, or of endurance; much less . . . self-
restraint, unselfishness, and a good heart'; and that 'the increased
resources of society are found in practice to be increased opportunities
for the skilful to make themselves masters of the weak'.[35] Clearly, it is
not that Dickens reflects something of the optimism to be found in
Harrison, but that Harrison, possibly recalling *Great Expectations*,
takes a somewhat less gloomy view of the modern world than Dickens.
Not only do Pip's aspirations bring misery, the story of Whittington or

Crusoe gone sour, but the society in which he moves is one where the spirit of acquisition has taken irreversible hold.

This bleak condition is expressed with particular force through the characters of Jaggers the lawyer, who is Pip's 'guardian', and his chief clerk Wemmick. They operate in a metropolitan setting that is all too clearly dominated by money-bags, cant, soot, hubbub, and ugliness. The last of these becomes immediately apparent to Pip as, arriving in the city, he is confronted by 'ugly, crooked, narrow and dirty' streets, a 'motheaten' hackney coach, the 'dust and grit' around Jaggers' office, the decay of his lodgings at Barnard's Inn, a 'miserable makeshift' of 'crippled flower-pot, cracked glass, . . . soot and smoke . . . dry rot and wet rot . . . rot of rat' (163, 165, 172). More important than outward dilapidation, however, is something on the inside, in the very workings of society and its institutions. Passing Newgate Prison, Pip is sickened by the casual violence of the courts when he hears that four are to be hanged in a row at eight the next morning; the trials and fate of the culprits are reduced to the site of a desperate opportunism, being touted as a tourist attraction by a barker whom Pip buys off with a shilling, and whose mildewed finery bespeaks a past bargain struck with the executioner (165–6). Hard currency, moral apathy, the seizing of the main chance everywhere prevail. As Wemmick says to his young charge, 'They'll do it, if there's anything to be got by it' (172).

Jaggers and Wemmick himself must be counted pre-eminently among the 'They'. Theirs is a subtle, highly efficient brutality. Famously dedicated to amassing 'portable property' (201, 204, 262), the rings, brooches, and other pieces he takes from Jaggers's clients as undeclared payment for interceding on their behalf with his elusive master, Wemmick's methods are suave, low-key but deadly, as is seen in the demonstration he mounts for Pip on their tour of Newgate, where he shakes hands with the 'Colonel', a forger of coins he knows to be certainly condemned to death but encourages to hope for a reprieve (' "I think I shall be out on this Monday, sir" . . . "Perhaps," returned my friend, "but there's no knowing" ') so as to extract from him the gift of virtually all he has left of value – a pair of prize pigeons (261–2). What is so chilling here is not only the predatory manoeuvres themselves, or the use of the handshake of good faith as a cover for false intent, but the complete indifference of Wemmick, who is not a bad man, towards the plight of others, his amoral assumptions, his inhumanity. So it is with his employer, though his is more the bludgeoning approach.

When we first meet Jaggers in London he is characteristically threatening people with his finger, frightening two men and an old woman into paying him, not for resolving their cases, but for keeping them mysteriously going. Then he berates another client, the hapless Mike, for daring to mention that he has found a witness who will swear 'anythink', while nevertheless having the disreputable stooge paraded outside the window so that he can weigh up how plausible he would be (169–70). To use his own formulation, Jaggers is an unscrupulous 'beater' in a world of 'beaters and cringers' (390) – though he can be submissive enough when serving the rich and therefore powerful, like Miss Havisham and Magwitch. It is no wonder that he likes the look of Bentley Drummle, whom he nicknames 'the Spider' (212); which is a designation, however, that, in its suggestions of laying traps and watching, seems much more applicable to himself than to the patently loutish Drummle. Jaggers is the bullying type, but he is also 'deep'. As Wemmick proudly remarks, 'If there was anything deeper, . . . he'd be it' (199).

Jaggers's mastery of others rests above all upon the rule of fear. His main instrument of control is the impression he constantly gives 'of knowing something secret about every one of us that would effectually do for each individual if he chose to disclose it' (136); and, sitting in the lawyer's office, Pip reflects upon the fact that the clerk 'had the same air of knowing something to everybody else's disadvantage, as his master had' (165). Jaggers seems to have inherited something of the divine attributes of unaccountability and all-seeingness, and nothing is more guaranteed to keep people in line than the certainty that nothing can be hidden, especially when accompanied by uncertainty about quite what the transgression might be. Wemmick again puts it in a nutshell when he avers that his master 'has 'em, soul and body' (263). Taking this together with Wemmick's description of the *modus operandi* whereby he, the 'subordinate', plays front man for the 'principal' who keeps himself apart and 'high' (263), and together with all the practical evidence, and we might say that they have the perfect racket, involving subterfuge and exploitation, even blackmail. Who, we might ask, are the criminals? But of course the Jaggers–Wemmick set-up is an allowed one, on the right side of the law – in fact the Law itself. They help to run, and are run by, a self-perpetuating system driven by self-interest, where relationships are structured as a pecking-order of gainers and losers, power and powerlessness. This is modern urban society. Indeed, we are prompted to take an even wider view: the place where the action is centred is 'Little Britain' (163, 264), suggesting a microcosm of the condition of the nation.[36]

Jaggers not only casts his finger at people, he bites it, symbolically consuming his victims no doubt but equally wounding himself. At the psychological level the strong as well as the weak are damaged by the system. The lawyer's other mannerism is the obsessive compulsion to wash with scented soap:

> he seemed to have been engaged on a case of a darker complexion than usual, for, we found him with his head butted into the closet, not only washing his hands, but laving his face and gargling his throat. And even when he had done all that . . . he took out his penknife and scraped the case out of his nails before he put his coat on. (210–11)

These repeated ablutions are the sign of Jaggers's subconscious and unrealizable wish to be cleansed of the filth of the profession in which he so brilliantly engages, and thus the symptom of a divided personality. For all his authority, he is no less trapped than anyone else.

Wemmick, it seems, *can* find an escape, or at least a refuge, from corruptness and constraint. This Englishman's home in the country is literally his Castle, on a small scale, complete with moat, drawbridge, arbour, lake, and working cannon. It is very much a repository of value in contrast to the urban rat race. It is a place of familial affection, with the cheerful 'Aged P' being well looked after and being so fond of 'his boy' (369); of instinctive communication and intimacy, not only in the customary tipping of nods to the delighted 'Aged' but in the remarkable courtship ritual of Wemmick and Miss Skiffins consisting of the former's arm gradually elongating itself again and again round the latter's waist and being again and again 'unwound' by her with 'greatest deliberation' (298); of farmyard and fresh vegetables, where pig, fowls and rabbits thrive alongside frames of cucumbers; of a healthy do-it-yourself mentality, where the proprietor is 'engineer', 'carpenter', 'plumber' and 'gardener' all in one (207); of frugality, warmth, and hospitality, with haystacks of buttered toast, home-produced sausage, jorums of tea, and something a little stronger which Wemmick and Miss Skiffins 'drank out of one glass' (298). We may compare this ambience, rich in ordinary human virtue and pleasure, comfortably ramshackle, with, say, the calculated excellence and tensions of Jaggers's dinner party, where Pip and his school-fellows end up quarrelling and their host shows off his housekeeper, Molly, 'a wild beast tamed' (202) – with all the legerdemain, deceit, competition, and disquiet of the urban scene.

It can also be said, of course, that the Castle at Walworth and the people in it are quite bizarre, even in some ways ridiculous. We have (in Pip's own words) a 'crazy little box of a cottage' (209) weirdly extended along the lines of a fortress and great country estate; the Aged's deafness transforms from the source of a display of unspoken love and respect between father and son to the basis of a joke when Pip, trying to converse, has 'not the faintest notion what he meant' (293); the cut of Miss Skiffin's dress made her figure 'very like a boy's kite' (294); and so on. The Aged's opinion that 'This spot and these beautiful works upon it ought to be kept together by the Nation, after my son's time, for the people's enjoyment' (208) appears to make fun at once of dotage, grotesque suburban taste, and the nation's addiction to preserving its heritage for democratic use. Yet, though this no doubt impugns a debased modern culture, there is, in what we have seen, nothing that seriously undermines the status of the Walworth episodes as a model of demeanour, relationships, and priorities in life, and it may indeed be that they gain greater effect as such through an atmosphere of sympathetic comedy. What does in the end compromise the standing of Walworth, however, is something in the nature of the relation between it and London.

The fortifications of the Castle draw a symbolic line between the private and the public, home and the world of business, so that the former is put apart, unable to connect with or influence the latter. A Union Jack flying on its battlements, the place at Walworth is another, different, little Britain. A division has set in at both the cultural and the personal levels. This makes, for example, Wemmick's activities as 'Jack of all Trades' at the Castle the expression of a nostalgia for a more integrated existence – such as still holds at Joe Gargery's forge – where work and daily life go along together. Wemmick has his 'Walworth sentiments' and his London or 'official sentiments', and they are kept entirely separate – 'must not be confounded together', as he tells Pip (291). Paradoxically, he keeps sane by accepting a kind of schizophrenia. Jaggers knows nothing of his property or of the Aged: 'Never heard of it. . . . Never heard of him. No; the office is one thing, and private life is another. When I go into the office, I leave the Castle behind me, and when I come into the Castle, I leave the office behind me' (208).

There are in fact two Wemmicks, physically and on the inside. As he journeys back from Walworth to the city, he by degrees 'got dryer and harder . . . and his mouth tightened into a post-office again' (210). When he and Pip dine with Jaggers, Pip is inclined to catch his eye 'in a friendly way', but he 'turned his eyes on Mr. Jaggers when ever he raised them from the table, and was as dry and distant to me as if there were twin Wemmicks and this was the wrong one' (389). But it is not only by reticence that he shuts out his Walworth self. The 'wrong twin' springs quickly into action to back up his employer when Jaggers summarily dismisses the distraught Mike whose daughter is under arrest on suspicion of shoplifting: ' "Get out of this Office. I'll have no feelings here. Get out." "It serves you right," said Wemmick. "Get out." ' (415).

This is all the more indicative of the reign of heartlessness for coming just after Jaggers has admitted to having 'poor dreams' of his own about having 'a pleasant home' someday, and to having saved Estella from the criminal underworld into which she was born by arranging for her adoption by Miss Havisham (412–13). Small things can be done to alleviate the cruelty of the system of self-interest, but they leave that system fundamentally unchanged. The same is true of Wemmick's occasional emergency application of a Walworth sentiment in a London context, as in his comradely warning to Pip to cover his tracks when he is hiding Magwitch. It makes no difference to how the modern world generally goes.

The understanding of the contemporary situation that we get from these parts of *Great Expectations*, however, does not stop at this sense of dichotomy where the humane is unable to negotiate with the acquisitive. In some respects there *are* connections between London and Walworth. On Pip's first visit to the suburbs the meal includes a fowl that Wemmick explains had been acquired as a thank-you from a cook's-shop owner whom he had reminded of the easy treatment he had received when acting as a Juryman – 'As far as it goes, property and portable' (204). Later, we are confronted in the midst of a 'warm and greasy' Sunday afternoon with Pip's suspicion that Miss Skiffins's 'classic brooch' was 'a piece of portable property that had been given her by Wemmick' (296–7). It may be, of course, that this piece has been purchased rather than extorted; but there is enough in these instances to show that the edenic Walworth bears the taint of fallen metropolitan ways. Wemmick speaks jokingly of being prepared should his 'little place' be 'besieged' (207), but his defences have in a sense already been penetrated, since the gains from the one style of life have been carried to the comfortable heart of the other. On a larger plane, moreover, it becomes apparent that the whole of Wemmick's fixed property has been built on the proceeds of the dubious business of the Law; for the Aged tells Pip that his son had given up the Wine-Coopering for the legal profession to earn the money to look after him, and 'little by little made out this elegant and beautiful property' (293). The worthiness of purpose, caring for an infirm parent, does not alter the fact that it is funded by hard-nosed means, and that the Castle is, as it were, the excess value of Wemmick's London labour. The opposing spheres are fundamentally of a piece; there is no getting outside the system of money and self-interest. The point is underlined elsewhere by Pip's only 'good' deed being to underwrite Herbert's engagement in trading for profit on the imperial stage; and, in a different way, by the language that describes the Newgate Wemmick, who is said to be in his 'conservatory' and to have 'walked among the prisoners, much as a gardener might walk among his plants' (260, 262). At the Castle he grows fruit and vegetables; in prison he grows people. The imagery reminds us that the split personality is, at the level of crude survival, the same man after all.

Against this background of irresistible social process the settled life of the Gargery household at the end of the novel seems even more peripheral than the Castle at Walworth – a comforting sidelight rather than a beacon for any real present or future; in David Trotter's words 'powerful nostalgia',[37] but nostalgia nonetheless. It is literally and figuratively a small corner of England, not only buried far from the city and the rising suburbs but edged closely around by the uneasy, go-getting provincial world of Satis House, where Miss Havisham's relatives scuttle about in search of pickings like the insects on her decayed wedding feast, and of the town, where the main chance is sought obsequiously by Trabb the tailor and pompously by Pumble-chook, whose narrow-mindedness seems to be reflected in his prem-ises with their myriads of 'little drawers' for shutting nature away in dried-up pieces, so that Pip, feeling the oppression, wonders if 'the flower-seeds and bulbs ever wanted of a fine day to break out of those jails, and bloom' (53). Do the tradespeople themselves ever want to break out, we wonder, when we learn that they form a chain of compartmentalized and lethargic voyeurs, or spies, with Pumblechook conducting his business 'by looking across the street at the saddler, who appeared to transact *his* business by keeping his eye on the coach-maker, who appeared to get on in life by putting his hands in his pockets and contemplating the baker', and so on and on (54). Standing in splendid isolation, the forge is more an enclave of utopian images than a working model for social organization at large; the considered but fundamentally desperate throw of a beleaguered intelligence.

Much the same limitation attaches to Joe Gargery himself in his exemplary guises as 'gentle Christian man' and one committed to filling ably his niche in the scheme of things. He is too much the exception and too much on the edge of things, or too deep in the rustic interior, ever to furnish a practical ideal of English manhood. Nostalgia is certainly an apt word to describe this portrait of a village smithy happy to observe the 'diwisions' in life and content with the place he is 'competent to fill, and fills well' (149). The disgruntled and ambitious Orlick is Joe's *alter ego*, as well as Pip's, though it is also worth noting that the relative status of the two men, the agreeable craftsman-proprietor and the recalcitrant journeyman, is another reflection of Dickens's conservatism in questions of social hierarchy.

Yet Joe is typical of something else in Dickens – a paradox. However nostalgic, the conception of Joe Gargery is in certain ways a challenging one, and a good instance of Dickens's propensity for entering contemporary debate from a radical angle. To understand this, we must briefly consider the current attitudes to the question of what constitutes a gentleman.

The straightforward traditional view comes from William Sewell, High Church clergyman, Oxford don, and headmaster of St Peter's College, Radley, the public school he helped to found in 1847. In his sermons to the boys Sewell proclaims quite simply that the 'divisions of mankind' are ordained by God, who has struck a line 'between those who are gentlemen, that is, of a higher and superior class, and those who are not':

> Some men he has made to rule and govern; some to be ruled and governed. And in England, the term gentleman is generally given to all those who are in those positions of society, in which they are trusted with power and authority, and are required to exercise the higher faculties of nature, in influencing, guiding, and benefiting others. And now you can see that in this sense the term gentleman is applicable to every one of you. You are all sons of gentlemen, of persons who, at least, are in liberal, respected professions and occupations. This place is not intended for any others.[38]

In 1854 Sewell sent Dickens a copy of the first volume of his *Sermons* (the above quotation is from the second), which the latter swiftly returned as a gesture of dislike.[39] For Dickens, the emphasis should lie on inner qualities, the 'higher faculties' themselves, not social rank, and he may have had Sewell's sweeping validation of privilege in mind when getting the trustworthy Herbert Pocket to condemn 'prejudice' while crediting his father with the sound principle that 'no man who was not a true gentleman at heart, ever was, since the world began, a true gentleman in manner' (181). This standpoint was itself very much a trend of the time. Writing on 'Gentlemen' in the *Cornhill Magazine* in 1862, for example, Sir James Fitzjames Stephen states that 'there is a constantly increasing disposition to insist more upon the moral and less upon the social element of the word, and it is not impossible that in course of time its use may come to be altogether dissociated from any merely conventional distinction'.[40] Ruskin, in 'Of Vulgarity', a section of *Modern Painters* (1860), looks at length at the characteristics of 'gentlemanliness', which he sees as deriving from a genetic inheritance that can be enhanced or degraded from generation to generation. 'Sensitiveness', 'sympathy', 'kindness and mercifulness', 'self-command', and 'truthfulness' are the key virtues in Ruskin's definition of the gentleman; and the 'fineness of nature' that they collectively represent is by no means incompatible with 'bodily strength', or with 'reserve', where the latter comes from constant habits of feeling: 'your gentleman has walked in pity all day long; . . . you thought the eyes were bright only; but they were wet'.[41] To this, which appeared in the same year as *Great Expectations*, we recognize an obvious resemblance in Joe, the one for whom 'lies is lies', the giant combining 'strength with gentleness', whose touch was as 'the rustle of an angel's wing', Pip's tender nurse (71, 141). The connection then seems all the closer when we find Ruskin lamenting as vulgar 'the assumption of behaviour, language, or dress unsuited to them, by persons in inferior stations of life' – Joe, we recall, knows he is 'wrong' in his London clothes, 'wrong out of the forge, . . . or off th'meshes' (224) – but stresses that 'provincial dialect' – which Joe so plainly speaks – is not.[42]

Yet there is more to Joe than a mirroring of relatively advanced ideas; something markedly distinct. Although Stephen and Ruskin, unlike Sewell, suppose in theory that gentlemanliness is independent of social position, in practice class bias persists, and is presumed in the very language and examples they use, as in Ruskin's quoted reference to 'persons in inferior stations' who act above themselves, or to the 'higher classes, being generally of purer race'.[43] Neither does Dickens, as we know, envisage any reordering of the 'divisions of mankind'; but by locating the gentlemanly qualities, if not quite exclusively in view of the kindly Herbert Pocket, then certainly squarely in a working man he unsettles the lines of the argument, shifting the weight of preference and attention to the lower stratum. Indeed, in driving a wedge between the two elements in the summarizing phrase 'gentle Christian man' he unpacks the whole concept of the gentleman, and the presuppositions about hierarchies of birth and wealth that cling to it. Ruskin, disliking the growth of competition and economic self-interest under capitalism, advocates ideals of quasi-feudal responsibility and chivalry as the salvation of conventional society, and advises 'all orders', 'higher' and 'lower', to be watchful in their breeding and conduct for the sake of the nation's health, since genetic process can both elevate and debase (and in fact will in the long run ensure the very fluidity of movement up and down the ladder that Ruskin does not want).[44] Dickens, while sharing the ideals, centres them in a blacksmith, and so puts the whole notion of social cohesion under pressure, not because Joe Gargery would ever challenge the system – though others of the low might – but because he is out on a limb, a tiny picture of well-being in a great landscape of disease, a sound working and family man but not a sufficient working model.

In the conceptions both of the forge and of Joe himself there emerges, thus, an impasse on the question of the condition and future prospects of England. Dickens appears to have been worried by this, and in *Our Mutual Friend* will return to and configure anew both the family and the gentleman as bases of social stability. In the same novel, moreover, he will revisit with a fresh sense of purpose a third major theme of *Great Expectations*, and the one that remains for us to consider – that of gender positions.

*

In an influential essay Lucy Frost considers the three main female characters of *Great Expectations*, Mrs Joe, Miss Havisham and Estella, as 'strong' women who are tamed into conformity with orthodox expectations of subservience and passivity. At first perceptively cultivating their qualities of independence and self-assertiveness, the novel proceeds to turn the tables and impose upon them 'a grim moral logic of repentance and conversion'.[45] Frost tracks this movement back to a personal fear of womankind on Dickens's part and to his natural complicity with patriarchal notions of the feminine, and ends up by stressing the loss of consistency and credibility that she sees arising in the story from the shift of perspective. For all the brilliance of her local insights, these emphases on author psychology and the deterioration of novelistic form ultimately blunt the force of the treatment of women in this text. Irrespective of Dickens's own leanings, his book exposes to scrutiny the very ideology it underwrites, and opens up the whole question of women's needs and place in society. This happens for two reasons: firstly, on account of the quality of his presentation of the problematics of female experience, which exists as much in indirect as in explicit portrayal; and secondly, because the positioning of women is expressed through the mind of a narrator, whose attitudes are themselves subject to appraisal.

Though it remains an important reference point throughout the novel, the admired model of Victorian womanhood makes only fleeting appearances, in the form of Herbert's Clara and more especially Biddy who supplies a familiar mix of comeliness and wholesome character, 'pleasant and . . . sweet-tempered', with 'thoughtful and attentive eyes . . . that were very pretty and very good' (125). Mrs Joe, to whom Dickens does devote a deal of imaginative energy in the earlier parts of the novel, is the anti-type of this ideal: 'tall and bony', always on the 'ram-page', liberally applying her cane 'Tickler' or using Pip as a 'connubial missile', dosing the boy with Tar-water, knocking Joe's head against the wall; her violent, sharp and unyielding temper being figured in the 'coarse apron' she almost always wears, fastened behind 'with two loops, and having a square impregnable bib in front, that was stuck full of pins and needles' (8–9, 11–12). Her marriage and family obligations in bringing up her orphaned brother are matters of endless complaint, for, as she announces to Pip, 'It's bad enough to be a blacksmith's wife (and him a Gargery) without being your mother' (9). Resentful of her station, she turns housekeeping into 'an exquisite art of making her cleanliness more uncomfortable and unacceptable than dirt itself' (23). This propensity is graphically illustrated in one of Pip's recollections. When his sister learned that she had been excluded by Miss Havisham from the discussions about his future, and had her illusions of reflected glory shattered by the news that he was to become a mere blacksmith's apprentice after all, she threw a candlestick, erupted into a fit of sobbing, took up her scrubbing-brush, and 'cleaned us out of house and home', wondering aloud why Joe hadn't married 'a Negress Slave' in the first place (98–9).

Mrs Joe's behaviour clearly matches the contemporary definition of hysteria. Writing in a *Dictionary of Psychological Medicine* of 1892, but recuperating ideas of the previous half century, Horatio Bryan Donkin describes the hysteric as one who is 'an individualist, an unsocial unit', and fails 'in adaptation to organic surroundings'.[46] Her mental abnormality is mainly evidenced by 'exaggerated impressionability or tumultuous emotion on apparently slight provocation'. Some types become 'inert', others (as Mrs Joe) 'actively mischievous'; the action or inaction result from 'the passion for sympathy or notoriety', and instances of this range from 'mere giving way to or exaggeration of suffering, to wilful imposture, simulation of all kinds'. It is apt to recall, in the light of the reference to pretence, that when Mrs Joe falls into a frenzy at being called names by Orlick during the row at the forge over who should get a half-holiday, she does not lapse suddenly but 'consciously and deliberately took extraordinary pains to force herself into it, and became blindly furious by regular stages' (114). We suspect her of what Donkin goes on to call 'subtlest craft' in working up a loss of self-control and drawing attention to herself. When her 'clappings and screamings', beating of her bosom, and other automatisms prompt Joe to lay successfully into Orlick in defence of her honour, she faints – though, as Pip tellingly speculates in a whispered aside, almost certainly not before she 'had seen the fight first' (115).

Pip has never a good word for his sister, and his account of her encourages the same response that Donkin enters in respect of the actions of headstrong and manipulative hysterics – 'contempt and aversion'. Yet there is another side to the issue. Judgemental though he can be, Donkin is also keen to stress that where hysterics are 'powerless to help themselves' they 'rightly excite our pity' rather than condemnation; and he is committed throughout his paper to the belief that female hysteria is due in large part to restrictions and prohibitions imposed by society: ' "Thou shalt not" meets a girl at almost every turn.' 'Repression and ignorance in sexual matters' is the primary agency, but there are, Donkin insists, 'all kinds of other barriers to the free play of her powers . . . set up by ordinary social and ethical customs'. 'Regular work and definite pursuits' can provide 'a safety valve' for women of all conditions, as they do customarily for men.

Implicit in Donkin's observations in fact is the view that *all* deviant behaviour in the field of hysteria, however abhorrent, is at bottom involuntary and attributable to causes outside the perpetrator's control. It constitutes symptoms that we should try to explain and understand, not simply denounce. In the light of this approach, Mrs Joe too becomes a case for scrutiny. Pip has a big axe to grind with the sister who has abused him, and, as we know, he had entertained thoughts of wanting her dead, but the alert reader of *Great Expectations* will wish to ask why she is as she is, and what her conduct and bearing mean.[47]

Not invited to the audience at Satis House, and objecting to being used as 'door-mats' under their feet, Mrs Joe asks Joe and Pip what 'company [they] graciously thought she *was* fit for' (98). This is a good question. Mrs Joe is a socially and economically ambitious woman, excited at the thought of prospects like Pip's, but who is inescapably tied to her narrow sphere, 'fit' only for the forge and its domestic routine. Her offensive in cleaning Joe and Pip out of house and home, in making their lives a misery, is to wage war from within, turning the terms of her restriction into weapons of assault. This seems more like frustration and driven defiance than the motiveless malignity that Pip consistently ascribes to, for him, this unqualified exemplar of 'violent women' (114). The same mixed impression attaches to the infamous 'coarse apron' that is at once Mrs Joe's strait-jacket and her armour. Pip somewhat sarcastically remarks that there was no reason why she should have worn it at all, or, if she did wear it, should not have taken it off, 'every day of her life' (8). But he has missed, or does not wish to see, the point. She parades the uniform of her enslavement with an air of belligerent martyrdom, expressing dissatisfaction with her lot. Her other notable appendage, Tickler, is a similar, and perhaps more telling, sign of her discontent; a phallic rod with which she so often brings her 'ram-paging' to a climax, it suggests that there are in her energies, like those of a man, which can find no outlet in her world, except in a bizarre form of masculinity. Mrs Joe's grotesque and aggressive demeanour is the untoward release of dammed-up force; or in Donkin's terms, 'nervous discharges, and an undue lack of determination of such discharges into definite channels'. Joe seems intuitively to see something of the problem when he says that she is a *'master*-mind', much 'given to government', for whom he is inclined to make allowances in view of his memory of his own mother as 'a woman drudging and slaving and breaking her . . . hart and never getting no peace' (48–9: italics mine). One woman's life is much like another's: desire ill matched with opportunity.

That Mrs Joe has an unfulfilled sexual appetite is also clear. She is a woman easily aroused, forever flirting with Pumblechook, and like Estella taking pleasure in watching men fight over her. Indeed, her posture in the aftermath of the fisticuffs at the forge, when Joe, the victor, carries her into the house, has something of the orgasmic about it, as she 'would do nothing but struggle and clench her hands in Joe's hair' (115). Even her way of cutting bread-and-butter seems to indicate a sensual streak, as she jams the loaf hard and fast against herself, spreads it with the creamy substance, and 'hew[s] it into two halves' (10). Most striking of all, however, is her relation to Orlick after he has bludgeoned her almost to death. Far from shunning or being afraid of him, or wishing to denounce him, she dotes on him. Having him summoned to her presence by drawing a hammer on her slate,

> [s]he manifested the greatest anxiety to be on good terms with him, was evidently much pleased by his being at length produced, and motioned that she would have him given something to drink. She watched his countenance as if she were particularly wishful to be assured that he took kindly to his reception, she showed every possible desire to conciliate him, and there was an air of humble propitiation in all she did, such as I have seen pervade the bearing of a child towards a hard master. After that day, a day rarely passed without her drawing the hammer on her slate, and without Orlick's slouching in and standing doggedly before her. (124)

This is an important passage in the movement whereby Mrs Joe, the disruptive woman, is made to submit to the ideology of male dominance and tranquil domesticity. Pip has already told us that in her battered state 'her temper was much improved, and she was patient'; and it is significant that the disabling of Mrs Joe is the occasion of Biddy, herself specifically 'sweet-tempered' and 'patient' (125, 283), moving in as a 'blessing to the household' (123), the fair displacing the diametrically foul.[48] The eagerness to 'conciliate' and 'air of humble propitiation' suggest a penitent, a transgressor brought to her senses and seeing the light; the shrew, whom Orlick had once perceptively accused of wanting to be 'everybody's master', tamed into child-like compliance with the domination – the purging – at the same time prefigured by the journeyman's threat, 'I'd hold you, if you was my wife. I'd hold you under the pump, and choke it out of you' (114).

Yet this normalization of Mrs Joe is not the only meaning of the passage. There is another over and above it, or rather under and below. The imbecility that quietens her, creating the conditions for her reformation, also clears a way for the surfacing of a deep-down and unspeakable truth. The hammer signifies not only phallic power, Orlick as the instrument of masculine authority and punitive correction, but the phallus itself, which is persistently the object of her desire. Philip Martin argues, interestingly, that in wanting Orlick to be given a drink Mrs Joe is recreated as the conventional mother-figure, ministering succour;[49] but it could also be that she wants him plied with the kind of liquor with which he habitually fortifies himself when on *his* rampages (as so markedly throughout the assault on Pip at the sluice-house). Perhaps she is not humouring Orlick during the scene of his attendance but trying to attract him, taking an instinctual pleasure in thoughts of being wildly acted upon, held 'under the pump' in whatever sense. This interpretation is in perfect keeping with the fact that her husband, though 'a sort of Hercules' in the forge and on the marshes, shows little or no manliness in the home, where he spends a lot of time in the kitchen and caring for Pip, decidedly 'a'nt a master-mind' or a 'ram-pager' of any kind, and exhibits a 'mild, good-natured, sweet-tempered, easy-going' character much like that of the passive Victorian woman (8, 49). Orlick exudes the unrestrained potency which in Joe is conspicuously absent.

Mrs Joe Gargery, then, will not fit the regularizing mould that is prepared for her. There is a dimension of her being – inherent, primitive, self-affirming – that it cannot contain and that threatens it with rupture. One of the first things we notice about her as a woman is her name, with its suggestion that her identity is subsumed under that of her spouse; the last thing is that in the event she never ceases to have her independent say, whether deliberate or from the unconscious. In a sense this is so even when she passes over into the silence of death:

> in the evening, just at tea-time, [she] said quite plainly, 'Joe.' As she had never said any word for a long while, I ran and fetched in Mr. Gargery from the forge. She made signs to me that she wanted me to put her arms round his neck. So I put them round his neck, and she laid her head down on his shoulder quite content and satisfied. And so she presently said 'Joe' again, and once 'Pardon,' and once 'Pip.' And so she never lifted up her head any more. (283)

This account of death-bed reconciliation and repentance assigns her definitively to the pattern of convention, 'content and satisfied', sorry for the trouble she has caused. Yet what credit can we give it? It is Pip's description of what Biddy has told him, and hearsay is not the safest of evidence. It is so neat in its orthodoxy, and so discontinuous from what we have seen before of Mrs Joe, as to appear far-fetched or a leap of faith; so in keeping with Biddy's values as to seem her naïve and dutiful projection of events rather than the reality. Biddy's ending for Pip's sister is no doubt what Dickens considers best for womankind, and to everyone's advantage; but it cannot cover up the Pandora's box of need, restriction, and refusal that his imagination has, wittingly or otherwise, laid open.

*

If Mrs Joe's psychology has an ingredient of sexual frustration, Miss Havisham's derives specifically from the tradition of the deserted woman, of which a major example had been the story of Marianne's derangement after her jilting by Willoughby in Jane Austen's *Sense and Sensibility*, where, as Philip Martin shows, we get the classic 'behavioural abnormalities such as self-neglect, self-forgetfulness and emotional abandonment'.[50] Marianne, developing 'the most nervous irritability', becomes 'wholly dispirited, careless of her appearance', and wrapped up in herself, 'lost in her own thoughts'; she takes to the house but is alternately prone to sitting before the fire 'in melancholy meditation' and too restless to remain long in one spot, moving 'from one window to the other', and later being unable to stay 'in the room a moment after she was dressed . . . requiring at once solitude and continual change of place'.[51] This is like the cases of erotomania documented in nineteenth-century medical discourse, such as that by J.E.D. Esquirol which tells of the young female who 'becomes sad and thoughtful':

> The countenance assumes a pale hue, the eyes sink in their sockets . . . The sufferer experiences turns of prostration, without previous exertion . . . Nothing diverts her, or engages her attention. On the contrary, every thing wearies her. She avoids her relatives and friends . . . Her appetite is feeble, and capricious. She does not sleep; or, if she does, her rest is disturbed, and she becomes emaciated. . . . She finally sinks into marasmus, and dies.[52]

Wasting is very much the first thing Pip sees in Miss Havisham:

> I saw that everything within my view which ought to be white, had been white long ago, and had lost its lustre, and was faded and yellow. I saw that the bride within the bridal dress had withered like

the dress, and like the flowers, and had no brightness left but the brightness of her sunken eyes. I saw that the dress had been put upon the rounded figure of a young woman, and that the figure upon which it now hung loose, had shrunk to skin and bone. Once I had been taken to see some ghastly waxwork at the Fair, representing I know not what impossible personage lying in state. Once, I had been taken to one of our old marsh churches to see a skeleton in the ashes of a rich dress, that had been dug out of a vault under the church pavement. Now, waxwork and skeleton seemed to have dark eyes that moved and looked at me. I should have cried out, if I could. (58)

The bright 'sunken eyes' in particular link this figure to those of the psychiatric studies, where we find not only Esquirol's detail of the 'eyes [that] sink in their sockets' but the foregrounding in Alexander Morison's mid-century *Physiognomy of Mental Diseases* of how one subject's 'face is flushed and her eyes are brilliant', another's 'eyes are red and brilliant'.[53] A further connection lies in the nature of Morison's text, which, complete with artists' sketches and accompanying written commentaries, parades the mad for the gratification of public curiosity. Miss Havisham likewise appears to Pip as an exhibit in a waxworks or an archaeological display. But the similarities end there. Miss Havisham is a freak of an unusual kind; her eyes, as it turns out, are not those of a passive spectacle but of proactive and mysterious intent, 'dark eyes that moved and looked at me'. This impression of a persistent, rudimentary life in the midst of deathliness (she is just afterwards described as 'corpse-like', her dress as 'grave-clothes' and 'shroud' (60)) is one with the whole paradox of Satis House, which though it is spread with dilapidation and decay, is inhabited with animated primitive forms, the blotchy spiders running in and out of the black fungus of the wedding feast, the mice rattling behind the panels, the beetles scurrying about the hearth – and Miss Havisham's squabbling relatives crawling about the rooms and corridors in quest of advantage. The clocks have stopped but time is ticking.

The antics of the unprepossessing Camilla, Sarah Pocket, and the other hangers-on make Satis House, with its 'dismal' air and barred windows (55), not so much a prison as a resort for the insane, with Miss Havisham the tormenting superintendent. But this is a mere sideshow to the main entertainment. Miss Havisham does not withdraw into helpless agitation like Marianne Dashwood, though she admits to 'sometimes hav[ing] sick fancies' (59), and certainly does not die like Esquirol's lovelorn female. Unlike the latter, whom 'nothing diverts' while she lives, or 'engages her attention', the mistress of Satis House impatiently 'want[s] diversion' (59), which she sets up in deadly earnest as a scheme to exact revenge on all men. She is the abandoned woman who fights back; the madwoman who takes up the cudgel, or more truly the wand, since the rare step Dickens takes in animating the commonplace sufferer involves conflating her with the archaic figure of the Witch (a word used of her quite early on (85)). Her seizing of the initiative is sometimes insinuated by her reaching out to lay hands on Pip, either directly, as when she 'twitched [his] shoulder', or through Estella, who 'touched [him] with a taunting hand' (64, 85). More often it is signalled by the force of her gaze, her watching rather than being watched; so that, for instance, she would 'look on, with a miserly relish' at the card games played by Pip and Estella, where Pip was ritually and humiliatingly 'beggared', and would be such an avid spectator of Pip's fascination with Estella's prettiness that she seemed to feed upon it, to 'enjoy it greedily' (95). This emaciated woman does not waste feebly away but takes nourishment from the unfolding of her plot. Pip does look at her on the day of their first meeting, but this is because she makes him:

> 'Look at me . . . Do you know what I touch here?' she said, laying
> her hands one upon the other, on her left side.
> 'Yes, ma'am.' (It made me think of the young man.)
> 'What do I touch?'
> 'Your heart.'
> 'Broken!' (58)

The broken heart becomes the sign, not of her weakness, nor even simply her hurt, but of her pained defiance, as she shows it off 'with an eager look' and a smile 'that had a kind of boast in it'. A similar reversal of polarities – the accepted locus of woman's vulnerability becoming the unexpected seat of proud mutinous strength – then emerges when the figures of fragmentation and death that are associated with dis-appointment in love are turned into the instruments of indictment and retribution, as, on the anniversary of her intended nuptials, she appoints the place and time for the grand finale of her destruction:

> 'When the ruin is complete . . . and when they lay me dead, in my
> bride's dress on the bride's table – which shall be done, and which
> will be the finished curse upon him – so much the better if it is done
> on this day!' (89)

She pronounces a curse upon a criminal other, rather than stands accursed through deficiencies of her own.

Of course there is also something questionable about all these actions and utterances – a desperation that is manic and brooding by turns, the grip of an *idée fixe* actually damaging to others (not least Estella) as well as to herself, and, in the passage we have just considered, self-delusion (for Compeyson, the man who swindled and jilted Miss Havisham, would be too obdurate ever to feel the weight of her rebuke). We cannot forget that she *does* have 'sick fancies', does grow regularly 'distraught' (89). From the beginning the presentation of her behaviour is pitched between respect and disapprobation. The issue is never altogether decided one way or the other, as we shall see, but it is true that on the whole the attitude of censure comes to prevail. Miss Havisham is another Dickens character whose rehabilitation means being brought into line. The turning-point arrives in the quarrel scene where we witness her reaping a bitter harvest from her schooling of Estella, as her pleas for 'love' are met only by the monstrous indifference she has herself bred in her adopted daughter:

> 'You stock and stone!' exclaimed Miss Havisham. 'You cold, cold heart!' . . .
> 'You should know,' said Estella. 'I am what you have made me. Take all the praise, take all the blame, take all the success; in short, take me.' (304)

The truth is that Miss Havisham does *not* 'know' the harm she has done, but is being forced to find out; and Estella then goes on to explain the sad repercussions of her upbringing, which, having taught her 'that there was such a thing as daylight, but that it was made to be her enemy and destroyer', has rendered it impossible for her 'to take naturally to the daylight' (306). Two things are happening to Miss Havisham. She is getting her comeuppance and being herself educated, taught to see the light. Moreover, this decisive movement in the text towards a corrective viewpoint coincides with more direct references than ever before to a deep-seated malady requiring a cure, hers now being plainly 'a mind mortally hurt and diseased', and to the suffering her scheming has caused Pip, which, with a similar diagnostic ring, he labels the product of 'a perversion of ingenuity' (302–303). Miss Havisham is being put back into the orthodox lines of psychomedical classification. In a clear turnaround of earlier impressions, she no longer wins a smouldering vitality from her mission but is pictured in the stasis of obsession, gruesomely consuming Estella's very existence, 'devouring the beautiful creature she had reared' (302) We notice at the same time that precedence in looking, the touchstone in power relations, passes over at this point to Pip, who, at the end of a long paragraph everywhere punctuated by the phrase 'I saw in this', recognizes in the spectral presence before him the image of a distorted life: 'I saw in this, Miss Havisham as I had her then and there before my eyes, and always had

had her before my eyes; and I saw in this, the distinct shadow of the darkened and unhealthy house in which her life was hidden from the sun' (303). Brooding female instability is set over against masculine clear-sightedness. And if we should think that Estella, in her analysis of her own fostering and its effects, displays a clarity of insight beyond Pip's compass, we must remember that this leaves her still helpless and incomplete, self-controlled but without control of herself and any capacity for fulfilment – 'I must be taken as I have been made. The success is not mine, the failure is not mine, but the two together make me' (306).

The ways in which Miss Havisham is 'improved' may seem reasonable enough. She is humanized in her feelings and responses. Softened no doubt by the cutting blows of Estella's plain speaking, she appears to sympathize with Pip when, on his next visit to Satis House, he gets the same treatment; while Estella reacts to his protestations of undying love 'merely with incredulous wonder' (for, chillingly, she knows love only as 'a form of words . . . nothing more'), her guardian dissolves, as Pip recalls, into a 'stare of pity and remorse' (362–4). This advance in disposition is then extended in her agreeing to Pip's request, after his own fortune has disappeared, for money to buy Herbert Pocket the partnership in Clarriker's, a deed which she recognizes as 'useful and good', offers as an earnest of there being something 'human in my heart', and follows up with a readiness also to 'serve' Pip in his own right should he so wish (396–7). Yet Miss Havisham is required to make amends much in excess of any ordinary moral regeneration. It is enough for Scrooge's reformation that he should love others and spread his money around, as Miss Havisham is happy to do here; but she must prostrate herself, confess her wrongdoing, and beg forgiveness. She hands Pip a pencil to go with the writing tablets he has taken from her, on which she has written instructions for Herbert's money to be paid out:

> 'My name is on the first leaf. If you can ever write under my name, "I forgive her," though ever so long after my broken heart is dust – pray do it!' . . .
> She turned her face to me for the first time since she had averted it, and, to my amazement, I may even add to my terror, dropped on her knees at my feet; with her folded hands raised to me in the manner in which, when her poor heart was young and fresh and whole, they must often have been raised to heaven from her mother's side. . . . I bent over her without speaking. She was not kneeling now, but was down upon the ground.
> 'O!' she cried, despairingly. 'What have I done! What have I done!' (398)

Again, recall of a previous occasion emphasizes just how far things have changed. On the spot where the youthful Pip, before first departing for London in Chapter 19, had gone down on his knees and kissed Miss Havisham's hand in deference, the grown-up Pip stands over her, receiving her supplication. The turnabout, however, is not simply a function of the passage of time, of Miss Havisham's stricken decline and Pip's ascendant maturity and undoubted claims upon her, but also of gender relationship and authority. Like Mrs Joe before her, Miss Havisham, the self-affirming man-hater, is humbled, reduced to childlike dependency, and made to recant. Writing is not exclusively the preserve of men in Dickens but it is predominantly so; and her action of yielding its wherewithal, the tablets and pencil, and seeking Pip's formal en- dorsement of her contrition, symbolically reflects and reinforces the hierarchy, the assumption of male precedence. The event is moreover encoded with other configurations of social and cultural status. The imagery of Miss Havisham raising her hands in prayer, as she must have done as a little girl at her mother's side, links Pip to the role of priest, or father-confessor, being asked for absolution. The idea of his literally underwriting her admission of guilt, or her penitence, evokes the figure of judge, or attorney, or other official, issuing a pardon. In Pip is epitomized the patriarchal guardian and dispenser of the law, religious and secular – God's surrogate.

But the harrowing of Miss Havisham does not end even there. Scrooge is left finally to get on with his better life; she goes up in flames. This is not that she might be purified, as could have been the symbolic case, but to give Pip another opportunity of asserting himself:

> I had a double-caped great-coat on, and over my arm another thick coat. That I got them off, closed with her, threw her down, and got them over her; that I dragged the great cloth from the table for the same purpose, and with it dragged down the heap of rottenness in the midst, and all the ugly things that sheltered there; that we were on the ground struggling like desperate enemies, and that the closer I covered her, the more wildly she shrieked and tried to free herself; that this occurred I knew through the result. (402)

This may be read as Pip's narrative construction, imagining himself in the part of hero, the prince or white knight swooping to cleanse the enchanted castle; yet that makes the passage no less an allegory of domination. The situation constitutes a weird version of the Sleeping Beauty or damsel-in-distress myth. The beautiful maiden is away with Bentley Drummle, and is in any case too frigid ever to be awakened, but something of the erotic content of the legend is strangely displaced into the encounter between Pip and Miss Havisham, who is both the wicked witch that must be overcome and the helpless woman that must be protected and saved. Pip throws himself upon her, wrestling like an adversary but also like a lover, holding her 'forcibly down with all [his] strength' in a pose suggestive of the exerting of sexual dominance. In the aftermath, he plants a kiss upon her lips: 'I leaned over her and touched her lips with mine, just as they said, not stopping for being touched, "Take the pencil and write under my name, 'I forgive her' " ' (403). She has been rescued, not so that she might be roused or revivified, but that she might go off with the cry of reverent submission once more on her breath. In the end, she has been deprived not just of writing but of the true power of speech, for all she can do is repeat automatically and 'innumerable times' the same set phrases:

> 'What have I done!' And then, 'When she first came, I meant to save her from misery like mine.' And then, 'Take the pencil and write under my name, "I forgive her!" ' She never changed the order of these three sentences, but she sometimes left out a word in one or other of them; never putting in another word, but always leaving a blank and going on to the next word. (402)

She has become the monumental cipher of her own cautionary and instructive tale.

The end of Miss Havisham and Pip's ascendancy over her are prophesied at earlier points in the narrative. They are foretold in the ruined landscape of Satis House, not least in the apparition of her hanging by the neck from a wooden beam which Pip sees on his first exploration of the grounds, 'a movement going over the whole countenance as if she were trying to call to me' (64), with its suggestions of crime and punishment, or suicidal deeds, and of apparent pleas for help. She had 'leaned on' Pip's shoulder to walk around the room, dependent on his support, and had developed a fondness for the song of masculine prowess, 'Beat it out, beat it out – Old Clem', which she would accompany with a low moan, as if of sexual pleasure (85, 96). The effect of these anticipations is to make the outcome – her guilt, her penitence, her submission – seem predestined, unalterable, in the true order of things.

Yet, there is an important final twist. At the moment of her plainest conformity to expectations, when she shows 'earnest womanly compassion' towards Pip and laments that she 'stole' Estella's 'natural heart' and 'put ice in its place', Miss Havisham suddenly reverts to her old troublesome self, tossing an awkward challenge at Pip – 'If you knew all my story, . . . you would have some compassion for me and a better understanding of me' (400). Pip replies that he does know the story, that it has inspired him 'with great commiseration', and that he hopes he understands it and 'its influences'. As Philip Martin points out, however, Pip 'has always mistaken knowledge for understanding';[54] he has been taught that facts are all he needs to take power, not least through the pre-eminent example of Jaggers, a true guardian to him in this respect, whose possession of others, 'soul and body' (263), extends, interestingly, to a double of Miss Havisham, Molly, the murderess he got acquitted (Miss Havisham's crime being the murder of Estella's womanly nature). Pip had learned the basic details of Miss Havisham's history from Herbert on the same occasion as he had received lessons in table-manners, the implication being that competence in the one sphere is on a par with competence in the other; both are helpful to his advancement as a gentleman, the former giving the background of his supposed benefactress and containing much instructive comment, too, about the 'true gentleman at heart' and the false varnish and ungentlemanly conduct of Miss Havisham's half-brother and her suitor (180). In the measured, somewhat stilted language of Pip's response to Miss Havisham's plea for 'compassion' and 'better understanding' – 'It has inspired me with great commiseration . . . ' – we hear the delicate formality and detachment of the gentleman he has become. She is looking for something more than this, for sympathy and insight rather than superficial comprehension, and intimates that this would be facilitated by his knowing *all* her story, including presumably her feelings and experiences, and not just the bare particulars and perceived effects.

This exchange Philip Martin glosses, helpfully, with Luce Irigaray's address prompting us to reach beyond the dominant codes – moral, social, political – through which women are spoken for, mediated and often corrected, 'to listen to her differently in order to hear an *"other meaning" which is constantly in the process of weaving itself, at the same time ceaselessly embracing words and yet casting them off to avoid becoming fixed, immobilized*'.[55] Miss Havisham with what Martin here terms 'the language of Satis House', and Mrs Joe with her eccentric actions and ideographic inscriptions, at once resist the prevailing centres and their systems of representation – even as they are suppressed by them – and speak for the urgency of their own desires. One very apt and so far unmentioned instance of this is when Miss Havisham, 'keeping Estella's hand drawn through her arm and clutched in her own hand, . . . extorted from her, by dint of referring back to what Estella had told her in her regular letters, the names and conditions of the men whom she had fascinated' (302). This is of course itself channelled through Pip's perspective, and he goes on to interpret the 'intensity' of Miss

Havisham's attention to the roll call as a sign of 'a mind . . . diseased'. But he also describes her as 'most weird', conceding something mysterious in her behaviour, something that resists the easy or received explanation, that slips his grasp. One thing that makes the spectacle particularly striking is that the two women have appropriated, on a regular basis, the instrument of masculine authority, the letter (and it was through a letter, received at the altar, that Miss Havisham was jilted), and have produced a catalogue of male types, of 'names and conditions of . . . men', all no doubt considered aberrant, which they can scrutinize as men do the psychomedical, or other, directories and vignettes of women. They have defiantly created their own female counterpart of Morison's *Physiognomy of Mental Diseases*. Does Miss Havisham's rapt absorption in the gallery of Estella's conquests signify a sadistic urge for control, or voyeuristic curiosity, or vicarious sexual pleasure, or some combination of all these and more? This is certainly listening – or in the present example, rather, visualizing – differently, so as to catch an 'other meaning'; seeing more, towards seeing 'all'.

When all is said, however, perhaps the point we are left with is not so much that there are whole stories which can be definitively known as that all stories are partial. In *Great Expectations* this goes as patently for the narrator's story as for anybody else's. When Pip recapitulates Miss Havisham's situation, saying that her mind had 'grown diseased, as all minds do . . . that reverse the appointed order of their Maker', and that she received 'her punishment in the ruin she was' (398), we find, not the summation of an unquestionable Truth and Authority, but a relative, culture-specific summary judgement. The novel opens up to discussion not only aspects of the woman question but the official centres of meaning themselves.

*

Estella is another woman who is tamed and 'improved'. The original, unpublished ending of the novel and the longer, published one agree that she has been, as she puts it in the latter, 'greatly changed' (483). Her coldness has been replaced by sensitivity; where there was once a steely void is now 'a heart', a concept that stands out through repetition in the sentence that concludes the earlier version, for everything about her gave Pip, at this unexpected meeting, 'assurance, that suffering had been stronger than Miss Havisham's teaching, and had given her a heart to understand what my heart used to be'.[56] In his revision Dickens expands upon this bare sentiment, with regard both to the nature of the transformation and its means. Pip sees what he had never seen before, 'the saddened softened light of the once proud eyes', and feels what he had never felt before, 'the friendly touch of the once insensible hand' (483). Estella confides in him, not only laying out her own claim to inward regeneration by saying of his remembered worth that 'I have given it a place in my heart', but also declaring on her own account that she has learned through affliction, 'when suffering has been stronger than all other teaching, and has taught me to understand what your heart used to be'. 'I have been broken, but – I hope – into a better shape' (484). The effect of moving from reported to direct speech is to give added sanction, from Estella's own mouth, to the violent ordeal she has undergone and the results it has produced. Neither ending pulls any punches in deprecating the man who has abused her, Drummle the wife-beater, who 'had used her with great cruelty, and who had become quite renowned as a compound of pride, avarice, brutality, and meanness' (482). But the emphasis lies not there but on Estella's gain. The beatings she has received have been all for the best – have done her good.

This reversion to stereotype, startling in its thoroughness and in that of Estella's complicity, is for Lucy Frost a shocking banality in comparison with the incisive mentality Estella had displayed in puzzling her way to an understanding of the mutilation caused in her by her foster-mother's relentless misrepresentation of love's 'daylight' as an enemy and a blight.[57] Fair enough. Yet that is not the only possible viewpoint. Some people, women as well as men, may prefer the mellower, reasonable Estella. Also, it can be argued that the change in her is continuous with a previous aspect of her character, for are there not stirrings of compassion, of a 'natural heart', in her shielding of Pip from the snares she lays for other men? 'Do you deceive and entrap him, Estella?' asks Pip of her relation to Bentley Drummle; to which she replies, 'Yes, and many others – all of them but you' (312). Seen squarely in the context of a first-person narrative, however, what this record of a curious intimacy and its extension in the book's coda express is not so much a for-better or for-worse model of female development in Estella as Pip's desire for her. From their earliest encounter she is the object of a fascination so complete as to defy all logic. She is the reason for his wanting to be a gentleman in the first place; and later, he confesses, he goes on loving her despite her faults and whatever the cost:

> The unqualified truth is, that when I loved Estella with the love of a man, I loved her simply because I found her irresistible. Once for all; I knew to my sorrow, often and often, if not always, that I loved her against reason, against promise, against peace, against hope, against happiness, against all discouragement that could be. Once for all; I loved her none the less because I knew it, and it had no

more influence in restraining me, than if I had devoutly believed her to be human perfection. (232)

Talking of the development of mental life, where individuals learn to limit their desires in the face of the 'difficulties of the external world', Freud observes that 'the pleasure principle long persists, however, as the method of working employed by the sexual instincts, which are so hard to "educate", and, starting from those instincts, or in the ego itself, it often succeeds in overcoming the reality principle'.[58] This is the case with Pip, who knows the uncomfortable reality of Estella's character and of his relationship with her – his 'sorrow' – but can do nothing about it and carries on his compulsive search for satisfaction. When, during the discussion at Satis House of her forthcoming marriage to Drummle, Estella tells Pip, 'You will get me out of your thoughts in a week', his answer is 'Never'; she is present somehow in everything he sees and does: 'You have been in every line I have ever read, since I first came here . . . in every prospect I have ever seen since – on the river, on the sails of ships, . . . in the woods, in the sea, in the streets. You have been the embodiment of every graceful fancy that my mind has ever become acquainted with' (364). In the softer 'figure of a woman' (482) that materializes in the book's final scene, then, is expressed something in Pip's mind – his fantasy of a different, accessible Estella. If Orlick had been his proxy in exacting revenge on Mrs Joe, Drummle is so in licking Estella into a shape where he can make closer and more balanced contact with her, thus following the 'tendency towards stability' and towards 'keeping the quantity of excitation as low as possible' that Freud identifies as the underlying direction of mental functioning.[59]

The revised ending, indeed, seems to reach beyond a balancing act or holding operation, with the pair in a transient pose of mutual understanding, to the projection of an *obtainable* Estella, even a union:

> I took her hand in mine, and we went out of the ruined place. And, as the morning mists had risen long ago when I first left the forge, so, the mists were rising now, and in the broad expanse of tranquil light they showed to me, I saw the shadow of no parting from her. (484)

The relative merits of this and the original conclusion have been widely debated, with some critics, for example, preferring the earlier, less optimistic, or harsher, approach as more in keeping with Pip's previous painful experience, and others (among them Dickens, who called it a 'pretty little piece of writing') finding the revision artistically and emotionally satisfying in the manner of a fairy-tale happy ending.[60] Yet aesthetic considerations and such a sharp divide fall away if we view the text as a mental topography expressive of Pip's need for an inner satisfaction – and also of his failure to attain it. Even the published revision is far from unambiguous. 'I saw the shadow of no parting from her' (serial and first edition) is an adaptation of the manuscript phrasing of 'I saw the shadow of no parting from her, but one', and was itself in turn modified for the 1868 edition into 'I saw no shadow of another parting from her'; but what all three variations have in common is that each gives a decidedly mixed impression, in that the future, though propitious, is envisaged in negative rather than positive terms – as a parting not seen rather than a union looked forward to. A 'shadow' is invoked even as it is denied.[61] Foreseen or not, separation remains a distinct possibility; at worst, in the phrase 'the shadow of no parting' 'shadow' may suggest an illusion, making the concept of 'no parting' unreal, a chimera. At best, then, this 'happy ending' speaks of hope and equilibrium, not certainty or fulfilment. The novel ends with the existentialist hero – trying not triumphant, hanging on in an unpredictable universe where 'tranquil light' is inevitably shaded by darkness.

Against this picture of an uncertain existence in an uncertain world we can at least set the consolation, however small, of the stable life of the forge, the loving Biddy and Joe, the close-knit family, children and the promise of fresh beginnings. Or can we? Critics, it is true, have sometimes spoken of the ending with Estella as if it were an irrelevant postscript, the design of the novel being complete when Pip returns after eleven years and takes his young namesake to the churchyard to show him the family gravestones, in scenes that signify 'a healing and a rebirth'.[62] As we have already seen, however, this return to the beginning may just as well be taken as a departure point for imagining the second Pip, whatever his advantages in the bosom of affectionate parents and a wise godfather, as another hostage to fortune, destined in his own way to repeat the first Pip's struggle through life. There can be no knowing. But there is another possibility, too, more unsettling still. Is Pip the younger really the son of Biddy and Joe, or of Biddy and Pip? The time-scale of Pip's absence is about right – eleven years (changed by Dickens from an equally plausible eight). As we know, what Pip sees as he enters the old place is 'I again!'; and Joe goes on to point a physical resemblance, for 'we hoped he might grow a little bit like you, and we think he do' (481). In an intriguing parenthesis near the close of the manuscript ending we are told that Estella 'supposed the child, I think, to be my child', which can be taken to fuel speculation about his paternity as much as to inhibit it. Pip asks Biddy to 'give' him the child one day, or at least 'lend' him, as if tapping a special understanding and

Fig. 4 'Joe Gargery, Pip, and Biddy' by Marcus Stone.

making some special claim; and the intimacy between the two seems strangely pointed for just old friends: as she puts her hand in his, 'There was something in the action and in the light pressure of Biddy's wedding-ring, that had a very pretty eloquence in it'. Does this act, the gentle, probing touch, speak only of an attractive matronly nature, or of instincts not so upright or innocent? Is there a skeleton in the Gargery domestic cupboard waiting to come out and shatter the reassuring bliss? If anyone should think that in suggesting this interpretation I am stretching the evidence too far (and I guess that some readers will), there can be no denying that it is entirely true to the prophetic evocation in *Great Expectations* of a severe, abrasive, even apocalyptic modernity where nothing is quite what it seems or can be taken simply at face value, where no set of values or ideology is safe from havoc, where self-interest rules, and where dysfunction spreads.

Notes

1. See William A. Cohen, 'Manual Conduct in *Great Expectations*', *English Literary History*, 60 (1993), 217–59 (pp. 233–5).
2. All references are to Charles Dickens, *Great Expectations*, ed. Charlotte Mitchell, with an Introduction by David Trotter (Harmondsworth: Penguin Books, 1996); hereafter cited in the text.
3. Thomas Hughes, *Tom's Brown Schooldays*, ed. Andrew Sanders (Oxford: Oxford University Press, 1999), Part II, Chapter 5, pp. 289–98 passim; hereafter *TBS*, with references given in parenthesis.
4. Andrew Sanders, ed. cit., p. xx: 'Sexuality . . . a silent area in this book'.
5. Quoted in Asa Briggs, *Victorian People: A Reassessment of Persons and Themes 1851–67* (1954; Harmondsworth: Penguin Books, 1990), p.152.
6. See *TBS*, Part II, Chapter 1, pp. 225–9, Chapter 6, pp. 311–15.
7. See my discussion of Uriah Heep, Chapter 4, pp. 136–9; also note 45, p. 171.
8. Cf. Hughes's address to his old school in 1891: the most marked characteristic of Rugby boys of his generation 'was the feeling that in school and close we were training for a big fight . . . a fight which would last all our lives, and try all our powers, physical, intellectual and moral, to the utmost' (quoted in *TBS*, ed. Sanders, p. x).
9. See Huw Richards, Review of Derek Birley, *English Cricket: A Social History* (London: Aurum, 2000), *Times Higher Education Supplement*, 18 February 2000, p. 23.
10. Peter Brooks, 'Repetition, Repression, and Return: The Plotting of *Great Expectations*, in *Charles Dickens*, ed. Steven Connor (Oxford: Blackwell, 1985), pp. 35–58 (p. 56); repr. from Brooks, *Reading for the Plot: Design and Intention in Narrative* (Oxford: Clarendon Press, 1994), pp. 115–42.
11. Jack Rawlins, 'Great Expiations: Dickens and the Betrayal of the Child', *Studies in English Literature, 1500–1900*, 23 (1983); repr. in *Great Expectations: Contemporary Critical Essays*, ed. Roger D. Sell (Basingstoke: Macmillan, 1994), pp. 79–97 (pp. 92–3).

12. Rawlins, p. 93.

13. See chapter 2, p. 51 above; also note 49, p. 60.

14. This distrust is, of course, the counterpart of the Puritan commitment to solid truth and the plain style, which is itself predicated on respect for the Word. In the introductory verse Apology to *The Pilgrim's Progress*, Bunyan controversially defends his use of figurative devices:

> Some men by feigning words as dark as mine,
> Make truth to spangle, and its rays to shine.
> 'But they want solidness.' Speak man thy mind.
> 'They drowned the weak; metaphors make us blind.' . . .
> My dark and cloudy words they do but hold
> The truth, as cabinets enclose the gold.
> (ed. Roger Sharrock (Harmondsworth: Penguin Books, 1984), pp. 33–4)

15. Beacon and gibbet are two of the main elements in Wordsworth's memory of his eerie experience of disorientation when he was lost as a young child on the bleak moor in the 'spots of time' episode in Book XII of *The Prelude* (1850, lines 208–87). The 'visionary dreariness' that attends these moments, when 'mind is lord and master – outward sense / The obedient servant of her will' (221–2), is, like the 'Blank misgivings of a Creature / Moving about in worlds not realised' in the 'Immortality Ode' (145–6), for Wordsworth evidence of a soul pre-existing and resisting the limits of earthly being. Dickens's recall of Wordsworth's detail throws into relief the former's concern with less transcendent aspects of the psyche – the effects of violence, the emergence of guilt, incipient moral sense – although the child's mental interaction with the landscape around him does play its part in the opening chapters of *Great Expectations*, as in such (very un-Wordsworthian) events as when 'The dykes and bank came bursting at me through the mist, as if they cried as plainly as could be, "A boy with Somebody-else's pork pie! Stop him!" ', or the cows came 'staring out of their eyes, and steaming out of their nostrils, "Halloa, young thief!" ' (17). These humorous passages read like a comic demystifying of Wordsworth's account of Nature's educative reproof of his early transgression when the cliff rises up to admonish him in the boat-stealing incident of Book I (lines 357 ff.).

16. Another instance of Joe's cautious outlook in matters of social position comes earlier, when, talking to Pip about the boy's visits to Satis House and hopes of rising in the world, he reflects 'Whether common ones as to callings and earnings . . . mightn't be the better of continuing fur to keep company with common ones, instead of going out to play with oncommon ones' (71).

17. We may recall once more the key episode in Bunyan's conversion where, sitting upon a 'settle' in the street, he imagined that the very stones and tiles 'did bend themselves against me, me-thought that they all combined together to banish me out of the World; I was abhorred of them, and unfit to dwell among them . . . because I had sinned' (*Grace Abounding*, ed. Roger Sharrock (London: Oxford University Press, 1966), pp. 60–61). The quality of experience is similar; the interesting difference is that whereas the distracted Bunyan envies the objects around him their solidity – 'they stood fast and kept their station, but I was gone and lost' – Pip identifies with

conditions of stasis and longs for a release, the power to move on, which he
finds in journeying back to the forge to do penance. Both protagonists,
however, suffer the paralysis of guilt and are seeking a way forward to grace
and salvation.

18. Brooks, p. 46.
19. Ibid.
20. 'Remembering, Repeating, and Working-Through', in *The Standard
    Edition of the Complete Psychological Works of Sigmund Freud*, ed. James
    Strachey, in collaboration with Anna Freud, 24 vols (London: Hogarth
    Press, 1953–74), XII (1958), 145–56 (p. 147).
21. The influence of Hollywood movies and the shape of popular conceptions
    are not, of course, unconnected. No one who has seen *Spellbound* is likely
    to forget the powerful sequence of Dr Edwardes's (Gregory Peck's) catharsis
    as he recollects the moment of his brother's (actually accidental) death on
    the spiked railings.
22. Freud, 'Remembering, Repeating, Working-Through', pp. 152, 156. An
    illuminating account of Freud's theory and practice of 'working-through' is
    given by Darien Leader, *Freud's Footnotes* (London: Faber and Faber,
    2000), pp. 88–119.
23. F.R. and Q.D. Leavis, *Dickens the Novelist* (1970; Harmondsworth:
    Penguin Books, 1994), pp. 417–18.
24. *Pilgrim's Progress*, p. 134.
25. Leader, p. 161, referring to R.B. Onians, *The Origins of European Thought*
    (1951; Cambridge: Cambridge University Press, 1988), pp. 321–33,
    378–82, 386–7. An interesting variation on the synthesis of beating and
    words is concentrated in Mrs Joe's ideographic representation of Orlick as
    the 'hammer'. Later, as we shall see, the 'improved' Miss Havisham
    formalizes her willing subordination to Pip by asking him to sign the words
    of forgiveness she has written out on her tablet. She is, in her symbolic
    attitude, asking to be 'beaten'.
26. Julian Moynahan, 'The Hero's Guilt: The Case of *Great Expectations*',
    Essays in Criticism, 10 (1960), 60–79 (p. 61).
27. Freud, 'Repeating, Remembering, Working-Through', p. 50.
28. Moynahan's article (note 26 above) forged a whole new critical direction in
    opening up this theme of 'doubling' and the displacement of Pip's repressed
    guilt. I take my lead from its main emphases.
29. *Pilgrim's Progress*, p. 94.
30. Compare, for example, the poet Cowper's experience at Southampton,
    recounted in his autobiographical memoir, *Adelphi* (written c.1767):

> The morning was clear and calm; the sun shone bright upon the
> sea . . . Here it was that on a sudden, as if another sun had been
> kindled that instant in the heavens on purpose to dispel sorrow
> and vexation of spirit, I felt the weight of all my misery taken
> off. My heart became light and joyous in a moment . . . I must
> needs believe that nothing less than the Almighty Fiat could
> have filled me with such inexpressible delight. (*The Letters and
> Prose Writings of William Cowper*, ed. James King and Charles
> Ryskamp, 5 vols (Oxford: Clarendon Press, 1979-86), I
> (1979), 9)

But these feelings of hope, like Pip's, soon depart, to be replaced with bouts of soul-trouble. They are intimations of rebirth, not the thing itself.

31. Trotter, Introduction to *Great Expectations*, ed. Mitchell, pp. xvii–xviii.

32. For Trotter (p. xviii), 'so powerful is the feeling of closure' conveyed by the scene at the forge 'that relatively little hangs on Pip's subsequent encounter with Estella'. This emphasis greatly underrates not only the force of the encounter itself (as we shall see) but also the implications of the young Pip's being projected out of the cosy frame of the present picture into an uncertain future.

33. Frederic Harrison, 'A Few Words About the Nineteenth Century', *Fortnightly Review*, March 1882; in *The Choice of Books and Other Literary Pieces* (London: Macmillan, 1887), pp. 415–47 (p. 425).

34. Robin Gilmour, 'Pip and the Victorian Idea of the Gentleman', in *Great Expectations*, ed. Sell, pp. 110–22 (p. 111); repr. from Gilmour, *The Idea of the Gentleman in the Victorian Novel* (London: Allen & Unwin, 1981), pp. 105–48.

35. Harrison, pp. 435, 436–7, 443, 446.

36. My reading of social structure and mechanisms concurs in general with that of Jeremy Tambling, 'Prison-bound; Dickens and Foucault', *Essays in Criticism*, 36 (1986), 11–31; see also, Tambling, *Dickens, Violence and the Modern State* (Basingstoke: Macmillan, 1995), pp. 17–47.

37. Trotter, p. xvii.

38. William Sewell, 'Gentlemanly Manners', *Sermons to Boys at Radley School* (1854–69), vol. II, pp. 453–4.

39. See *Letters of Charles Dickens*, ed. Madeline House et al. (Oxford: Clarendon Press, 1965–), VII, 307.

40. Unsigned [Sir James Fitzjames Stephen], 'Gentlemen', *Cornhill Magazine*, 5 (March 1862); repr. in *Charles Dickens: Great Expectations*, ed. Graham Law and Adrian J. Pennington (Peterborough, Ontario: Broadview Press, 1998), pp. 560–62 (p. 560).

41. John Ruskin, 'Of Vulgarity', *Modern Painters*, Vol. V (1860), Part IX, Chapter 7; repr. in *Great Expectations*, ed. Law and Pennington, pp. 563–71 (quoted passim).

42. Ruskin, pp. 569–70.

43. Ruskin, p. 564.

44. Ruskin, p. 564.

45. Lucy Frost, 'Taming to Improve: Dickens and the Women in *Great Expectations*', *Meridian*, 1 (1982), 11–20; repr. in Sell, pp. 60–78 (p. 60).

46. Horatio Bryan Donkin, 'Hysteria', in *A Dictionary of Psychological Medicine*, ed. Daniel Hack Tuke, 2 vols (London: J. and A. Churchill, 1892), I, 619–21 (quoted passim). For the popularity of the attitudes to be found in Donkin, and their early development in the works of John Conolly, E.J. Georget and others, see *Embodied Selves*, ed. J.B. Taylor and S. Shuttleworth (Oxford: Clarendon Press, 1998), pp. 166–7.

47. Among novelists, 'Mark Rutherford' (that is, William Hale White) offers in *Catharine Furze* (1893) a singularly sustained and broadly sympathetic exploration of female 'hysteria'. This novel develops a specific link with *Great Expectations* in the account of how one character, Mrs Bellamy, in the absence of other outlets for her energies, pursues, like Mrs Joe, a neurotic interest in housework, duplicating defence upon defence against the encroachments of dust and dirt. It is through the portrayal of Catharine

herself, however, who dies from the influences of pent-up, unrealizable 'force', and especially unsocial erotic desire, that the debate on questions of woman's psyche and restrictions of role and conduct is significantly advanced. See my 'Mark Rutherford's Salvation and the Case of Catharine Furze', in *Mortal Pages, Literary Lives*, ed. V. Newey and P. Shaw (Aldershot: Scolar Press, 1996), pp. 172–203.

48. The David Lean film adaptation picks out the Mrs Joe/Biddy inverse doubling very effectively by making them look-alikes.

49. Philip W. Martin, *Mad Women in Romantic Writing* (Brighton: Harvester Press, 1987), p. 118. Martin's incisive and challenging account of women characters in *Great Expectations* in the context of contemporary psychological theory is unsurpassed in critical responses to this area of the novel.

50. Martin, p. 96.

51. Jane Austen, *Sense and Sensibility*, ed. Ros Ballaster (Harmondsworth: Penguin Books, 1995), pp. 145, 148, 152.

52. J.E.D. Esquirol, *Mental Maladies: A Treatise on Insanity*, translated with additions by E.K. Hunt (Philadelphia, 1845), p. 338.

53. Sir Alexander Morison M.D., *The Physiognomy of Mental Diseases*, 2nd edn (London, 1843; repr. New York: Arno Press, 1976), accounts of 'A.A.' and 'M.S.P.' (no page numbers).

54. Martin, p. 120.

55. Elaine Marks and Isabelle de Courtivron, *New French Feminisms* (Brighton: Harvester Press, 1981), p. 103; quoted by Martin, pp. 94, 122.

56. The original ending is reprinted as Appendix A of *Great Expectations*, ed. Mitchell, pp. 508–509 (p. 509).

57. Frost, pp. 68–9.

58. Freud, *Beyond the Pleasure Principle*, in *Freud: On Metapsychology*, ed. Angela Richards (Harmondsworth, Penguin Books, 1984), p. 278.

59. *Beyond the Pleasure Principle*, pp. 277–8.

60. See the summary of relevant criticism in *Charles Dickens: Great Expectations*, ed. Robin Gilmour (London: Dent 1994), p. 446.

61. Gilmour (ed.), *Great Expectations*, p. 447.

62. Martin Meisel, 'The Ending of *Great Expectations*', *Essays in Criticism*, 15 (1965), 326–31.

CHAPTER SIX

Our Mutual Friend

Retrospective and Reform

'Society': or, 'Life with the Lammles'

The last of Dickens's completed novels, *Our Mutual Friend* gathers up and pushes to the limit themes that have gone before. Among these reiterations is an extreme sense of the bleakness of modern life. As the book opens, the riverside, in *Oliver Twist* the narrow resort of criminals, is now a drab and sprawling wasteland in which human 'birds of prey' scavenge for survival.[1] Gaffer Hexam, hand-trawling from his 'dirty and disreputable' boat, turning out the pockets of corpses and turning the bodies in for a price, reminds his daughter Lizzie, who is repelled by the cull at which she assists, that it is their 'living', their 'meat and drink' (43, 45). We soon learn, however, that Gaffer and those like him are not – to use the word of his associate, Rogue Riderhood – the only 'wulturs' (46) at work. Feeding off people is by no means unique to the urban underclass. Lawyer Lightwood's remark to his skittish tormentor, Lady Tippins, that when he left his desert island (where she has placed him in her playful imagination because of his long absence from her company) the savages 'were becoming civilized . . . At least they were eating one another, which looked like it' (888), infers an apt summary of how the upper classes conduct themselves in *Our Mutual Friend*. To be 'civilized' in their world is to be predatory, often vicious. Gaffer at least waits for folks to die before robbing or trading off them. 'Society' practises its cannibalism on the living, and on its own.

While Gaffer belongs to the murky depths the Veneerings, who throw a banquet in the second chapter, are all surface. They are the *nouveaux riches*, products of the system of capital investment and 'traffic in Shares' (159), set in a terrain of 'high varnish and polish', surrounded by everything 'bran-new', house, friends, a plethora of material possessions, even a 'bran-new baby' (48). Yet the signs of atrophy already show in the glittering façade, which everywhere exudes 'a fatal freshness' (50). The gloomy butler summons the party to table as with a prophecy of doom – 'Come down and be poisoned, ye unhappy children of men!' (51). This is a love-less gathering. The ageing Lady Tippins flirts with many, attracts none, a gruesome parody of the *femme fatale*. Boots and Brewer, who have no opinions of their own but parrot the loudest around them, exemplify a suppression of intelligence and personality, their names equating them with the lines they are in. Similarly present are 'a Member, an Engineer, a Payer-off of the national Debt, a Poem on Shakespeare, a Grievance, and a Public Office' (49). To Twemlow, the minor aristocrat, not even function but virtual anonymity attaches, for he is uncertain whether he is Veneering's 'oldest friend, or newest friend', and is mistaken by one delayed guest for the host himself. This late entrant is Podsnap, apogee of commerce and the risen middle class, an archetype of Arnoldian 'Philistinism', manifest in him above all as myopic respectability, which over-particularly reduces his daughter Georgiana, 'the young person' to whose cheek no blush must be brought, to a nervous wreck, and as a mindless monoculturalism, which dismisses the manners and customs of other countries, everything 'Not English', out of hand, or rather with 'a flourish of the arm' (174–5). The company, which covers a good cross-section of the well-born and the well-to-do, is neither cohesive circle nor set of rounded individuals, but an unstable mix of grist to the mills of Veneering's ostentation and ambitions, which is ground to some advantage later when everyone dashes around getting him elected to the parliamentary seat of Pocket-Breaches. Rotten politics is also in view.

Of all the characters of the beau monde, it is in the Lammles, Alfred and Sophronia, that the rule of heartless self-interest is perhaps most glaringly exposed. If Podsnap is all too visibly egotistical, blustering, slightly mad, they practise a subterranean and insinuating contrivance – firstly upon themselves. Showing the versatility of his art, which vis-à-vis *Our Mutual Friend* will be a specially important consideration, Dickens reaches into the macabre cavalcade and extracts a story. He 'a mature young gentleman', she 'a mature young lady' (159), each misleads the other into betrothal on the pretence of having property. The scene of recrimination on the sands at Shanklin when the honey-mooners realize they have been duped is a gruesome study in the sour fruits of mutual deceit. There is asperity enough in the calculated ver-bal assaults – 'Do you pretend to believe', says Mrs Lammle to her new husband, that 'when you talk of my marrying you for worldly advantage, that it was within the bounds of reasonable probability that I would have married you for yourself?' (170) – but a deeper and heavier bitterness of soul is caught in the symptoms of stabbing resentment and brooding impotence, the 'moody humour', of a passage for which the illustrator Marcus Stone memorably appropriated Dickens's ironical tag, 'The Happy Pair':[2]

> for the lady has prodded little spirting holes in the damp sand before her with her parasol, and the gentleman has trailed his stick after

THE HAPPY PAIR

Fig. 5 'The Lammles' by Marcus Stone.

him. As if he were of the Mephistopheles family indeed, and had
walked with a drooping tail.

. . . A taunting roar comes up from the sea, and the far-out rollers
mount upon one another, to look at the entrapped impostors, and
to join in impish and exultant gambols. (168, 170)

We may note that there is something both of the devil – Mephistopheles
– and of the wild beast in Lammle, who is described elsewhere as having
'too much sparkle . . . in his teeth' (53). Once their plight has sunk in, he
takes the lead in establishing a contract with his wife 'to work together
in furtherance of [their] own schemes' (173). Out of a marriage from hell
comes an unholy alliance. Having 'both been biting, and . . . both been
bitten' (172), they resolve to sink their jaws into others. First, they plot
to arrange a marriage between the innocuous Georgiana Podsnap and
Fledgeby the money-lender, who agrees to pay them a thousand pounds
for getting his hands on the girl's fortune. When this plan falls through,
the 'happy pair of swindlers' (619) switch their attention to the good Mr
Boffin, hoping he will reward them for unveiling the supposed
machinations of his secretary, Rokesmith. Boffin rumbles their design,
and pays them off with a £100 note. In turn, Fledgeby, forcing the
sympathetic Jew, Mr Riah, his debtor, to act as a front for his covert
business in bill-broking, rounds on Lammle, buys in his outstanding
accounts, and makes him bankrupt. When the Lammles see through
Fledgeby's cover, Alfred mercilessly beats him up. This seems less a case
of people eating people than of dog eats dog. Sure enough, Fledgeby is
described as a 'slow Retriever' and a 'cur' (318, 320).

Like so many of Dickens's narratives, the vignette of 'Life with the
Lammles' does come up with a positive surprise. Of the novels we have
considered, *Our Mutual Friend*, in keeping with its place in the oeuvre,
contains the most diverse reappraisal of the position and potential of
women, and against all the odds even the rebarbative Sophronia
Lammle attracts some sympathy. When Alfred congratulates her, not
very gently, for having wheedled her way into Georgiana's confidence –
'You have done so well to-day, Sophronia, that you must be tired. Get
to bed' (319) – we feel not simply revulsion at so barren a relationship
but the extra privation of being the subordinate partner, curtly
dismissible like an obliging child. Alfred all along has the advantage of
Sophronia, enjoying a freedom unavailable to her as a woman. He is the
callous adventurer whose devious pursuit of wealth represents a choice,
a gambler's bluff, while it is not easy to see what she, an impoverished
spinster of forty-five, could have done otherwise to secure her future. At
least her subterfuge is the less blameworthy in absolute terms, though
the less allowable according to the rules of the Victorian mating game,

where the cards are stacked in favour of the male. She was trapped before she started; and this can explain why she eventually takes steps to extricate Georgiana from the snare being laid for her (by secretly warning Podsnap of his daughter's peril), where her motivation may be seen both as revenge against her tyrannical husband and an elder-sisterly feeling for another of life's female victims.

These questions of gender relations, and that of the Lammle marriage as inverse configuration of the domestic ideal, are relevant to Dickens's subsequent remodelling of his ideology of the family in the exemplary unions of John Harmon and Bella Wilfer and Eugene Wrayburn and Lizzie Hexam. The immediate point, however, is that the strains of empathy in the portrayals of Sophronia and Georgiana are about the only bright spots in a picture of high 'Society' that is overwhelmingly grim – one other being an unfolding respect for the basic decency of Twemlow, who is reserved for a significant role at the end of the book. The realm of the Veneerings and the rest is in the main perceived as dehumanized and dehumanizing. The animal imagery that we have already noticed – avian, canine, piscatorial – is widely spread. Mrs Veneering is introduced as 'aquiline-nosed and fingered' (52), and at the Lammles' wedding breakfast there is an account of the antipathy between Lady Tippins and the bride's aunt who combines the petrifying stare of the snake-haired gorgon with the incessant 'snort' of the pig (167).

This side of the novel resonates with Dickens's continuing interest in Malthusian and Darwinian ideas of the competitive state of nature (which he takes seriously but will ultimately deem acceptable only in part); but, though the antagonists are certainly (in Tennyson's words) 'red in tooth and claw', they have descended from the noble struggle of the wilds to the squabbling, scratching and strutting of the menagerie.[3] Mrs Podsnap, it appears, belongs not so much even to the zoo as to the laboratory or display case, for she is 'a fine woman for Professor Owens' (52), by whom Dickens means Sir Richard Owens, Head of the Natural History Section of the British Museum, whose expertise lay in the field of extinct species.[4] When she then becomes 'quantity of bone, neck and nostrils like a rocking-horse', we shift firmly into this other dominant register, where people are conflated with *things*. Lady Tippins, for example, lets slip the mercenary instincts of her caste by putting amity on a par with ownership, calling the Veneerings in the same breath 'my exclusive property [and] the dearest friends I have' (301), while Fledgeby uses his own body, as he does Mr Riah, as a lure for the unwary, since he 'was sensible of the value of appearances as an investment, and liked to dress well' (324). Fledgeby's movables, from the coat on his back to the china on his table, possess a charm for him in proportion, not simply to the mean bargain he has struck in acquiring them, but to their force as trophies of the hunt, representations of 'somebody's ruin or somebody's loss'. The most striking development of the motif of objectification, however, is in the depiction of the brash materialism of 'Podsnappery'. Here it is the things that act and speak:

> Four silver wine-coolers, each furnished with four staring heads, each head obtrusively carrying a big silver ring in each of its ears, conveyed the sentiment up and down the table, and handed it on to the pot-bellied silver salt-cellars. All the big silver spoons and forks widened the mouths of the company expressly for the purpose of thrusting the sentiment down their throats with every morsel they ate. (177)

The sentiment that the anthropomorphic tableware rams home is 'I am so many ounces of precious metal worth so much an ounce; – wouldn't you like to melt me down?'. Not only men and women but the objects themselves conform to a fetishism of monetary value.

The impression in *Our Mutual Friend* of a world thus degraded to impersonality and the cult of the pecuniary reaches well beyond the contexts of the metropolitan elite and their proletarian counterparts along the water's edge. The dust-mounds that overshadow several strands of the action are veritable goldmines for those who, like old Harmon and his legatee Boffin (the 'Golden Dustman'), have the right to gather, sift and sell them; there is no refuse that cannot be recycled for profit.[5] At least with the dust business there is some sense of lively and productive industry. Elsewhere there is only an eerie and creeping attenuation of life. Deep in the City the buildings have an 'air of death' about them. One set of ghostly figures brushes litter into the gutters while another emerges to pick it over, as 'melancholy waifs and strays of housekeepers and porter sweep melancholy waifs and strays of paper and pins into the kennels, and other more melancholy waifs and strays explore them, searching and stooping and poking for anything to sell' (450). It is easy to imagine among these scavengers not only those looking for bits and pieces to swell the stock of the familiar street-sellers of stationery but also such categories of the poor as the cigar-end finders and the 'Pure-finders', or collectors of dogs' dung, of which Dickens would have encountered ample notice in Henry Mayhew's *London Labour and the London Poor*.[6] Sometimes it seems that human life has disappeared altogether, supplanted by a swirling miasma of paper:

> That mysterious paper currency which circulates in London when the wind blows, gyrated here and there and everywhere. Whence

can it come, whither can it go? It hangs on every bush, flutters in every tree, is caught flying by the electric wires, haunts every enclosure, drinks at every pump, cowers at every grating, shudders upon every plot of grass, seeks rest in vain behind the legions of iron rails. (191)

This envisions the stirrings of catastrophe. Banknotes and share certificates have become, not mere litter, but an insidious invasive matter. The arid, blustery London spring transforms into apocalyptic process: 'currency' is an autonomous and alien form, without apparent origin or purpose, that has worked its destructive will, is all but spent, and is being subsumed in the primitive energy of nature. The land, laid waste, returns to its primordial state.

Dickens's Art and a Typology of the Artist

This, however, is as gloomy as *Our Mutual Friend* gets. From the beginning there are positives to set over against the evidences of degeneracy, degradation and impending doom. One of these is the sheer vigour of Dickens's art, even where it treats what are, abstractly considered, negative conditions or subject matter. As T.S. Eliot saw when conceiving his own approach to an uncongenial modernity in *The Waste Land*, Dickens makes fresh capital from his imaginative investment in the materials of a botched and failing civilization.[7] The reference amidst the Veneerings' dinner party to the 'great looking-glass above the sideboard, reflect[ing] the table and the company' (52) situates and frames the assembled characters as a set of images, not real persons, and concedes, even highlights, the distortive effects of mirror perception.[8] The grotesque exhibits of the menagerie or of the playroom (that is, the rocking-horse Mrs Podsnap) are there to pleasure the curious reader-onlooker as much as to deprecate the stalwarts of fashionable society. Indeed Dickens's writing in these sections of the novel, though adroit social criticism, prophesies the self-sufficient animated forms of Surrealism, where what matters is, in the words of David Gascoyne's title, 'The Very Image' itself – 'And all these images / and many others / are arranged like waxworks / in model bird-cages / about six inches high.'[8] The same connection with modern tradition holds for the oneiric street scenes we have also touched on. More than any other of Dickens's works *Our Mutual Friend* can be read for its poetic ingenuity.

This is to say that the role of existentialist hero that in *Great Expectations* had fallen to Pip, dogged survivor in a changing and dispiriting world, is in *Our Mutual Friend* transferred to the author himself, the resilient artist. Yet there are also instances of resistance from inside the bounds of social degeneration, rather than only from the creative margins. Tucked away in a corner of the Temple, for example, is Blight, clerk to the client-less lawyer Lightwood, who invents lists of appointments and callers – 'Mr Aggs, Mr Baggs, Mr Caggs, Mr Daggs . . . ' – to stop his mind being 'shattered to pieces' by lack of occupation (131). Blight's problem is a general intolerance of inertia but is associated with the specific atmosphere of indolence and futility that at this stage of the novel surrounds the semi-aristocratic sphere of the reluctant professionals Lightwood and Wrayburn. Down the scale, Miss Abbey Potterson, landlady of the Six Jolly Fellowship Porters, fights against a cruder threat; not only drunkenness, which is as likely to afflict the idle rich as the labouring poor, but the criminal inclinations of figures such as Rogue Riderhood, who is banned from her premises, as is Gaffer Hexam when he too is suspected (on Riderhood's false evidence) of killing a man. The redoubtable Miss Potterson, champion of order, organizes her customers as a good schoolmistress would a group of potentially wayward pupils:

> Gaffer was not there, but a pretty strong muster of Miss Abbey's pupils were, who exhibited, when occasion required, the greatest docility. On the clock's striking ten, and Miss Abbey appearing at the door, and addressing a certain person in a faded scarlet jacket, with 'George Jones, your time's up. I told your wife you should be punctual,' Jones . . . gave the company good-night and retired. . . . Nor, was Miss Abbey's vigilance in any way abated by this submission, but rather sharpened; for, looking round on the deferential faces of her school, and descrying two other young persons in need of admonition, she thus bestowed it . . . (109)

If this well-run public house is like a school, the police station, where the supposed body of John Harmon lies, resembles a religious house complete with library, the Night-Inspector, who is the 'quiet Abbot' of the place, 'with pen and ink, and ruler, posting up his books in a whitewashed office, as studiously as if he were in a monastery' (66, 69). The nearby incessant shrieking of a woman calling for someone's liver reminds us of the untamed energies that the forces of the law hold tenuously in check, not only, on the evidence of this episode, by the proverbial strong arm but also by a 'neat and methodical' (66) hand, where that long-standing instrument of control, writing, has become well and truly of the essence.

That the inn is like a school and the police station like a monastery may somehow suggest confusion within the fabric of society. But we are witnessing not a pure reality but Dickens's vision of how things are. The cross connections indicate that the Dickens of *Our Mutual Friend*, in sharper distinction than ever from the two Arnolds or Thomas Hughes, holds no brief of respect for the great institutions of Church and education, or their grand arc of influence, but can raid them as a source of metaphorical support for the idea of people battling on in limited ways for the principles of coherent and civilized existence. The positions we have considered, of Blight, of Miss Abbey, of the Inspector, and of the author himself, all represent in some degree holding operations in the face of the threat of chaos. This aspect of the novel leads Nancy Aycock Metz to assert that it offers 'no promises of social regeneration'.[9] She has not, however, grasped the whole story. *Our Mutual Friend* does contain messages of hope, and these include templates for social renovation. Thinking of some of the major characters, Metz comments that the book produces 'significant affirmations . . . of the power of individuals to come to terms with their pasts, to learn from their errors, to find purpose, and to build lasting relationships', but these are 'separate and more or less self-contained victories'. The point is that these 'victories', and not only they, set standards for conduct, for framing goals, for constructing a better society. They comprise, as we shall discover, a programme for personal and national progress such as Pip's estranged survival and Joe and Biddy's out-of-the-way family idyll cannot.

Even Miss Abbey and the Inspector are minor beacons: decent, competent people; diligent middle managers, one in local business, the other a public servant; salt of the earth. (Blight is a different matter. He just hangs on, going nowhere, and in this and his string of rhymes constitutes a small-scale parallel to the arrested artist, a sort of amateur exponent of automatic writing as against the sophisticated surrealist.) The Boffins are a more fulsome, though still relatively straightforward, exemplary pair. They embody and apply basic Christian virtues amid a welter of immorality. The 'soundest of sound hearts', they adopt the orphans Johnny and Sloppy, dispense charity to the destitute Betty Higden, epitomize 'high simplicity' in contrast to the 'low cunning' personified in their implacable enemy, the 'wily' Silas Wegg (234). From Wegg's evil their goodness is symbolically inseparable in the moral scheme of the book, to which they are central. In Wegg is lodged all the greed, dissimulation and ruthless ambition of the self-interested spirit. The equivalent of the Veneerings or Podsnap at street, or gutter, level, he is Dickens's last and arguably most zealous condemnation of the social climber – a role Wegg plainly takes on when explaining himself to Mr Venus as one dedicated to the 'prospect of getting on in life and elevating

myself by my own independent exertions' (127). Not only does he plot
to relieve Boffin of his rightful inheritance by crooked means, he vows
to make him suffer and squirm, to 'put [him] to the grindstone', to
'break him and drive him' (646). This propensity for gratuitous violence
is linked, as is Uriah Heep's subtler aggression, to envy, which is but one
deadly sin of which Wegg is a dedicated practitioner. The hardness and
deficiency of character, and the unbalanced nature, denoted by his
wooden leg are accompanied by lust, though not for the fair sex but for
money, thoughts of which give that same appendage an erection, as it
'started forward under the table, and slowly elevated itself' as he read of
the famous miser Dancer's habit of burying piles of banknotes in heaps
of manure (544). In his recalcitrant jealousy Wegg denounces Boffin as
'the minion of fortune and the worm of the hour', 'usurper' of the
wealth that should rightly be his; but it is to Wegg himself, later directly
named by the narrator 'Evil Genius' and 'Serpent', that the demonic
epithets really apply (360–61, 554, 564, 648). Equally and opposite, the
'ignorant and unpolished' Boffins are exemplars of a 'religious sense of
duty and desire to do right', and of 'moral straightness', excited, like the
redeemed Scrooge, not by wealth itself but by prospects of 'the good
[that] will be done' with it (146).

Another notable feature of the presentation of Wegg is that he, like
Blight, is one of the several versions of the figure of the artist in *Our
Mutual Friend*.[10] He is 'a literary man', a street-seller and composer of
poems and songs, and is employed by Boffin to read to him the 'Decline-
And-Fall-Off-The-Rooshan-Empire' (93, 96). That is, he belongs to a
semi-literate culture of popular entertainment, where the doggerel of his
own verses jostles snatches quoted from Moore's Irish ballad of
'Eveleen's Bower' or Dibdin's ballad-opera *The Waterman*, and where
literature is tied up with the business of scraping a living.[11] In him
literary production and the profit motive are closely intertwined; we are
indeed told on his first meeting with Boffin of 'visions rising before his
mercenary mind, of the many ways in which this connexion [with
his new acquaintance] was to be turned to account' (101). Even when
his mind's eye appears to be working innocently something questionable
emerges; so that his peopling of the house at the corner where he pitches
his stall with imaginary inmates, 'Miss Elizabeth', 'Master George',
'Aunt Jane' and 'Uncle Parker', and his arranging of its interior
'according to a plan of his own', becomes a fantasy of possession when
he later explodes in a frenzy of resentment against Boffin for occupying
the – *his* – property (88, 554). The ingenuous, the 'undesigning' (234),
Boffin himself looks as if he will be the anti-type of the artist, making up
or envisioning nothing. Yet this impression is contradicted on at least

two important counts: firstly by his elaborate pretence that he has changed into a horrible miser, the plot or happy deception that shocks Bella Wilfer out of her misguided assumption that only material riches matter; and secondly by his impulse, which he shares with Mrs Boffin, for keeping faith with the past. When the pair show their secretary, Rokesmith (young John Harmon, their former charge, going incognito), round the Bower, which they have inherited from old Harmon, they point out, among other things, the staircase by which the 'poor child' had visited his overbearing father, and on which they had comforted him, 'sitting with his little book':

> 'Ah! And his poor sister too,' said Mrs Boffin. 'And here's the sunny place on the white wall where they one day measured one another. Their own little hands wrote up their names here, only with a pencil; but the names are still here, and the poor dears gone for ever.' (232)

To this Boffin responds, 'We must take care of the names, old lady . . . We must take care of the names. They shan't be rubbed out in our time, nor yet, if we can help it, in the time after us' (232–3). Whereas Wegg exists only in and for the present and future of his own narrow desires, the Boffins preserve the lives and memory of others. They could join the Ghost in teaching Scrooge – of whom we are of course reminded by the image of the lonely boy and his book – a thing or two. They are a force for redemption.

Our Mutual Friend is a self-reflexive creation in which characters and action mirror different orders of creativity. In Wegg and the Boffins are projected contrasting sides of Dickens's own art. The whole ambit of the former's profession reminds us of Dickens's association with the streets and the music hall, and of that mischievous, transgressive streak that propelled him, above all in *Oliver Twist*, to the haunts and subjects of low culture; but more obviously Wegg's 'mercenary mind' reflects the Dickens who drove himself, and hard bargains, for economic gain, and could suffer nights of hysterical fever when his writing yielded less than the expected proceeds.[12] Boffin, on the other hand, is the production and expression of his worthier creative self, which, moreover, replicates itself throughout the novel. Boffin's salutary design vis-à-vis Bella is reproduced in the author's histories of John Harmon and Eugene Wrayburn. These accounts of personal development may be said to sustain something important from Dickens's past, for they resurrect his conviction, crystallized in the *Carol*, that the individual may change for the better, and that this has implications for the greater well-being of humankind. Similarly, the Boffins are a configuration of a long-standing clutch of Dickensian values, and an affirmation of his belief in the power of these values constantly to renew their shape and influence. The future for Dickens does not lie with Wegg, who is unceremoniously, and literally, dumped in the muck cart; nor with the Veneerings or the Lammles, both of whom go bankrupt and flee the country; but with the old mores of liberal humanism, aptly reconstituted for the needs of the time.

The nature of Dickens's genius in *Our Mutual Friend*, its depth and breadth, can finally be brought further into focus through reference to the character that more than any has been seen by critics as a salute to the spirit of creation – Mr Venus, taxidermist and articulator of skeletons.[13] Venus recovers coherence out of fragments, and is associated with the thrill of things coming to life:

> Mr Wegg, looking back over his shoulder as he pulls the door open by the strap, notices that the movement so shakes the crazy shop, and so shakes a monetary flare out of the candle, as that the babies – Hindoo, African, and British – the 'human warious', the French gentleman, the green glass-eyed cats, the dogs, the ducks, and all the rest of the collection, show for an instant as if paralytically animated; while even poor little Cock Robin at Mr Venus's elbow turns over on his innocent side. Next moment Mr Wegg is stumping under the gaslights and through the mud. (130)

Venus's little dominion is an oasis of magical transformation amidst the glare and dirt that are the natural element of destructive go-getters like Wegg. Within the obvious allegorical circuit, where Venus stands for the novelist at work in an age of sordid materialism, the detail of the 'human warious' forges a particular connection with Dickens and his renowned fecundity of characterization. Yet the relationship is plainly not one of simple parallels. Creation in Venus's sphere is either, as in the above passage, an illusion, a trick of the light or of an electric atmosphere, or has no meaning beyond itself; it is artifice and end-stopped. In so far as his work has any outcome it is to make money in the medical and curio markets. These facets draw an ironic attention to Dickens's art, which, at one level or another, shares all three; but they also throw into relief how far it outreaches their limits. It includes and transcends them. The same goes for its relation, say, to Jenny Wren's visions of birds and flowers and bright slanting rows of happy children saying 'Come and play with us' (290), or to her intimations of the afterlife as she kneels on the roof and loses herself in the celestial sight of 'golden arrows pointing at the mountains in the sky from which the wind comes, and you feel as if you were dead' (334). Dickens writes for serious purposes and in confrontation with real life – as he does in this enactment of the crippled Jenny's extraordinary game of being 'dead', which realizes both the persistence of her pain, physical and inner, and her resilience in countering it.[14] Only in the abstract are Jenny's mental pictures merely sentimental or escapist. Both Jenny and Mr Venus, moreover, elsewhere come to represent Dickens in proactive postures, rather than as short measure; the former in her function as 'Mrs Truth', revealing the hidden natures and motives of other characters, often to themselves as well as to the reader, the latter when he takes up articulation of a new sort – 'I will articulate the details', he says (641) – by explicating Wegg's subterfuge to Boffin, and so helps to plot the fall of evil and the triumph of right.

The three-core intent of Dickens's mature novels, moral, ontological and socio-political, is not only maintained in *Our Mutual Friend* but is highlighted by those ingredients which privilege creation for creation's sake. The socio-political aspect, so far not addressed explicitly in this chapter, has featured not only in the anathematizing of the new bourgeoisie, the Veneerings and the Podsnaps, and of the rebellious lower-class Wegg, but in the raising up of the Boffins, 'faithful servants . . . honest and true' (147), downstairs versions of Joe and Biddy who know their place in the scheme of subordination but become kingpins of the liberal-humanist establishment. Dickens's thinking on matters of social stability and progress then in its final movement takes, at least in theory, a radical turn, in the alliance of the working-class Lizzie and the aristocratic Eugene, and in other ideas for the revaluation of group categories and relations. Before coming to these areas of the novel, however, there is one other upward-climber to consider – a damnable experiment in social engineering, Bradley Headstone the schoolmaster, whose story is among the greatest Dickens wrote.

A Haggard Head, with the Tale of Little Rogue Riderhood

'There's no royal road to learning; and what is life but learning?' (751), says R. Wilfer, Bella's father, neatly. 'The school of life', learning the hard way, is a central motif in *Our Mutual Friend*, as it had been in *David Copperfield* and *Great Expectations*. Yet this novel, like *Hard Times*, takes up education not only as an experiential or moral theme but also as a pressing social topic.[15] From the early 1840s, when he became almoner to Miss Burdett-Coutts, Dickens had developed a strong interest in the voluntary 'Ragged Schools', set up to provide instruction to children of the very poor. These institutions he appears to have considered well-meaning but in practice misguided, and the fact that Charley Hexam, Lizzie's brother, has attended one supplies an opportunity to relaunch a favourite complaint about the unsuitability of the reading books which they used:

> young women old in the vices of the commonest and worst life, were expected to profess themselves enthralled by the good child's book, the Adventures of Little Margery, . . . unwieldy young dredgers and hulking mudlarks were referred to the experiences of Thomas Twopence, who, having resolved not to rob (under circumstances of uncommon atrocity) his particular friend and benefactor, of eighteen-pence, presently came into supernatural possession of three and sixpence. (263–4)

A degree above came the National Schools of the kind headed by Bradley Headstone and his nearby counterpart Miss Peecher, where Charley is now a pupil-teacher under the former's direction. These were working-class establishments run by Anglican and Nonconformist agencies but partially subsidized by the state, and taught by men and women who rose from the ranks and exited through the training colleges, which were a mid-nineteenth-century attempt to put the profession on a sounder, more rational footing. Though by no means a novelty at the time of *Our Mutual Friend* (government support had begun in 1833, inspection in 1839), these schools were proliferating rapidly during the sixties, and for Dickens supplied a conspicuous addition to the spreading urban territories, 'newly built, . . . so many like them all over the country, that one might have thought the whole were but one restless edifice with the locomotive gift of Aladdin's palace' (267). They were currently very much in the news, moreover, as teachers agitated against the 'Revised Code' legislation of 1863 that made the payment of state aid contingent upon results in examinations conducted by approved visitors, and left those at the pedagogic seam hard-pressed, potentially culpable, and no better off for any particular successes they achieved.

That Dickens approved of the spread of literacy is suggested by the narrator's observation on the difference it has made to Charley Hexam as he awaits Mortimer in the Veneerings' 'library of bran-new books': 'he glanced at the backs of the books, with an awakened curiosity that went below the binding. No one who can read, ever looks at a book . . . like one who cannot' (60–61). The admirable Miss Potterson is an avid reader of newspapers, and, as we know, the Inspector's good work depends to a large extent upon his command of the pen. Overwhelmingly, however, Dickens is concerned in *Our Mutual Friend* not so much with the advantages of education either to individuals or the community as with its adverse effects on those caught up in the new system as its products and functionaries. Far from any broadening of his mind and horizons, the result of Charley's scholarly success is a hybrid and stunted personality, a snobbish and bigoted outlook, and status anxiety. He is described on first appearance as wedged in a half-formed state between cultural extremes, 'a mixture . . . of uncompleted savagery, and uncompleted civilization' (60). In a classic example of class- and kin-betrayal, he grows ashamed of the sister whose sacrifices have given him his chance, complaining, for example, of her companionship with the impoverished Jenny Wren, by which he thinks himself 'disgraced': 'I am trying my best to get on in the world, you pull me back' (278, 281). He similarly resents Eugene Wrayburn's arranging for Lizzie's tuition because this will damage *his* reputation: 'I am raising myself in the scale of society by my own exertions and Mr Headstone's aid, and have no right to have any darkness cast upon my prospects, or any imputation upon my respectability' (343).

Blind to any but his own interests, he sees everyone, beneath or above, solely as instruments of his betterment or as hindrances to it. Lizzie's refusal of Bradley Headstone's suit so angers him that he casts her aside, with the amazingly obdurate reproach that *she* is acting insensitively, 'a pretty piece of disinterestedness': 'And so all my endeavours to cancel the past and to raise myself, and to raise you with me, are to be beaten down by *your* low whims' (459). Renunciation of the past, the lack of sensitizing memories and stabilizing roots, is one thing which connects Charley with the 'bran-new' Veneerings and distinguishes him from the 'good' characters, the Boffins, or Lizzie herself, who vainly appeals to their 'old days . . . together' (461) as a claim upon her brother's kindness. In the end, Charley rejects Bradley Headstone as well, when the schoolmaster falls under suspicion for the attack on Wrayburn. His speech of farewell revisits all the desert places of his chronic self-regard: the absence of any 'softening old time behind him'; the cool conviction of being always in the right and everyone against him, for he proclaims that 'every effort I make towards perfect respectability, is impeded by somebody else through no fault of mine'; a purblind projection of his own short-sightedness onto others, in arraigning Headstone for being 'so concentrated upon yourself, that you have not bestowed one proper thought on me' (780–81).

No one among the critics has a good word to say for Charley. George Gissing, in his early study, set the pace: 'This youth has every fault that can attach to a half-taught cub of his particular world. He is a monstrous egotist to begin with, and "school" has merely put an edge on to the native vice.'[16] In stressing the natural defect, the 'native vice' that is 'merely' exacerbated by his schooling, Gissing appears to be following a lead in Dickens, who, in remarking on Charley's 'hollow empty heart' and 'selfishness', talks of a 'vice in human nature' (780). All in all, however, it is popular education itself that comes in for the severest criticism in the novel. If not entirely responsible for the monstrosity Charley has become, it carries most of the guilt. It may even be that, although his egotism repels our sympathy, we can at least understand his conduct as the driven defensiveness of one placed in a precarious position, drawn inescapably into the march, or grind, upwards in society but fearing rejection or a fall. Whether or not Dickens intends this dash of potential sympathy, he is certainly set upon exposing the worst in Charley's acquired attitudes of mind, which at some points he serves with the additional black mark of the discourse of business relations, as the young man concedes, not love for his sister, but a liability to repay what he 'owe[s]' her, or weighs her value against that of his mentor and concludes that Headstone is 'worth fifty' of her (279, 459). The hard-nosed rationale of basic arithmetic, rote learning and getting on invades the field of relationships. Seeing the unattractive and troubled Charley, we must be inclined to agree with his father, Gaffer, who charges him, not with any natural vices, but with being turned into an 'unnatural young beggar' by his 'schooling' (121). (Looking back to *David Copperfield*, one implication of all this seems to be that if the lowly but bright like Charley are to be educated at all, then better treat them to an environment like that at Dr Strong's excellent academy – and introduce the state grammar school. Not for the first time Dickens emerges as at once radical and socially conservative.)

Charley's problems are writ large in Bradley Headstone, fully-fledged example of the new race of teachers, 'highly certificated stipendiary schoolmaster' (265). He and Miss Peecher have been reduced almost to automatons by their training and their profession. She is the sum of her job and its appurtenances, a walking compendium of fixed poses, offices and objects – 'shining, neat, methodical . . . A little pincushion, a little housewife, a little book, a little workbox, a little set of weights and measures, and a little woman, all in one' (268). Headstone, too, has been turned into 'things'. He is the 'mechanical' man; robotic stockholder and dispenser of facts from the several branches of elementary knowledge:

> He could do mental arithmetic mechanically, sing at sight mechanically, blow various wind instruments mechanically, even play the great church organ mechanically. From his early childhood up, his mind had been a place of mechanical stowage. The arrangement of his wholesale warehouse, so that it might be always ready to meet the demands of retail dealers – history here, geography there, astronomy to the right, political economy to the left – natural history, the physical sciences, figures, music, the lower

mathematics, and what not, all in their several places – this care had
imparted to his countenance a look of care . . . There was a kind of
settled trouble in the face. (266–7)

Once again the system of education suffers guilt by derogatory
association with the fields of trade and consumerism, and vice versa;
Dickens gets two pet hates with one figurative swipe – indeed with one
(Head)stone. Yet it is clear from the striking close-up of the 'settled
trouble' in the schoolmaster's face, as it never quite is in the picture of
Charley Hexam, that Dickens is interested in the person behind the
functionary, and in the individual drama behind the surface of an ill-
conceived social policy. Something of the same impression arises with
the sudden interpolation of the phrase 'a little woman' in the inventory
of Miss Peecher's attributes, but in her case its development is limited to
the superficial facts of her unrequited hopes of marrying Mr Headstone.
With Headstone himself Dickens goes far and deep.

Bradley's 'trouble' is explained on one level as the result of a constant
effort to hold on to the freight he has toiled so hard to amass: he 'always
seemed to be uneasy lest anything should be missing from his mental
warehouse, and taking stock to assure himself' (267).[17] His greater
difficulty, however, is that he is trapped in the impossible situation that
we have already identified as Charley's incipient fate – adrift from his
past yet not at home in his present. This comes out in the awkwardness
with which he wears the uniform of his profession – 'decent black coat
and waistcoat, and decent white shirt, and decent pantaloons of pepper
and salt [they smart, he smarting beneath], with his decent silver watch
in his pocket and its decent hair-guard round his neck [it protecting, he
being strangulated beneath]' (266). Not only is he in a strait-jacket, he
does not fit the mould it represents; cannot, that is, make a satisfactory
transition from one class to another: he 'was never seen in any other
dress, and yet there was a certain stiffness in his manner of wearing this,
as if there were a want of adaptation between him and it, recalling some
mechanics in their holiday clothes'. This last clause reminds us of the
trussed-up Joe Gargery visiting Pip in London, and humbly conceding
that he is out of his element, not 'right', and returning with relief to the
forge and his working garb. But Bradley Headstone cannot switch back;
he has only the one 'dress', the one identity, to wear, however ill-fitting.
There is in the image of the discomforted schoolmaster a vein of
characteristic Dickensian deprecation of processes of upwards social
movement; whereas Joe, as we know, is an exemplary model of
conformity to a fixed scheme of difference and subordination, Bradley
Headstone is a dire warning of the price to be paid for taking the
meritocratic high road. It is even intimated that he would have done

better to have taken a track more suitable for 'a pauper lad'; for there was enough of what was 'animal, and of what was fiery (though smouldering) still in him, to suggest that if . . . [he] had chanced to be told off for the sea, he would not have been the last man in a ship's crew' (267). There would be no hubris, no comeuppance, and no unsettlement of the established order in a lively low-born spirit making his way – at least so far – in the circumscribed, distant, and time-honoured orbit of naval service. Yet this persistent strain of ideological conservatism does not preclude, and indeed goes hand in hand with, a liberal imaginative grasp of the predicament of the uprooted, the unclassed. These early stages of the analysis end with a sharp reminder of the cleft stick of being forever unable to take strength from one's background and equally unable to leave it behind. 'Regarding that origin of his, he was proud, moody, and sullen, desiring it to be forgotten. And few people knew of it' (267). To desire to have something forgotten is to have it constantly in mind; if few people knew of it, then some always did.

The shadow of his humble origins and his uncertain identity are aspects of Headstone's plight that are then actively dramatized in the remarkable confrontation with Eugene Wrayburn prompted by the latter's interest in Charley's sister, a scene reminiscent of Steerforth's humiliation of Mr Mell but more harrowing. The episode seethes with class antagonism. Wrayburn is not looking for a fight, but proves a formidable enemy when challenged, mercilessly probing his opponent's points of weakness. Refusing to use Headstone's proper name, he relentlessly taunts him with the title of 'Schoolmaster', simultaneously denying him individuality or selfhood, transforming his one badge of respect into a mark of ridicule, and underlining the unpleasant truth that he is stuck on a relatively lowly rung of the social ladder – that mobility has ironically begotten paralysis of opportunity, release has brought restriction. Eugene's mention of the 'low obscure people' around Lizzie touches the rawest of nerves in Bradley, who immediately takes it as a reference to his own 'meanness of birth' (346–7); that the former's subsequent rebuttal of the charge rings true only increases our sense of the latter's psychological insecurity. Headstone, unlike Mell, does fight back, asserting his claims as an achiever against the odds: 'You reproach me with my origin, . . . you cast insinuations on my bringing-up. But I tell you, sir, I have worked my way onward, out of both and in spite of both, and have a right to be considered a better man than you, with better reasons for being proud.' Yet it is plain throughout the interview that he knows the limits of his power in the face of Eugene's high breeding and ease of manner, and at one point he admits this: 'That lad who has just gone out could put you to shame in half-a-dozen branches of knowledge in half an hour, but you can throw him aside like an inferior. You can do as much by me, I have no doubt' (344). People like Headstone had to contend not only, as Philip Collins puts it, with 'lower-class prejudices against the man who deserts his kind, and middle-class prejudices against the *parvenu*', but with their own acute self-consciousness and frustration, which can surface in physical symptoms no less than in words, as the 'passionate' schoolmaster, lamenting his lack of control over himself, breaks off to wipe the perspiration from his brow 'as he shook from head to foot', and spoke in 'a very agony, and . . . followed it with an errant motion of his hands as if he could have torn himself' (345).[18]

As the two men face each other, they are described as having 'some secret, sure perception between them, which set them against one another in all ways' (341). This is not a 'doubling' of opposites in mental life, such as is primary in the variance between the upright Copperfield and the sensual Uriah Heep, the Jekyll-and-Hyde syndrome, but that other kind, implicit in a minor way in the earlier relationship, which is the clash of rival entities in society – the state-educated public servant versus the well-born public-school-educated member (if in Wrayburn's case reluctantly) of the learned professions. Headstone's intensity, pride, and in themselves effective lines of argument prophesy a real and prolonged struggle, which is still with us, though it has resolved itself into an uneasy accommodation rather than open warfare, and has been significantly modified by the (one-way and selective) crossing of boundaries enabled by progressive expansion of advanced and higher education.

Dickens, however, is confronting a fresh phenomenon, an early stage in the battle for social space and power, and the victory goes, with his approval, to Eugene Wrayburn. There is something of the freak and the madman about Headstone – Eugene finds him 'an entertaining study' and 'curious monomaniac' (345, 347) – which makes him the masculine counterpart of the women in Dickens, Mrs Joe or Miss Havisham, who are 'not right' and must be put down – although, as with them, the extended portrayal of an unnatural condition, summarized vis-à-vis Headstone as 'suppression' (267), opens up the whole issue of social constriction. It was not only Victorian females that suffered from limited outlets for their energies, as Headstone himself implies when declaring that there is something in him that is stifled yet fundamentally unchecked: 'Do you suppose that a man, in forming himself for the duties I discharge, and in watching and repressing himself daily to discharge them well, dismisses a man's nature?' (345). Dickens tenders not just the 'sociology' of the new breed of college-trained teachers, which is how Philip Collins sees it,[19] but that of an incipient era in the redisposition of agencies and forces in modern society, and at the same time considers in Headstone the 'man' the human costs involved, the experiential side of the question.

In the longer run, however, the quality of Dickens's attention to this character, which in magnitude comes to surpass anything accorded to Mrs Joe, Miss Havisham and the like, lifts it out of history to the timeless plane of high tragedy. As with Bill Sikes, though in gloomier colours, a kind of subfusc, Dickens's sense of the heroics, or anti-heroics, of passion, transgression and enraged introversion take over. Once the sociological focus softens and falls away the protagonist emerges in full view, a figure of stringent pathos, even a curious nobility. The story of Bradley Headstone and Lizzie Hexam is one of those areas of Dickens which make complete nonsense of the old idea that he is no good at psychology. In this narrative he overturns Victorian suppositions about the sexes and offers a study in *male* erotomania. With Headstone the cliché 'love at first sight' comes to frightening life, his being a nature that 'may lie by for years, ready on the touch of an instant to burst into flame' (396). The energy that has lain actively dormant in him, neither absorbed nor expressed in routine existence, which the narrator has called 'animal' and 'fiery' (267), attaches itself to Lizzie as the object of desire; thoughts of her set his 'head hammering at one fixed idea' (396). His formal declaration, in the interview in the ominous churchyard setting, must be the strangest courtship ever to have happened, opening as it does with his reproachful lament that she is 'the ruin' of him, and that the time they first met was 'a wretched, miserable day' (452). Yet the phrases are, in this earnest proposal, the dead metaphors of lover's sighs made painfully literal. Lizzie is no woman to be conventionally wooed but an obsession, or, in her suitor's own words, a 'tremendous attraction which I have resisted in vain, and which overmasters me' (454). The man is looking for release from something within him rather than fulfilment from something, or someone, without. He is the victim of his own uncompromising emotions, unable to act of his free will; and what makes his situation the more poignant and terrifying is that he knows how much is at stake, which is no less than his destruction or survival, the damnation or salvation of his being:

> It is [not] voluntary in me to be here now. . . . You draw me to you. If I were shut up in a strong prison you would draw me out. I should break through the wall to come to you. . . . You could draw me to fire, you could draw me to water, you could draw me to the gallows, you could draw me to any death, you could draw me to anything I have most avoided, you could draw me to any exposure and disgrace. This and the confusion of my thoughts, so that I am fit for

nothing, is what I mean by you being the ruin of me. But if you
would return a favourable answer to my offer of marriage, you
could draw me to any good – every good – with equal force.
(454–5)

Headstone can clearly express his feelings, but can find no aid in that,
no talking cure.

In all of this Dickens treats Headstone seriously and with respect. He
speaks, for example, of his 'less than ordinary', rather than aberrant,
constitution (396); in describing his 'animal' and 'fiery' impulses he
gives them a natural dignity, whatever threat they may pose to himself
or others; he is articulate in his self-knowledge, however powerless to
help himself; and even his violence, as when he wrenches mortar from
the wall of the graveyard and, at Lizzie's final refusal, strikes the stone
'with a force that laid the knuckles raw and bleeding' (456), represents,
not just blind fury, but the awesome ferocity of an all-or-nothing, larger-
than-life temperament. In giving him this stature, and in giving him his
say, Dickens repays a debt to the maligned Heep and demonized Orlick
– though without yielding an inch on the question of the social climber's
demands for recognized status and positive valuation. The same ambivalence – committed imaginative embrace and upvaluing accompanying silent socio-ideological denial – continues in the next phase of
the story of Bradley Headstone, which returns us to the conflict with
Eugene Wrayburn. Once convinced that he has no hope with Lizzie,
Headstone immediately transfers his passionate feelings onto his rival,
speaking in jealous rage of how this other has crushed him 'in the dirt
of his contempt' (458). Status anxiety and the desire for Lizzie are intertwined in him, and together target Wrayburn as the source of his
tormented sense of failure. He says to Lizzie that Wrayburn is 'the text
of the little I have left to say' (457). 'Text' is an apt word, for in pursuing
vengeance upon his enemy he does what so many in *Our Mutual Friend*
do – he hatches a plot. This of course is the hunting of Wrayburn to
destruction, an action already prefigured and acted out in literal
substitution in that hitting of the burial-ground coping with such force
that it left him 'holding out his smeared hand as if it held some weapon
and had just struck a mortal blow' (456). But the design involves not
only a definite quarry but a putative tool, in the form of yet another
plotter – and type of the artist – Rogue Riderhood.

Riderhood, like Wegg, is a weaver of false tales. He spreads the
rumour that Gaffer has killed a man, when he himself has long been
under strong suspicion of having done that very thing; he insists that he
is the virtuous labourer 'as earns his living by the sweat of his brow'
(573), just as he terrifies the hapless Betty Higden into handing over her

last few coins; far from being thankful for his resurrection from death by accidental drowning, he concocts a scheme, though it never quite matures, for getting damages from the company whose steamer had the audacity to bump into him in the dark. However one might judge his misdemeanours, however, there can be no denying the deftness and appeal of his performance; if not a lovable Rogue, he does prompt a sneaking admiration in his puckishness and incorrigible defiance of the official line. Headstone, when he first makes his close acquaintance, appears at once to establish ascendancy over the man by declaring knowledge of his name, and imagines he might make use of him against Wrayburn – ' "Your name is Riderhood." . . . "I'm blest if it ain't," returned that gentleman. "But I don't know your'n." . . . "Here is an instrument. Can I use it?" ' (614). But Riderhood has ploys of his own, subtle and impressive. Though he does not know the schoolmaster's name, he can quickly pin a title on him; where Lightwood is 'The Governor' and Wrayburn 'T'other Governor', Headstone becomes 'T'otherest Governor' (611). This most untutored of creatures systematically 'declines' people as scholars do their grammar; while this systematization gives him no actual power over others, it does help to bring his world and those who have entered it under control, to make the latter manageable by clothing them in an insolent (dis)regard – as it were discounting their independent and unpredictable reality. Riderhood can be explained as a study in the great instinct to survive and have presence, which operates in him through native wit, uncompromising self-belief, and a practised aloofness to the life around him. There is something in him of the Shakespearian Fool, with his tendentious acumen; something of a lower-order Falstaff. He is the inverted toff; as is brought out by his so often being ironically termed 'that gentleman' by the narrator (for example, during the above-quoted exchange about his name (614)), and in the fact that he has much in common with Eugene Wrayburn. When he contrasts himself with the latter the effect is to point a similarity between them:

> 'Look here, T'otherest Governor,' replied the man, becoming hoarsely confidential. 'T'other Governor he's always joked his jokes agin me, owing, as *I* believe, to my being a honest man as gets my living by the sweat of my brow. Which he ain't, and he don't.' (611)

At this stage of the novel, neither man is a byword for industry, neither above a bit of sharp practice in chasing his own ends. Riderhood's statement both connects him with Wrayburn, rendering them rakish doubles at opposite ends of the social scale, and illustrates another function of the former within the narrative, which is that of commentator and interpretative guide, for he makes plain aspects of Wrayburn's character from which that indolent socialite lawyer and dubious suitor of the vulnerable Lizzie must in due course be redeemed. The same role, moreover, is apparent in the trio of 'Governor', 'T'other' and 'T'otherest', which produces a hierarchy of ardour and audience expectation – the decent, unexceptional Lightwood, the odd, unsettling Wrayburn, the positively outlandish Headstone.

There is, however, yet a further way of understanding Riderhood's place in *Our Mutual Friend*, which is as Dickens's agent in the mortification of Bradley Headstone. Where Wegg's plotting had been developed only to be punished in the name of goodness, Riderhood's is put to the service of sinister authorial intent. To remind the schoolmaster that Wrayburn makes fun of 'honest' people – 'jokes his jokes agin ['em]' – is to fuel his resentment, to egg him on along his disastrous course. When Headstone then copies the lock-keeper's clothes to throw the blame on him for the impending attack on Wrayburn, Riderhood soon cottons on, locates the discarded garments after the assault has taken place, and confronts Headstone with the damning evidence in a climactic scene at the school. Riderhood becomes, bizarrely, H.M. Inspector in Headstone's classroom, examining the children while the appointed teacher agonizes, though not for reasons of pedagogic unease:

> 'Wot's the diwisions of water, my lambs? Wot sorts of water is there on the land?'
> Shrill chorus: 'Seas, rivers, lakes, and ponds.'
> 'Seas, rivers, lakes, and ponds,' said Riderhood. 'They've got all the lot, Master! Blowed if I shouldn't have left out lakes, never having clapped eyes upon one, to my knowledge. Seas, rivers, lakes, and ponds. Wot is it, lambs, as they ketches in seas, rivers, lakes, and ponds?'
> Shrill chorus (with some contempt for the ease of the question): 'Fish!'
> 'Good a-gin!' said Riderhood. 'But wot else is it, my lambs, as they sometimes ketches in rivers?'
> Chorus at a loss. One shrill voice: 'Weed!'
> 'Good agin!' cried Riderhood. 'But it ain't weed neither. . . . It's suits o'clothes.'
> Bradley's face changed.
> 'Leastways, lambs,' said Riderhood, observing him out of the corners of his eyes, 'that's wot I my own self sometimes ketches in rivers. For strike me blind, my lambs, if I didn't ketch in the river the wery bundle under my arm!'
> The class looked at the master, as if appealing from the irregular entrapment of this mode of examination. The master looked at the examiner, as if he would have torn him to pieces. (866–7)

This is brilliant black comedy; but it is followed by a profoundly serious moment that silences all laughter, and that is all the more arresting for coming closely upon the measured accelerando of the question-and-answer session. On first entering the room, Riderhood had asked the master to write his name on the blackboard, which had been done – 'Bradley Headstone'. Now, with Bradley knowing he has been found out, the action is reversed: 'They looked at each other. Bradley, slowly withdrawing his eyes, turned his face to the black board and slowly wiped his name out' (867). Thus ends up the last of Dickens's low-born pretenders to middle-class status and authority – in self-obliteration. Riderhood is not Dickens's only accomplice in producing the cautionary outcome; Bradley Headstone is made, in a pose of ultimate humiliation, to co-operate in erasing his own identity. The suggestion is that the parvenu has within his very condition the seeds of an inevitable and terrible failure. There is, moreover, a third person present here in spirit – Eugene Wrayburn. Riderhood and he are, as we know, soulmates when it comes to opposing Headstone, the one from beneath, the other from above; and the connection is re-emphasized just after this scene, when, in the lock-keeper's shack, Riderhood, taunting his victim and 'smoking' (871), merges strangely in our minds with the image of Headstone's erstwhile tormentor, nonchalantly 'blowing the feathery ash from his cigar' (343). Headstone suffers his torture in a space between extremes, the force of the world from which he came and the force of that to which he aspires. Riderhood's triumph over him figures the victory of Wrayburn which is central to the final ideological scheme of the novel.

Yet the story of Bradley Headstone does not end even there. Before launching his examination of 'the lambs' Riderhood had enquired of Headstone whether he knew someone of his own build answering to a name sounding like 'Totherest'. 'I think I know the man you mean.' Extending our reading of Headstone's act of wiping out his name, we may see it as a cancellation not of a complete identity but of one side of a split self; Bradley Headstone dies, T'otherest lives. The moment returns us with a resounding whimper to the plane of tragedy because, as well as being the finale of Dickens's deprecation of social experimentation, it renders in symbolic attitude the climax – or anticlimax, all passion spent – of a history of self-separation and struggle between daylight existence and the dark, primitive inside of the psyche. The 'one' at last concedes to the 'other(est)'. Whether this is a pitiful surrender or an enabling embrace of a new certainty, is a question I shall come back to.

The last fall guy of Dickens's reactionary view of social re-formation is also the most sustained of his radical, sociologically disturbing, studies of the outsider. Headstone, as I have said, recalls Bill Sikes, but gone is the link to a tradition of colourful, swashbuckling criminality, which had taken the robber-turned-murderer, not unglamorously, through fire and to the rooftops. The physical supplies a telling point of contrast. Sikes's solid bodily presence signifies rootedness, in the lower order and as a distinct national type, and (not least in its violent and erotic aspects) provides focus and outlet, in Dickens's readers, for middle-class attitudes of repulsion and attraction. Sikes is an icon that allows the audience both to define and transgress cultural limits. Headstone simply unsettles presuppositions. He has no body at all, only disparate and unco-ordinated parts: the carcass 'ungainly and undecided'; the face that turns from 'burning red to white, and from white back to burning red'; the fingers that 'wiped his forehead and hands'; the fist that makes the churchyard wall crumble; the nose that sends out 'a great spirt of blood' (399, 400, 401, 456, 704). He is reduced at one stage, during the period of his frantic pursuits of Wrayburn through the night streets, to just a head; he goes in the dark 'like a haggard head suspended in the air', and as a 'haggard head' floats up the staircase (608, 610). Appearance does not signal an inability to throw off lower-class origins – we think of Pip's embarrassment when his rowing instructor says he has a blacksmith's arm – but the absence of any coherence of being, wholesome or un-wholesome, that they might bring. Headstone is a 'weirdo' of modern times, a 'head case', a 'nutter'; one who can neither connect with a past nor, as Pip does, adjust to the pressures of the present. It is the 'haggard' in 'haggard head' that positively signifies, for Dickens is interested in the mental strain. All along, Headstone's problem has been not only inner conflict but lack of integration. Thus, in his conversation with Lizzie there is on the one side the dry, tight-lipped civility of his argued proposal – 'My circumstances are quite easy, and you would want for nothing. My reputation stands quite high, and would be a shield for yours . . . ' (455) – and on the other the throbbing urge to possess her; and the same dichotomy between rationality and emotion then mani-fests itself in the division of his life between his day job and night-time recreation:

> Tied up all day with his disciplined show upon him, subdued to the performance of educational tricks, encircled by a gabbling crowd, he broke loose at night like an untamed wild animal. Under his daily restraint, it was his compensation, not his trouble, to give a glance towards his state at night, and to the freedom of its being indulged. (609)

There are echoes in Headstone of another 'schizoid' personality, cleft between professional and non-professional existence, Wemmick, but the hopeful message of Wemmick's garnering of blessed relief in suburban domesticity has been exchanged for the disquieting, and historically no less prophetic, factor of the 'compensation' of lawless abandon.

Headstone's is the fragile 'ego' of classic Freudian theory, a husk, an underdeveloped and artificial construct (by dint of role-specific training), uninformed by energies passed over from the 'id', the domain of the instincts. The mechanisms of self-censorship, which are seated in the 'ego' and 'super ego', are consequently also weak; and it is noticeable that when the schoolmaster does direct punishment upon himself it takes the form of masochism rather than self-regulation, as when he broodingly aggravates his murderous state 'with a kind of perverse pleasure akin to that which a sick man sometimes has in irritating a wound upon his body' (609), or when he is fascinated by sight of the pit of the river lock, suicidal, 'a troubled soul, set upon some violence, . . . hover[ing] between that violence and another' (703). Once on the road to a terrible misdeed, there is nothing to stop him:

> If great criminals told the truth – which, being great criminals, they do not – they would very rarely tell of their struggles against the crime. Their struggles are towards it. They buffet with opposing waves, to gain the bloody shore, not to recede from it. . . . All his pains were taken, to the end that he might incense himself with sight of the detested figure in her company and favour, in her place of concealment. And he knew as well what act of his would follow if he did, as he knew that his mother had borne him. (609)

The deed done, there is no remorse, only the dread of discovery and the agonizing reproach that it might have been done more efficiently:

> The state of that wretch who continually finds the weak spot in his own crime, and strives to strengthen them when it is unchangeable, is a state that aggravates the offence by doing the deed a thousand times instead of once; but it is a state, too, that tauntingly visits the offence upon a sullen unrepentant nature with its heaviest punishment every time. (777)

Whatever the status of these insights as a general account of the criminal mind, they certainly make impressive sense in their context.

The reference to an 'unrepentant nature' and its 'heaviest punishment' may suggest a judgemental stance: that Dickens is concerned to underline the inevitability of retribution for evildoing. But religio-moralistic truth is less important to him than existential truth. At one point we are actually moved to direct sympathy for the suffering sinner, when Charley Hexam, the only support and bright spot in Bradley Headstone's life, repudiates him:

> Was it strange that the wretched man should take this heavily to heart? Perhaps he had taken the boy to heart, first, through some long laborious years; perhaps through the same years he had found his drudgery lightened by communication with a brighter and more apprehensive spirit than his own; perhaps a family resemblance of face and voice between the boy and his sister, smote him hard in the gloom of his fallen state. For whatever reason, or for all, he dropped his devoted head when the boy was gone, and shrank together on the floor, and grovelled there, with the palms of his hands tight-clasping his hot temples, in unutterable misery. (781–2)

Headstone is reduced, or raised, simply to a 'man', stricken by the agony of rejection The final pose, grovelling, devoted head dropped, palms tight-clasped, raises religious associations – an imagery of prayer and even penitence itself – only to subsume them in a picture of sheer bodily and mental pain; the movement whereby the hands are pressed, not, as might be expected, in supplication, but in 'unutterable misery' sums up the elevation, in the whole passage, of humanistic vision and response. While Dickens resists consigning Headstone's 'fallen state' to didactic purposes, however, making of it an orthodox exemplum, he does take another figurative route, that of mythopoeic elaboration. The posture we have just considered reminds us of a world of grace from which Headstone is excluded. When we are then told, later, of 'the steady pressure of the infernal atmosphere into which he had entered' (863) the reference is not to his surroundings, though in the city and on Riderhood's desolate riverbank they can be bleak enough, but to his inner state, 'racked and riven' (862). He carries hell within him – like Milton's Satan: 'Me miserable! Which way shall I fly / Infinite wrath, and infinite despair? / Which way I fly is hell; myself am hell.'[20] Bradley has come to re-enact the archetypal psychodrama of the imprisoned self in a corner of Victorian England. The typological connection puts him, of course, on a grand scale, though, paradoxically, the measure of his tragic condemnation becomes the littleness to which his universe has contracted:

> He took heed of nothing but the ice, the snow, and the distance, until he saw a light ahead, which he knew gleamed from the Lock House window. . . . In the distance before him, lay the place where he had struck the worse than useless blows that mocked him with Lizzie's presence there as Eugene's wife. In the distance behind him, lay the place where the children with pointing arms had seemed to devote him to the demons in crying out his name. Within there, where the light was, was the man who as to both distances could give him up to ruin. To these limits had his world shrunk. (868)

The preoccupation with Lizzie and Eugene forges a further link with Satan, who had looked enviously upon the bliss of Adam and Eve in Paradise;[21] but there is also a distinction to be made between precursor and legatee, which is highlighted in a passage where we follow Bradley's thoughts as he moves from this same central obsession to a general reflection upon his predicament:

> For, then he saw that through his desperate attempt to separate these two for ever, he had been made the means of uniting them. That he had dipped his hands in blood, to mark himself a miserable fool and tool. That Eugene, for his wife's sake, set him aside and left him to crawl along his blasted course. He thought of fate, or Providence, or be the directing Power what it might, as having put a fraud upon him – overreached him – and in his impotent mad rage bit, and tore, and had his fit. (863)

Satan, and Milton's readers, know who the enemy is, who it is that mounts the master-plot against them. Headstone (satanized again by the imagery of a crawling beast) is likewise sure there is a 'directing Power', of which he has become the sport, but he cannot put a name to it. This reflects the uncertainty of an age that doubted the existence of God. Indeed, it can be said to do more. By locating the sense of a greater Authority in the unbalanced mind of the protagonist it queries the whole idea of a purposive Order. Do we live in a merely spectacular universe? Is the impotent individual the jest only of his own psychological processes?

Whichever the reason, external or internal, there is no free will. That is the message of the closing scenes of the Headstone saga. 'T'otherest' is liberated from all restraint when 'Bradley Headstone' is rubbed out, but only to become a driven force. Something of the compulsion with which he acts comes out in the way he is drawn to the Lock House for the last showdown with Riderhood, and enters it without thinking:

> He mended his pace, keeping his eyes upon the light with a strange intensity, as if he were taking aim at it. When he approached it so nearly as that it parted into rays, they seemed to fasten themselves to him and draw him on. When he struck the door with his hand, his foot followed so quickly on his hand, that he was in the room before he was bidden to enter. (868)

The influence of *Paradise Lost* gives way at this point to the old favourite, *The Pilgrim's Progress*, for the Lock House is the negative configuration of the Wicket Gate – the biblical strait gate – through which Bunyan's hero passes before starting on the road to salvation: ' "Do you see yonder Wicket Gate?" The man said, "No." Then said the other, "Do you see yonder shining light?" He said, "I think I do." Then said Evangelist, "Keep that light in your eye, and go up directly thereto." "[22] The denouement of this strand of *Our Mutual Friend* is Dickens's gloomiest account of the human condition, not only because there is no salvation but because there is no damnation either. The climax is a telling one precisely because it does not take us beyond the literal facts of two struggling bodies going over into the 'smooth pit' of the Lock, and being discovered under the ooze and scum: 'Riderhood's hold had relaxed, probably in falling, and his eyes were staring upward. But, he was girdled still with Bradley's iron ring, and rivets of the iron held tight' (874). There is nothing in this of the abyss of eternal reprobation and ultimate despair that lies in wait for Satan beyond his present misery, 'in the lowest deep a lower deep / Still threatening to devour [him]', the Hell beyond the living hell.[23] There is no place in modernity for an eternity of any kind, the transcendently bright or the abysmally dark.

The ending is satisfying nonetheless. This is because we are on Headstone's side. We see in him our own vulnerability as beings in a field of force, psychic, social, and *perhaps* providential, and take pleasure in his being on top (he literally lies 'upon' Riderhood as they fall), if only in an act that brings his destruction. Conversely, we have no sympathy for Riderhood, who has by now become one of Dickens's grossest examples of the ethic of cold-blooded self-interest, it being his plan to blackmail Bradley first and then unforgivably drain dry the latter's admirer, the harmless Miss Peecher. At the same time, the spotlight swings upon Riderhood in another and more significant way. He, who had seemed immune to the universal law of adverse agency, going his own way, turns out to be as subject to that law as anyone. He finally gets the plot badly wrong when he thinks he can 'get money out of a schoolmaster'; for his antagonist, thinking in altogether different terms, is determined to prove that 'You can't get blood out of a stone' (871). This is not the most serious mistake Riderhood makes, moreover. He believes he cannot be drowned, saying, as Headstone locks him in his iron grip, 'You can't drown Me. Ain't I told you that the man as has come through drowning can never be drowned' – before perforce yielding to the other's invitation to 'Come down!' (874). Riderhood's failed superstition underscores, in parodic form, the power of error and the hopelessness of belief. No one can control their destiny, or grasp what larger scheme, if any, there is beyond.

Rake

The lack of free will and ultimate purpose does not for Dickens, however, divest us of the responsibility to do the best we can to advance our individual and collective welfare – any more than for the old Calvinists, in so many ways his forebears, a world of rigid pre-destination banished responsibility for regulating conduct and caring for the state of the soul.[24] In *Our Mutual Friend*, he focusses his hopes and constructive ideas above all in Eugene Wrayburn and those associated with him, particularly, though not exclusively, Lizzie and the parallel partnership of John Harmon and Bella Wilfer. In all these characters the theme of personal development is bound up with that of the social good.

Eugene himself is in a double sense the reformation of a familiar Dickensian character-type, which we may at this point usefully track back. Steerforth, as gentleman rake, is relevant, as, from the same novel, is Jack Maldon, a summary example aptly described by John Lucas as signifying 'essential triviality and predatory sexual instinct'.[25] The nearer model, however, is James Harthouse in *Hard Times*, a sustained but tight-edged portrayal of a cluster of qualities, or defects, we have come to think of under the head of Decadence, a phenomenon which Arthur Symons, in his essay of 1893 on 'The Decadent Movement in Literature', termed 'an interesting disease' typical of an over-luxurious civilization, whose symptoms were 'an intense self-consciousness, a restless curiosity in research, an over-subtilizing refinement upon refinement, a spiritual and moral perversity'.[26] That Harthouse is the starting point for the 'perversity' from which Wrayburn is eventually reclaimed is implicit in the first, sarcastic description of the former, 'a thorough gentleman made to the model of the time, weary of everything, and putting no more faith in anything than Lucifer'.[27] But things are not so simple, for we can also trace in the earlier figure a certain am-bivalence that predicts the more complex later conception. A brief account of Harthouse will illuminate the direction of Dickens's thinking in his return to and reconstruction of the type.

Harthouse is physically self-indulgent (he smokes a lot, as Wrayburn does), and ostentatious in dress and appearance (on close encounter the novice decadent Tom Gradgrind perceives him admiringly through a cigar haze as all 'waistcoat' and 'whiskers'). He has abandoned a succession of career choices and travel plans as 'a bore', and at the time of the action of the novel is 'going in for' politics with the same lack of serious commitment. He tells Bounderby's young wife, Louisa,

> I assure you I attach not the least importance to any opinions. The

> result of the varieties of boredom I have undergone, is a conviction (unless conviction is too industrious a word for the lazy sentiment I entertain on the subject), that any set of ideas will do just as much good as any other set, and just as much harm as any other set . . . What will be, will be. It's the only truth going. (133)

His guiding principle lies in having none, his sole creed in taking things as they come.

The picture, however, is not an entirely negative one. Dandyism always has its attractions (as in real nineteenth-century life Byron and Disraeli famously saw when making names for themselves).[28] Harthouse is appealing not only in his wit, colour and ease of manner but in a sensitivity – or, to recall Symons, 'restless curiosity' – indicative of the artistic temperament. There is something of the poet in his early response to the mystery of Louisa, whose complex bearing 'baffled all penetration' (132); something of the novelist's powers of analysis in his reflections on the Bounderbys' 'cheerless' house and Louisa's singular reliance on her ungracious brother as an object of her love, which reveals to him how 'much the greater must have been the solitude of her heart, and her need of someone on whom to bestow it' (135). His indifference, which is linked to his upper-class origins, brings him an insouciant freedom that surfaces both as active mobility – as the narrator puts it, one who finds 'everything to be worth nothing' is 'equally ready for everything' (128) – and a capacity, like that of the satirist, for exposing hypocrisy, as when he frankly admits to the Utilitarians' ability to 'prove anything' by statistics, and to his own motive in joining them because on their political wing they form 'the largest party' and give him 'the best chance' (134).

Yet ambiguity is one thing, endorsement quite another. We are not, of course, meant to approve of James Harthouse. Within the network of evaluative metaphor that Dickens constructs in this novel, he is described as a 'demon' and as 'the tempter' (138, 139). He visits Louisa on horseback and speaks to her like a knight in a romance, saying, for example, 'There never was a slave at once so devoted and ill-used by his mistress' (211); but this is the ploy of the seducer, not the obeisance of the genuine errant adventurer; and the more circumspect rhetoric of persuasion with which he regularly addresses Louisa, expertly distinguished by Roger Fowler as an 'elaborated code' dominated by complicated syntax and verbal device, 'a literary, educated form',[29] marks him not only as upper-class, a 'fine gentlem[a]n' (128), but as an agile exponent of fiendish legerdemain. He is in a line of descent from Milton's Satan through the Lovelace of Richardson's *Clarissa*. When, later on, in his exchanges with Sissy Jupe, Harthouse himself calls the progress of his steps with Louisa 'perfectly diabolical' (234), it is as part of an attempted self-justification: something was happening beyond his control. With Sissy, however, no amount of special pleading will even begin to work; his devilish nature is simply, and literally, put to flight by her innocence – her 'child-like ingenuousness', her 'modest fearlessness', her 'truthfulness' (233) – rather as Comus is by the Lady in Milton's masque. This scene is followed by a wonderfully pointed exposure of Harthouse's corruptness, his shallow egotism, in another of those moments of social and moral illumination that are Dickens's outward-looking counterpart to the self-sufficient Romantic epiphany. We would, the narrator tells us, expect Harthouse to have valued his prompt retreat from Coketown as a way of making some amends for the 'very bad business' arising from his previous actions; in fact, 'A secret sense of having failed and been ridiculous . . . so oppressed him, that what was about the very best passage in his life was the one of all others he would not have owned to on any account, and the only one that made him ashamed of himself' (238). This is the last we hear of him. For this lost soul there is no call to redemption.

Eugene and Lizzie and John and Bella

Wrayburn replicates Harthouse, but in a finer tone. As late as Chapter 10 of the third book of *Our Mutual Friend* he appears in the stereotypical pose of the 'decadent' gentleman, standing 'half amused and half vexed, and all idle and shiftless' beside the bench of Jenny Wren, the dolls' dressmaker. Although such elementary traits are there for almost all the novel, however, they are rarely so isolated or so superficially paraded. When we first encounter Wrayburn it is as 'the gloomy Eugene', 'indolent', languidly upper-class and 'public school', repelled by the word 'energy' and lacking all commitment to his profession; but this lassitude is interestingly linked to positive neglect (he uses the word 'hate' of his attitude to his job) and the denial of family plans: 'It was forced upon me', he says, 'because it was understood that we wanted a barrister in the family. We have got a precious one' (57, 61–2). Later the rejection is more specifically of the filial duty and paternal authority in which the stability and very continuance of the dynasty are vested; for Eugene's mockery of his calling to legal eminence is one with the conscious irreverence he shows towards his father's wishes in being, as he puts it, 'the married man I am not' (193). It is in the areas of marriage and the family that he will in due course most obviously, and very importantly, reverse his attitudes.

Eugene is also cast from the start in the moulds of snob and seducer. The former trait comes out in two notable episodes. One is the taunting of Bradley Headstone, which we have already considered. In the other he literally fumigates Jenny Wren's wretched alcoholic father, whom he has named 'Mr Dolls', with a shovel of live ashes (600–603). Eugene has a trick in common with Rogue Riderhood, but uses it sadistically. By naming others on his own terms, at the level of a social function, 'schoolmaster', or an object of amusement, 'Mr Dolls', or a racial type, for he says of the good Mr Riah '*I* give him the name of Aaron' (598), is to exercise an aggressive domination.

Lizzie Hexam's possible fate at the hands of Eugene is memorably implied in the *double entendre* of his remark to Jenny Wren, 'I think of setting up a doll, Miss Jenny', and in her pointed retort, 'You are sure to break it. All you children do' (288–9). Eugene's plan to arrange an education for Lizzie, daughter of a Thames body-scavenger, is not born of philanthropic altruism or any levelling instinct. But it is in his relation to her that we are most immediately struck by an ambiguity and possibly saving grace in his character. When he first sees her, through the window of her waterside hovel, it is with the voyeuristic gaze of the sensual aesthete:

> It showed him the room, and the bills upon the wall respecting the drowned people starting out and receding by turns. But he glanced slightly at them, though he looked long and steadily at her. A deep rich piece of colour, with the brown flush of her cheek and the shining lustre of her hair, though sad and solitary, weeping by the rising and the falling of the fire. (211)

The poetic sensibility that elsewhere negligently indulges in 'contemplation of the sky' (340) warms into a lingering caress of beauty in living cipher. This scene is reminiscent of Satan's rapt attention to Eve caught unawares in paradise in Milton's epic.[30] It is not only predacious threat we are reminded of, however, but also the fact that Satan is, if only fleetingly, disarmed of his malice by the sight of 'graceful innocence'.[31] The mixture of delinquency and worthier disposition that exists for only a moment in Satan, and adds an intriguing depth to Harthouse's early reactions to Louisa, is a clear thread in Wrayburn's personality, suggesting a capacity for a constructive engagement with, at least, womankind. Lizzie Hexam comes to him as something between potential prey and a promise of renovation in the midst of death – the pictures of the drowned people literally forming a background and contrast to her lustrous vitality, while the rising and falling of the fire casts an undecided pattern of darkness and light, tragic and regenerative possibilities, simultaneously with the evocation of erotic aura and energies, themselves redolent with both peril and hope. Her appealing image represents the creative, if dangerous, side of an imaginative temperament in Eugene of which the solipsistic reverse is his obsessive authoring of Headstone as a quarry to be viciously destroyed:

> I goad the schoolmaster to madness . . . Having made sure of his watching me, I tempt him on, all over London. One night I go east, another night north, in a few nights I go all round the compass . . . I seek those No Thoroughfares at night, glide into them by means of dark courts, tempt the schoolmaster to follow, turn suddenly, and catch him before he can retreat. Then we face one another, and I pass him as unaware of his existence, and he undergoes grinding torments. (606)

These are the 'pleasures of the chase' (606). The story of Eugene and Lizzie is different, as we shall see; linear rather than moving in ever-decreasing about-turns. As soon as he stops spying on her a better self emerges, pointing forwards. He experiences remorse: 'If the real man feels as guilty as I do . . . he is remarkably uncomfortable' (212).

Eugene is always a two-sided, enigmatic character; in his own words, 'an embodied conundrum' (339). Harthouse is entirely amoral, while Steerforth has but flashes of incipient compunction, as when he confides in David, 'Daisy, I believe you are in earnest, and are good. I wish we all were!' (377). In Eugene, on the other hand, the insouciance of the 'decadent', and the freedom it brings, are under constant pressure from the constraints of conscience: he can feel 'a little ashamed' even of his treatment of 'Mr Dolls' (604). It is above all in a capacity for self-scrutiny and for reflecting upon his own situation and behaviour that he differs from his Dickensian precursors. His development is by and large the history of the enhancement of this faculty under the influence of Lizzie herself (whereas Harthouse, we recall, was altogether impervious to the goodness of Sissy Jupe); until, when the two meet secretly in the countryside to which Lizzie has retreated, he receives such 'a deep impression' from the 'purity' with which she expresses her own love and her own suffering that he falls suddenly into an assessment of their relationship and respective natures. In himself he recognizes the deficiencies, the carelessness and self-regard, inclined to exact 'pains and penalties all round'; but there is a voice within that at the same time speaks what we already suspect, that he is at bottom a serious young man capable of genuine commitment, who dares anyone to tell him that his feeling for Lizzie is 'not a real sentiment on my part, won out of me by her beauty and her worth, in spite of myself, and that I would not be true to her' (765). Set against his earlier flippant conceit on the value of his unused kitchen as a constellation of 'moral influences expressly meant to promote the formation of domestic virtues' (349), this riverside monologue gives the measure of Eugene's progress in sensitivity and psychological health.

Inward advance, however, is no point of resolution. There remains in Eugene a current of what the narrator calls outright 'wickedness', which surfaces to prompt a dilemma: ' "Out of the question to marry her," said Eugene, "and out of the question to leave her. The crisis!" ' (766). The impasse is so emphatic and summary as to suggest a deliberate contrivance by Dickens, a coil from which to launch a definitive movement in the text, which thereafter drives towards patent affirmation of 'domestic virtues', or, that is, of middle-class 'domestic ideology'.[32] This ideology functions throughout the novel, as in the conception of Lizzie in terms of ideals of selfless devotion (towards her father and brother), purity (she loves Wrayburn but flees his unsolicited approaches), and, most tellingly of all in view of her technical working-class status, genteel speech and manners.[33] In the later reaches of *Our Mutual Friend*, however, we are much more aware of a programmatic discourse. The conventional happy ending and the cleansing of 'decadence' become contexts for Dickens's last framing of a code of best social practice and regulation. This is most obvious, however, in the marriage of the novel's other central couple, John Harmon and Bella Wilfer, which is at once important in itself and a background for assessing the nature and meaning of the union of Eugene and Lizzie.

The early chapter in which Harmon, known as Rokesmith, returns to the scene of his near-death experience at the hands of robbers reprises the theme of the precariousness and elusiveness of identity that Dickens had so often explored. His recollection of the moment at which he had almost drowned, and had caught a glimpse of someone else in his clothes and in his place, forms an allegory of how easily the 'I' may be lost or destroyed; that of his sudden return to self-consciousness and successful struggle to the surface forms one of the 'I''s resilience and capacity for being reborn, as through baptism: 'I could not have said my name was John Harmon. . . . There was no such thing as I, within my knowledge. It was only after a downward slide through something like a tube . . . that the consciousness came upon me, "This is John Harmon drowning! John Harmon struggle for your life. John Harmon, call on Heaven and save yourself!" ' (426). In the present of his reflections he can forge no certain direction through the alleys and rooms of the landscape of his memory, but moves again and again in a circle, finding himself 'at the point from which he had begun' (422). John makes the interesting comparison between his condition and narratives of escape from prison, where 'the little track of the fugitives in the night always seems to take the shape of the great round world'; the challenge is to break out of the confines of his own mental vortex, and so uncover the 'I [that] lie[s] buried somewhere else'.

The sense of existential combat figured here counts for nothing in the novel's account of Harmon's subsequent development, which is so bland and low-key that G.K. Chesterton could feel that it is not 'so easy to say what he is intended to be'.[34] What John is intended for is to be the very model of a modern patriarch – a successful 'City man' and loving husband, caring less for the profits that got taken to the Bank than for his wife, who is a 'most precious and sweet commodity . . . that never was worth less than all the gold in the world' (750). In a sense his progress remains circular, for it moves backwards to the recovery of his father's legacy, which is, however, cleansed of its original filthiness – legitimized – by its passing to a new generation, by the heir's healthy disregard for money *per se*, and by the wholesome domestic purposes to which he puts it. Significantly, John and Bella move into their new home on the day the last pile from the dust-mounds is being carted away. Allowing for differences of family circumstance, John Harmon ends up just like Ebenezer Scrooge, an impeccable rich man responsibly dispensing his innocent bounty. John says to Bella that it is 'natural' that he should wish her to have a carriage to ride in, rather than soil the shoes on her pretty feet (748). It is implied through this whole segment of the text, of course, that is also natural for some people to have the wherewithal to sustain a comfortable and fashionable lifestyle. Dickens is a notable champion of the down-trodden, but no less a supporter of the well-heeled.

The underlying purpose of Bella Wilfer's life, as seems to be inscribed in the letters of her name, is for her to become the perfect wife. Much of her story is taken up with her being brought, through Boffin's pious fraud in pretending that he has fallen victim to avarice, to shed her fascination with money; to move from the shallow obsession of 'I love money, and want money – want it dreadfully' to the recognition of how 'morally uglier' her changed benefactor has become – 'capricious, hard, tyrannical, unjust' – and a plea to be made herself 'poor again', and so 'more innocent, more sorry, more glad' (81, 521, 661). The uncomplicated lesson and straight switch from cupidity to simplicity and sentiment read like melodrama, and indeed the liveliest portions of the episode are provided by Boffin's pantomime antics and feigned interest in the lives of famous misers, one of whom warmed his dinner by sitting upon it. Yet this change in Bella is all part of the bigger picture of her education. At one point she says she has been 'saved . . . from

[her]self' and just afterwards is described, by her father, as 'much improved' (671, 681); becoming a better and happier person is one with being made fit for the womanly role. When Lizzie in her rural hiding-place confides in her about her secret love for Eugene and her determination to cherish it in silence – 'When I think my life may be but a weary one, I am proud of it and glad of it. I am proud and glad to suffer something for him, even though it is of no service to him, and he will never know of it or care for it' – Bella learns both the example of 'deep, unselfish passion' and of something that needs correcting in her own character, which she suddenly views as 'a mere impertinent piece of conceit', that of a 'cold, worldly, limited little brute' (591–2). The percipient Lizzie knows better of her new friend, in whom she divines a courageous and steadfast spirit – 'A heart well worth winning, and well won. A heart that, once won, goes through fire and water for the winner, and never changes, and is never daunted' (592). This encouragement and Bella's own insights prepare the way for a life of service and being served.

The moral and practical aspects of Bella's progress come together when she proves herself worthy of John by putting his worth above her own and all worldly possessions; as she tells Boffin, she would rather John 'thought well' of her 'though he swept the street for bread' than that she had the regard of one who 'splashed mud upon him from the wheels of a chariot' (665). Of course, she doesn't have to put up with the poverty she is ready to accept; the largesse she receives from her husband includes a 'chariot', as we know, and extends even to the blatantly luxury item of an aviary of tropical birds! Her dreams of wealth and its pleasures come true once she has conscientiously broken free of them. This outcome reinforces Dickens's message for his female readers – a case of virtue and self-abnegation rewarded (curiously like the improving tale of Tommy Twopence which Dickens had considered such incongruous fare for the pupils of the Ragged Schools). It also situates the man as provider.

Hierarchical in some respects the relationship certainly is: later, we hear Bella conceding directly that John is 'so much stronger, and firmer, and more reasonable and more generous' than she (755): 'He for God only, she for God in him'.[35] When she does lay claim to a fighting spirit it is to declare her undying support, the sacrifice of her own existence to his: that 'if all the world were against him, she would be for him; that if all the world repudiated him, she would believe him; . . . that, under the worst unmerited suspicion, she could devote her life to consoling him, and imparting her own faith in him to their little child' (830). Interestingly, this pledge of devotion is introduced with a reference to

'her own little natural pathetic way', the words fixing her on a lower
scale, doing once more what comes naturally, displaying the ductile
emotion proper to womankind. Separate spheres there certainly are, too.
He belongs explicitly to the world of 'business', she to the 'home', where
she applies herself to the newspaper, so that she may better be his
'companion', and (mirroring in a minor way the relation of Dickens's
reader to his text) to the *Complete British Family Housewife*, of which,
daunting though it is, Bella makes a much surer conquest than David's
incompetent Dora had made of her book of instruction (749–50). These
are described specifically as her – woman's – 'branch[es] of study',
marking her off from the larger arena of intellectual striving.

Just how far any of her activities and commitments stretch her in
what she says she wants to be, which is 'something so much worthier
than the doll in the doll's house' (746), is debatable; and there are terms
of affection that undoubtedly set alarm bells ringing if we trouble about
the objectification of women: 'most precious and sweet commodity',
making Bella eminently ownable and consumable, we have already
encountered, and on the same page comes, not the familiar 'angel', but
the rather more serviceable 'bright light in the house' (750). But what
Dickens intends for his own time he achieves. The Harmons are his most
thorough and successful construction of the functioning bourgeois
family unit; a model of complementarity that is both attractive (the
humour of the presentation helps in this) and workable, can be warmed
to and aspired to.

Romantic love had long had a place in the Dickensian domestic ideal,
but a muted one. It appears, we may remember, in Scrooge's vision of
Belle's happy life, as a splendour he has forfeited. It is developed as an
element in the bonding of Agnes and David – though in that same novel
the transgression of Steerforth and Emily and, in a different way, David's
infatuation with Dora show also its errant force. With John and Bella,
however, the concept is put at the very core of the institution of
marriage, a *sine qua non* of the dynamic interdependence that works in
its several ways to mutual advantage. As Bella says, 'It all comes of my
love, John dear' (750). And with love, in *Our Mutual Friend*, comes sex.
In comparison with earlier heroines the striking thing about Bella, as to
a lesser extent about Lizzie, is her physicality; body and spirit, separated
out in the lower-class Nancy and middle-class Rose Maylie, struggling
to get together in Agnes, are in Bella conspicuously united, and this
represents a revised understanding not only of the woman herself but
of that component of cultural organization in which she is the twin
icon. We are frequently treated to Bella's displays of sensuousness, her
touching and feeling, her flirting and forwardness. In one chapter, she

cannot wait 'to draw her arm through his, and delightedly squeeze it'; recalls how they 'have run away together often' and, evoking the frisson of bodily contact, how 'I made you carry me, over and over again'; offers 'a kiss' (371, 375). In another scene, she provocatively parades before her man in a dress he has bought her, soliciting an intent scrutiny of 'her figure' and the cry of 'splendid female'; she tightens 'her arm a little closer about him' and her 'hand stole gradually up his waistcoat to his neck'; and on one especially intimate occasion, he 'had become alarmingly limp . . . from the knees upward', and 'Bella sprinkled him with kisses instead of milk, but gave him a little of that article to drink; and he gradually revived under her caressing care' (668–71, 673). No retiring Victorian young person, this.

But, of course, the man in question in all these passages is Bella's father, Rumty Wilfer. What are we to make of that? Is Dickens indulging the reader's covert instincts by generating moments of excitement in the safe, innocent context of a father–daughter relationship? Or, contrariwise, is he titillating the reader by arousing thoughts of the forbidden, incest itself? Both reactions are possible, and both are clearly indicated by the inescapable *double entendre* of the last quotation, the incident of Rumty's fainting fit and revival. Moreover, in view of the contemporary preoccupation with the literal fact of widespread incest among the working classes, an ultimate depravity linked to crowded living conditions, the ambiguous, wholesome/unwholesome, quality of the physical side of Bella's and her father's interaction may be said to reinforce, but in some way also to question, the middle-class sense of elevation and apartness.[36] One other effect is certain, however. Dickens realizes Bella's sexuality so that it may be transferred from the paternal sphere to that of the husband. The reassignment is signalled quite deliberately in a brief pageant when Bella, on the very spot where she and her father had earlier enjoyed a spree like a courting couple, the hotel at Greenwich, seals the refiguration of relations with a ritual double kiss:

> Bella sat between Pa and John, and divided her attentions pretty equally, but felt it necessary . . . to remind Pa that she was his lovely woman no longer.
>
> 'I am well aware of it, my dear,' returned the cherub, 'and I resign you willingly.'
>
> 'Willingly, sir? You ought to be brokenhearted.'
>
> 'So I should be, my dear, if I thought I was going to lose you.'
>
> 'But you know you are not, don't you, poor dear Pa? You know that you have only made a new relation, who will be as fond of you and as thankful to you . . . .' Bella put her finger on her own lip, and then on Pa's, and then on her own lip again, and then on her husband's. (734–5)

Bella is always much less demonstrative with John than with Pa, and when the betrothed unite she virtually disappears into him – 'seemed to shrink to next to nothing in the clasp of his arms, partly because it was such a strong one on his part, and partly because there was such a yielding to it on hers' (671). This is both the suppression and the preservation of her erotic energy. Sex is present in her marriage but retreats behind closed doors, all part of a serious, satisfying, co-ordinated, healthy reciprocity. That it *is* there is proved, if nowhere else, by Bella's gentle, tentative climax to thoughts about ships sailing from the mysterious seas: 'I think . . . among them . . . there is a ship upon the ocean . . . bringing . . . to you and me . . . a little baby, John' (756).

Bella's sea imagery reminds us of that sense of 'unknown' destiny that pervades *Our Mutual Friend*. The relationship of John and Bella, how-ever, is an instructive showpiece in how people can bring order and success to their lives both on the personal level and within the evolving social frame and historical process. It upvalues private mutuality and love while aligning them with a powerful regard for wealth, lineage and inheritance. In Chapter 12 of the fourth book, conjugal bliss is rendered complete only when John, to soothe his lurking 'uneasiness' (826), lays public claim to the considerable patrimony of which he has already secretly taken possession; and a bouncing baby does duly appear to consolidate the present and secure the future. The ivory casket full of jewels for Bella and the nursery for his child on which he splashes out are immediate tokens of affection but also disguised long-term in-vestments in family bonding and forwards prosperity.

The union of Eugene and Lizzie is suffused with comparable values, though the 'normalization' that it represents is often more curiously textured. Lying at death's door following Headstone's murderous as-sault, Eugene is presented by his friend Mortimer Lightwood, after a great deal of fuss and searching for a healing spell, with 'a word' – 'Wife' (811). That the real name of Jenny Wren, who actually comes up with the magic word and slips it to Lightwood, is Fanny Cleaver suggests another transfer and regulation of sexual energies, this time their translation from wayward appetite to sanctioned disposition; an effect enforced by the way Jenny's delicately sensuous ministration as sickroom nurse – a 'touch upon his breast or face', an easing of the pressure of the bedclothes, a kiss upon his cheek or 'poor maimed hand' (809–11) – subsumes the libidinal in the chaste and intercedes to defer, while also predicting, a caring and carefully managed bodily intimacy between the intended couple.[37] At the same time, the manifest homoerotic dimension in Eugene's history is conclusively dissolved at the very instant of its strongest expression, when Lightwood, the companion to whom he had ever been 'strongly attached' (337) and with whom he had shared a home, goes off to summon Lizzie for the bedside ceremony: 'Touch my face with yours, in case I should not hold out till you come back. I love you, Mortimer' (812).

Matrimony itself gives solid effect to the repentance Eugene has come to feel – 'I have wronged her enough in fact . . . still more in intention' (808) – and puts his whole life on a new course, steadying the coming and going, the 'wandering away I don't know where' (807), which in the aftermath of his illness has replaced yet still echoes his former aimlessness. No longer can he say, as he once said to Mortimer, 'I have no design whatever. I am incapable of designs' (348). Gone is any such urge as had driven him on his night stalking of Bradley Headstone, the constantly repeated outcome of which had been the gentleman 'glid[ing]' into 'dark courts' and 'tempt[ing]' the schoolmaster to follow, climaxed by the suspended animation of one kind of compulsion, sophisticated, aristocratic, meeting another, earthy, crude, bestial, where the two men 'face one another . . . and [Headstone] undergoes grinding torments' (606). The images evoke very strikingly the world of same-sex conflict and intercourse from which Eugene has been extricated in a self-consuming excess of masculine violence – his being bludgeoned from behind by Headstone in the near-fatal attack on the riverbank symbolizes an unleashing and emptying out of male-on-male potency – and by Lizzie's saving feminine presence. Where Bella's lawful uniting with John represents a transcending of daughter–father love, that of Eugene with Lizzie is a leaving behind of self-pleasure and fantasy (we recall Eugene's peeping at Lizzie in her riverside shack), heterosexual rapaciousness, and homosexual impulse.

Lest we miss the fact of Eugene's redemption as it is expressed in the motifs of journeying and orientation, delirium and recovery, there is a clear-sighted exchange at the end of the next chapter in which he regrets his 'trifling wasted youth' and 'humbly hope[s]' to do better henceforth (825). The regularization of his relations with Lizzie is then carefully extended outwards to embrace the approval of his father, which is reported in language that implies the sanctity of the larger, collective interest and makes the defence of social status a holy cause. Eugene talks of his marriage receiving 'paternal benediction' and 'being thus solemnly recognized at the family altar' when it is suggested that Lizzie should have her portrait painted (884) – presumably for the ancestral gallery, which would draw her formally into line. The beauty that Eugene had once threatened to plunder as he viewed it through the frame of the hovel window has now become a propitiatory offering and legitimate family possession. The rejection of dynastic authority with which his story commenced has been comprehensively reversed.

Not only 'love of families'[38] but the several standard components of middle-class ideology are reaffirmed in *Our Mutual Friend*. Even the virtue of honest work gets in as Eugene, announcing a change of attitude in his professional life, creates a motto: 'In turning to at last, we turn to in earnest' (885). Yet there are, nonetheless, some distinctive manoeuvres on Dickens's part that merit attention. For one thing, as we have seen, concern for and discipline of the body assumes a new importance in his thinking. For another, he goes out of his way to insist, more emphatically than ever before, upon a redefinition of the concept of the gentleman, when, of all people, the hitherto timorous Twemlow is given the honour, in almost the last words of the novel, of publicly putting down 'Society', which disapproves of Eugene marrying beneath his station:

> 'Pardon me, sir,' says Twemlow, rather less mildly than usual, 'I don't agree with you. If this gentleman's feelings of gratitude, of respect, of admiration, and affection, induced him (as I presume they did) to marry this lady . . . I think he is the greater gentleman for the action, and makes her the greater lady. I beg to say, that when I use the word, gentleman, I use it in the sense in which the degree may be attained by any man.' (892)

Worth goes with sound sentiment and conduct, rather than with title, money, or connections. The gentleman as unaccountable upper-class adventurer, like Harthouse or Steerforth, or Eugene in an earlier guise, gives way to the gentleman as man of feeling, good husband and responsible scion. Any man may achieve the designation. Another, more striking redrawing of social boundaries lies in the very fact of the union of Eugene and Lizzie, who is at this stage a factory girl. It is as if Harthouse had learned his lesson and married Sissy Jupe, or Steerforth had done the decent thing by Little Emily – though, again, it must be remembered that Lizzie's attributes and disposition, so improbable by standards of verisimilitude, already qualify her for her upwards relocation.

The ideological preferences of *Our Mutual Friend* continue those of *David Copperfield* but with a loosening and reordering of class relations. Pure meritocrats like Headstone and Charley Hexam make no more headway in Dickens's approbation than Uriah Heep had done, whatever his imaginative respect for the tormented schoolmaster; but, while David had unproblematically married a solicitor's daughter of straight middle-class pedigree, Eugene does have to adjust his lifestyle and thinking to the solid ground around and, in taking Lizzie, beneath him. To the end the reactionary and radical strands in Dickens are intertwined. We may recall that when our student of mass periodicals in

Eliza Cook's Journal applauds their effect in 'strengthen[ing] the bands of society' the phrasing suggests a commitment to the principles both of hierarchical structure, 'banding', and of promoting cohesion, 'bonding'; and in *Our Mutual Friend* Dickens extends his own pursuit of these twin objectives by prioritizing nobility of *character* and by crossing dividing lines.

Dickens was not alone in doing this. The most dedicated of all propagators of Victorian values, Samuel Smiles, did not publish the volume actually entitled *Character* until 1871, but Dickens may well have been influenced by the earlier *Self-Help*, which proclaims this theme alongside the gospel of work and had already gone into four editions and eight reprints between 1859, the year of publication, and 1864 when the first part of *Our Mutual Friend* came out. There is, for instance, a close parallel between Dickens's definition of the true gentleman and that formulated at length in the final chapter of Smiles's guidebook to national standards in conduct and achievement: 'Riches and rank have no necessary connexion with genuine gentlemanly qualities. The poor man may be a true gentleman – in spirit and in daily life. He may be honest, truthful, upright, polite, temperate, courageous, self-respecting, and self-helping.'[39] It is high-mindedness and behaviour that matter in life, not birth or material possessions. Smiles's specific reference to 'the poor man' renders transparent his, and Dickens's, outflanking of the problem of inequality and possible conflict between the classes by moralizing the measure of human standing and success. The treatment of Joe Gargery at the lower end of the social ladder complements that of Eugene at the upper. The collapsing of hierarchy on ethical grounds safely preserves it in social and economic terms.

Smiles was also instrumental in circulating that other great prescription for social stability with which we have seen Dickens so substantially involved: the doctrine of 'home' and 'separate spheres', the association of men with the realm of business and the charge upon women to maintain what Ruskin famously, or notoriously, called the 'temple of the hearth'.[40] Smiles's highest term of praise is 'manly', and among his most important indicators of desert are the discretion and forbearance with which a man '*exercise*[s] *power* over those subordinate to him', of which 'women and children' head the list.[41] The records of heroes and their exploits that pack the pages of *Self-Help* are ghosted by the wives and mothers whose special duty was moral guardianship and service in the home as, in the words of one contemporary journalist, a 'place of happiness . . . which alone can make compensation for all the troubles . . . with which men of all classes must meet in public life, and business, and occupation of any description'.[42] And such is the impression that is continued in the penultimate chapter of *Our Mutual Friend*, where, on a visit to the Harmons, 'Mr Eugene Wrayburn' imparts to 'Mrs John Harmon' the confidence that 'please God, she should see how his wife had changed him', and Lizzie appears on cue to fill out the image of regenerative sway and constant support: ' "But would you believe, Bella," interposed his wife, coming to resume her nurse's place at his side, for he never got on well without her: "that on our wedding day he told me he almost thought the best thing he could do, was to die?" ' (883–4).

Thus, we see Dickens once more at work in the field of contemporary debate, addressing issues of how life should be lived and organized, pointing directions, processing and building ideology. There is one remaining area in this regard where *Our Mutual Friend* offers a distinct reformulation of attitudes, and strikes a cardinal note for the future – that, not of Eugene, but eugenics.

Eugenics: A New Liberal Dispensation

One example of Dickens's blurring of received opinion is that in Bella he challenges the widespread assumption that active sexuality was the prerogative of the working-class woman and in Lizzie the notion that moral beauty belonged all to the middle class.[43] What these two always have in common, however, is that they are perfect female specimens. Both are called 'the boofer lady', one by the young orphan Johnny, the other by his great-grandmother Betty Higden (575, 387); and we can certainly believe what springs from the mouths of babes and the tender-hearted. The first thing Lizzie and Bella do on meeting is to exchange compliments about how 'pretty' each looks. John Harmon, duly smitten by the latter, tells her, 'Just as you are attracted by her beauty – by her appearance and manner, she is attracted by yours' (582, 587).

Such details might appear inconsequential, were it not for the then strong current of interest in the function of feminine attraction in the welfare of the race. No less a figure than Herbert Spencer, for example, writing in 1861, mounts a vigorous argument against granting women a higher education on the grounds that 'forcing', or excessive study, produces physical decline: 'Mammas anxious to make their daughters attractive, could scarcely choose a course more fatal than this, which sacrifices the body to the mind. . . . Men care little for erudition in women; but very much for physical beauty, good nature, and sound sense. . . . [A] cultivated intelligence based on a bad *physique* is of little worth, since its descendants will die out in a generation or two'.[44]

Spencer's unfortunate young ladies are 'pale, angular, flat-chested'. Swarthy, lustrous, robust – 'a dark girl of nineteen or twenty' (43) – and more delicately vivacious, with 'brown eyes and brown curls' and 'a pretty figure' (77, 79), Dickens's heroines are mirror opposites of a flourishing shared ethnicity; and in uniting them with the emphatically eligible Harmon and Wrayburn, offspring respectively of successful middle-class trade and established upper-class families, he treads the path of an elementary eugenics. Thinking back to Herbert Spencer, it is interesting that Lizzie should be educated by Eugene up to a certain standard of literacy, for this makes her fit to be his consort without the slightest danger of unhealthy brain-forcing. Though Dickens saw in Lizzie the source of an invigorating infusion of both new blood and moral sense into a failing upper class, and was happy to cut through assumptions that the classes should not intermix, he proceeds conservatively, putting careful cultural controls on the process of cross-influence.

The emplacement of evolutionary ideals is reinforced within *Our Mutual Friend* by the several portraits of degenerates, where in some notable instances defect of character is linked to physical defect. We may recall the 'rocking-horse' figure of Mrs Podsnap, all bone, neck and nostrils, fit for Professor Owens's laboratory for the study of failing species. In the money-lender Fledgeby and in Silas Wegg a criminal mentality is associated with a particular brand of deficiency or imbalance – hormonal. Fledgeby's distinguishing feature is that he cannot grow whiskers; which is not a problem for the hirsute Alfred Lammle, whose full-frontal approach to deception and revenge contrasts directly with the former's subtle wiles. Lammle could do with some feminine instincts, Fledgeby (whom in fury he thrashes almost to death) with some manliness. In Fledgeby pecuniary accretion and possession of others body and soul are commensurate with, and a compensation for, sexual enervation. In Wegg they are more a perversion of energy; as we have already seen, not only does a missing limb signify his generally faulty nature but its wooden replacement, erecting itself under the table at the mention of buried treasure, tells an altogether more precise diagnostic story. Fetishism aside, Wegg, with his violent outbursts, blind aggression and shameless self-interest, and penchant for the easy life, conforms closely to the criminal type outlined in a treatise by the medical and scientific thinker Sir Francis Galton: 'The ideal criminal has marked peculiarities of character: his conscience is almost deficient, his instincts are vicious, his power of self-control is very weak, and he usually detests continuous labour.' And when Galton then proceeds to underline the astonishing 'absence of genuine remorse for their guilt' in criminals, and their 'utter untruthfulness . . . however plausible their statements may be', it strikes us how well his definition also covers the chronically disingenuous Rogue Riderhood. Galton was in fact the man who coined the term 'eugenics' for selective human breeding, and he is discussing here, as he puts it, 'the practicability of supplanting inefficient human stock by better strains and [considering] whether it might not be our duty to do so by such efforts as may be reasonable, thus exerting to further the ends of evolution more rapidly . . . than if events were left to their own course'. The project, though Galton never quite comes to a decision as to the exact means, is to root out 'vicious instincts' on the basis that they are 'transmissible by inheritance', and not susceptible to reform through the application of 'altruistic sentiments'.[45] Dickens of course does not go this far, but neither does he, like Venus, deal neutrally in 'Miscellanies of . . . human species' (559). Built into Dickens's presentation of the 'stock of human warious' (558) is a pattern, a taxonomy, whereby the genetically desirable is distinguished from the undesirable. There is little chance of the under-sexed Fledgeby propagating his kind; nor of Wegg: but for good measure the former is incapacitated and tucked away in the proverbial dummy's box and the latter is consigned to where he truly belongs, the rubbish cart.

Dickens's vehement attacks on jingoism in the caricature rhetoric of Podsnap, who considers all foreign countries 'a mistake' (174), does not preclude a proactive care for the nation's make-up and well-being. His concept of the common weal, however, is finally determined as much by inclusion as exclusion, by what he surprisingly puts in as well as what he wants to see cast out. The good Mr Riah is the obvious case in point. Dickens goes out of his way to stress Riah's Jewishness while at the same time insisting that he is 'a man': 'A venerable man, bald and shining at the top of his head . . . A man who with a graceful Eastern action of homage bent his head and stretched out his hands with palms downward' (328). Not only is the Jew respected as one of the kindest persons in the book, especially in his support of Lizzie (for whom he finds protective employment amidst others of his people) and Jenny Wren (who calls him her 'godmother'), he is made the medium of a rallying-call for self-esteem among an oppressed race when he confesses to hating himself for his subservience – 'in bending my neck to the yoke I was willing to wear, I bent the unwilling necks of the whole Jewish people' (795). Thus Dickens moves to correct the 'great wrong' Mrs Liza Davis had told him he had perpetrated in the portrayal of Fagin; successfully so, it appears, since the same correspondent sent him a copy of Bernisch's Hebrew and English Bible in 'grateful and admiring recognition' of his 'atoning for an injury'.[46]

In Riah Dickens tolerantly, indeed affirmatively, clears an honourable space for the outsider. Less dramatic, but just as important, is his situating of Jenny and Sloppy. These are from the ranks of the disabled and the disadvantaged; but each is granted a symbolic triumph that distinguishes them from the degenerate characters and underlines their status as, if we may use the word, 'desirables': Jenny has the pleasure of sprinkling pepper on the plasters of brown paper and vinegar she applies to Fledgeby's injured back, Sloppy is the one who actually throws Wegg into the scavenger's cart. Jenny, as a conception, is a clear and direct challenge to widespread theories of degeneration predicated on a belief in the overwhelming power of inheritance, or that, as the influential psychiatrist Henry Maudsley succinctly put it, 'the . . . ill of the parent becomes the inborn infirmity of the offspring'.[47] Genetically understood, she is a mass of contradictions that makes nonsense of any straight application of the principle of heredity, where, quoting this time from Théodule Ribot's classic exposition of the 'biological law' of repetition, generations 'transmit to their descendants at least a predisposition to imperfections like their own'.[48] Drunkenness and moral degradation are often linked together by the exponents of this law, including Maudsley in a family tree illustrating 'the natural course of degeneracy',[49] but Jenny, daughter of a depraved alcoholic who sells Lizzie's whereabouts to Eugene for the price of a drink, has an inclination to neither. On the contrary, sound moral instincts and discipline are among her great strengths, evident in her dealings with everyone she meets or knows, with Lizzie, her friend Riah, Fledgeby, whom she always distrusts, Eugene, whom she at first suspects of dishonest motives towards Lizzie but ends up caring for 'with an earnestness that never relaxed' (809), with her father, whom she looks after. Rather, the caution is against the immediate and practical damage, and especially the psychological danger, that can radiate from weakness of character: Jenny's reactive casting of her father in the role of her 'troublesome, bad child' (291) reveals not only her resilience in finding strategies for survival but also a distortion in family relations that she cannot altogether rise above, both of which – the resourcefulness and the peril – are shown in the 'scolding' scene where she becomes a frenzied 'little quaint shrew' (294) when her 'child' misbehaves; in keeping things functioning she takes a desperate gamble with the pressures of dysfunction. Jenny does have innate physical problems; 'a dwarf – a girl – a something', crippled with a 'bad' back and 'queer' legs (271). Maudsley might well have explained this in terms of a generally degraded line of descent, since his illustrative genealogy shows regular linkages of bodily with mental deformity.[50] Yet in Jenny lack on the one hand is compensated by intelligence on the other; she is constantly alert and perceptive, our 'Mrs Truth' who sees through Eugene's plans for 'setting up a doll', or is a step ahead of Lizzie in understanding her feelings for Eugene and coaxes her into articulating her half-formed emotions by getting her to read in the fire a story of a 'beautiful lady' winning the man she loves and rescuing him from his 'failings' (404–405). So much, too, for Maudsley's observation that 'chronic alcoholism in the parent may directly occasion idiocy in the child'.[51]

With Jenny, then, Dickens not only projects a secure and active place for the disabled in his good society, he scrambles standard lines of approach to disability itself, seeing complexity and even value and quality instead of simply privation and a threat to posterity that had better be rooted out. Something similar happens with Sloppy. In a *Household Words* contribution of 1853, written in collaboration with W.H. Wills, Dickens had surveyed advances in the treatment of idiocy and had praised the new method of Dr Guggenbühl's mountain clinic in Switzerland, which produced extraordinary improvements in 'idiot' children, transforming them from 'stunted withered skeletons' to persons moving 'rapidly towards perfect development'.[52] A follow-up article on the subject, unsigned but usually attributed to Harriet Martineau, though assuming inherited factors, also lays stress on the efficacy of training and education, and at one point remarks upon the common phenomenon of the mother discovering 'the wonderful faculty her child had in some one direction'.[53] Sloppy's great and famous gift, over and above his talent for turning the mangle in the child-minder Betty Higden's parlour, is that he reads the newspapers aloud and 'Do the Police in different voices' (246). That he is literate in any degree, let alone adept at mimicry, suggests of course that he is not an 'idiot' at all, in spite of his propensity for uttering the occasional 'howl' (392) and his odd, ungainly make, with 'a very little head, and an open mouth of disproportionate capacity that seemed to assist his eyes in staring, . . . [a] considerable capital of knee and elbow and wrist and ankle . . . [that] he didn't know how to dispose of . . . to best advantage, but was always investing it in wrong securities' (245, 249). Sloppy is a 'love-child' brought up in the Poor-house, a 'weak ricketty creetur' taken in by Betty who thought she might 'do something with him' (247, 249); he was, Betty explains, once 'thought to be no better than a Natural' – that is, in the archaic sense, an 'idiot' (247, 249).[54] The lesson of *Our Mutual Friend* is not that 'idiots' ought to be helped and cared for – though Dickens certainly held this view – but that we should not judge by origins (Sloppy's illegitimacy) or appearances, and that we should nurture the best in everyone. (There is something of this argument implicit in Martineau's paper, for she tells of seeming cases of idiocy, defined by 'popular prejudice', where, without any formal tuition, the child learned to read, and even write, and to do sums.)[55] In the longer run it turns out that Sloppy has two other notable gifts. One is that he is exceptionally 'amiable', a model of 'tenderness of heart' in his attachment to his benefactress (249, 392), a type of the blessed innocent; the other, by contrast practical, that he is excellent at making and mending things, a broken mangle or piece of furniture, toys, the pieces of 'a foreign monkey's musical instrument', his ingenious fixing of which drew a crowd of onlookers (442–3). Mr Boffin takes the considerate and useful step of paying for him to learn the trade of cabinet-making.

Sloppy meets Jenny. Perhaps Dickens's most audacious move with regard to the crippled woman is that he recognizes her sexuality, which is symbolized by her voluptuous 'fair hair' (402–403) and expressed in her frequent talk of the man who will enter her life, 'the party who is coming to court me when the time comes' (402). The book thus speaks out emphatically in an area where even nowadays we would expect a relative silence. Sloppy, it seems, is the one Jenny has been waiting for. She draws him in by referring to 'Him who is coming to court and marry me', which makes Sloppy jealous, and by shaking her hair down, which prompts admiration – 'What a lot, and what a colour!' (881–2). In the middle of this flirtatious encounter, to which Dickens is entirely sympathetic, we are firmly reminded of Jenny's 'imperfections', for she calls herself 'a queer little comicality' and frankly declares to Sloppy 'I am lame'. The prediction of an eventual union then compounds the force of Dickens's line in cutting through and contradicting nineteenth-century anxieties about hereditary decline, or 'unkinding',[56] the risk of which Ribot, for one, saw as being paradoxically enhanced by improvements in medicine, for 'the assistance of medical science, more certain, and possessed of more resources, makes more and more certain the future of children, by saving the lives of countless weak, deformed, or otherwise ill-constituted creatures that would surely have died in a savage race, or in our own a century or two ago'.[57] We are meant to rejoice in Sloppy's final words, which lead us to believe that the two will marry; after meaningfully pledging to take more care of the doll he has come to collect than if she were 'a gold image', he exits with a touch and a promise – 'and there's both my hands, Miss, and I'll soon come back again' (883).

Dickens stands against evolutionary/social engineering in important particulars but on a wider front has his own agenda of discrimination and relative value; necessarily so, since his are realistic, not utopian, concerns. Inclusiveness does not mean equality. The Wrayburns and the

Harmons are at the top of the pyramid and at the head of the line; the Wilfers, the Boffins, and so on down to Miss Abbey or the boy in Lightwood's office or Sloppy and Jenny themselves, are below and behind. The double metaphor is usefully suggestive, because Dickens is involved in projecting both a synchrony of immediate social structuring and a diachrony of forwards policy. Of the novels we have closely considered, *Our Mutual Friend* is closest to *Oliver Twist* in having this socio-political focus; yet whereas the earlier novel valorizes middle-class types, values and authority in contradistinction from a robust lower order, transgressive, violent, vaguely heroic, the latter ends up with a single and discreet configuration of social organization, a blueprint for the workings of a liberal consensus that we recognize as our own. The respect for Sloppy and Jenny signifies not only humane and politically correct attitudes but an underpinning of the place of manual labour – Sloppy's mechanical and wood-working skills – within the hierarchical scheme and of the core role of domesticity – their union replicates the twin motivation of love and advantage that operates in the other good marriages – as a bonding agent within and between layers. In comparison with *Oliver Twist*, the bourgeois hegemony has become less contestable because more broadly based, less specifically located in terms of class and setting. Neither does there seem any real alternative to Dickens's preferred order of things. The voice of high Society does raise itself again in the very last chapter; Podsnap protests that his 'gorge rises' (889) against the alliance of Eugene, who is one of them, and Lizzie, who comes from the bottom of the scale, and Lady Tippins seconds his opinion. But this group, though it hasn't gone away (and still hasn't), seems in these closing pages more than ever a retrograde and narcissistic laughing-stock, an irrelevance. There is no viable ruling class visible in *Our Mutual Friend*; and what might stand for one it makes nonsense of. All the more forcibly does the book hail its readers for a system – an ideological regime.

John Forster, in his *Life of Dickens*, also connects *Our Mutual Friend* with *Oliver Twist*, but in terms which bring in a more specific aspect of Dickens's sociological standpoint. 'Betty Higden finishes what Oliver Twist began.'[58] Betty is a mouthpiece for Dickens's continuing offensive against the Poor Law Amendment of 1834 and its consequences for the workhouses, over which fresh controversy had erupted in the mid-sixties because of the rising death rate among inmates, official complacency, and a *Lancet* report on the appallingly unsanitary, 'foul and dirty', conditions.[59] 'Kill me sooner than take me there', says Betty on her first appearance; 'God help me and the like of me! – how the worn-out people that do come down to that, get driven from post to pillar, and pillar to post, a purpose to tire them out! Do I never read how they are put off, put off, put off – how they are grudged, grudged, grudged, the shelter, or the doctor, or the drop of physic, or the bit of bread?' (248). It is unclear how far Dickens believed in a public welfare programme; certainly he accepted the necessity of support for the needy, and pragmatically worked to improve a facet of the existing arrangements as a member of the Association for the Improvement of the Infirmaries of the London Workhouses. In current practice, however, he saw only pretentious failure, and an increase of misery in the form of a terror, as Betty puts it, of being 'brick[ed] up in the Unions' (440).[60] In a telling biblical reference, he indicts the inversion of true charity: 'It is a remarkable Christian improvement, to have made a pursuing Fury of the Good Samaritan' (569).

Yet Betty must be read not simply as a conduit for social criticism but also as a positive model of that spirited independence which is always near the top of Dickens's priorities for human survival and success. She is another exemplar of the doctrine of self-help. She labours at her 'Minding-School', sews her meagre savings into her clothes to guard against the indignity of a pauper's funeral, and when she decides to 'run away' to leave Sloppy free to live with the Boffins insists on receiving from the pair, who would happily 'set [her] up like a queen', nothing more than a small 'loan' to start her off as an itinerant knitwear-seller. What she wants is to 'get my own bread by my own labour, . . . to be of a piece like, and helpful to myself right through to my death' (441). The gospel according to Smiles has adherents not only in reformed Wrayburns but in the striving honest poor. Society existed for Dickens, but was not coterminous with the State; government intervention and administration, whether central, as in the 'Circumlocution Office', which gets its latest rap in the Postscript to *Our Mutual Friend*, or local and devolved, as in the workhouse boards, bred only monstrous travesties of a well-wrought existence. Betty Higden brought up Sloppy where the authorities nearly killed him; the Boffins granted her the means of survival where they would have ignored or confined her; the 'fresh airy' (385) charitable hospital in which the orphan Johnny dies – based upon Great Ormond Street Hospital for Sick Children, for which Dickens raised considerable amounts of money[61] – puts their creations to shame. What faith he had Dickens lodged, not in State provision, but in hard-working and well-intentioned individuals, families and groups doing the best for themselves and for others – mutual friends.[62] Nowhere does Dickens more obviously ply a definite political doctrine, recognizably Victorian, sociable but in no way socialist. The broader point, however, is that ideology is never just the circumscription or the produce of Dickens's writing but a field of contest in which he strives and which sets out the contours of our own preoccupations and possible choices.

Self-Subverting Artefacts

It is with that other great prolepsis in Dickens's texts that we must conclude – their reverse operation as self-subverting artefacts. And this brings us back to Eugene and Lizzie.

Some critics have taken a very dim view of the ending of *Our Mutual Friend*. Eve Kosofsky Sedgwick, for example, an influential analyst of culture formation, talks of 'this homophobic reinscription of the bourgeois family' that is especially 'crippling' to Lizzie, who is 'unrelentingly . . . diminished by her increasingly distinct gender assignment'.[63] There is a point here of course: the 'wife' (the term becomes so ubiquitous as to be an identity tag) who assumes 'her nurse's place' at her husband's side and has to be persuaded by her friend Bella to go out for ride (884) certainly lacks the appealing individuality, drive and mystique of the veiled figure rowing a scavenger's boat on the Thames. To accommodate Lizzie to the presiding ideology requires her diminution, her sanitization.

But are things ever straightforward in Dickens? The conclusion of *Our Mutual Friend* is as self-querying in its afterlife as anything in the novels. Core affirmations are undermined and called in question on several levels. The continual foregrounding of 'wife' as a word – Chapter 10 of the fourth book is actually entitled 'The Dolls' Dressmaker Discovers a Word' – exposes marriage as a constituent in a symbolic order, rather than a necessary or natural state; in human terms, it becomes an option that can be accepted or refused. Similarly, the idea of gentlemanliness with which the book ends is so isolated and bracketed off as the unlikely utterance of a minor character, Twemlow, that it inevitably declares its part as a tactic in a design that, as we have seen, at once supports and hides inequality. Most notable in the light of Sedgwick's misgivings, however, is the fact that whatever the falling-off in Lizzie's independence and vitality Eugene is actually a great deal more depleted and put down. Determined to argue that Eugene is privileged over Lizzie, Sedgwick writes that he 'already, by the end of the novel, looks almost "as though he had never been mutilated" ';[64] but this is unfaithful to the text, which actually says that the glow on his face as he talked of defending Lizzie to the last against her detractors 'so irradiated his features that he looked, *for the time*, as though he had never been mutilated' (886: italics mine). The recovery of viripotence is provisional and uncertain – particularly when we recall the previous information that 'it was declared by the medical attendants that he *might not be much disfigured by-and-by*' (883: italics mine).

Far from Eugene's position being, as Sedgwick claims, 'awash with patriarchal authority',[65] the overwhelming impression at last is of his dependency, as he walks 'resting on his wife's arm, and leaning heavily upon a stick' (883). She may be the womanly 'nurse', but he is the patient; and, what is more, his physical incapacity is matched by a psychological one, for all he can do when Lizzie is away – *she* retains some degree of mobility – is 'look . . . forward to [her] coming back' (886), like a child missing its mother. Whereas he had once led Headstone a merry dance all over London, he can now only sit waiting for his spouse to return from an outing. The figuring of middle-class domestic ideology is achieved at the price of Eugene's disfigurement and unmanning. The whole edifice of that ideology is destabilized, even as it is being built, by a quirkiness in the design and distortions in the relation of parts. We can turn Sedgwick around and say that in the misalignment of gender positions, which is all the more apparent in comparison with the normative Harmon household, we detect the distinct outline of a female empowerment. On second thoughts, the two marriages are not so symmetrical as they seemed. The one unsettles the settled resolution of the other. At the very point of closure the novel stores the germ of an unpredictable future. What interpellates the reader for an ideology in one age may in another feed alienation from it.

When all is said, the tensions we have just identified in *Our Mutual Friend* can also be viewed in another light. The subordination of Eugene and Lizzie to the purposes of ideology is, in a sense, the continuing sacrifice of Dickens's imaginative art. It repeats on a sparer canvas the conflict that had emerged in full colour in the elevation of the world of Mr Brownlow and the Maylies at the expense of that of Fagin, Sikes and their associates. Dickens never could escape the struggle of order against energy, or of narrative – that is, the teleology of middle-class values – against the life of fiction. Recalcitrance, the grotesque, the violent, the piquant ingredients of Dickensian fictionality, persist most dramatically, as we have seen, in the untameable Bradley Headstone; but they are present too, in a lower key, in the unreclaimed Eugene Wrayburn, not least in his 'goad[ing] the schoolmaster to madness', where the syntax attaches the madness equally to the hunted and the hunter. There is in this side of Eugene a doubling of the darker authorial temperament itself,[66] just as in his steady contemplation of the solitary Lizzie in her hovel he enacts a sensuous aestheticism that is both creative and predatory. The reactions of generations of readers (including Sedgwick) have indicated, however, that, though ideology overrules imagination in *Oliver Twist* or *Our Mutual Friend*, it does not subjugate or cancel its appeal. Dickens's last finished novel technically cleans up 'decadence' yet really remains its host. This is a characteristic irresolution – another way in which his texts abidingly question themselves.

Notes

1. All references are to Charles Dickens, *Our Mutual Friend*, ed. Stephen Gill (Harmondsworth: Penguin Books, 1985). The phrase 'birds [or bird] of prey' appears three times in quick succession (pp. 45, 64, 65).
2. Stone supplied forty plates for the first volume-form edition, 1865.
3. *The Origin of Species* had appeared in 1859; for its immediate influence on Dickens, see Goldie Morgentaler, 'Meditating on the Low: A Darwinian Reading of *Great Expectations*', *Studies in English Literature 1500–1900*, 38 (1998), 707–21. Paul Davis asserts that in *Our Mutual Friend* Dickens is challenging Darwin by 'satirically reducing life to elemental terms and denying mutuality' (*The Penguin Dickens Companion* (Harmondsworth: Penguin Books, 1999), p. 376); but the truth is that he accepts the Darwinian theory of evolutionary struggle in this part of the novel while later affirming, against this bleak background, the saving grace of a co-operative spirit by which it can be alleviated. For Malthus and Dickens, see Chapter 3, pp. 65–7 above. The Tennyson quotation is from *In Memoriam*, lyric 56.
4. Professor Sir Richard Owens became head of the Natural History Section of the British Museum in 1856, having previously held the position of Hunterian Professor of comparative anatomy and physiology at the Royal College of Surgeons. His work had been lauded in an article, 'Owens's Museum', in Dickens's periodical *All the Year Round*, 27 September 1862.
5. In contemporary suburban London domestic refuse was collected by contractors and dumped in private dust-yards, where the heaps were sorted into their various constituents and sold. R.H. Horne, in a contribution to Dickens's *Household Words*, 'Dust; or Ugliness Redeemed' (13 July 1850), lists an amazing array of materials recovered by the gangs of sifters, ranging from coal and crockery, the latter to be used in road construction, through bones for soap-making and rags for paper, to ashes, which were valuable as 'brieze' to brick makers. A detailed account of the business, including graphic descriptions of yards with as many as 127 men and women simultaneously at work, appears in Henry Mayhew, *London Labour and the London Poor* (1861–62), repr. in 4 vols, with introduction by John D. Rosenberg (New York: Dover Publications, 1968), II, 166–79 (p. 169). The value of the mounds was legendary: Horne and Mayhew give examples of them fetching from £10 000 to £40 000. Dickens's indebtedness to Mayhew's great study is substantial. Most of the parallels are discussed in Harland S. Nelson's 'Dickens's *Our Mutual Friend* and Henry Mayhew's *London Labour and the London Poor*', *Nineteenth-Century Fiction*, 20 (1965–66), 207–22.

A lively debate among critics as to whether the heaps contained human excrement and thus give rise to Freudian symbolic overtones equating money and faeces – 'filthy lucre' – found summation in Harvey Peter Sucksmith, 'The Dust-heaps in *Our Mutual Friend*', *Essays in Criticism*, 23 (1973), 206–12.

6. See Mayhew, I, 261–72; II, 142–6.

7. Eliot drew from the novel not only the first title of his poem, 'He Do the Police in Different Voices', but also character-types and situations, not least those of urban high society and its world of brash surfaces, and aspects of his symbolic organization, especially the motifs of death and resurrection, where the polar experiences of water, drowning and baptism, feature prominently in both texts. The ability to 'do the Police in different voices' belongs to Sloppy, the foundling adopted by Betty Higden (*Our Mutual Friend*, p. 246). Dickens's involvement in snatching creative affirmation from the jaws of a degraded modernity is the theme of Nancy Aycock Metz's 'The Artistic Reclamation of Waste in *Our Mutual Friend*', *Nineteenth-Century Fiction*, 34 (1979–80), 59–72: 'the artistic reclamation of waste as practiced . . . in *Our Mutual Friend* is convincing in its example of how chaos may be made livable' (p. 72).

8. David Gascoyne, 'The Very Image', lines 26–30, in *Poetry of the Thirties*, ed. Robin Skelton (Harmondsworth: Penguin Books, 1964), p. 235. Nicholas Royle ('Our Mutual Friend', in *Dickens Refigured*, ed. John Schad (Manchester: Manchester University Press, 1996), p. 48) puts an interesting spin on this aspect of Dickens, remarking that 'the Veneerings are presented to us in a discourse that is neither realism nor caricature but something dislocating the two, that is to say what we might call veneerrealist discourse or social veneerrealism'. Royle appeals here to the insight in J. Hillis Miller's 'fine evocation of Veneering, "gradually manifest[ing] himself like an ectoplasmic vision at a séance"' (Miller, *The Form of Victorian Fiction* (Notre Dame: University of Notre Dame Press, 1968), p. 41). In this work Miller addresses the use of the mirror above the Veneerings' dinner-table as a symbolic way of showing how art reflects and transforms social reality. We may additionally note that T.S. Eliot, in the 'Game of Chess' section of *The Waste Land* (lines 77–85) (London: Faber and Faber, 1962), employs a similar device, 'the glass / Held up by standards' and the 'Reflecting . . . table', to this effect but also to point the self-regard, the inward-looking and narcissistic cast, of fashionable society. Both meanings are present in Dickens.

9. Metz, 'The Artistic Reclamation of Waste', p. 60.

10. Metz apart, particular attention is given to this theme by Albert D. Hutter, 'Dismemberment and Articulation in *Our Mutual Friend*', *Dickens Studies Annual*, 11 (1983), 135–75. Authorship as an 'imperative for survival' among various characters is explored by Robert Kiely, 'Plotting and Scheming: The Design of Design in *Our Mutual Friend*', *Dickens Studies Annual*, 12 (1983), 267–83.

11. It is common knowledge that Wegg belongs to the class of street ballad-sellers known as 'pinners-up', 'men and women . . . who sell songs which they have "pinned" to a sort of screen or large board, or have attached them in any convenient way, to a blank wall' (Mayhew, I, 272; cf. *Our Mutual Friend*, p. 87: 'the unfolded clothes-horse displayed a choice collection of halfpenny ballads and became a screen'). But Wegg also com-

poses songs of his own, and alters existing ones. Dickens thus conflates two distinct types, the sellers and what Mayhew terms 'the street poets and authors', to which *London Labour and the London Poor* devotes a separate account (I, 278–80).

12. We may recall that disappointment at the profit accruing from *A Christmas Carol* made Dickens ill: 'Such a night as I have passed! I really believed that I should never get up again, until I had passed through all the horrors of a fever' (quoted in Peter Ackroyd, *Dickens* (London: Minerva, 1991), p. 439).

13. This is Hutter's position, pp. 152–7: thus, 'Venus is in effect a comic version of Dickens the novelist' (p. 157). Cf. Kiely, p. 282: 'Venus, the articulator of bones, seems an author after Dickens [*sic*] own heart.' See also Metz, pp. 63–5.

14. A parallel may be drawn between Jenny's 'fancies' and the imaginings of the eponymous subject of Blake's song of Innocence, 'The Chimney Sweeper'. The boy's heavenly vision of sweepers who 'wash in a river, and shine in the Sun . . . / Then naked & white, all their bags left behind, / . . . rise upon clouds and sport in the wind' (lines 16–18) brings provisional relief from suffering but leaves it fundamentally untouched and through contrast intensifies our sense of its reality (William Blake, *Poetry and Prose*, ed. Geoffrey Keynes (London: Nonesuch Press, 1961)). Garrett Stewart offers an excellent assessment of the force and the limitations of Jenny's 'transcendental visions' in 'The "Golden Bower" of *Our Mutual Friend*', *English Literary History*, 40 (1973), 105–30. Stewart concludes that the recurring tragedy of Jenny's life is 'that fancy is an unreliable refuge from drudgery, that what is beautiful in her life must inevitably evaporate, the lovely lapsing away into what is mean and demeaning', but that she must nonetheless keep open 'the apertures to wonder' (pp. 119, 121). At one point, taking a cue from Hillis Miller's *Charles Dickens: The World of His Novels* (Cambridge, MA: Harvard University Press, 1958), he talks of the history of nineteenth-century fiction being in part that of 'its internalization for individual characters of that Romantic experience previously restricted to the extraordinary imagination of the gifted poet' (p. 116). My example from Blake shows that visionary experience was by no means thus restricted in the Romantic period, and was extended, among many other characters, to a poor sweep.

15. See Richard D. Altick, 'Education, Print, and Paper in *Our Mutual Friend*', in *Nineteenth-Century Literary Perspectives*, ed. Clyde de L. Ryals (Durham, NC: Duke University Press, 1974), pp. 237–54, to which I am indebted for knowledge of the contemporary background. The fullest previous discussion of the subject is in Philip Collins, *Dickens and Education* (1963; repr. with alterations, London: Macmillan, 1964), pp. 159–71.

16. George Gissing, *Charles Dickens: A Critical Study* (London: Gresham Publishing Company, 1902), p. 257.

17. The troubled Headstone may also be seen as a victim of the evils of 'brain forcing', which were widely discussed within the context of an expanding state education system. James Crichton-Browne, for instance, a specialist in the nervous diseases of children, considered them as most likely to arise 'under a system of "cram" or spurt teaching, . . . or of learning by rote or by rule, without any real understanding of what is being learned', and as

particularly apt to occur 'after the imposition of heavy tasks upon the memory'. The consequences of injudicious forcing, Crichton-Browne goes on to say, are dullness, 'loss of mental balance', 'eccentric[ity] in manner and conduct', even the 'outburst of madness'. Headstone would obviously qualify on all counts. A further intriguing element in Crichton-Browne's article is that he takes as a key exemplification of the crippling effects of cramming the account of Dr Blimber's establishment in *Dombey and Son*! Dickens clearly enjoyed credit with the professionals for his observations of medical phenomena. Crichton-Browne acclaims his 'quick insight and sympathy with the right'. See James Crichton-Browne, 'Education and the Nervous System', in *The Book of Health*, ed. M.A. Morris (London: Cassell, 1883), pp. 350–52, 379–80.

18. Collins, p. 159. Altick, p. 240, quotes a highly relevant professional paper of the time, *The School and the Teacher*:

> It is no strange thing that men who in education, tastes and habits have all the qualifications of 'gentlemen' should regard themselves as worthy of something very much higher than the treatment of a servant and the wages of a mechanic. What in short the teacher desires is that his 'calling' shall rank as a 'profession'; that the name of 'schoolmaster' shall ring as grandly on the ear as that of 'clergyman' or 'solicitor'; that he shall feel no more that awful chill and 'stony British stare' which follows the explanation that 'that interesting young man is only the schoolmaster'.

In the light of such a passage we can appreciate all the more precisely the cutting effect of Wrayburn's repeated contemptuous use of 'Schoolmaster', 'a most respectable title' (341).

19. Collins, p. 159.
20. Milton, *Paradise Lost*, IV. 73–5, in *The Poems of John Milton*, ed. John Carey and Alastair Fowler (London: Longmans, 1968).
21. *Paradise Lost*, IV. 505ff.
22. *Pilgrim's Progress*, ed. Roger Sharrock (Harmondsworth: Penguin Books, 1984), p. 41.
23. *Paradise Lost*, IV. 76–7.
24. See, for example, Cowper's statement:

> Charge not, with light sufficient, and left free,
> Your wilful suicide on God's decree.
> > ('Truth', lines 19–20, in *The Poems of William Cowper*,
> > ed. John D. Baird and Charles Ryskamp, 3 vols
> > (Oxford: Clarendon Press, 1980–95))

25. John Lucas, *Charles Dickens: The Major Novels* (Harmondsworth: Penguin Books, 1992), p. 63.
26. Quoted in *The Concise Oxford Dictionary of Literary Terms*, ed. Chris Baldick (Oxford: Oxford University Press, 1990; paperback edn 1991), p. 51.
27. References are to Charles Dickens, *Hard Times*, ed. Kate Flint (Harmondsworth: Penguin Books, 1995).

28. See Andrew Elfenbein, *Byron and the Victorians* (Cambridge: Cambridge University Press, 1995), pp. 213–18.

29. Roger Fowler, 'Polyphony and Problematic in *Hard Times*', in *The Changing World of Charles Dickens*, ed. Robert Gittings (London: Vision Press, 1983), pp. 100–101.

30. *Paradise Lost*, IX. 444–72.

31. *Paradise Lost*, IX. 459.

32. This is the phrase recurrently used by Catherine Waters in *Dickens and the Politics of the Family* (Cambridge: Cambridge University Press, 1997), which contains an insightful chapter on *Our Mutual Friend*.

33. See Waters, p. 199.

34. G.K. Chesterton, *Criticisms and Appreciations of the Works of Charles Dickens* (London: Dent, 1933), p. 216.

35.   For contemplation he and valour formed,
         For softness she and sweet attractive grace,
         He for God only, she for God in him:
         His fair large front and eye sublime declared
         Absolute rule . . .
                   (*Paradise Lost*, IV. 297–301)

36. See Frank Mort, *Dangerous Sexualities: Medic-moral Politics in England since 1830* (London: Routledge & Kegan Paul, 1987); repr. in *Sexuality*, ed. Robert A. Nye (Oxford: Oxford University Press, 1999), pp. 96–98 (p. 97):

> Incest was the most common form of moral anxiety, precisely because it dramatically disrupted middle-class norms of family propriety. But these representations contained rather more than the perception that sexual immorality resulted from an impoverished and overcrowded environment. Sexual immorality was defined through the significations of dirt, disease, squalor, corruption and the political threat of an urban working class populace.

37. See Miriam Bailin, *The Sickroom in Victorian Fiction: The Art of Being Ill* (Cambridge: Cambridge University Press, 1994), pp. 103–104.

38. The phrase is from 'Cheap Reading', *Eliza Cook's Journal*, 1 (1849), 2; see Chapters 1 and 3, pp. 6–7 and 77 above. The most vigorous brief account of 'love of families' as a keystone in the edifice of the bourgeois hegemony is given in E.J. Hobsbawm, *The Age of Capital 1848–1875* (1975; London: Abacus, 1995), pp. 278–83.

39. Samuel Smiles, *Self-Help, With Illustrations of Conduct and Perseverance* (1859; London: John Murray, 1908), p. 470.

40. John Ruskin, 'Of Queen's Gardens', *Sesame and Lilies* (1865; London: Everett & Co., n.d.), p. 97.

41. *Self-Help*, p. 477.

42. 'Women in Domestic Life', *Magazine of Domestic Economy*, 1 (1836), 66. Smiles outlines the duties of women directly in Chapter 2 of *Character* (1871; London: John Murray, 1910), entitled 'Home Power', where, for example, command of the useful art of preparing food is contrasted with the pointless aspiration of having the vote.

43. It is interesting to note that when Lizzie and Bella meet the former is working in a factory, which was, in Victorian opinion, the major site, and cause, of the corruption of females. Jeffrey Weeks, in *Sex, Politics and Society: The Regulation of Sexuality since 1800* (London: Longman, 1989), pp. 57–8, discusses the concern of government and bourgeois intellectuals with the mores, or lack of them, among working women:

> Because of the developing ideology of woman's role in the family and her very special responsibility for society's well being, it was women working outside the home who received the most attention from the parliamentary commissioners . . . Moreover, most attention was paid not to the conditions of work as such but to the moral and spiritual degradation said to accompany female employment. Ashley [later Lord Shaftesbury] wrote, 'In the male the moral effects of the system are very sad, but in the female they are infinitely worse . . . It is bad enough if you corrupt the man, but if you corrupt the woman, you poison the waters of life at the very fountain.'

When Eugene locates the runaway Lizzie he might reasonably have expected her to be an easy target for his powers of persuasion.
44. Herbert Spencer, *Education, Intellectual, Moral and Physical* (London: Williams and Norgate, 1861), pp. 186–8.
45. Francis Galton, *Inquiries into Human Faculty and Its Development* (London: Macmillan, 1883), pp. 2, 61–5; repr. in *Embodied Selves*, ed. J.B. Taylor and S. Shuttleworth (Oxford: Clarendon Press, 1998), pp. 330–32.
46. See Hawes, *Who's Who*, p. 198; citing Edgar Johnson, *Charles Dickens: His Tragedy and Triumph* (London: Gollancz, 1953), pp. 1010–12.
47. Quoted by Taylor and Shuttleworth, p. 287.
48. Théodule A. Ribot, *Heredity: A Psychological Study of its Phenomena, Laws, Causes and Consequences* (1873; 2nd edn, London: Henry S. King, 1875), pp. 10, 303.
49. Henry Maudsley, *Body and Mind: An Inquiry into their Connections and Mutual Influence, Specially in Reference to Mental Disorders* (London: Macmillan, 1870); repr. in Taylor and Shuttleworth, pp. 326–9 (p. 327).
50. Taylor and Shuttleworth, pp. 327–8.
51. Taylor and Shuttleworth, p. 327.
52. 'Idiots', *Household Words* (4 June 1853), 315.
53. 'Idiots Again', *Household Words*, 9 (15 April 1854), 197–200; repr. in Taylor and Shuttleworth, pp. 322–5 (p. 324).
54. Gill, *Our Mutual Friend*, p. 902, glosses 'Natural' as 'illegitimate' or possibly 'idiot'. Gill's preference cannot be right, for Betty has just explained he was a 'love-child (247), and would hardly raise the matter again as a debatable one.
55. 'Idiots Again', pp. 323–4.
56. Maudsley, *Body and Mind*, in Taylor and Shuttleworth, p. 329.
57. Ribot, *Heredity*, p. 303.
58. John Forster, *The Life of Charles Dickens* (1872–74; London: Chapman & Hall, n.d.), Book IX, Ch. 5, p. 812.
59. See Gill, *Our Mutual Friend*, n. 3, pp. 910–11. In April 1865 *The Lancet* announced its intention to set up a fact-finding enquiry into the state of

the workhouse hospitals, prompted by the decision of an 1864 Select Committee to recommend no alterations to the system and by a sense of a change in social mood whereby there was increasing 'kindly feeling between the higher and middle classes and the poor'. Dickens's own views were very much in tune with The Lancet Sanitary Commission's devastating report, and Gill quotes from a letter of February 1866 in which he thinks it no wonder that 'the poor should creep into corners and die rather than fester and rot in those infamous places'.

60. As Dickens insists in the Postscript to *Our Mutual Friend*, Betty Higden was no piece of fantasy; there really were 'deserving Poor who prefer death by slow starvation and bitter weather, to the mercies of some Relieving Officers and some Union Houses' (894). Mayhew (II, 145) describes his interview with a sixty-year-old widow, a pure-finder, who like Betty prefers death out-of-doors to the workhouse:

> I could never bear the thought of going into the 'great house' [workhouse]; I'm so used to the air, that I'd sooner die in the street, as many I know have done. I've known several of our people, who have sat down in the street with their basket alongside them, and died. . . . I'd sooner die like them than be deprived of my liberty, and be prevented from going about where I liked. No, I'll never go into the workhouse.

61. See Ackroyd, *Dickens*, pp. 846, 849.
62. To my knowledge, the only critic to take seriously the idea of such a commitment to mutuality in Dickens is John P. Farrell, 'The Partners' Tale: Dickens and *Our Mutual Friend*', *English Literary History*, 66 (1999), 759–93.
63. Eve Kosofsky Sedgwick, 'Homophobia, Misogyny, and Capital', repr. in *Charles Dickens*, ed. S. Connor (Oxford: Blackwell, 1985), pp. 193–4.
64. Sedgwick, p. 193.
65. Sedgwick, p. 193.
66. Bailin, *Sickroom in Victorian Fiction*, mounts a strong argument along these lines, seeing Headstone's and Wrayburn's 'macabre "chase"' as the allegorized 'feverish inversion' of narrative project in 'a sick man's compulsory "task"' (pp. 96–8).

Bibliography

Charles Dickens: Texts

Main references throughout are to the Penguin Classics editions of Dickens's fiction specified below.

A Christmas Carol. 1843. Volume 1 of *Charles Dickens: The Christmas Books*, ed. Michael Slater, 2 vols, Harmondsworth: Penguin Books, 1971, repr. 1985.
David Copperfield. 1849–50. Ed. Trevor Blount, Harmondsworth: Penguin Books, 1985.
—— ed. Nina Burgis, Oxford: Clarendon Press, 1981.
Great Expectations. 1860–61. Ed. Charlotte Mitchell, Harmondsworth: Penguin Books, 1996.
Hard Times. 1854. Ed. Kate Flint, Harmondsworth: Penguin Books, 1995.
The Haunted Man. 1848. Volume 2 of *Charles Dickens: The Christmas Books*, ed. Slater (see above).
Oliver Twist. 1837–9. Ed. Peter Fairclough, Harmondsworth: Penguin Books, 1985.
—— ed. Fred Kaplan, New York: W.W. Norton & Co., 1993.
Preface to the first Cheap Edition of *Oliver Twist*. 1850. *Charles Dickens: Oliver Twist*, ed. Steven Connor, London: J.M. Dent, 1994, pp. xli–xliv.
Our Mutual Friend. 1864–5. Ed. Stephen Gill, Harmondsworth: Penguin Books, 1985.
The Dent Uniform Edition of Dickens's Journalism, ed. Michael Slater, 4 vols, London: J.M. Dent, 1994–2000.
The Pilgrim Edition of the Letters of Charles Dickens, ed. Madeline House, Graham Storey, Kathleen Tillotson, et al., 11 vols to date, Oxford: Clarendon Press, 1965–.

Criticism, Biography, and Literary-Historical Studies

On Dickens

Ackroyd, Peter. *Dickens*, London: Minerva, 1991.

Altick, Robert D. 'Education, Print, and Paper in *Our Mutual Friend*', in Clyde de L. Ryals (ed.), *Nineteenth-Century Literary Perspectives*, Durham, NC: Duke University Press, 1974, pp. 237–54.

Bayley, John. '*Oliver Twist*: "Things As They Really Are"', in John Gross and Gabriel Pearson (eds), *Dickens and the Twentieth Century*, London: Routledge, 1962, pp. 49–64.

Bowen, John. 'The Transformation of Scrooge', *English Review*, 3.1 (September 1992), 38–40.

Brooks, Peter. 'Repetition, Repression, and Return: The Plotting of *Great Expectations*', *Reading for the Plot: Design and Intention in Narrative*, Oxford: Clarendon Press, 1994, pp. 115–42.

Buckwald, Craig. 'Stalking the Figurative Oyster: The Excursive Ideal in *A Christmas Carol*', *Studies in Short Fiction*, 27 (1990), 1–14.

Chesterton, G.K. *Criticisms and Appreciations of the Works of Charles Dickens*, London: Dent, 1933.

Cohen, William A. 'Manual Conduct in *Great Expectations*', *English Literary History*, 60 (1993), 217–59.

Collins, Philip. (ed.) *Charles Dickens: The Critical Heritage*, London: Routledge & Kegan Paul, 1971.

—— *Dickens and Crime*, 1962; 3rd edn, Basingstoke: Macmillan, 1994.

—— *Dickens and Education*, London: Macmillan, 1964.

Connor, Steven. *Charles Dickens*, Oxford: Blackwell, 1985.

—— (ed.) *Charles Dickens*, Longman Critical Readers, London: Longman, 1996.

—— '"They're All in One Story": Public and Private Narratives in *Oliver Twist*', *Dickensian*, 85 (1989), 3–16.

'David Copperfield and Pendennis', Unsigned review, *Prospective Review* (July 1851).

Davis, Paul. *The Penguin Dickens Companion*, Harmondsworth: Penguin Books, 1999.

Dellamora, Robert. 'Pure Oliver: or, Representation Without Agency', in Schad (ed.), *Dickens Refigured* (see below), pp. 55–79.

Eisenstein, Sergei. 'Dickens, Griffith, and the Film Today', *Film Form*, New York: Harcourt, 1949, pp. 195–255.

Engel, Monroe. *The Maturity of Dickens*, Cambridge, MA: Harvard University Press, 1967.

Farrell, John P. 'The Partners' Tale: Dickens and *Our Mutual Friend*', *English Literary History*, 66 (1999), 759–93.

Flint, Kate. *Dickens*, Brighton: Harvester Press, 1986.

Forster, John. *The Life of Charles Dickens*, 1872–4; Fireside Edition, London: Chapman and Hall, n.d.

Fowler, Roger. 'Polyphony and Problematic in *Hard Times*', in Robert Gittings (ed.), *The Changing World of Charles Dickens*, London: Vision Press, 1983, pp. 91–108.

Frank, Lawrence. *Charles Dickens and the Romantic Self*, Lincoln, NE: University of Nebraska Press, 1984.

Friedman, Stanley. 'Dickens' Mid-Victorian Theodicy: *David Copperfield*', *Dickens Studies Annual*, 7 (1977), 128–50.

Frost, Lucy. 'Taming to Improve: Dickens and the Women in *Great Expectations*', *Meridian* 1 (1982), 11–20.

Garnett, Robert R. 'Why Not Sophy? Desire and Agnes in *David Copperfield*', *Dickens Quarterly*, 14 (1997), 212–31.

Gilbert, Elliot L. 'The Ceremony of Innocence: Charles Dickens' *A Christmas Carol*', *PMLA*, 90 (1975), 22–31.

Gilmour, Robin. (ed.) *Charles Dickens: Great Expectations*, London: Dent, 1994.

Gissing, George. *Charles Dickens: A Critical Study*, London: Gresham Publishing Co., 1902.

Gold, Joseph. *Charles Dickens: Radical Moralist*, Toronto: Copp Clark, 1972.

Hawes, Donald. *Who's Who in Dickens*, London: Routledge, 1993.

Holderness, Graham. 'Imagination in *A Christmas Carol*', *Etudes Anglaises*, 32 (1979), 28–45.

Hughes, Felicity. 'Narrative Complexity in *David Copperfield*', *English Literary History*, 41 (1974), 89–105.

Hutter, Albert D. 'Dismemberment and Articulation in *Our Mutual Friend*', *Dickens Studies Annual*, 11 (1983), 135–75.

Ingham, Patricia. *Dickens, Women and Language*, Hemel Hempstead: Harvester Wheatsheaf, 1992.

Jaffe, Audrey. 'Spectacular Sympathy: Visuality and Ideology in Dickens's *A Christmas Carol*', *PMLA*, 109 (1994), 254–65.

—— *Vanishing Points: Dickens, Narrative, and the Subject of Omniscience*, Berkeley, CA: University of California Press, 1991.

Johnson, Edgar. *Charles Dickens: His Tragedy and Triumph*, London: Gollancz, 1953.

Jordan, John O. (ed.) *The Cambridge Companion to Charles Dickens*, Cambridge: Cambridge University Press, 2001.

—— 'The Medium of *Great Expectations*', *Dickens Studies Annual*, 11 (1983), 73–88.

Kiely, Robert. 'Plotting and Scheming: The Design of Design in *Our Mutual Friend*', *Dickens Studies Annual*, 12 (1983), 267–83.

Lane, Lauriat. 'The Devil in *Oliver Twist*', *Dickensian*, 52 (1956), 132–6.

Leavis, F.R. and Leavis, Q.D. *Dickens the Novelist*, 1970;
    Harmondsworth: Penguin Books, 1994.
Lucas, John. *Charles Dickens: The Major Novels*, Harmondsworth:
    Penguin Books, 1992.
—— *The Melancholy Man: A Study of Dickens's Novels*, London:
    Methuen, 1970.
Marcus, Steven. 'Who Is Fagin?', *Dickens: From Pickwick to Dombey*,
    London: Chatto & Windus, 1965, pp. 358–78.
Meisel, Martin. 'The Ending of *Great Expectations*', *Essays in
    Criticism*, 15 (1965), 326–31.
Mengham, Rod. *Charles Dickens*, Tavistock: Northcote House, 2001.
Metz, Nancy Aycock. 'The Artistic Reclamation of Waste in *Our Mutual
    Friend*', *Nineteenth-Century Fiction*, 34 (1979–80), 59–72.
Miller, J. Hillis. *Charles Dickens: The World of His Novels*, Cambridge,
    MA: Harvard University Press, 1958.
Morgentaler, Goldie. 'Meditating on the Low: A Darwinian Reading of
    Great Expectations', *Studies in English Literature, 1500–1900*, 38
    (1998), 707–21.
Morris, William E. 'The Conversion of Scrooge: A Defense of That
    Good Man's Motivation', *Studies in Short Fiction*, 3 (1965), 46–55.
Moynahan, Julian. 'The Hero's Guilt: The Case of *Great Expectations*',
    Essays in Criticism, 10 (1960), 60–79.
Needham, Gwendolyn. 'The Undisciplined Heart of David Copperfield',
    Nineteenth-Century Fiction, 9 (1954), 81–107.
Nelson, Harland S. 'Dickens's *Our Mutual Friend* and Henry Mayhew's
    London Labour and the London Poor', *Nineteenth-Century Fiction*,
    20 (1965–66), 207–22.
Newey, Vincent. 'Dickensian Decadents', in Michael St John (ed.),
    Romancing Decay: Ideas of Decadence in European Culture,
    Aldershot: Ashgate, 1999, pp. 64–87.
Newman, S.J. *Dickens at Play*, Basingstoke: Macmillan, 1981.
Nussbaum, Martha C. 'Steerforth's Arm: Love and the Moral Point of
    View', *Love's Knowledge: Essays on Philosophy and Literature*, New
    York: Oxford University Press, 1990, pp. 335–64.
Orwell, George. 'Charles Dickens' (1940), *'Decline of the English
    Murder' and Other Essays*, Harmondsworth: Penguin Books, 1965,
    pp. 80–141.
Palmer, William J. *Dickens and New Historicism*, Basingstoke:
    Macmillan, 1997.
Pykett, Lyn. *Charles Dickens*, Basingstoke: Palgrave, 2002.
Rawlins, Jack. 'Great Expiations: Dickens and the Betrayal of the
    Child', *Studies in English Literature, 1500–1900*, 23 (1983), 667–83.

Royle, Nicholas. 'Our Mutual Friend', in Schad (ed.), *Dickens Refigured*, pp. 39–54.

Sadrin, Anny. *Parentage and Inheritance in the Novels of Charles Dickens*, Cambridge: Cambridge University Press, 1994.

Schad, John. (ed.) *Dickens Refigured: Bodies, Desires and Other Histories*, Manchester: Manchester University Press, 1996.

Schlicke, Paul. *The Oxford Reader's Companion to Dickens*, Oxford: Oxford University Press, 1999.

Sedgwick, Eve Kosofsky. 'Homophobia, Misogyny, and Capital: The Example of *Our Mutual Friend*', *Between Men: English Literature and Male Homosocial Bonding*, New York: Columbia University Press, 1985, pp. 163–79.

Sell, Roger D. (ed.) *Great Expectations: Contemporary Critical Essays*, New Casebooks, Basingstoke: Macmillan, 1994.

Shires, Linda M. 'Literary Careers, Death, and the Body Politics of *David Copperfield*', in Schad (ed.), *Dickens Refigured*, pp. 117–35.

Slater, Michael. *Dickens and Women*, London: Dent, 1983.

Smith, Grahame. *Charles Dickens: A Literary Life*, Basingstoke: Macmillan, 1996.

Spilka, Mark. '*David Copperfield* as Psychological Fiction', *Critical Quarterly*, 1 (1959), 292–301.

Stewart, Garrett. 'The "Golden Bower" of *Our Mutual Friend*', *English Literary History*, 40 (1973), 105–30.

Stone, Harry. 'Dickens and the Jews', *Victorian Studies*, 2 (1959), 223–53.

Sucksmith, Harvey Peter. 'The Dust-heaps in *Our Mutual Friend*', *Essays in Criticism*, 23 (1973), 206–12.

Sutherland, John. 'Why Is Fagin Hanged and Why Isn't Pip Prosecuted?', *Can Jane Eyre Be Happy?: More Puzzles in Classic Fiction*, Oxford: Oxford University Press, 1997, pp. 52–63.

Tambling, Jeremy. *Dickens, Violence and the Modern State*, Basingstoke: Macmillan, 1995.

—— 'Prison-bound: Dickens and Foucault', *Essays in Criticism*, 36 (1986), 11–31.

Tracy, Robert. '"The Old Story" and Inside Stories: Modish Fictions and Fictional Modes in *Oliver Twist*', *Dickens Studies Annual*, 17 (1988), 1–33.

Trotter, David. Introduction to *Great Expectations*, ed. Charlotte Mitchell, pp. vii–xx.

Walder, Dennis. *Dickens and Religion*, London: George Allen & Unwin, 1981.

Waters, Catherine. *Dickens and the Politics of the Family*, Cambridge: Cambridge University Press, 1997.

Westburg, Barry. *The Confessional Fictions of Charles Dickens*, Dekalb: Northern Illinois University Press, 1977.

General

Bailin, Miriam. *The Sickroom in Victorian Fiction: The Art of Being Ill*, Cambridge: Cambridge University Press, 1994 (pp. 79–108, 'Charles Dickens: "Impossible Existences" ').

Beer, Gillian. *Darwin's Plots: Evolutionary Narrative in Darwin, George Eliot and Nineteenth-Century Fiction*, London: Routledge, 1983.

Blake, Andrew. *Reading Victorian Fiction: The Cultural Context and Ideological Content of the Nineteenth-Century Novel*, Basingstoke: Macmillan, 1989.

Davis, Philip. *Memory and Writing from Wordsworth to Lawrence*, Liverpool: Liverpool University Press, 1983 (pp. 196–225 on Dickens).

—— 'Why Do We Remember Forwards and Not Backwards?', in Newey and Shaw (eds), *Mortal Pages, Literary Lives*, pp. 81–102.

Elfenbein, Andrew. *Byron and the Victorians*, Cambridge: Cambridge University Press, 1995.

Gilmour, Robin. *The Idea of the Gentleman in the Victorian Novel*, London: Allen & Unwin, 1981 (pp. 105–48 on *Great Expectations*).

Hayward, Jennifer. *Consuming Pleasures: Active Audiences and Serial Fictions from Dickens to Soap Operas*, Lexington, KY: University Press of Kentucky, 1997 (pp. 41–83 on *Our Mutual Friend*).

Kucich, John. *Repression in Victorian Fiction*, Berkeley, CA: University of California Press, 1987 (pp. 201–83 on Dickens).

Martin, Philip W. *Mad Women in Romantic Writing*, Brighton: Harvester Press, 1987 (pp. 113–22 on *Great Expectations*).

McCarthy, Justin. 'Novels with a Purpose', *Westminster Review*, 82 (July 1864).

McKeon, Michael. *The Origins of the English Novel 1600–1740*, Baltimore, MD: Johns Hopkins University Press, 1987.

Miller, D.A. *The Novel and the Police*, Berkeley, CA: University of California Press, 1988 (pp. 4–10 on *Oliver Twist*, pp. 192–220 on *David Copperfield*).

Miller, J. Hillis. *The Form of Victorian Fiction*, Notre Dame, IN: University of Notre Dame Press, 1968.

Newey, Vincent. *Cowper's Poetry: A Critical Study and Reassessment*, Liverpool: Liverpool University Press, 1982.

—— 'Goldsmith's "Pensive Plain": Re-viewing *The Deserted Village*', in Thomas Woodman (ed.), *Early Romantics: Perspectives in British*

Poetry from Pope to Wordsworth, Basingstoke: Macmillan, 1998, pp. 93–116.

—— 'Mark Rutherford's Salvation and the Case of Catharine Furze', in Newey and Shaw (eds), *Mortal Pages, Literary Lives*, pp. 172–203.

—— 'Wordsworth, Bunyan, and the Puritan Mind', *English Literary History*, 41 (1974), 212–34.

Newey, Vincent and Shaw, Philip. (eds) *Mortal Pages, Literary Lives: Studies in Nineteenth-Century Autobiography*, Aldershot: Scolar Press, 1996.

Qualls, Barry. *The Secular Pilgrims of Victorian Fiction*, Cambridge: Cambridge University Press, 1982 (pp. 85–138, 'Transmutations of Dickens' Emblematic Art').

Sales, Roger. *English Literature in History 1780–1830: Pastoral and Politics*, London: Hutchinson, 1983.

Tanner, Tony. Introduction to *Pride and Prejudice* by Jane Austen, Harmondsworth: Penguin Books, 1985, pp. 7–46.

Thackeray, William. 'A Box of Novels', *Fraser's Magazine*, 29 (February 1844), 143–69.

Background, Context, Theory

Acton, William. *The Function and Disorders of the Reproductive Organs in Childhood, Youth, Adult Age, and Advanced Life Considered in their Physiological, Social and Moral Relations*, 1847; 4th edn, London: John Churchill, 1865.

Althusser, Louis. 'Ideology and Ideological State Apparatuses', *Lenin and Philosophy, and Other Essays*, trans. B. Brewster, London: New Left Books, 1971, pp. 127–86.

Ambrose, Isaac. *Prima, Media & Ultima*, vol. 2, London, 1654.

Arnold, Matthew. *Culture and Anarchy*, 1869; ed. J. Dover Wilson, Cambridge: Cambridge University Press, 1969.

Austen, Jane. *Sense and Sensibility*, 1811; ed. Ros Ballaster, Harmondsworth: Penguin Books, 1995.

Babcock, Barbara. *The Reversible World: Symbolic Inversion in Art and History*, Ithaca, NY: Cornell University Presss, 1978.

Baldick, Chris. *The Concise Oxford Dictionary of Literary Terms*, Oxford: Oxford University Press, 1991.

Baxter, Richard. *The Saints Everlasting Rest*, 1650; 4th edn, London, 1653.

Bennett, Tony. *Formalism and Marxism*, London: Methuen, 1979.

Blake, William. *Poetry and Prose*, ed. Geoffrey Keynes, London: Nonesuch Press, 1961.

Briggs, Asa. *Victorian People: A Reassessment of Persons and Themes 1851–67*, Harmondsworth: Penguin Books, 1990.

Bunyan, John. *Grace Abounding to the Chief of Sinners*, ed. Roger Sharrock, London: Oxford University Press, 1966.

—— *The Pilgrim's Progress*, ed. Roger Sharrock, Harmondsworth: Penguin Books, 1984.

Byron, George Gordon Noel, Lord. *Complete Poetical Works*, ed. Jerome J. McGann, vol. 2, Oxford: Clarendon Press, 1980.

Campbell, Joseph. *The Hero with a Thousand Faces*, 1949; 2nd edn, Princeton, NY: Princeton University Press, 1968.

Carlyle, Thomas. *Sartor Resartus*, 1836; Introduction by. W.H. Hudson, London: Dent, 1967.

—— *The Works of Thomas Carlyle*, ed. H.D. Traill, 30 vols, London: Chapman and Hall, 1896–1901.

Carpenter, William Benjamin. *Principles of Mental Physiology*, 1874; 2nd edn, London: Henry S. King, 1875.

'Cheap Reading', *Eliza Cook's Journal*, 1 (1849).

Child, Mrs D.L. *The History of the Condition of Women*, London, 1835.

Cobbe, Frances Power. 'The Fallacies of Memory', *Hours of Work and Play*, London: N. Trübner and Co., 1867.

Coleridge, Samuel Taylor. *The Portable Coleridge*, ed. I.A. Richards, New York: Viking Press, 1950.

Cowper, William. *The Letters and Prose Writings of William Cowper*, ed. James King and Charles Ryskamp, vol. 1, Oxford: Clarendon Press, 1979.

—— *The Poems of William Cowper*, ed. John D. Baird and Charles Ryskamp, 3 vols, Oxford: Clarendon Press, 1980–95.

Crichton-Browne, James. 'Education and the Nervous System', in M.A. Morris (ed.), *The Book of Health*, London: Cassell, 1883.

Defoe, Daniel. *Robinson Crusoe*, 1719; Afterword by Harvey Swados, New York: New American Library, 1961.

De Quincey, Thomas. 'Suspira de Profundis', *Blackwood's Edinburgh Magazine*, 57 (June 1845).

Donkin, Horatio Bryan. 'Hysteria', in Daniel Hack Tuke (ed.), *A Dictionary of Psychological Medicine*, vol. 1, London: J. and A. Churchill, 1892.

Drysdale, George. *Elements of Social Science, or, Physical, Sexual and Natural Religion*, 1854; 13th edn, London: Truelove, 1873.

Eagleton, Terry. *Walter Benjamin: Towards a Revolutionary Criticism*, London: Verso, 1981.

Eliot, George. *Middlemarch*, 1871–2; ed. W.J. Harvey, Harmondsworth: Penguin Books, 1985.

Eliot, T.S. *Complete Poems and Plays*, London: Faber and Faber, 1962.

Engels, Friedrich. *The Condition of the Working Class in England*, 1845; trans. W.O. Henderson and W.H. Chaloner, Oxford: Blackwell, 1971.

Esquirol, J.E.D. *Mental Maladies: A Treatise on Insanity*, trans. E.K. Hunt, Philadelphia, 1845.

Feurbach, Ludwig. *The Essence of Christianity*, 1841; trans. Marian Evans [George Eliot], 1854; New York: Harper & Brothers, 1957.

Fiske, John. 'British Cultural Studies and Television Criticism', in Robert Allen (ed.), *Channels of Discourse: Television and Contemporary Criticism*, London: Methuen, 1987, pp. 254–90.

Foster, John. 'On a Man Writing Memoirs of Himself', *Essays in a Series of Letters*, London: Holdsworth and Ball, 1865.

Foucault, Michel. *The Order of Things: An Archaeology of the Human Sciences*, London: Tavistock, 1970.

Freud, Sigmund. *Beyond the Pleasure Principle* (1920), in *Freud: On Metapsychology*, ed. Angela Richards, Pelican Freud Library, vol. 11, Harmondsworth: Penguin Books, 1984, pp. 269–337.

—— 'Creative Writers and Day-Dreaming' (1908), in *Freud: Art and Literature*, ed. Albert Dickson, Pelican Freud Library, vol. 14, Harmondsworth: Penguin Books, 1985, pp. 129–41.

—— 'Remembering, Repeating and Working-Through', in *The Standard Edition of the Complete Psychological Works of Sigmund Freud*, ed. James Strachey, vol. 12, London: Hogarth Press, 1958, pp. 145–56.

—— 'The "Uncanny" ' (1919), in *Freud: Art and Literature*, ed. Dickson (see above), pp. 335–76.

Froude, J.A. 'England and Her Colonies', *Short Stories on Great Subjects*, vol. 2, London, 1888.

Galton, Francis. *Inquiries into Human Faculty and Its Development*, London: Macmillan, 1883.

Gay, Peter. *The Naked Heart*, London: HarperCollins, 1996, vol. 4 of *The Bourgeois Experience: Victoria to Freud*, 4 vols, 1984–96.

'Gentlemen', *Cornhill Magazine*, 5 (March 1862).

Goldsmith, Oliver. *The Vicar of Wakefield*, 1766; ed. Stephen Coote, Harmondsworth: Penguin Books, 1986.

Hall, Joseph. *Occasional Meditations*, 3rd edn, London, 1633.

Harrison, Frederic. 'A Few Words About the Nineteenth Century', *Fortnightly Review*, March 1882; *The Choice of Books and Other Literary Pieces*, London: Macmillan, 1887.

Haskell, Thomas. 'Capitalism and the Origins of the Humanitarian Sensibility', *American Historical Review*, 90 (1985), 339–61.

Hawthorn, Jeremy. *A Concise Glossary of Contemporary Literary Theory*, London: Edward Arnold, 1994.

Hobsbawm, E.J. *The Age of Capital 1848–1875*, 1975; London: Abacus, 1995.

Holland, G. Calvert. *An Inquiry into the Moral, Social, and Intellectual Conditions of the Industrious Classes of Sheffield*, London, 1839.

Hood, Thomas. *Memorials of Thomas Hood*, ed. by his daughter, 2 vols, London, 1860.

—— *The Works of Thomas Hood*, ed. by his son and daughter, 11 vols, London, 1882–4.

Horne, R.H. 'Dust; or Ugliness Redeemed', *Household Words* (13 July 1850).

Hughes, Thomas. *Tom Brown's Schooldays*, 1857; ed. Andrew Sanders, Oxford: Oxford University Press, 1999.

Hutton, R[ichard] H[olt]. Review of *Is Life Worth Living?* by W.H. Mallock, *The Spectator*, 12 July 1879.

Huxley, T.H. *Evolution and Ethics*, London: Macmillan, 1893.

'Idiots', *Household Words* (4 June 1853).

'Idiots Again', *Household Words* (15 April 1854).

Jaynes, Julian. *The Origin of Consciousness in the Breakdown of the Bicameral Mind*, 1977; rev. edn, Harmondsworth: Allen Lane, 1979.

Johnson, Samuel. 'Review of [Soame Jenyns,] *A Free Enquiry into the Nature and Origin of Evil*' (1757), in *The Works of Samuel Johnson, LL.D*, vol. 11, London: W. Baynes and Son, 1824.

Jones, Ernest. *The Life and Works of Sigmund Freud*, 1953–57; ed. and abr. Lionel Trilling and Steven Marcus, Harmondsworth: Penguin Books, 1964.

La Capra, Dominick. *Rethinking Intellectual History*, Ithaca, NY: Cornell University Press, 1983.

Lallemand, Claude François. *A Practical Treatise on the Causes, Symptoms, and Treatment of Spermatorrhoea*, 1836–42; trans. and ed. Henry J. McDougall, London, 1847.

Law, Graham and Pennington, Adrian J. (eds) *Charles Dickens: Great Expectations*, Peterborough, Ont.: Broadview Press, 1998.

Leader, Darien. *Freud's Footnotes*, London: Faber and Faber, 2000.

Lessing, Doris. *Under My Skin*, London: HarperCollins, 1994.

Liddon, Henry. 'Sermon 9 June 1876', repr. in *Culture and Society in Britain 1850–1890: A Source Book of Contemporary Writings*, ed. J.M. Golby, Oxford: Oxford University Press, 1986, pp. 122–5.

Mallock, W[illiam] H[urrell]. *Is Life Worth Living?*, London: Chatto & Windus, 1880.

Malthus, Thomas Robert. *An Essay on the Principle of Population*, 1798; ed. Geoffrey Gilbert, Oxford: Oxford University Press, 1993.

—— *Essay on the Principle of Population*, 2nd edn, London, 1803.

Marks, Elaine and de Courvitron, Isabelle. *New French Feminisms*, Brighton: Harvester Press, 1981.

Mason, Michael. *The Making of Victorian Sexuality*, Oxford: Oxford University Press, 1995.

Maudsley, Henry. *Body and Mind: An Inquiry into their Connections and Mutual Influence, Specially in Reference to Mental Disorders*, London: Macmillan, 1870.

Mayhew, Henry. *London Labour and the London Poor*, 1861–2; repr. with an Introduction by John D. Rosenberg, 4 vols, New York: Dover Publications, 1968.

McCord, Norman. *British History 1815–1905*, Oxford: Oxford University Press, 1995.

Mill, John Stuart. *Autobiography*, 1873; Foreword by Asa Briggs, New York: New American Library, 1964.

Milton, John. *Paradise Lost*, in *The Poems of John Milton*, ed. John Carey and Alastair Fowler, London: Longman, 1968.

Moral Reformer 1 (1831).

Morison, Alexander. *The Physiognomy of Mental Diseases*, 1838; 2nd edn, London, 1843; New York: Arno Press: 1976.

Mort, Frank. *Dangerous Sexualities: Medic-moral Politics in England since 1830*, London: Routledge, 1987.

Nye, Robert A. (ed.) *Sexuality*, Oxford: Oxford University Press, 1999.

Onians, R.B. *The Origins of European Thought*, 1951; Cambridge: Cambridge University Press, 1988.

Pascal, Blaise. *Pensées*, in *Oeuvres Complètes*, ed. J. Chevalier, Paris: Pléiade, 1969.

Pelham, Camden. *The Chronicles of Crime; or, The New Newgate Calendar*, London: Miles & Co., 1887.

'The People's Portrait Gallery', *People's Journal*, 1 (3 June 1846).

Pope, Alexander. *Poetical Works*, ed. Herbert Davis, London: Oxford University Press, 1966.

Ribot, Théodule A. *Heredity: A Psychological Study of its Phenomena, Laws, Causes and Consequences*, 1873; 2nd edn, London: Henry S. King, 1875.

Richards, Huw. Review of *English Cricket: A Social History* by Derek Birley, *Times Higher Education Supplement*, 18 Feb. 2000, p. 23.

Rieff, Philip. *The Triumph of the Therapeutic: Uses of Faith after Freud*, 1966; Harmondsworth: Penguin Books, 1973.

Rivkin, Julie and Ryan, Michael. (eds) *Literary Theory: An Anthology*, Oxford: Blackwell, 1998.

Ruskin, John. 'Of Queen's Gardens', *Sesame and Lilies*, 1865; London: Everett & Co., n.d., pp. 78–128.

—— *The Works of John Ruskin*, ed. E.T. Cook and Alexander Wedderburn, 39 vols, London: George Allen, 1903–12.

Said, Edward. *The World, The Text, and The Critic*, 1984; London: Vintage, 1991.

Sewell, William. *Sermons to Boys at Radley School*, 1854–69; extract repr. in Law and Pennington (eds), *Charles Dickens: Great Expectations* (see above), pp. 562–3.

Simmel, Georg. 'The Adventure', trans. David Kettler, in *Georg Simmel, 1858–1918: A Collection of Essays, with Translations and a Bibliography*, ed. Kurt H. Wolff, Columbus: Ohio State University Press, 1959, pp. 243–58 (trans. of 'Das Abenteuer', *Philosophische Kultur: Gesammelte Essays*, 1911; 2nd edn, Leipzig: Alfred Kröner, 1919).

'Simplex'. *An Enquiry into the Constitution, Government, and Practices of the Churches of Christ*, Edinburgh, 1808.

Skelton, Robin. (ed.) *Poetry of the Thirties*, Harmondsworth: Penguin Books, 1964.

Smiles, Samuel. *Character*, 1871; London: John Murray, 1910.

—— *Self Help, With Illustrations of Conduct and Perseverance*, 1859; London: John Murray, 1908.

Spencer, Herbert. *Education, Intellectual, Moral and Physical*, London: Williams and Norgate, 1861.

—— *The Principles of Psychology*, London: Longman, 1855.

Stallybrass, Peter and White, Allon. *The Politics and Poetics of Transgression*, London: Methuen, 1986.

Sulloway, Frank J. *Freud: Biologist of the Mind: Beyond the Psychoanalytic Legend*, London: Fontana, 1980.

Taylor, Jenny Bourne and Shuttleworth, Sally. (eds) *Embodied Selves: An Anthology of Psychological Texts 1830–1890*, Oxford: Clarendon Press, 1998.

Thackrah, Charles Turner. *The Effects of Arts, Trades and Professions, and of Civic States and Habits of Living: With Suggestions for Removal of Many of the Agents which Produce Disease, and Shorten the Duration of Life*, 1831; 2nd edn, London: Longman, 1832.

Thompson, John B. *Ideology and Modern Culture*, Cambridge: Polity Press, 1990.

Tosh, John. 'Home? It's Where the Heart Is', *Sunday Times*, 22 Dec. 1996, sec. 3, p. 9.

Turner, Graeme. *British Cultural Studies: An Introduction*, 2nd edn, London: Routledge, 1996.

Weeks, Jeffrey. *Sex, Politics and Society: The Regulation of Sexuality since 1800*, London: Longman, 1989.

Williams, Raymond. *The Country and the City*, St Albans: Paladin, 1975.

Winslow, Forbes Benignus. *On Obscure Diseases of the Brain and Disorders of the Mind*, 1860; 4th edn, London: John Churchill, 1868.

'Women in Domestic Life', *Magazine of Domestic Economy*, 1 (1836).

Wordsworth, William. *Poetical Works*, ed. Ernest de Selincourt and Helen Darbishire, 5 vols, 1940–49; 2nd edn, Oxford: Clarendon Press, 1952–4.

——— *The Prelude*, ed. Ernest de Selincourt; 2nd edn, rev. Helen Darbishire, Oxford: Clarendon Press, 1959.

Wright, L. *Clean and Decent*, New York: Viking Press, 1960.

Wright, T.R. *Theology and Literature*, Oxford: Blackwell, 1988.

Index

Endnote references have been selectively indexed, as have characters from Dickens's novels.